Leon Forrest

Leon Forrest:
Introductions and Interpretations

edited by John G. Cawelti

Bowling Green State University Popular Press
Bowling Green, OH 43403

Kenneth Warren, "The Mythic City: An Interview with Leon Forrest."
Kenneth Warren, "Thinking Beyond the Catastrophe: Leon Forrest's *There Is a Tree More Ancient Than Eden*"
Danille Taylor-Guthrie, "Sermons, Testifying and Prayers; Looking Beneath the Wings in Leon Forrest's *Two Wings to Veil My Face.*"
John G. Cawelti, "Earthly Thoughts on *Divine Days.*"
All from *Callaloo.* Copyright (c) 1993. Reprinted by permission of the Johns Hopkins University Press.
Stanley Crouch, "Beyond Tribalism." From *The All-American Skin Game* by Stanley Crouch. Copyright (c) by Stanley Crouch.
Reprinted by permission of Pantheon Books, a division of Random House, Inc.
Sven Birkerts, "*Invisible Man* by Sven Birkerts: *Divine Days* by Leon Forrest." Copyright (c) 1993 by *The New Republic.* Reprinted by permission.
Craig Werner, "Leon Forrest and the AACM: The Jazz Impulse and the Legacy of the Chicago Renaissance." Copyright (c) 1993 by *The Black Scholar.* Reprinted by permission.

Copyright © 1997 Bowling Green State University Popular Press
Library of Congress Cataloging-in-Publication Data
Leon Forrest : introductions and interpretations / edited by John G.
   Cawelti.
      p.   cm.
   Includes bibliographical references.
   ISBN 0-87972-733-0. ISBN 0-87972-734-9 (pbk.)
   1. Forrest, Leon—Criticism and interpretation. 2. Afro-Americans in
literature. I. Cawelti, John G.
PS3556.0738Z75 1996
813'.54--dc21   96-3951
                                                                          CIP

Cover design by Dumm Art, Cleveland, Ohio.

To The Memory Of

PERRIN LOWREY

Contents

Acknowledgments

First of all, I am deeply grateful to Leon Forrest, not only for his help in creating this volume but for a long-term friendship which has been one of the great pleasures of my life, and, of course, for his wonderful novels.

I am also very grateful to the contributors. In particular I would like to thank A. Robert Lee for his support, advice and encouragement.

My colleague Arthur Wrobel did a heroic job in helping me edit the long essay "The Labyrinth of Luminosity." He is certainly responsible for whatever stylistic virtues the piece may have, though he should not be blamed for any of its shortcomings.

Leigh Anna Mendenhall was my editorial assistant in the last stages of preparation and was greatly helpful in matters of editing and formatting. She also brought the bibliography up to date.

The staff of the Department of English at the University of Kentucky helped with typing, copying and other tasks which made my life easier. I would particularly thank Lucy Combs, Pat Current, Melissa Thompson and Imogene Foster. The support of Professor David Durant, Chairperson of the Department for this project was indispensible.

A grant from the College of Arts and Sciences of the University of Kentucky, Richard Edwards, Dean, enabled me to take advantage of editorial assistance to bring the volume to completion.

Perrin Lowrey, to whom this volume was dedicated, played a very important role in my life and that of Leon Forrest. At the time of his tragically early death he was a Professor at the University of Chicago and my colleague and friend who introduced me to what became a permanent interest in Southern and African-American literature. As my introduction indicates, he was also a very important teacher for Leon Forrest. Finally, it was Perrin Lowrey who brought me together with Leon Forrest many years ago.

Without the constant support and inspiration of my wife, Mary Catherine Flannery, I would never have been able to do this.

Leon Forrest:
The Labyrinth of Luminosity:
An Introduction

John G. Cawelti

Lodged in the innermost heart of America is a fatal division of being, a war of impulses. America knows that a split is in her and that that split might cause her death; but she is powerless to pull the dangling ends together. An uneasiness haunts her conscience, taints her moral preachments, lending an air of unreality to her actions, and rendering ineffectual the good deeds she feels compelled to do in the world. America is a nation of riven consciousness . . . . Chicago is the city from which the most incisive and radical Negro thought has come; there is an open and raw beauty about that city that seems either to kill or endow one with the spirit of life.   Richard Wright (1945)
(Introduction to *Black Metropolis*)

Art has to do with the process of reaching down into repressed values and giving it some luminosity.   Ralph Ellison (1972)
(Interview with Leon Forrest in *Muhammad Speaks*)

Biography

Leon Forrest was born on January 8, 1937 in Cook County Hospital, an enormous public hospital about a mile west of Chicago's Loop, the commercial and financial center not only for the city but for its vast midwestern hinterland. "County" is also on the boundary of Chicago's South and West sides, home of most of Chicago's African-American population of approximately one and a half million.[1] This is the area which Forrest has re-created into the fictional space of Forest county, locale of his four novels. Perhaps this point of birth between the great white power center and the teeming slum neighborhoods which it exploited, dominated, and bewailed gives some initial clue to the character and concerns of Leon Forrest's writing, which has consistently reaffirmed the vitality of the African-American heritage and insisted on its creative importance for modern American culture as a whole.

Forrest grew up on the South Side in a five room apartment at 3704 South Parkway (now Martin Luther King Dr.), an area not too far distant from both the wretched slum apartment where Richard Wright's *Native Son* begins and from the elegant mansion in the then lily-white area of the University of Chicago where Bigger Thomas accidentally commits the murder which seals his doom. In the opening scenes of *Native Son*, Bigger and his friends go to the Regal Theater at 47th and South Parkway, only about ten blocks away from the Forrest apartment.[2] However, the family and the neighborhood of Forrest's youth were very different from the tragic and psychologically destructive world of Bigger Thomas. Forrest's parents were solidly lower-middle-class African-Americans. His father, a mulatto from Bolivar County, Mississippi, was never acknowledged by his own white father and had been working since the age of six. A man of many abilities, he had risen to become a bartender on the Santa Fe railroad, one of the best positions open to blacks in the late 1930s. His mother was descended from a large New Orleans Creole family which had also migrated to Chicago. Both of Forrest's parents had literary and musical talents; his father wrote lyrics for songs some of which he recorded, and his mother wrote short stories and passed on a passionate interest in jazz singers to her son.

The complex interplay between the Catholic culture of his maternal family and the Protestantism of his father's side profoundly influenced Forrest's development and became a major element in his writing.[3] As a child he attended both the Pilgrim Baptist Church, where his father had been a member of the choir, and St. Elizabeth's Catholic Church, where one of his maternal aunts ran the cafeteria and where he received religious instruction.[4] Forrest was "deeply impressed" by the complex order of the Catholic ritual and he eventually became a Catholic communicant; but he never lost his feeling for the passionate rapture and spiritual questing of black Protestantism and "learned to love the art of the folk preacher and particularly the sprituals and gospel singing" (*Relocations* 13). Forrest's paternal aunt, Maude Richardson, was a devoutly religious woman and one of his major mentors: "she taught Bible in the Protestant tradition, which in her ethos was something of a commingling of Baptist and Methodist interpretation, recombined with Negro peasant savvy. She and her husband maintained the ethos of the

South, and the Negro values of genuine effort and God-fearing connections. . . . In the very heart of the slums, where they live, you will find a little Southern patch of vegetables growing in the backyard and Uncle Eddie's flower garden growing in the front—untouched, and even respected, by winos and lost souls of the neighborhood" (*Relocations* 15-16).

The neighborhood on South Parkway where Forrest grew up figures prominently in his first novel. He renamed South Parkway DuSable Street in honor of the legendary first settler of Chicago, probably a black man (in actuality the street was renamed for Dr. Martin Luther King, Jr). *There Is a Tree* describes a vibrant and diverse urban neighborhood, showing signs of blight and decay, but still thriving with a Jewish grocery store on the corner and several other small businesses in the vicinity:

And I could smell the wine from the broken bottles running the streets. . . . And the Bar-Be-Que sauce sour and yet sweet swimming at the nostrils from the House of the Soul, where a huge blood-red pig, the color of the wine running running running the streets, turned slowly slowly slowly on a wire rotisserie in the window, next-door to Winestein's Grocery Store. . . . And I could smell the loud stench of burning bits of hair streaming from the House of the Brown-Skinned Goddess Salon, where a picture of a brown-skinned version of Jean Harlow running an ancient Madame Walker straightening iron through her wavy, black, shoulder-length hair stood in the freshly washed and wiped down sharply windowpane. (*Tree* 47)

Forrest attended Wendell Phillips grade school, an all-black neighborhood school, where he remembers the teachers emphasizing pride in the African-American heritage. In the early 1950s, he enrolled at Hyde Park High School which had started to integrate after World War II, although a few blacks had attended Hyde Park earlier in the century. Hyde Park was about 20-25 percent African-American when Forrest entered as a freshman. This large high school served the University of Chicago area and was one of the great urban high schools with one of the highest academic ratings for a public high school in the country. Forrest was not outstanding as a student, but began to show promise in creative writing, inspired by a white teacher, Mrs Edythe Thompson, who encouraged him in his efforts.

After graduating from high school, Forrest attended Wilson Junior College for a year, but in 1956 Forrest's parents divorced.

His mother married an accountant and opened a liquor store at 79th and South Park. During this time Forrest worked at the liquor store, an experience which would furnish material for his fourth novel, *Divine Days*. He also attended classes at Roosevelt University and the University of Chicago until he dropped out of college in 1960 and was drafted.

The middle 1960s was a crucial formative period in Forrest's life and he later re-created some of the central formative elements of this time in *Divine Days*. Two years of army service (1960-62) took him to Germany where he became a Public Information Specialist, writing articles for the 3rd Armored Division newspaper *Spearhead*. In 1962, Forrest returned to Chicago where he again worked at his mother's liquor store, took some courses in creative writing at the University of Chicago, and began working as a journalist on small weekly papers on the South Side. During this time he began his career as a writer and made the crucial decision to become a novelist instead of the poet and playwright of his original ambition. It was also at this time that he lost some of the people most important to him. His mother died of cancer in 1964, a loss which powerfully influenced the writing of *There Is a Tree More Ancient than Eden*. Leon Forrest, Sr. succumbed to diabetes in 1971; and in 1965, Perrin Lowrey, a Southern born writer and teacher at the University of Chicago who strongly influenced Forrest's writing, was killed in an automobile accident.

Though full of loss and grief, this crucible period was also a time of setting forth. In 1966, Forrest's first creative publication appeared in a small literary magazine, *Blackbird*; a sketch entitled "That's Your Little Red Wagon," it would become part of *Tree*. Also in 1966, Forrest met the distinguished African-American educator and University of Chicago Professor Allison Davis, who would become one of his long-term friends and a great source of wisdom and insight about Black Chicago. Forrest ended his apprenticeship as a journalist when he joined the Black Muslim newspaper *Muhammad Speaks* as an associate editor in 1969. And most importantly, he successfully courted his wife, the former Marianne Duncan, whom he married on September 25, 1971.

In the early 1970s, Forrest met two other major African-American writers, Ralph Ellison and Toni Morrison. Ellison became a friend and supporter until his own death in 1994, while Morrison, then an editor at Random House and interested in discovering African-American writers, became the publisher's editor for Forrest's first three novels. Morrison played an important role in these early works. She not only suggested their titles, but inspired Forrest to write the "Lives" section of *Tree*. This important creative relationship continued until the publication of *Two Wings to Veil My Face*, when Morrison left Random House to become the Schweitzer Professor at SUNY Albany in 1983, and then a professor at Princeton University. With Morrison's help, Forrest published his first novel, *There Is a Tree More Ancient than Eden* in 1973. The book was launched with high praise from both Ralph Ellison and Saul Bellow; in that same year Forrest left *Muhammad Speaks* for a teaching post at Northwestern University. From that time on his career as a writer and teacher has continued with major benchmarks being the publication of his next three novels; *The Bloodworth Orphans* (1977), *Two Wings to Veil My Face* (1984), and *Divine Days* (1992); his promotion to Full Professor at Northwestern (1984) and his nine year service as chair of the African-American Studies Program there. During this time, Forrest's reputation as one of the most important, albeit one of the most difficult and challenging, of African-American novelists has increased and his works are becoming ever more widely known and commented upon. While the relatively small sales of the first three novels discouraged Random House from publishing the enormous manuscript of *Divine Days*, Forrest had fortunately met Lee Webster, the founder and publisher of Another Chicago Press, who agreed to bring out paperback editions of *Tree*, *Bloodworth*, and *Two Wings* and to become the publisher of *Divine Days*. After a fire destroyed some of the remaining stocks of *Divine Days*, W.W. Norton reissued the book in both hardcover and paperback editions. In addition, Forrest published, in 1994, an important collection of essays, *Relocations of the Spirit*. He is presently working on another novel, which is structured as a series of novellas.

Mentors and Influences

The influences which shaped Forrest's growth as a writer and the teachers who helped him develop his talent reflect the diversity and complexity of his work. The initial influence was two-sided: the world of Black Chicago (or "Bronzeville" as it was known at the time of his growing up) was one side of the mold and the two churches, Protestant and Catholic in which much of his life and feeling was invested was the other. We've already noted the profound influence of Forrest's double religious background on the development of his consciousness, but the world of the streets also tugged at the young man, perhaps in something like the way it pulls at young Nathaniel Witherspoon: "I was always falling in love with the sounds and shapes abounding in the streets and the sadness of people and places, and often times inimtating consciously, and unconsciously, those latter influences which indeed represented authority. . . . I found myself revering certain fragments of personalities, which were glorious or demonic, but always grand (*Tree* 5). Just as Forrest's writing continually recreates the forms and emotions of two churchly traditions—the ecstatic lyricism of the Protestant sermon and the rich symbolic order and complex cultural heritage embodied in Catholic ritual[5]—his style is also pervaded by the lore and and the rituals of the streets—folktales, the "dozens," "signifying," nicknaming, and many other forms of street culture.

But there was one major area of African-American culture where the two worlds of the church and the streets continually flowed together, that of black music. The spirituals had influenced the blues, which in turn had shaped soul and gospel music and in many ways all of this came together in that most remarkable of all African-American musical inventions: jazz. Of the many influences which shaped the young Forrest as a writer, the impact of jazz was perhaps the greatest of all. As Forrest later reflected:

One of the literary constants of Afro-American literature is the Reinvention of life. Or, the cultural attribute of black Americans to take what is left over or, conversely, given to them (either something tossed from the white man's table . . . or let us say, at the other end of the spectrum, the Constitution, or basketball) and make it work for them, as a source of personal or group survival, and then to place a stamp of elegance and elan upon the reinvented mode; to emboss upon the basic form revised, a highly individualistic style, always spun of grace, and fabulous rhythms...a kind of magical realism. Of course the improvisational genius of jazz is the epitome of what I am getting at here. (*Relocations* 23)

Jazz provided a structural and stylistic model for Forrest as well as a continuing source of inspiration. In fact, the idea of becoming a sort of literary counterpart to the great jazz musicians in their ability to bring together and reinvent the complex currents of African-American life has surely been Forrest's deepest artistic intention. In his most eloquent and charged moments, Forrest's prose does approach the power he ascribes to the music of Ironwood "Landlord" Rumble:

Ironwood became the high priest of the tribe, extemporizing upon his royal golden flute, with a faint jangle of the whispering tambourine, a psalm of memory to Lady Day. Celebrating in tongues her time-freezing, prison-love, muted-hypodermic-jellied, sight-blinding, knocking-bones, lean-honed, aching vision in the frigid, dehydrated valley of bleached dry bones of love, Ironwood's rage-muted violin-sounding flute; and behind *that*, talking, dancing, spirit, meat shaking off their bones, as Big Maybelle, like the huge-hearted felt-flesh life, like Bessie inside the body and blood of Lady's delicate violin song of sorrows. . . . Singing them all back to the foundling child in the path-road, tiny enough to fit into a mailbox. (*Bloodworth* 301)

These basic cultural influences were molded as well by the influence of particular individuals who became mentors and examples for the aspiring young writer. Beyond his gifted and diverse family, Forrest was probably first given a push in the direction of his ultimate vocation by a remarkable woman, Lenora Bell, who lived for a time with his family. In an autobiographical sketch, Forrest begins his account with Miss Bell, referring to her as a "magical seamstress, a lady who was always transforming life; first the cloth, now the body, and then the very spirit of the recreated person before our eyes. Like any good beautician or barber, my Kentucky aunt knew what her clientele said they wanted, and she knew what would work wonders on her *characters*, transforming them into new ladies" (*Relocations* 3).

According to Forrest, Lenora Bell first gave him an inkling of the possibilities of reinventing life—"my seamstress 'aunt' put her stamp or style of reinvention upon her inspired art: here indeed was the body and the spirit transformed"—and thus introduced him to what would be the most important theme in all his work. But Miss Bell was also apparently a great romantic. Forrest says that though she never married she had a lifelong facination with love and love stories. He later recreated her as the character Bella-Lenore Boltwood in *The Bloodworth Orphans*:

Bella-Lenore often dreamed about the romantic, even though she despised actual, outward touching of sexual passion of any kind: it should never be discussed; men should always wear the dinner jacket. But several well-thumbed copies of *Wuthering Heights* were locked away in her huge trunk—that still housed her trousseau. And after four tall glasses of Foxhead Four-Hundred, Bella-Lenore would recall all of the myths of the great lovers and especially that of Orpheus and Eurydice. (*Bloodworth* 89)

Lenora Bell's mythical dreams helped open the young Forrest's mind to the powerful allure of high romanticism. With this in view, it is not surprising that one of the first major literary influences on the young writer was Dylan Thomas, and that Forrest dreamed of being a poet and dramatist long before he decided to try the novel.

Forrest remembers that two other early literary influences were dramatists: Tennessee Williams, who would surely have delighted in the character of Lenora Bell-Bella-Lenore Boltwood, and Eugene O'Neill, who gave the would-be playwright the example of the long dramatic monologue which he later transformed into the sermon and the extended internal monologue. In fact, the taproot of Forrest's talent seems to be his feeling for voice. He's a highly gifted natural mimic, but his mimicry seems to reflect a more complex ability to become the creative channel for many voices; this ability, which he ascribes to Joubert Jones, the narrator of *Divine Days*, is undoubtedly a key to Forrest's own fictional creativity:

I'm too hypersensitively attuned to the sound of voices, babblings, otherworldly and worldly tongues. I never forget the nuances of sounds within voices. Sometimes my imitation of voices—as a kind of avocation—can delight a party and for a long time my so-called gift was in demand. I also read palms. A good way to get a pretty girl onto your lap, for starters. The plague of inner voices so riddled me—because you see I have no control over those moments when these voices, or a specific voice might hit me, or what he'll say, or what she might demand of me. I had to stop doing these imitations, lest they unleash certain spirits from within. I now rely entirely on my palm-reading powers for social entree. For when a voice hits me, I'm like a man caught up in a shooting gallery. (*DD* 11)

Forrest's feeling for voices is reflected in his distinctive style which, as many critics have noted, has a powerfully spontaneous, improvisatory, oral quality. Forrest's first longer literary creations were drafts of poems which he was encouraged to create by his first important teacher of writing, Mrs. Edythe Thompson, a white teacher of creative writing at Hyde Park High School. At the time Forrest attended, 1951-55, Hyde Park High School was a top-quality urban high school serving the University of Chicago community and its surroundings and Forrest was able to attend it by using the address of one of his father's associates on the Santa Fe Railroad.

It was after his two-year stint in the Army in 1960-62, most of which he spent as a reporter for Army newspapers in Germany, that Forrest returned to Chicago and began seriously pursuing the idea of becoming a writer. While working at his mother and stepfather's liquor store and bar on South 79th St., he began to take extension courses at the University of Chicago. Through his involvement with the University he met two men who were to have a deep influence on his life and writing.

The first was Perrin H. Lowrey, a white Southerner whose family came from the Faulkner country of Northern Mississippi, but who had grown up in Baltimore and done graduate work at the University of Chicago. Lowrey had recently returned to Chicago to head one of its extension programs and to teach in the Humanities Section of the University of Chicago College. Himself a fiction writer, Lowrey was a profound student of contemporary Southern and African-American literature, and when Forrest signed up with him for a creative writing workshop and a course on the modern novel, Lowrey helped him read Faulkner's *The Sound and the Fury*, introduced him to James Joyce's *A Portrait of the Artist as a Young Man*, and inspired him to reread Ellison's *Invisible Man* and to understand the great importance of that novel for the first time. These three writers, along with Dostoyevsky, Shakespeare, and the Bible, have remained the most powerful literary influences on Forrest's work.

In many ways, Lowrey presided over the emergence of Forrest as novelist: he encouraged him to continue the creative experiments that led to his first novel, and suggested some of the basic literary models that enabled Forrest to create his own distinctive narrative techniques and style. The examples of Joyce, Faulkner, and Ellison helped Forrest see how a writer might create significant fiction by exploring the struggles of a talented and sensitive young man to understand and give expression to his world. In addition, Ellison's own use of traditional African-American forms, like the sermon and jazz, offered Forrest a crucial example of how he might reinvent his own cultural heritage.

Ironically, Perrin Lowrey gave Forrest one final gift. When Lowrey was killed in an accident in his early forties, Forrest published a deeply moving tribute to his teacher. It was in part through this tribute that Forrest met Ralph Ellison, who had known and liked Lowrey; this meeting marked the beginning of a long personal friendship. Ellison offered Forrest the wisdom of an older African-American writer and observer of American life; another person who played a similar role was the distinguished black educator and sociologist Allison Davis. Forrest met Davis at the University of Chicago in 1966 and the two were good friends for nearly twenty years until Davis died in 1983. Davis's sharing with Forrest his profound understanding of the social and cultural patterns of black Chicago undoubtedly helped Forrest add significant depth to his understanding of the world he was in the process of reinventing as the fictional Forest County. An intellectual of great brilliance who offered Forrest an important personal model of wisdom and elegance, Davis's interest in traditional African-American culture was also permeated with a deep concern for the destiny of the black underclass.

Allison knew with the folklore of the past that it makes no difference how far a turtle extends his two front feet, he cannot move his body until he does something about his hind legs. Thus Allison sought to uplift thinkers, teachers, and administrators with his findings and his knowledge so that we might find ways to bring up the economic rear of the race, and the underprivileged—the economically deprived black underclassses now unto the third generation. How to heed the ancient ancestral commandment—pull up as you lift up, in our time. (*Relocations* 256)

Yet Forrest was painfully aware of the degree to which the new black middle-class was indifferent to Davis's message and this was an aspect of Davis's situation that he stressed when he reinvented him as the character Dr. Allerton Jamesway in *Divine Days*:

This aristocratic-looking Negro looked like a majestic envoy on a mission for the United Nations. This man who was so exquisitely educated—and yet so alone. Always alone. It was his aloneness that troubled me so—for him; the implications of the intellectual life, if you were a thoughtful Negro, and a creative one. Naturally, though, my fears for him were fears I felt for myself and for my future in the arts. . . . Dr. Jamesway was unappreciated (almost unknown among the black middle-class) even though many of the teacher-class had read his works in college probably force-fed upon them. However, since they never read anything worthwhile after graduation, if they could help it, most of the Negroes in the middle class that I knew assumed that Dr. Jamesway was dead. But he was very much appreciated in Williemain's barbershop. There he was on a national stage, if you spoke to anyone of his discipline. He was legend in the South—much like DuBois—among the educated yet an all but mythical, invisible soul in the Yankee-Negro under-educated North. (*DD* 89)

Forrest's years as a reporter and editor at *Muhammand Speaks* followed the critical "beginning time" of the mid-1960s when he worked at a variety of jobs while he flexed his wings— bartender, reporter on community newspapers, office boy, Catholic Interracial Council speaker. At *Muhammad Speaks*, Forrest was strongly influenced by the paper's dynamic early editor Richard Durham and deeply, if ambiguously, impressed by Elijah Muhammad. Durham and Forrest were the last non-Muslim editors of *Muhammad Speaks* and they brought to the paper a great interest in the strength and vitality of traditional "Negro" culture. In contrast, the Muslims rejected this tradition, and the grounds that "'soul,' as the definitive yeast of black ethos, was pollution in the light of Elijah's eyes" (*Relocations* 70). In addition to teaching him more about writing, Durham reinforced Forrest's commitment to the art and vitality of African-American cultural traditions. In his essay on Elijah Muhammad and his own experience with *Muhammad Speaks*, Forrest notes that, though ideologically a Marxist, "Durham enjoyed Negro culture and didn't see it as a tool to the worldwide revolution...but rather as a rich resource upon which blacks could and had based a thriving culture; and as a certain evidence of how a people maintained their humanity amid an attempt to destroy the souls of these black folk (*Relocations* 87).

The complexity of Forrest's response to Elijah Muhammad and the Black Muslim movement is reflected in the essay "Elijah" in *Relocations of the Spirit* and in several characters and episodes in the novels. First of all, Forrest insists that, for all its limitations, the Muslim movement was one of the few contemporary social movements that seriously addressed the problems of despair and self-destruction endemic to the black underclass:

(Elijah) must also be judged by the lives he saved by dint of the obsessive faith he conjured, and the self-help programs he developed. All of this must be placed into the equation; because after all America didn't extend its noble hand of up-lift and opportunity to this peculiar branch of the defeated black American, but rather cast them below the demarcation of humanity, where they could not be seen. Elijah came along and extended to them a life-raft. (*Relocations* 115-16)

Yet, for all this, Forrest sees the Muslim movement as narrow and fanatical, and criticizes its failure to recognize the importance of new roles for women, its anti-semitism, its blind rejection of the positive values of the African-American cultural heritage, and its lack of appeal to younger urban blacks. Forrest's own interest in the power of myth led him to see the new mythology promulgated by Elijah Muhammad as a brilliant example of the misuse of that power; in both *The Bloodworth Orphans* and *Divine Days*, the Muslim movement is satirized in the figure of W.A.D. Ford, a mythical trickster based loosely on the mysterious figure of the legendary incarnation of Allah, W.A.D. Fard, who supposedly gave the Muslim message to Elijah Muhammad. Indeed, one of the underlying themes of *Divine Days* is the archetypal clash between Ford as mythical con-man and emissary of darkness, and Sugar-Groove, the archetypal hipster who represents the survival and tranformative vitality of the African-American cultural tradition.

Forrest broke off his association with *Muhammad Speaks* on the eve of the publication of his first novel *There Is a Tree More Ancient than Eden* in 1973, in part because he felt that his fictional representation of the movement would be resented. One of his last published essays in *Muhammad Speaks* was a feature article on Ralph Ellison which appeared in December, 1972.[6] And it was Ellison, who, along with Saul Bellow, helped launch Forrest's first novel with strong praise for its originality and power. The conjunction of these two major American writers of the postwar period was not accidental for, as Forrest developed as a writer, he moved away from the early modernist influence of the James Joyce of *Portrait* and the Faulkner of *The Sound and the Fury* and began to evolve new fictional forms more similar to the later Joyce of *Ulysses* and the Faulkner of *Absalom, Absalom!* and *Go Down, Moses*. These forms were less concentrated and more expansive, more pervaded by the archetypal patterns of myth, more historically oriented, and, in Faulkner, more directly related to the history of the South and of racism in America. Ellison and Bellow also reflected these artistic changes and became important models for Forrest's later work.

At this time, Forrest also began his editorial relationship with Toni Morrison. Though their work is very different both in content and style, there were important similarities in their development during the time of their association. After their first novels, both turned increasingly to the history of slavery and racism in America for their subjects, a trend reflected in different ways in Morrison's *Song of Solomon* and *Beloved* and in Forrest's *The Bloodworth Orphans* and *Two Wings to Veil My Face*. Moreover, in these novels the two writers used patterns of folklore and mythology much more extensively as they expanded the historical horizons of their fictions. In this respect both writers reflected the growing interest in African-American cultural history which blossomed in the black studies movements of the 1970s and in the enormous popularity of Alex Haley's *Roots* as book and television miniseries.

At this time, Forrest himself received an appointment to the new African-American studies program at Northwestern University; his encounter there with the distinguished tradition of African studies at Northwestern increased his own knowledge of the African background of black American culture and had considerable influence on his later fiction. Though now a teacher as well as a published writer, Forrest continued his own studies in anthropology and in the literary traditions of Western civilization. Between the writing of *There Is a Tree* and the conception of *The Bloodworth Orphans*, Forrest read and was deeply influenced by Lord Raglan's study of archetypal mythic patterns in *The Hero* and *Jocasta's Crime*, and Raglan's analysis helped him shape the mythical dimension of *The Bloodworth Orphans*. In addition, Forrest continued his extensive studies of the Bible, Dostoyevsky, Joyce, Woolf, Proust, and Shakespeare under the guidance of Marvin Mirsky, a remarkable teacher of literature in the Continuing Education Program of the University of Chicago. These studies have resulted in an increasingly rich and complex texture of mythical and historical allusions in Forrest's work.

Central Themes

In one of Forrest's earliest written passages, Nathaniel Witherspoon, devastated by the loss of his mother, and feeling desperately alone in the world, dreams of himself as an angel struggling to rise beyond his suffering:

My arms aching like apple-tree ladder ascending (seeing now through my frozen tears) and aching from my wings to my fingertips, full of the stuffings of patches. . . . The wings, lamblike on the outside but yellowed like an ancient scroll, greasy, black and purplish blue, like bruised blood, tough and wolfish underneath. . . .

Ascending now towards the cathedral spire of chained but falling stars, that were pealing and sobbing some song (a valley of cross-eyed rosary beads laced about the dazzling wine cups)—yes, and inside their sobbing did I hear heartthrob drums *talking* about troubles and sorrows, Lord God...? (Tree 42-43)

Here, several of Forrest's recurrent themes intersect in the dream-driven consciousness of this motherless child struggling to rise above his grief and suffering on wings which are themselves aged and torn by experience and pain. Forrest's protagonist finds that he must "make a way out of noway," a phrase that Forrest puts in the mouth of such diverse but analogous charac-ters as Sweetie Reed, Nathaniel's devoutly Christian grandmother, and Sugar-Groove, the transcendent hipster of *Divine Days*. Nathaniel must not only accept the loss of his mother and his aloneness in the world, but try to rise to the example of those of his African-American ancestors who transformed the chaos, injus-tice, and pain of their existence into something transcendent and redemptive.

Nathaniel's personal suffering begins his initiation into the fate of his race, which is prefigured in his nightmarish vision of the crucifixion in *There Is a Tree* and continued in the tragic histories of the Bloodworth and Witherspoon families as revealed in *The Bloodworth Orphans* and *Two Wings to Veil My Face*. Yet, at the same time that he encounters the terrible history which has shaped the lives of his family, his friends, and his race, Nathaniel is also learning the lesson of re-invention—developing the ability to transcend the horrors of African-American history through the power of re-creation which Forrest believes has been the true genius of African-American or "Negro" culture.[7] Most significantly the culture has accomplished this through the transcendent force of black religion, but it has also sought "a way out of noway" though spirituals, jazz and other musical transformations and through the rich oral poetry, drama, and narration of the streets. The drama of Forrest's two major protagonists, Nathaniel Witherspoon and Joubert Jones, is not only one of encountering the tragedy of Africans in America, but of realizing the redemp-tive power of the African-American cultural heritage and of rec-ognizing the need to re-create this power in their own lives. In this way, they begin to learn the meaning of the awesome charge laid on the young Nathaniel by his beloved Aunt Hattie Breedlove at the end of *There Is a Tree*: "and nathan as you catch up in this sense of time in your power and your power in time you become humbled more by the grace and restraining glory of god and what he's allowed for you to see: the honor and glory of lighting a candle down the forest of the night; yet you got a responsiblity and a voice to man, as well, and that is in building up your city" (*Tree* 156).

The city which Nathaniel might have created if he had been real is Forest county, the mythical landscape based on black Chicago which Leon Forrest has richly spun out for us through his novels. The creation of this city as an imaginative transformation of the African-American cultural heritage represents the forging of a culturally significant and even redemptive literature seeking "a way out of noway." This is Forrest's most important and recurrent theme.

In the "appletree" passage from *There Is a Tree*, the transcendent and redemptive powers of religion and art are symbolized, as is often the case in Forrest's work, by images of angels. There are, for example the two plaster angels set up as yard decorations at the Reed plantation which witness the terrible events that take place there. But these plaster angels are symbolically transformed into the angel of the spiritual which helps the suffering soul rise to glory:

> Hurry, Angel, hurry! Hurry down to the pool.
> I want you to trouble the waters this morning.
> To bathe my weary soul.
> Angel got two wings to hide me away
> Two wings to fly me away. (*Two Wings* 249)

Surely the most delightful—and perhaps most significant—improvization on angels in Forrest's work is the wonderful tall tale of Sugar-Groove in heaven told by the great folk historian and story-teller of the barber shop Oscar (Williemain). In Williemain's account, Sugar-Groove has died and gone to heaven, where, in spite of the used wings he has been outfitted with, he so amazes and outrages the other angels by his high-flying along the restricted Sky-Blue Freeway that St. Peter calls him in for a reprimand:

For what was the saga all about (when all is said and done) in the barbershop concerning Sugar-Groove. . . How once Sugar-Groove got to heaven and was given a used set of wings. . . . He was in fact issued an old patched-up set of shattered wings thrown in the Catholic salvage section and over in the Free Will bin where other angelic vestments were tossed away, and cast asunder . . . And not only that but how Sugar-Groove had to fly around heaven with one wing on the right, roped off and tied behind him. . . . And how he reinvented himself out of all that so much so that St. Peter himself was startled to amazement. (*DD* 1134)

Sugar-Groove stands for a complex pattern of re-creation: he himself has surmounted rejection by his white father and the darkness of his beginnings to become a consummate artist of life, a master of style in the highest African-American tradition; in turn, by telling this tale of Sugar-Groove in heaven, Williemain reinvents the character and transforms him into an archetypal legendary hero within the oral tradition of black culture; finally, by recreating Williemain's story into an important episode in a modern African-American novel, Joubert Jones (and Leon Forrest) continue the process of transformation by which Sugar-Groove becomes a transcendent symbol of the creative vitality, passion for survival, and human richness within African-American history and cultural traditions.

Other key themes of Forrest's work also express the quest for transcendence of the chaos and suffering of African-American history through spiritual and artistic re-creation. The first three novels, those that deal with the Witherspoon-Bloodworth families, center around stories of the destruction and recreation of families. Many characters are orphaned, either through death or through the effects of miscegenation resulting from the sexual exploitation of black women by white men. Families are reconstructed when other black women take on the rearing of orphans, but sometimes the chaos of the past cannot be overcome. Two of the Bloodworth orphans are brought to their doom when ignorance of their actual relationship leads them into a passionate but incestuous love, while two others are killed by the emptiness of their lives and their inability to come to terms with their identities. On the other hand, though Nathaniel Witherspoon loses his mother, and even discovers that his father is not the biological child of his beloved grandmother, the loving care and spiritual strength of his grandmother is strong enough to have recreated the disrupted family ties she reveals to Nathaniel in the course of *Two Wings to Veil My Face*.

Forrest remembers this ready willingness of black families to take on adoptive children as one of the great strengths of the traditional African-American culture, and another of those important ways in which that culture improvised and recreated to "make a way out of noway." Joubert Jones, the narrator of *Divine Days*, has also been orphaned by the death of his parents, but has been adopted by his aunt and her husband. On the other hand, Sugar-Groove, whose mysterious fate becomes one of the central pivots of Joubert's memories, ruminations and investigations in the course of the novel, has been denied by his white father and raised by a black aunt and uncle. The unresolved ambiguities of this background of miscegenation and denial have made it impossible for Sugar-Groove to establish a family of his own.

This swirling complexity of disrupted family lines and ambiguous identities is reflected in the importance of naming, renaming, and nicknaming, which symbolizes the shifting and uncertain identities of the citizens of Forest County.[8] In Forrest's novels, the characters' original names are more often than not lost or superseded by adoptive names. Thus, Regal Pettibone and La Donna Scales are actually the children of P.F. Bloodworth and a black woman, but have been re-named by their adoptive parents, as have Industrious and Carl-Rae Bowman, sons of Rachel Flowers and Arlington Bloodworth II, her white exploiter.

These adoptive names often prove to be highly ironic and sometimes even seem to be a sort of curse on their possessor. For example, another Bloodworth orphan is the son of William Body, himself a half-white Bloodworth offspring and his half-sister. This orphan is renamed Abraham Dolphin "for a completely freshwater start and for the strength of the name." Though Dolphin flees the South by hiding in a coffin and is resurrected in the North as a highly successful doctor and owner of the Eden Lounge, his naming as the great patriarch becomes increasingly ironic in light of his work as an abortionist, and his resurrection is cancelled when he commits suicide.

In a world where official names are often misleading or ironic, nicknaming assumes a particular importance. This is particulaly problematic for African-Americans since the official name was often either given by or taken from the slave master or arbitrarily assigned by the Freedman's Bureau. The Black Muslims made renaming a crucial part of the process of conversion as a testimony to this aspect of black history, assigning X's to Muslim converts to symbolize the loss of the original African identity in the course of enslavement. A large number of Forrest's characters are best-known by nicknames or street names and some, like Sugar-Groove, are known in no other way, having become completely identified with and by their nicknames. Forest County nicknames have several different, sometimes interlocking, significances. They are almost always the direct reflection of some characteristic, quality, event, or saying which is special or unique to the person, thus emphasizing the person's unique and individual identity as opposed to the standardization and, in the case of blacks, the built-in alienation of official names. Thus we have Milton "Beefeater" Raines from the character's well-known love of gin; or "Opera Slim" McSpilvens, the willowy opera-loving hospital attendant; or Rev. Wilbur "Spiffy" Lumpkins, ("he was known in Williemain's Barbershop and elsewhere as Spiffy, because of his natty dress" (*DD* 446)). Such nicknames reflect the re-creative, transformative poetry of the steets. They are also often semi-secret, their real meaning known only to the inner circle of friends; in this way, nicknames affirm the brotherhood and sisterhood of fellow sufferers as the true source of identity.

Nicknames undercut the fixed and standarized identity symbolized by official names with more personal and semi-secret aliases which sometimes help individuals elude the victimization, exploitation and degradation directed by white society at the official name. Moreover, the presence of a nickname opens up the possibility of new transformations and re-creations of identity which we see carried out with dazzling virtuousity in the case of Sugar-Groove whose many names reflect his continual self-re-creation and his unwillingness to be confined by the limitations of the past. Yet through all these many nicknames there also remains a common element—the presence of sugar—which symbolizes the continuity in the whirling chaos of his many transformations:

Sugar-Groove had so many none-such nicknames, but all were based in Sugar. Or should I say sugar-soaked. There was Sugar-Ditch, for his home town, but the only others that I was aware of (Sugar-Dripper, Sugar-Dipper, Sugar-Groove, Sugar-Grove, Sugar-Spook, Sugar-Goose...Sugar-Stagger, Sugar-Saint, Sugar-Spine, Sugar-Dick, Sugar-Stud, Sugar-Loaf, Sugar-Smoke, Sugar-Shit, Sugar-Eyes, and Sugar-Shark) referred to various tributes paid to his revealed sexual merriment and moxie or prowess; or his cunning at dice, cards, gambling tables and other games of chance. (*DD* 97-98)

Sugar-Groove's own life provides the material for his transformations. Forrest presents this as an important artisic form in traditional African-American culture, where other artistic accomplishments were closed off by racism and poverty. Many vibrant passages in Forrest's work, particularly in *Divine Days,* describe this kind of artistry in life. For example, there are "older Negro waiters":

The sophisticated refinement of many of their number was meshed with a down, tough, boss and embossing, angular view of reality; full of fine grace, street savvy, aristocratic bearing and training, discipline, salty language. Many retrained the wealthy in everything from table manners to the latest dance step. Certain waiters defined what it meant to be unsquare, long, long, ago in this old world, to the new world. They turned accoutrements into artful fashions, which were constantly being stolen, or misread. (*DD* 523)

Nicknaming is one basic form of the poetry of the streets and expresses the creative impulse to transform the chaos of reality through artistry into richer conceptions of identity. Naming is also importantly connected with that other great resource of the African-American tradition: religious spirituality. Even when he is most deeply torn by grief for his lost mother, Nathaniel Witherspoon senses that his one hope of escaping the pit of despair is through the redemptive hope of faith in Christ. He dreams of that redemption in the metaphor of an old gospel song, as a form of name changing: if Jesus would give him his ultimate nickname and finally reveal his real identity, the chaos of his life could be transformed into hope for the future: "And somehow now upon the porches of my reverie-bent heart, I could hear myself singing Jesus—JESUS JESUS told me that the world would hate me, Lord, if HE changed my name/But I told my Jesus, MY FATHER WHO art—It would be, yes it would indeed be all right if he changed my name/My name/My Name" (*Tree* 74).

For Forrest there is a close connection between the artist's re-creation of chaos into order and the religious experience through which the suffering and evil of this world is redeemed by the realization of God's love. Like W.E.B. DuBois and others, Forrest believes that religion has been one of the greatest cultural creations of African-Americans and his novels are full of evocations of its depth and power. Here, for example, the men's choir at the "Anchor of Zion Baptist Church" embodies ages of historical transformations in the profundities of the religious experience:

Voices of ancient men, in the well of the church, standing in a semi-circle (like a hovering Greek Chorus). And I suddenly heard changing field shouts and cries of warning, anchored in slavery; sobbing, wailing, warbling, groaning, whooping, grunting, awe-swept. Transforming the memory of the human voice into a celebrating instrument, echoing an articulation out of the memory bank of time, tribulation, and suffering, celebration and escape, dire warnings and reshapen blood-curdling shrieks. Admonishment beyond words but then the shocking moment of a miracle—expressed now to me as an awakening to the sudden smell of terror. At the frontier of feeling, and intelligence, when gesture, dance, gasp, moan, pantomime (hush), backbone strut, and bending knee-bones spoke for the soul's angularity of flight, horror and wonder. But that was not enough. For in the beginning was The Word. (*DD* 475)

Forrest's double religious heritage shapes his treatment of religion. Catholicism appears in his rich cultural allusivness and interest in the complexities of spiritual tradition and ritual. However, African-American Protestanism is the central focus of Forrest's attention. Black Protestantism in Forest County is represented by characters, by important episodes involving church services, by forms like the sermon and the testimony, and by its deep influence for good or ill on most of the central characters through the portrayal of religious experiences like the traumatic ecstasy of conversion.

The most important figures representing religion are those powerful older women who have such an impact on Nathaniel Witherspoon's life: his aunt Hattie Breedlove Wordlaw, who comforts him at the time of his mother's death, and his adoptive grandmother, Great-Momma Sweetie Reed Witherspoon, who narrates her history and that of her father to Nathaniel in *Two Wings to Veil My Face*. Rachel Carpenter Flowers, the tragic adoptive mother of Regal Pettibone in *The Bloodworth Orphans*, plays a somewhat similar role in that novel.

These African-American matriarchs may reflect the influence of William Faulkner's celebrated Dilsey, and they may even be a kind of transformation of the stereotypical black mammy figure. They are also based to some extent on important figures in Forrest's own family, most notably his great-grandmother, a deeply devout woman who lived with the family when Forrest was young, and his two aunts, Maude Richardson and Maude White, to whom *Two Wings to Veil My Face* is dedicated.[9] Forrest's older women are wonderfully vital and different characters who possess transcendent powers of endurance and sacrifice drawn from the depths of their religious faith. They are towers of strength and courage in their own lives and embody the community's most important spiritual traditions. For Nathaniel, they become models of the imaginative transformation of the chaos of everyday life into spiritual truth; along with Sugar-Groove and others who represent the wisdom of the streets, these women are important guides in how to "find a way out of noway."

Yet each of these apostles of faith is a unique individual and plays a different role in Nathaniel's life. There's an edge of corruption, decadence, and madness to Rachel Flowers' faith, and, in a hilarious episode she nearly drowns Nathaniel in an overflowing bathtub in her zeal to baptize him (*Bloodworth* 74-76). The blind Rachel is such an extremist that

she commanded total sacrifice and submission from man. Nathaniel never heard her mention the concept of *mercy*. To bear witness and total sacrifice to Almighty God, not in exchange nor as a hopeful ritual for the knowledge and wisdom, about what was constantly expected in the way of daily sacrifice, as well as the long-haul sacrifice, but as the needle-eyed honed way to eternal life, for that was already inherent in the Word Itself, and too much knowledge was surely a dangerous thing, she drew up from her many cliche bags. (*Bloodworth* 58-59)

Nathaniel's Aunt Hattie Breedlove, on the other hand, is more purely selfless and comforting in her faith, more concerned with endurance and transcendence and less with sin. Indeed, for her, sinning is part of the process of redemption: "then all of a sudden, just as you beginning to gain some understanding of the understanding, you starts to backsliding and forgetting who you are, and where you been, and that there's always yet another river to cross, yes, and you starts to falling and he knows falling is important to true believing and righteous rising 'cause son he can't wash your sins away until you've sinned" (*Tree* 88). It is Breedlove who gives Nathaniel his initial understanding of the relationship between religious experience and artistic transformation and leads him toward his vocation as a builder of the city recreated by artistry.

Great-Momma Sweetie Reed is the most complex and fascinating of these figures. This remarkable character reveals to Nathaniel, her adopted grandson, some important information about his family history in *Two Wings to Veil My Face*, including the fact that she is his adoptive instead of his real grandmother. In a coda to *There Is a Tree* entitled "Transformation" and added to the book in 1988, Sweetie, at age 100, writes an amazing letter to President Johnson commenting on the current racial scene. Born two years after the end of the Civil War and carrying in her memory the history narrated to her by her father at his death in 1906 (he was born in 1827) Sweetie's memory extends well back into the time of slavery, and she has endured many of the horrors of racism, including the rape and murder of her beloved mother by white outlaws when she was only seven years old. Married at a very young age to Nathaniel's redoubtable grandfather, Jericho Witherspoon, an escaped slave who has become a distinguished lawyer and judge in the North, Sweetie has also had to endure the early childhood deaths of all of her children, and finally, her husband's fathering on another woman the child who becomes Nathaniel's father.

As she narrates her history, Sweetie becomes Forrest's richest example of the extraordinary power of African-Americans to survive not only the chaos and evil of slavery and racism, but the extraordinary transformations of "The Great Migration" and the new life in the ghettos of cities like New York, Chicago, Detroit, and Los Angeles. Her incredible life has intensified Sweetie's sense of responsibility for her fellow human beings and she has long devoted herself to feeding the homeless at the ghetto kitchen she has inherited from Lovelady Breedlove. The depth of Sweetie's religious convictions has only honed the sharpness of her tongue and her wit, and this remarkable combination of loving nurture and selfless dedication to the unfortunate, with acid-sharp perceptions and ruthless integrity, enable her not only "to play the dozens with our Founding Fathers (some of whom might even truly be our American cousins)" but to bring the troubled and uncertain Nathaniel to a new level of understanding and spiritual insight:

Commanding him to silence, cursing, praying, denouncing, rendering up counter-memoirs, phrases from scriptures, spirituals, then only gestures: the gestures of sign language, and homemade ones spun up from the grievousness of her soul's captivity in a windstorm; in flight as two wings unveiling her soul . . . an unfolding and a parting away. . . . Only grief-stricken gestures, as her soul chased and chastened his words, long and deep into the night and unto the dawning light of the new day. (*Two Wings* 295-96)

For Forrest, such women are the deepest embodiment of the African-American religious tradition and representatives of that extraordinary matriarchy which has engineered its survival through the worst. However, the official spokesmen for the churches are male preachers. Forrest's representation of their amazing sermons is a very important dimension of his art. These preachers are a complex group, and they range from the largely admirable Pompey c.j. Browne, who "has become something of a transformation of Adam Clayton Powell, Martin Luther King, Leon Sullivan and Richard Pryor, to the demonic trickster W.A.D. Ford, whose magical cult of "DIVINE DAYS" satirizes the worst excesses of evangelical religion both white and black. In between there are a number of spell-binders who are quite capable of rising to true insights when the spirit moves them, but also inclined to self-righteousness, jealousy of other preachers, the quest for personal power, and the manipulation of the credulous.

The majestic, charismatic six foot seven inch Browne (based in part on the legendary African-American preacher J.C. Austin) is an authentic man of the spirit, who is able to bring his congregations into a whirlwind of ecstasy through his furious eloquence. As he preaches, he becomes transformed into something beyond himself, ultimately seeming to become an embodiment of the word itself:

And the moldering soul of Rev. Browne coming through the wilderness of grumbling now grunting, moaning now chanting rage-eloquence and glory-majesty and humility and shocking elegance *sang* through a series of humming voices spun out to tongues . . . words beyond words into The Word, his trembling flesh alive, and leaping within the huge frame. The material of his robes winging like the old clothes of a scarecrow, caught in a windstorm. (*Two Wings* 130-31)

The Easter sermon which Nathaniel remembers hearing with his grandmother is a vibrant example of black sermonizing with its combination of vernacular language, folk images, biblical allusions, and profound emotion, and is worth comparing with Faulkner's representation of the Rev. Shegog's Easter sermon in *The Sound and the Fury* and with the powerful sermons in Ellison's *Invisible Man*. Among other things, Rev. Browne has modernized and urbanized his rhetoric, introducing the rhythms and the language of the streets. In the following passage from the Easter sermon, Rev. Browne attacks his congregation's obsession with material possessions by pointing to their love for their automobiles and then contrasting this with Christ's entry into Jerusalem:

Why I hear tell some of you trying to pour off that sardine oil into the carburator towards the end of the month. You're out there celebrating that chrome like you annointing, buffing and accelerating the Word into chrome—making it whiter and lighter than snow, with your steaming wet-wash rags as prayer cloths worshiping up your lily-white mule machines which are as stubborn as you are . . . Church, you've strapped down the radiance of your ancestral memory like those despair-filled slaves who delivered up the word on the runaways' route to the slave catchers in the days of our previous condition. But my master and our Jesus spun into Jerusalem sweet, cool and low in the saddle upon a jackass; that was his surrey and his chariot. What do you think the old folks meant when they sang, *Ride on, King Jesus, no man can hinder me.* You, Church, are looking for a miracle to medicate the malice within our maladies; but I say upon this Easter Sunday morning, Arise, turn about and come on out of the wilderness and turn a new face to God's Radiance. (*Two Wings* 129-30)

Rev. Browne's vernacular but prophetic eloquence is also on display when he preaches a brilliant eulogy of Nathaniel's grandfather and a moving sermon on the twelfth anniverary of Dr. Martin Luther King's death. Yet even Browne is not immune to the temptation of using his religious power for personal ends. As Danille Taylor-Guthrie points out, "His service at Easter is closer to a James Brown performance than a religious observance. He is resurrected not as Christ, J.C., but like J.B., who in a seeming fit of exhaustion is covered by a cape only to throw it aside in a renewed ouburst of energy. This act could be judged, as Sweetie does, as profaning the sacred; but it is also evidence of the thin line that exists between the sacred and secular in African-American culture." But the ultimate example of the corruption of religion in Forest county is the nefarious and diabolical "tricknology" of the demonic W.A.D. Ford. Ford uses the power of religion entirely for fraudelent, decadent, and sinister purposes. Appearing mysteriously in Forest County after a dubious career down South, this false messiah sets up a series of religious cults, including one known as DIVINE DAYS to which he attracts followers, milks them for all they are worth, and then mysteriously disappears. A fabulous charlatan and showman, Ford uses magic tricks like his version of the Indian rope trick, to lure in the credulous and deceive the unwary. His religious services are outrageous parodic pastiches of Christian and pagan myth and ritual:

old Ford, or Bishop St. Palm, as he now calls himself, has begun a forty-day fast in a golden coffin, for "divine guidance," with an Egyptian cobra in a veiled water tank, made like a pit, twenty-five feet beneath him. Apparently they arrested Ford for a few hours and accused him of operating a "moonshine still," beneath the very altar of the Anointed One Church, and for peddling that "holy wine" to his growing congregation. (*Bloodworth* 326)

Wizard Alpha Decathalon Ford, as one of his many aliases names him, surrounds himself with a mythology of origin similar to that promulgated about the Black Muslim messenger W.A.D. Fard, and an Effete Elite (a takeoff on the Muslim "Fruit of Islam"); he also makes use of a monstrous dog (resembling the classical Cerberus, guardian of Hades) known as ALL SOULS to help keep the faithful in line; and he has a beautiful young white mistress known as "Gay-Rail" (which plays on both the symbology of the grail and the racist canard that black men especially desire white women) with whom he indulges his epic carnal appetites. Gay-Rail even participates in his dubious rituals:

Ford declared before the assembled press conference . . . that he would stay perched in the golden gobbler coffin—like a burnished golden Easter egg—and arise on Easter Sunday morning from the coffin and give his congregation the word on the wine. . . . But by the time the police arrived a golden blonde, not a golden egg, was now dancing, inside of the tank, the dance of seven veils with a wine-drugged Egyptian cobra snake about her throat. (*Bloodworth* 327)

Where Ford represents the demonic evil inherent in any religious or spiritual power, most of the preachers of Forest County, are, at worst, tempted to self-dramatization, like Pompey c.j. Browne, or to using their ministerial positions to indulge their personal appetites like the appropriately named Rev. Honeywood "Sweet-Briar" Cox, or the Rev. Clay, J. Lightfoot, who:

was something to behold with the diamond rings on his fingers, his floweriness of contrived, sterling and preening phrases (vaulting over his actual modesty of his own intellectual angularity of ideas, his only touchstone to modesty); his baby-blue silk shirt, with laced french cuffs and rhinestone cufflinks; his dark-blue, three-piece suit (hand stitched in London, his advance copy on the back of the church program duly noted); his spit-shined, ebony wing-tips; his flowing "three-layered-wave-dip" stylized hair. . . The Rev. Clay J. Lightfoot made a most powerful imprint upon the church sisters. (*DD* 478)

Despite such temptations Forest County preachers, on the whole, struggle to live up to their roles as religious and cultural leaders and to use their power for good, at least as they understand it. Unlike Joyce, who came to view the Irish church as a betrayal of the hopes and dreams of the faithful, Forrest is more positive about African-American religion. For Joyce, the artist as high priest of the imagination, must strive to replace the power of the decadent priesthood with a new humanistic revelation. Though Forrest shares Joyce's view of the high seriousness of the artist's mission, he does not see the same basic conflict between religion and art. For him, the artist must draw on the great spiritual power and religious strengths of the African-American tradition just as good preachers draw on the skills of the artist, the dramatist, and the musician to raise the spirits of their congregations. A good novel or drama is like a powerful religious service in its celebration of the transformative powers of the imagination, and, at times, Forrest's fiction takes on the wild, ecstatic, and overpoweringly dramatic quality that shines forth in black religious services, as in the following description of a church choir in full tilt:

Voices somersaulting out of themselves—sleeves out of arms, arms out of sleeves—*now* hieroglyphical etching of voices with the mathematical precision of magicians pinching large, flagrantly gorgeous handkerchiefs, breath-taking in a rainbow, and then slipping them through the eye of a needle . . . Flourishing rhythms, now turning into dance patterns reconnnected to the backbone out of the Blues gone bad turned to good. Six young dudes are throwing good after bad-hipbone boogie-bold-butt for Jesus as the spirited spectators try to catch their breath in relief. (*DD* 700-01)

While Ford's orgiastic rituals use a combination of mystification, fear, eroticism and cheap tricks to arouse and manipulate his followers, the better preachers of Forest Country are deeply concerned with the authenticity of their message and the inner meaning of their visions. In this respect, they offer the artist real insight into the creative process. Though he shows a healthy youthful scepticism about the inflated claims and egotism of successful ministers, Joubert Jones is nonetheless impressed by the deeply spiritual sense of the religious exprerience he receives from certain preachers. One of them tells him:

Sometimes when I'm really preaching, the force of the Holy Spirit will lift me up . . .the mix of ideas expressed through me as a vessel of the Holy Spirit, as a means of God using me as a mechanism of communication to the people—and I get lost in myself, I get actually hypnotized. Now the Holy Spirit takes over. Then I say "the Preacher has come." This gives me that extra wind, like a marathon runner. I go on sometimes and eclipse my best efforts; and the people say, you were never better, Reverend Hines. That's when you are really preaching, when you have a meshing with the people's hearts and minds and all go up with you to the Mountain of God, to the City of God. (*DD* 491-92)

In another discussion with a minister he has been assigned to interview for the *Forest County Dispatch*, Joubert asks the Rev. Maurice Roper when and how he felt the call to preach the Word. The connection between this question and Joubert's own uncertainty about his future as a writer is evident and he is deeply struck, though still sceptical, about the Rev. Roper's answer, which takes the form of an extended parable about a family picnic in which he wanders away and becomes lost in the cellar of a mysterious decaying house. Here, in the depths of his despair, Rev. Roper says that he heard what he refers to as a "Daddy voice" come to rescue him and the other children from their confusion and lostness:

Come to me like a huge-hearted heralding wing wind to the North to the South, side-winders to the East streak-a-lean to the West—robing me up in every color, robing my body in a shade of the rainbow . . . out of the clearing into the great-gathering-up, unfolding. Then reclothing; then stripping me away . . . and once I started to rise it helped sweep me up that I . . . that I had wings. The Daddy voice had me re-directed in my mis-guidance. Pouring light and healing to my hapless condition. Son of Man, can these dry skeleton bones live? The Amazing Grace of it all. (*DD* 464)

Joubert remains unable to "buy into this brandywine of faith" (465), but by the end of *Divine Days* he has come to realize that the spiritual re-birth that Rev. Roper spoke of in his picnic story is a religious analogue for the imaginative power of re-creation, the greatest gift of the writer. The imaginative transformation of the religious tradition which, along with its music, constitutes the most important African-American cultural heritage, is one major way in which the black writer can become a significant part of that great tradition, as well as help map out the difficult road ahead. In this way Forrest's two central themes of the initiation of the culturally significant artist and the quest for spiritual power to make a way out of noway become united.

Forrest's deepest recurrent impetus in his manifold fictions is toward a fusing of the religious and the artistic imaginations which re-invents the redeeming and saving African-American cultural genius:

No doubt that religion is the opiate of the people, but it is an opiate that we cannot get along without. But it is the Negro in them that saves them. Even as they (the Black Muslims) were commanded that they must drop that old Negro name and assume an X. What saved them from the dead was that some remnant, some streak was still there of Negro, not African, and not European, but Negro—with that fabulous impulse to reinvent, to make a way out of noway. The Negro-American's will to transform, reinvent, and stylize until Hell freezes over. (*DD* 1127-28)

Works: The Witherspoon Trilogy

Forrest's first three novels center around crucial moments in the life of Nathaniel Turner Witherspoon, born like his creator in 1937.[10] *There Is a Tree More Ancient than Eden* (1973) represents Nathaniel's complex exploration of his consciousness, both conscious and unconscious, individual and archetypal, personal and historic as he is reluctantly forced to probe the meaning of his existence in the traumatic aftermath of his mother's death. In the course of this exploration, the reader is introduced to Nathaniel's complex family tradition, the seething and tragic multiplicity of his cultural and historical heritage, and the chaotic world of Forest County in the early 1950s.

The Bloodworth Orphans (1977) moves ahead to the early 1970s when Nathaniel, still undecided about his life, has reached the highly symbolic age of 33. At this time, in the early 1970s, Forest County has entered an era of civic breakdown marked by widespread violence and rioting in the inner city. In this novel Nathaniel is less a voyager through the jungle of his own inner consciousness and more a witness to the tragic fate of the doomed offspring of a family of mixed race sired by the sexual depredations of the white Bloodworth clan.

Finally, in *Two Wings to Veil My Face* (1983) Nathaniel at the age of 21 is confronted by his grandmother, Sweetie Reed Witherspoon, with the true history of his family in the beginning times of slavery and in its aftermath. This novel reveals more fully the origins of the ambiguous familial and cultural heritage, which the mature Nathaniel had confronted in *The Bloodworth Orphans*. Thus, *Two Wings* actually precedes *The Bloodworth Orphans* in the chronology of Nathaniel's life and development, and I will treat the novels in that order rather than in the sequence of their writing.

There Is a Tree More Ancient than Eden

Forrest's first novel is also his most difficult and densest work, chacterized by complex internal monologues representing many different layers of consciousness and by the attempt to set forth as one critic put it, an archeology of black consciousness. To accomplish this purpose, Forrest eschews the usual novelistic conventions of plot, episode, and chronological narrative. With respect to its fictional predecessors, *There Is a Tree* most resembles Faulkner's *The Sound and the Fury*, which Forrest was studying at the time he began writing. Like Faulkner's masterpiece, Forrest's novel is structured around a series of internal narratives, but where Faulkner gave his different sections over to different narrators, Forrest's novel is largely made up of sections representing different layers of a single narrator's consciousness. In addition, where Faulkner later wrote an "Appendix" explaining the history of the Compson family,[11] Forrest wrote the "Lives" section that introduced the major characters of *There Is a Tree* on Toni Morrison's suggestion that readers needed some such information to understand what was going on in Nathaniel Witherspoon's swirling consciousness. Later, when *There Is a Tree* was reissued by Another Chicago Press in 1988, Forrest added a final section "Transformation" which must now be considered part of the text of *There Is a Tree*.

The eleven chapters of *There Is a Tree* (excluding the two parts of "Transformation") are divided into five sections: The Lives; The Nightmare; The Dream; The Vision; and Wakefulness. Though these divisions were a later addition to the manuscript, they roughly correspond to different stages of the complex inner process of "troubling, remembering, revealing" which Nathaniel goes through in the course of the novel.

The "Lives" section introduces the major characters who will dominate the novel, in particular, Nathaniel Witherspoon and his family—his father, Arthur, his late mother, Madeline, his aunt Hattie Breedlove, and his powerful grandfather, Jericho Witherspoon—and friends, particularly the ill-fated, but deeply devout M.C. Browne, the rebellious Jamestown Fishbond, and Maxwell "Black-Ball" Saltport, who becomes a Black Muslim. The last part of the "Lives" section, which includes brief comments on Louis Armstrong, Frederick Douglass, Harriet Tubman, and Abraham Lincoln, implicates levels of historical and cultural meaning beyond the personal life of Nathaniel Witherspoon.

The different layers of Nathaniel's consciousness are represented as a narrative of his nightmares, dreams, and visions, and are articulated through a number of central symbols whose transformations represent the encounter between the different levels of Nathaniel's conscious-unconsious mind as he is driven by grief for his dead mother into new realms of knowledge. Nathaniel, in effect, embarks on a dream-quest, searching for knowledge which can guide and order his life.[12] The symbol of the "tree more ancient than Eden," which appears in the novel's title is a good example of this. The Eden tree is, of course, the most famous tree in the history of Western civilization, the tree of the knowledge of good and evil from the biblical account of creation in the Book of Genesis. This tree is connected to the "apple-tree ladder ascending" that Nathaniel experiences at the beginning of his nightmare (*Tree* 42) and which refers to the climb into knowledge forced upon him by his mother's death. But the realization which Nathaniel confronts as he climbs higher and deeper is that the tree of Eden is also the tree of the crucifixion and that man's struggle toward knowledge is marked by suffering and sacrifice. This stuggle toward knowledge through nightmare, dream and vision leads to Nathaniel's attempt to deal with his life in the state of "Wakefulness" which follows the dream-quest of the novel.

The image of a tree "more ancient than Eden" suggests an archetypal tree which underlies the many different legendary trees of human mythology and religion. For example, in early Germanic mythology, which may well predate the Biblical account of Eden, there is the myth of Ygdrasil, the Earth tree, from which all things originate. Another implication of the "more ancient tree" is the idea that there are human civilizations older than Western civilization and its Biblical roots, particularly in Africa.

Such hints of the African origins of mythic archetypes relate to Nathaniel's dream-driven journey into the historical memory of his people, where he encounters the historical tragedy of African-American slavery and the victimization of blacks. This leads his questing consciousness to the lynching tree, one of those "Southern trees bearing strange fruit—Blood on the leaves and blood at the root" from Billie Holiday's powerful song, which Forrest cites as the epigraph to *There Is a Tree*. In "The Vision," the fourth section of the novel, Forrest uses the structural framework of one type of African-American Easter sermon in which the preacher describes the events of the crucifixion and resurrection as if he were an eye-witness of the scene,[13] to represent the crucifixion as a lynching and thus to suggest an analogy between Christ's redemptive suffering and the historical fate of black Americans.

These different layers of archetypal, historical, and personal realization come together in an extraordinary passage from Nathaniel's dream in which he see death's pursuit of his beloved mother, not only as Satan's entry into Eden but as the white master's pursuit of a runaway slave:

and she/Mother listening down the warning woods (apparently mother hadn't seen the lion) for the clacking equestrian's hoof uprooting the snow-skinned earth and watching for the first glinting warnings of spurs, of his pearl handles, in the midnight depths of the alabaster encircled forests . . . and the flakes falling like mountains (yet the land unconscious of the downing down and the flaking, and the yelping hound dogs) as the brooding black madonna sat under the tree . . . Waited under that tree that looked like a bleeding scarecrow while the rider, curled about the tree from its roots to its leafless tops, looking like the twisted vertebrae of a snake with its blood-red rose dripping from his lapel into the snow-laden tree more ancient than Eden. (*Tree* 84)

As Nathaniel's traumatic grief drives him higher and deeper into realms of consciousness accessible only through the powers of dream and vision, he encounters at least four different levels of meaning. These intersect in clusters of symbols, like those connecting the Eden tree, the cross, and the lynching tree. The first level is that of Nathaniel's own personal life and his experiences of family and friends. Second, there is the historic experience of blacks in America, to which Nathaniel is related not only through history, but through the memories of older members of his family, most significantly the aged Jericho Witherspoon who was born in slavery and escaped from it. Another of Nathaniel's relatives, his Aunt Hattie Breedlove, represents another level of consciousness, associated with the Bible and its mythical-spiritual view of the world. Finally, there are the hints of archetypal meanings going back to the earliest origins of human life, which have been transformed into many different specific forms in the course of human cultural evolution. These can be known only through the deepest probings of the visionary imagination.[14]

Nathaniel's journey into consciousness is symbolized by the most elaborately developed image in *There Is a Tree*, that of the wagon or train. The first published section of the novel, and probably the earliest written, developed this image. It was based on the red wagon belonging to the watermelon peddler, Noah Dickson, and driven by his stepson, Jamestown Fishbond, when Dickson became ill. Nathaniel remembers a scene when the deeply black Jamestown was turned away from the door of Nathaniel's middle-class mulatto Uncle DuPont and retaliated by throwing a cantaloupe back at him. Uncle DuPont grabbed his .45 pistol and shot wildly after the retreating Jamestown as he drove his wagon up DuSable Street shouting back, "that's your little red wagon."

Though hilariously comic, this scene has very serious undertones in that it reveals the way in which American racism has separated the light-skinned African-American middle class from the darker-skinned underclass, alienating American blacks from each other as well as from whites. In his nightmare, Nathaniel associates Jamestown's wagon with his mother's funeral procession which followed the same route. By a similar process of dreamwork, the mother's funeral procession becomes Lincoln's funeral train, symbolizing martyrdom to the cause of human freedom; it also comes to represent the freedom train, carrying slaves to the north and the hope for a better life. This train also transmutes at various points into the slave ships carrying Africans to America and into a celestial train-chariot, carrying souls to heaven like the chariot in the famous spiritual:

(and my soul felt driven and dumb and colorless yet full of color; lost like a voice on stilts warning of the hour of Sabbath and of the clearing of bloody rootless and nameless plantations of Eden and trangressions and transfigurations and tribulations upon a hanging cross past cotton Christ chains and trains and golden slippers and lead and chariots and gardens and bruised-blood biddings and drums and the sepulcher-like coffin boats) (*Tree* 69-70)

Nathaniel's dreaming journey goes through three major stages which are marked off by the three main sections of his dream. The Nightmare section begins with Nathaniel striving to reach across death to find his dead mother. This quest is portrayed in images of climbing the apple tree of Eden and flying through cosmic space, yet even here the traditional image of heaven as "milk-white angels" dancing on stars is quickly replaced by a vison of black angels, suggesting that racism even extends into the myths of heaven. The flying Nathaniel soon encounters "those other angels—black skeletons tossed and driven, clacking together, as if they had been hatcheted down from the uppermost tops of the most massive trees in Eden" (*Tree* 42). Even as his dreaming soul tries to escape from the human tragedies of death and suffering, Nathaniel hears to the west the whistle of a train "crying down a long-ago-gone switch-blading track (like that streaking scar on old man Dickson's face) . . . (*Tree* 43).

This basic symbolic opposition of flying and climbing as opposed to trains, wagons, and symbols of movement along the earth continues throughout Nathaniel's dreaming. In general, the train symbolism is associated with the tragedy of history, with funerals, enslavement, and the inescable suffering of the past. Flying is an expression of the will to transcend, to escape, to find freedom. The tree becomes an intermediate symbol between earth and heaven, between history and transcendence; Nathaniel discovers that climbing the tree of sin and suffering is the only way to escape from the martyrdom of history.

The nightmare section is full of images of violence and death. Some are reflections of things Nathaniel has himself experienced, like the clash between his Uncle and Jamestown Fishbond, the burning of a neighborhood building in which children died, parental beatings of his friends Black-Ball Saltport and M.C. Browne, and his mother's death and funeral. But these personal images are mixed with others: the contemporary tragedies of great African-American artists like Charlie Parker and Billie Holiday—both destroyed by drugs—and historic images of slave ships, the pursuit of runaway slaves, lynchings.

The two figures of Jamestown and Aunt Hattie Breedlove emerge as powerful antagonists in Nathaniel's mind. The rebellious Jamestown, named for the colony where African-American slaves were first brought to America, is a gifted artist who is not allowed to express his anger at American racism in his paintings and turns instead to revolutionary politics. He becomes a sort of symbolic conductor on the train of history that Nathaniel dreams up in his nightmare. Aunt Hattie, the devout exponent of religious transcendence, speaks instead for trust in God and belief in the redemption of heaven.

As the nightmare section reaches its ending, Nathaniel is riding Jamestown's train toward the valley of death where he later experiences the terrible vision of the crucifixion; yet even as he is pulled toward this horror, he hears the voice of Aunt Hattie Breedlove's preacher quoting St. Paul: "For we know that if our earthly house of this tabernacle were dissolved, we have a building of God and a house not made of hands; eternal in the heavens" (*Tree* 75).

In the dream section Nathaniel begins to realize how his personal grief for the death of his mother is emblematic of the whole history of African-American anguish and loss. This new awareness gradually moves him from an obsession with the nightmare of reality to an exploration of some of the transcendent dreams of freedom and redemption that have characterized the African-American tradition.[15] The section is particularly marked by three dialogues (chaps 6, 8, and 9) in which traditional African-American religious, social and political ideals are subjected to interrogation. The first is between Nathaniel and his Aunt Hattie Breedlove in which the latter tells Nathaniel that, through faith in Christ, he can turn his grief over his mother's death into the power to transform himself and others. Aunt Hattie represents African-American spirituality and its remarkable ability to turn suffering into redemptive force. Chapter 8 is Jamestown Fishbond's account to Nathaniel of how his grandfather tried to make Jamestown's onerously named father, Moses Booker Fishbond, accept the ideology of Booker T. Washington and become a great "race leader." Jamestown's father chose, instead, a life of hustling and an early death. Finally, in chapter 9, Nathaniel dreams of a debate between the rebellious Jamestown and Nathaniel's own grandfather, Jericho Witherspoon, over the past and future of African-American history. Witherspoon still believes that African-Americans can best struggle to improve their lot by working politically within the framework of American democracy: "you come from a people who have a history of never currying favor but rather making do out of the dust,transforming the most rudimentary thing into utilitarian survival kits of usefulness" (*Tree* 110). Jamestown, however, insists that only violent revolution and a complete overturning of the present society can bring about black freedom: "Bloodshed is the only infusion guaranteed to shock the slumbering spirit and fire the magical Soul-Furnace for FREEDOM" (*Tree* 111).

The unresolved debate between accomodationists and revolutionaries leads Nathaniel's dreaming spirit back to the train of history and the valley of death and crucifixion. The fourth section of the novel, "The Vision," is a remarkably sustained and horrifying narrative of a crucifixion-lynching that reflects the archetypal history of human sacrifice from the earliest blood rituals and classical myths of sacrifice like Orpheus and Prometheus through Christ's crucifixion and the terrible lynchings, burnings, and castrations which were so horrifically endemic to the American South between Reconstruction and World War II.[16] To create this narrative Forrest uses the device of the African-American Easter sermon in which the preacher seeks to arouse the emotions of his congregation by making them feel like eyewitnesses of the crucifixion itself. In addition, Forrest uses a language permeated with Biblical and Shakespearian phrases, as well as images taken from crucifixion, lynchings, and other forms of sacrifice to suggest the extent to which human history is pervaded by such acts of violence.

However, Nathaniel's vision of the crucifixion culminates in a scene of resurrection and transcendence. For after the victim has been lynched, crucified, and dismembered, his eyes still seem to be alive, haunting the crowd. But as the crowd moves to destroy these prophetic eyes a group of angels appears who themselves bear the marks of enslavement: "a band of bruised-blood angels were now seen moving to the rhythm of the people—wearing stained tunics, which I had not seen before, yes and those chains upon their left ankles (*Tree* 145). These angels gather up the dismembered parts of the victim and reunite them and then, in a scene of apoclyptic strangeness and wonder, the victim seems both to rise toward his resurrection and to sink back into the chaotic reality of the world:

LORD FATHER HE WAS FLYING, his wings wretched, wrongsided, rotten rank—like the hag's rags, yet step-ladder climbing (moving on upwards as if he heard some secret drum drum drum) with a tambourine undercurrent/a long ways from home/homeward . . . And the wings splattered with wine, blood, dung, rain water, snow, soot, holes, patches, icicles, grease, duck butter, sperm—NOTHINGNESS—*and back down into a huge black pit and round and round back down into the night.* (*Tree* 147)

Nathaniel's vision powerfully evokes both the horror and the eternal recurrence of human suffering and sacrifice. But it also suggests the possibility, however uncertain and ambiguous, of the transformation and transcendence of the horror. Here we come to the heart of *There Is a Tree.* The complex discovery which Nathaniel makes as he travels through the visionary world of nightmare, dream, and vision driven by the hope of some kind of reunion with his dead mother, is that grief, loss, suffering and sacrifice are the common lot of human beings; yet he also learns that African-Americans, because of the almost unrelieved tragedy of their history, have developed amazing spiritual and artistic resources for transforming this suffering into redemptive power. Nathaniel must now begin to grow out of his childish immersion in grief and start to develop the spiritual force that will enable him to re-create his world without his mother's sustaining love. This is the subject of the novel's fifth section, "Wakefulness."

In some of the most richly poetic language of a novel which is full of linguistic pyrotechnics, "Wakefulness" begins with Nathaniel's "hawk-haunting" spirit struggling both to acknowledge the reality of death ("the old fouled and dawning deed yoking the word into a waxy horror") and the tenuous possibility of redemption ("the neon cross etched against the moon shaving, oscillating upon the pavement gutters and breaking across a scarecrow plantation [*Tree* 151]). The rhythm of rising to a vision of redemption and falling into the grief and despair of mortality, which appeared at the beginning of the "Nightmare" section, dominates Nathaniel's waking reflections as he struggles to come to terms with his mother's death as well as the historical tragedy of his race and its continuing exile in an increasingly decaying city.[17] Seeking to escape from the pit of despair, he turns for comfort and wisdom to his Aunt Hattie Breedlove, who tells him that he must accept the knowledge of death and the inevitability of suffering and sacrifice, but that in spite of this he can "ride on king jesus no man can hinder you—you can make a way out of noway" by building the city of the spirit in the ruins of history.

Once again Nathaniel remembers his mother's funeral procession through the same streets he dreamed of in his nightmare vision, but now he understands more fully the implications of this archetypal journey and the kind of spiritual rebirth and acceptance of reality he must endure to pass from childhood into manhood. At the end of the section, Nathaniel has arrived at that terribly painful moment between the death of childhood and the birth of maturity. He is desperately torn between continuing to hide himself away from knowledge and emerging into the torment and difficulty of being an adult human being and an African-American man:

And the fist of my bloody right hand coming down hard and well-deep into the pit of my stomach and howling as if death's mothering-birthing switchblading force had sliced across my face, as i did come up from underneath the bed and stood in all of my nakedness before my mother's body-length mirror, locked away in all the enframing reflection as my bloody hands clasped away at my loins and i crumbled upon the floor rising and falling rising and falling and rising and falling. (*Tree* 163)

This is where Forrest left Nathaniel at the end of the original version of *There Is a Tree*. However, as we shall see, he further developed the character and his life in his next two novels, and then, in a final section, he later added to *There Is a Tree*. This new ending is entitled "Transformation."[18] It contains two sections, both of which take place considerably later than the earlier novel. One, "The Epistle of Sweetie Reed," is dated 1967, when Nathaniel is 30 rather than in the early 1950s when Nathaniel was in his teens.[19] Historically, Sweetie Reed's letter reflects the time when the first great victories of the Civil Rights movement had been consolidated into legislation by Lyndon Johnson, but when the Vietnam War was deeply dividing the American public and drawing attention and energy away from the struggle for equality.

The second episode is a sermon "OH JEREMIAH OF THE DREAMERS" preached in a tavern in the early hours of the morning of the twelfth anniversary of Martin Luther King's assassination. It is 1980 and Nathaniel, now 43, is among a group of "bitter city dwellers" who have gathered to "assess the meaning" of King's life. This is post-Vietnam America where conservatism and racism are beginning to emerge again and where many of the great hopes which animated the time between Nathaniel's original dream-quest and this final section have been profoundly disappointed.

The New Testament also ends with epistles and prophecies and the connection has a certain appropriateness. "Transformations" offers both apocalyptic warning and redemptive hope to an America which seems to be losing its way after the great surge of possibility generated by the Civil Rights movement. An older, but still uncertain Nathaniel has become the witness and historian of the tragic legacy of slavery and racism in *The Bloodworth Orpans* and *Two Wings to Veil My Face*; and in this final section of *There Is a Tree* he becomes involved in two highly symbolic events. One is an epistolary confrontation between Sweetie Reed and the President of the United States who has begun a war on poverty which Sweetie feels is long overdue but misguided. In addition, Sweetie encounters representatives of the radical student and black power movements of the sixties which she views as pathetically self-indulgent compared with the Civil Rights movement.

"The Epistle of Sweetie Reed" surely deserves a place among the major vernacular narratives of American literature. It is a marvelous tour de force of style and voice, which brings the vibrant character Forrest created in *Two Wings to Veil My Face* back to life and deploys her wit and wisdom to explore the state of politics, racism, and protest in America. Her advice to President Johnson about his War on Poverty and her criticism of the corruption and folly which have turned it from a beacon of hope into a pork barrel are permeated with the feisty spirit and the deep experience of this centennarian, who in spite of her years, and the horrors she has seen, is still animated by her faith in God and vibrantly alive with hope and vitality:

Mr President, you might say that I was framed by the framers, who tried to keep me out of the picture some three hundred and fifty years ago; however, I am not writing you to play the dozens with our Founding Fathers. . . . But, Mr. President, there is an eagle in my soul, and so I am writing to you personally . . . to set the record straight, yet it won't get straightened out until you and I are straight, and we won't be straight until God straightens us all out in a desgregated graveyard—and He returns to gather up His elect and holds one grand-finale-grave eruption-supreme court hearing over this troubled land. (*Tree* 168)

Sweetie's hilarious account of a sixties-style student protest is her warning to the president of how the war against poverty has gone astray. But the episode has another important meaning as well in that it illustrates the terrible gulf between young black people and the wisdom and style of the great African-American tradition. The novel's final part, the sermon on Martin Luther King delivered by Pompey c.j. Browne, expresses instead the power, the continuity and the continued relevance of that tradition even in the face of seeming failure and destruction as it celebrates the spirit and the legacy of Martin Luther King.

This final sermon brings *There Is a Tree* full circle, but with a difference. First of all, while the book began with Nathaniel's highly personal grief for his dead mother, it ends with a group ritual in which Nathaniel joins with others in memorializing not only a great leader of his people, but of all Americans, ranked by some as the greatest American leader of the twentieth century. Thus, King's story not only enacts the archetypal ritual of crucifixion which Nathaniel envisioned in the course of his dream-quest, but very specifically parallels the life of Abraham Lincoln, whose martyrdom was described in the "Lives" section and whose funeral train was one of the central images weaving its way through Nathaniel's nightmares. Though martyrdom and crucifixion thus continue to be at the still point of the turning wheel of history, Nathaniel has learned that his individual grief is connected to a larger historical reality of suffering and death. This realization of the place of individual suffering in a larger pattern opens up the possiblity of transformation and transcendence.

Second, the "Midnight Mass" at the Crossroads Rooster Tavern brings together the world of the streets and the world of the spirit. Not only is Pompey Browne's sermon full of the rhetoric of the streets, but it occurs as the climax of a ritual which uses many of the forms of street culture: "a wild talk fest, filled with curses, and moments of celebration; hyperbole, wild jokes, laconic speil, tall tales, horror stories . . . Moments when the slain King is both eulogized and then scandalized" (*Tree* 204). In this context, Browne's sermon becomes a weaving together of the two great strands of African-American culture. And as he evokes King's great crusades in Montgomery, Birmingham, and Chicago and then the terrible day in Memphis when the leader was assassinated, Browne rises to a whirlwind of eloquence out of which he cries for his hearers to take up the cross of King, whose voice still cries out in the wilderness. This furious, thundering climax gives a final expression to the interwoven combination of despair and hope that weaves throughout Nathaniel's nightmare journey across the dream landscape of African America. Browne's appeal to the heroic martyrdom of King shows that there may be more than one way to climb the tree of sin and suffering more ancient than Eden and "give birth to a dancing star."[20]

Two Wings to Veil My Face

I'm discussing *Two Wings* out of the order of its composition because, in terms of Nathaniel Witherspoon's story it precedes *The Bloodworth Orphans*. Its key event, Sweetie Reed's narrative to Nathaniel occurs in 1958, while most of *The Bloodworth Orphans* takes place in the early 1970s. In addition, I think there is a number of ways in which Forrest used *Two Wings* to reorient and unify his trilogy. Therefore the events and discoveries of *Two Wings* shed an interesting backward light and help us to understand more fully what happens in *The Bloodworth Orphans*. I will deal with Forrest's second novel after discussing *Two Wings*.

Forrest's third novel is a story within a story within a story, a complex structure which is necessary to represent a situation in which truths about the past lie hidden within the assumptions of the present and must be uncovered and revealed.[21] The ostensible date of the telling is 1958. Nathaniel has turned 21 and his grandmother Sweetie Reed Witherspoon finally tells him the story that she undertook to tell him in 1944, when Nathaniel was seven and his grandfather Jericho Witherspoon died at the age of 117. Sweetie, separated from her husband since 1905, had promised to explain this, as well as her strange behavior at Witherspoon's funeral, when Nathaniel reached his majority. Now, in 1958, Nathaniel is 21 and a college dropout very uncertain of his future. At Sweetie's insistence he hears and writes down her story.

However, this story, while it does eventually explain Sweetie's long separation from her husband, turns out to be much more complicated than that. Sweetie feels compelled to tell Nathaniel not only about the crucial events of her own past, but also the personal history narrated to her by her father, I.V. Reed, a house slave and later servant at the Rollins Reed plantation in Mississippi, which Sweetie heard at her father's death bed in 1906. I.V. Reed's deathbed apologia to his daughter parallels the aged Sweetie's account of herself to her grandson; Nathaniel is acute enough to realize that what he has been asked to participate in is much more than a story or even a family history. Actually, he is being asked to become part of the ongoing consciousness of his family and his people: "Nathaniel . . . wondered if all the story-telling, the loving, the harsh disciplining, the praying and the direction had been but a preparation for the day, *this* day, when he would have to take over her memories, and business, and even participate in the state of her soul's progress. So that he would have to be many kinds of men brought together as one, in one flesh, and soul, and mind" (*Two Wings* 5).

The tale which Sweetie bears is a remarkable one going back to what she calls the "beginning" or "*backwater*" time. It might almost be called a reverse creation story in which the Garden of Eden becomes a hellish plantation, with the cruel slavemaster Rollins Reed as Satan and Sweetie's mother Angelina as Eve. And like the account in Genesis, Sweetie's story "troubles and reveals" by questioning the past both historically and morally. Most importantly, Sweetie is carrying within her a good deal of unfinished business, not only resulting from her own ambiguous relationships with her father, her husband, and her adoptive son and grandson, but from the horrible trauma of slavery which threatened to destroy the humanity of an entire people.

I.V. Reed's story is a final attempt to justify and explain his life. He wants not only to clear himself with his long-estranged daughter, but with his beloved wife Angelina, Sweetie's mother, who has been dead for many years. In fact, as he begins his account, Reed confuses Sweetie with her mother, a confusion which reflects the many unresolved ambiguities which have developed over his long life. Born in 1827, Reed is an exception-ally quick and talented young man who becomes a house slave and body servant to his master Rollins Reed. Though alienated from the rest of the slaves, his remarkable memory and musical gifts have made him a repository of traditional African songs and rituals, which he performs for the other slaves while hiding in a tree.[22] Reed's peculiar position between the house and the field is a profoundly ambiguous one and also leads him into evil, when he uses his position and his cleverness to gain revenge against the powerful slave leader Reece Shank Haywood. Reed is jealous of Haywood's sexual prowess, and he tries to bring Haywood to heel by getting him in trouble with the "blackbirding" master who has been sexually using Haywood's woman.

However, this plan backfires and Haywood nearly kills the master before he is driven off with a rock from Reed's slingshot. In despair Reed calls on the old African healer, Auntie Foisty, who not only restores Rollins Reed to health, but uses her magic to transform him into a kinder master. In spite of this, Reed's wife, Mistress Sylvia, has Reece Shank Haywood tracked down and tortured to death. Since Reed's wounding of Haywood with a stone made it impossible for him to escape his trackers, Auntie Foisty lays a curse on Reed that he must forever be the servant and the shadow of Rollins Reed, thus fulfilling the symbolism inherent in his initials, I.V. (we never know exactly what Christian names they stand for).[23] Reed's place becomes a pallet under the master's bed and he occupies this place until Master Rollin's death, when he finally moves to the top of the master's bed for his own death. This is where Sweetie finds him dying and hears the long death-bed confession and attempt as self-justification which she recounts to Nathaniel.

Sweetie presents Reed's story in his own words. Since she is still struggling to resolve her long-lasting anger at her father, her sense of justice demands that her grandson hear this testimony as straightforwardly as possible. In fact, as Sweetie's story nears its end, Nathaniel finally begins to understand how this complicated family history implicates him and he becomes something of a defender of old I.V. Reed before the bar of Sweetie's wrath.

Sweetie's anger at her father has several sources. Above all, she hates him for having been a white master's devoted servant and toady and for having sought his own comfort and security and his master's welfare, even to the point of being responsible for Reece Shank Haywood's horrible death. Moreover, Sweetie was born 11 years after her father's marriage and felt unwanted by him. I.V. Reed married and passionately loved the beautiful Angelina, daughter of Master Rollins Reed and a slave woman, possibly the same woman loved by Reece Shank Haywood. Angelina was given to Reed as a wife in 1855 as a reward from his master, but Sweetie was not born until 1867 and Reed seemed to resent her intrusion on his relationship with Angelina. Thus, a second source of Sweetie's bad feelings about her father is the long conflict between them over Angelina's love and memory which each of them would like to monopolize.

The conflict between Sweetie and her father was intensified when, in 1874, at the age of seven, Sweetie was stolen with her mother and taken to another plantation by a group of Southern racists who intended to re-enslave them. When the distraught Rollins Reed sends a group of "patrollers" to recover his daughter and grandaughter, Sweetie undergoes the horror of seeing her beloved mother raped and killed before she, herself, can be rescued.

When Sweetie returned to the Reed plantation, her father seemed to blame her for the loss of Angelina and refused to have anything to do with her. As soon as she had arrived at puberty, he suggested to Rollins Reed that they arrange for Sweetie's marriage to Jericho Witherspoon, now well established as a lawyer and judge in the North and willing to pay a sizeable fee for the marriage. The reason is that Witherspoon also loves Angelina, who he saw once as he passed through the Reed plantation on his flight to freedom. Only fifteen years old, Sweetie is sent north to marry Jericho Witherspoon, who, she discovers, is really marrying her in order to possess his memory of her mother.

The age disparity between Sweetie and Jericho—she is fifteen and he is fifty-five at the time of their marriage—make their early relationship more like one of father and child than husband and wife, but Witherspoon is deeply anxious to become himself a father. After years of miscarriages and early deaths of children, Witherspoon despairs of being able to have a child with Sweetie and fathers a son on another woman, Lucasta Jones, with whom he has a brief affair. When he returns home on June 5, 1905, with the one-month-old baby boy who becomes Nathan's father, Arthur, Sweetie agrees to raise the child, but insists on separating from Jericho; she maintains that separation until his death in 1944, devoting herself to the raising of her adoptive son and to her work of charity at the ghetto kitchen she has taken over from Lovelady Breedlove and Hattie Breedlove Wordlaw. Finally, Nathaniel remembers that when he himself was seven, Sweetie suddenly appeared at Jericho Witherspoon's funeral, topping the eulogy delivered by Pompey c.j. Browne with her own astonishing testimony.

This amazing story, compounded of Nathaniel's memory of his grandfather's funeral, Sweetie's recounting of I.V. Reed's deathbed apologia, and her own story, is gradually unveiled in *Two Wings to Veil My Face*. But even more important than the story, itself, is the process of "troubling and revealing" which it initiates. Sweetie and Nathaniel intuitively sense that understanding and accepting the traumatic horrors of African-American history is a necessary beginning to the transformation of this historical tragedy into redemptive spiritual force. As Nathaniel points out at the beginning of the novel, Sweetie is a woman who has an extraordinary capacity for giving comfort, both physical and spiritual, to others. In a wonderful passage describing Nathaniel's childhood memories of Sweetie's perennial baking of rolls, biscuits, and muffins for her missionary work, keeping her breads warm in sleeves made from towels, Forrest evokes the extraordinary sense of security and creativity bound up in Nathaniel's childhood memories of Sweetie:

The steam was always great for delivering the boy into the kingdom of daydreaming, even as the moist breathing of the breads opened him up to Great-Momma Sweetie Reed's story-telling powers and recollecting of leftovers to be remade once again by the boy when Great-Momma Sweetie unveiled the last of the sleeves and his imagination produced a vision of preserved mummies sliding forth (perhaps because of the thinning, see-through condition of the warm-up jackets) as if to play a joke on himself, but instead (as always) a bevy of life-giving celebrants of bread emerged almost bursting with life, not crumbling. (*Two Wings* 4)

Yet, this loving, giving force has come from a lifetime of experiencing and suffering evil and this has left terrible spiritual scars. Though Sweetie has become a model of selfless service to others, she still remains profoundly alienated from those closest to her:

Great-Momma Sweetie Reed had sought out healing all of her life and what had it rendered her privately? The world of her riddled soul and a dropout for a grandson. Privately, then and now, she was still at war with her father, I.V. Reed, and her estranged husband, Jericho Witherspoon . . . You could save the world, at least a piece of it; but you could also lose your way and your soul in the inner circle of the family. (*Two Wings* 18)

Sweetie Reed symbolizes the spiritual power and wisdom embodied in the African-American tradition. But her situation also shows how this power has been gained at great human cost by enduring and surmounting the terrible events of slavery and its racist aftermath, events which have disrupted families, destroyed many individuals, and created terrible misunderstandings and separations not only between whites and blacks, but between black parents and children, men and women. Whether these wounds can be healed remains uncertain, but Forrest is sure that no healing can begin without the recovery of the traumatic historical memory of the "beginning times." This is what he dramatizes in *Two Wings to Veil My Face*. Sweetie, at the end of her long life, sets out to trouble the waters, remembering and revealing the terrible secrets of the past, hoping at last to find that angel, bound up for her with the memory of her beloved mother, Angelina, who can hide her away from the world's horrors and help her fly away.

Like Sweetie, or rather with Sweetie as vehicle-medium, Leon Forrest undertakes the frightening journey from Forest County, Illinois, to Forrest County, Mississippi, from the world of the 1980s to the world of the 1850s, '60s and '70s, seeking a deeper understanding of the human implications of the enslavement of African-Americans. In the course of this imaginative journey, he (and Sweetie) encounter many hard truths about the complex relationships of masters and slaves and of men and women under the harsh and dehumanizing conditions of slavery, and some equally difficult things about the lingering effects of this historic tragedy in the lives of individuals and families. Yet, at the end of this quest rises the dauntless human spirit, whether expressed in the selfless giving and soaring vitality of a Sweetie Reed, or in the resilient manhood of Wayland Woods, whose letter to his former master and mistress is one of the final truths revealed by Sweetie.

Woods' letter is dated January 1, 1864, and is addressed from his present position in the Union Army to his former masters Rollins and Sylvia Reed. Reed's letter celebrates his new-found freedom and threatens a terrible justice if the Reeds harm his family or subject his daughters to the kind of sexual exploitation that so often defiled the world of the plantation. But above all Woods' letter is a prophetic indictment of slavery and a ringing affirmation of his manhood and his belief that the Lord's justice is at hand:

OH THEY MAY BURY ME IN THE EAST. YOU, ROLLEY MAY BURY ME IN THE WEST. BUT I HEARS THE TRUMPET'S LONG SONG AS A LOG IN THE LONG WOODS DROPPING OFF INTO THE SPRING WATER NEAR THE PRAISE HOUSE, AS THE SPRING TO EVERY DAY'S WITNESS SABBATH LIGHTNING SOUL TREMBLING IN ITS TERRIBLE SWIFT TIME . . . I'M OUT IN THIS WORLD SOMEWHERE, COMING AFTER YOU ALL . . . SOMEWHERE. (*Two Wings* 290)

The Bloodworth Orphans

Forrest likes to say that when critics found *There Is a Tree* too internalized and impressionistic, he decided to write enough different characters and actions into his second novel to satisfy everyone. *The Bloodworth Orphans* does teem with characters, whose situations are triply complicated by the fact that many of them, without being aware of it, are closely related to each other. This legacy of the sexual exploitation of African-American women by white men has helped make Forest County a world full of lost souls. These "orphans" futilely seek the love they feel is missing from their lives, and dream of recovering the families and heritages that have been ripped away from them. However, so tangled are the blood lines of black America that these quests often end in terrible tragedy. In many ways, Forrest's novel is the antithesis of Alex Haley's *Roots*, which had been published two years earlier. Haley's saga portrayed the struggle of an African-American family not only to survive but to retain some memory of lineage and heritage. Forrest, however, feels that there is a more tragic side to the African experience in America which must be acknowledged. The many individual tragedies of *The Bloodworth Orphans* grow out of a past of racist and sexual exploitation which has led to a disruption of families and denial of children, and ultimately to a catastrophic breakdown of lineage and culture.

Characters and events in *The Bloodworth Orphans* take on increasingly mythical dimensions reminiscent of the surrealistic nightmare-like quality of such episodes in Ellison's *Invisible Man* as the prologue, the battle royal, the paint factory sequence, and the violent race riot which drives the protagonist into his underground hideaway. In his treatment of the Bloodworth catastrophe, Forrest veers increasingly away from the conventions of realistic narrative in order to present a more archetypal and mythical vision in which, like Ellison, his treatment of individual characters and their fates links the American tragedy of racism with larger currents of human history and destiny. Such a narrative practice has its roots not only in Ellison but in the "magic realism" of contemporary writers like Gabriel Garcia-Marquez and in modern poets and novelists like Eliot and Joyce. In particular, Forrest makes recurrent use of the myths of Orpheus and Oedipus to underline the archetypal patterns he perceives in the Bloodworth tragedy.

Nathaniel Witherspoon is an appropriate witness to the Bloodworth calamity, because he has known both the deep security of a close family life and the terrible emptiness which can result from its withdrawal. In the first of the Witherspoon novels, *There Is a Tree More Ancient than Eden*, Nathaniel had to confront the great vacancy in his life caused by the death of his beloved mother. In the second, *Two Wings to Veil My Face*, he learned that the woman he had loved and leaned on all his life, his grandmother, Sweetie Reed, was actually not his real grandmother but an adoptive one. Now, twelve years after Sweetie Reed's revelation of the truth about his family past, Nathaniel has still not quite made his peace with life. He remains the "college dropout" that he has been for over a decade, resisting commitment to the stream of life. He has neither created a family of his own nor wholly given himself to a life of imaginative recreation. He remains a kind of spiritual orphan, searching for a family to attach himself to. This need draws him to the magnetic figures of Regal Pettibone and his fanatically religious stepmother Rachel Flowers, and through them into his involvement in the tragedy of the Bloodworth lineage.

The Bloodworth Orphans begins on Palm Sunday, 1970 with Nathaniel Witherspoon riding toward the River Rock of Eden Baptist Church in the elegant Lincoln Continental limousine of the highly successful singer, businessman, and playboy, Regal Pettibone. Pettibone is on his way to pick up his adoptive mother, Rachel Flowers, after the evening service, and is looking forward to Easter Sunday when, in his once-yearly appearance in the church, he will participate in a musical service with his mother. The novel ends about a year later in a Shakespearean apocalypse, reminiscent of *Hamlet, Macbeth,* and *King Lear.* Regal and most of his family have been tragically killed, the church has been destroyed by a terrible storm, Nathaniel has been arrested and incarcerated in a mental institution, and the city has erupted into anarchy and gang warfare.

So overpowering is this sequence of catastrophes that they seem to invoke or contain within themselves the shadow of some terrible doom or curse, the fatality of the Bloodworth lineage. The Bloodworth name is mentioned in the other two Witherspoon novels, but it is here that the history and significance of the family is fully developed. The Bloodworth clan is a family of white slaveholders in Mississippi, like the Reed family of *Two Wings.* Founded by Arlington Bloodworth, Sr., who was born in 1817 and lived to 1917, the family has produced a large number of progeny both black and white, spawned by the son and grandson of the original Bloodworth and by the mysterious P.F. Bloodworth, an adoptive son. The novel centers around Nathaniel's encounter with the lives and tragic fates of six of these Bloodworth "orphans:" Abraham Dolphin, the two Bowman brothers, and the three tragic siblings Regal Pettibone, La Donna Scales, and Amos-Otis Thigpen.

The novel is divided into two large sections (chapters 1-7, and 8-12) and these sections hinge around two events, the suicide of Abraham Dolphin and the death by cancer of Rachel Flowers. These deaths appear to set loose the catastrophic doom of the Bloodworth curse in ever widening circles until it has not only wiped out most of the remaining Bloodworth orphans, but has spread throughout the city bringing terrible storms and social breakdown in its wake. Even the ritual killing and dismemberment of the charismatic Regal as well as the lynching of the city's mayor cannot seem to satisfy the apocalyptic bloodlust that these events unleash. The novel ends in an ambiguously mythical way with Nathaniel and the one surviving Bloodworth orphan fleeing the city with a baby they have found in the ruins. In this final movement, themes of classical and Christian mythology converge with African themes: the Orphean sacrifices of Regal and Dolphin seem to make way for the Christian hope of rebirth, presided over by the figure of a Shaman-Wizard who has learned how to survive in a world of chaos and tricksters.

After the introduction of Nathaniel and Regal, most of the novel's opening three chapters are taken up with the story of Rachel Flowers, "an overwhelming Christian woman, whose love, adoration and service to Almighty God (and her blindness) made her seem more and more 'otherworldly' to the flock at River Rock of Eden Church, where she led the choir and everyone else" (*Bloodworth* xxxiv). Deeply religious, like the Hattie Breedlove Wordlaw of *There Is a Tree* and the Sweetie Reed of *Two Wings*, Rachel represents the great strength and power of African-American spirituality. However, in Rachel's case this power has been twisted into an all-consuming fanaticism and a greed for sanctification and dominance over the lives of others, shown by her equivocal position as a church leader and her bizarre marriage with the obscenely obese diabetic Bee-More (Money Czar) Flowers.

Rachel's strange marriage to Bee-More Flowers is an external sign of her spiritual malaise. This once beautiful man has become grotesque and ugly through obsessive indulgence in every sort of sensual pleasure. Now a diabetic who needs regular insulin injections to keep himself alive, he still gorges himself on enormous quantities of food. His indulgences, the very opposite of Rachel's obsession with sacrifice and purgation, seem to represent the counter-part of her excessive self-discipline, as if the more she flays herself with penance and abstention the more she needs to encourage Bee-More's gluttony as a means of vicariously experiencing that which she increasingly denies herself. For Rachel has achieved her leading position in the church through the dramatic power of her legendary self-denial:

She doted on sacrifice; she prayed for and lived by and around the ultimate circumambulatory moment of sacrifice. . . and like the fasting obsession of some of the Muslims streaking to Allah in an almost weightless condition lest the Devil catch up with them, and drag them back into the underground world of the appetites . . . purging and purging and purging, perhaps to get rid of their blackness. (*Bloodworth* 61)

Such seemingly selfless piety has aroused the jealousy and enmity of many of the other leading members of the church who resent both her power and the stringency of her discipline. Significantly, Nathaniel's Aunt Hattie Breedlove, the voice of a balanced and loving spirituality refuses to condemn Rachel, recognizing the true religious impulse that lies behind Rachel's excessive and ultimately destructive piety.

The ambiguity of Rachel's spirituality is symbolized by her blindness. Like the prophet Tiresias, Rachel is an problematic seer. Her prophetic insight doesn't enable her to save those she cares about from the doom which stalks them. Ironically, there is good reason for Rachel's mania, for she has unwillingly become a participant in the Bloodworth doom. Seduced (raped) by Arlington Bloodworth, III, third-generation scion of the Bloodworth plantation, she has borne him two mulatto sons, Industrious and Carl-Rae. Driven to madness by her white lover's bestial perversity, Rachel leaves her sons to be cared for by a black minister and, after a period of wandering, is violently converted to Christianity by an itinerant African-American preacher. She moves to Forest County and is eventually reunited with her sons, who have grown up to exemplify the divided fate of many African-American males. Industrious is a hard worker who spends much of the money he has made by his labor trying to help his brother Carl-Rae who has become a gambler and a hustler. Ironically, both are killed in the same year, and Rachel's despair at their deaths and at her inability to save them from their doom has driven her deeper into fanatical piety. Though she has tried to make up for her lost sons by adopting the foundling Regal Pettibone, she is ultimately unable to escape from the Bloodworth doom. Her death from cancer midway through the novel is one of the events which prepares the way for disaster.

Another pivotal event in the novel occurs around the same time as Rachel's death. This is the suicide of Abraham Dolphin, whose life seems to represent the height of African-American success within white society. Dolphin is a brilliant doctor, who specializes in abortions. He is also a fabulously successful entrepreneur and investor. As owner of the Eden Basement Lounge, one of Forest County's most successful nightspots, Dolphin is a powerful figure in the African-American community and an important ally of the white political elite. A big game hunter and bon vivant, Dolphin is a friend and confidant of the most powerful men in the state and the nation. He seems to be at the very height of his glory when he falls into despair and self-destruction, another victim of the Bloodworth curse.

Though he has no idea of his real origin, Dolphin is also a Bloodworth foundling, the grandson of Arlington Bloodworth II and the son of Bloodworth's mulatto son William Body. Left to die by his mother, Dolphin is discovered in the river mud, like Moses, by the half-mad daughter of another plantation magnate, Governor Masterson. Treated almost like a son by the governor, whose own sons are degenerate wastrels, Dolphin remains aware that he is black and that his background is different. He has even killed a white man in a New Orleans bar, without knowing that this was his uncle, Paxton Bloodworth.

Helped through medical school by a bequest from Governor Masterson, Dolphin's first success is as a doctor for black patients in the South. During the 1952 election he tries to use his medical practice to arouse his patients to some form of political action, but this premature Civil Rights agitation leads to death threats. Eventually Doctor Dolphin is forced to flee the South in a coffin carrying the body of a black veteran of the Korean War to the North.

Having arrived in Forest County, the now twice-born Dr. Dolphin builds the great career which finds him, in the novel's present of 1970, at the very apex of the African-American community. Yet in spite of his double rebirth, Dr. Dolphin continues a fruitless and desperate search for his identity. His profound personal uncertainties drive him to destroy the lives of his wife and two daughters by continually trying to make them over into a confirmation of his own ambiguous identity. Being unable to father a son eats at his soul and erodes his sense of personal accomplishment. His attempts to discover the truth about his own genealogy are unsuccessful and a desperate retreat into the mountains in quest of spiritual illumination is a failure. Finally, when he discovers that he has accidentally killed the son of the war veteran whose coffin he had shared on his flight to the North, Dolphin can stand no more and takes his own life.

The two deaths of Rachel Carpenter and of Abraham Dolphin are both discovered by Nathaniel Witherspoon, who has been close to each of these tragic figures. Nathaniel is deeply traumatized by the destruction of these powerful, though warped and twisted lives. But this is far from the end of the catastrophe. Not only is the River Rock of Eden Church destroyed in a terrible storm, but three more of Nathaniel's acquaintances turn out to be Bloodworth orphans and are unveiled as siblings of each other. One of these doomed children is Nathaniel's dear friend and idol, Regal Pettibone, who has become involved in a passionate love affair with a woman who turns out to be his sister, La Donna Scales. A third sibling, Amos-Otis Thigpen, a former associate of Abraham Dolphin, becomes the *deus ex machina* who reveals this incestuous relationship and then accidentally shoots his sister and brother, before he finally turns the gun on himself. In the aftermath of this tragedy the wounded Regal is torn to pieces by maddened members of his mother's church.

As the action mounts to a level of mythical catastrophe, we realize that the Bloodworth curse is Forrest's metaphor for the devastating and destructive loss of black identity in American society where the actuality of racial and cultural mixing has been pathologically denied, and the myths of white supremacy and racial purity have exacted a profound and lasting cost on the lives of individuals, both black and white. Now, in Forest County in the present time represented in the novel, the effects of this curse are unleashed and a long suppressed primordial chaos begins to emerge. An incessant rain announces the world's return to a beginning time of myth, while a breakdown of social order results from the failure of society's patterns of racial suppression to contain the forces of violence and chaos that have long festered beneath the surface.

In this apocalyptic context mythic forces emerge from the depths and erupt into the historic present. In many ways, the narrative world of Part Two of *The Bloodworth Orphans* (chapters 8-12) resembles the biblical world of Genesis as much as it does the American historical reality of 1970. Instead of chronological sequence, this mythic period is dominated by patterns of archetypal recurrence and return which break down our sense of the socio-historical context as it is usually defined. The distinction between generations, places, and times is no longer clear. Though the Bloodworth orphans, Regal, La Donna, and Amos-Otis appear to be in their mid-thirties or perhaps even younger during the first half of the novel, the story of their birth, which their half-brother Noah Ridgerook Grandberry tells to Nathaniel toward the novel's end, makes it appear that they must be at least a generation older. But this is precisely because their story reflects a mythical reality in which archetypal repetition is more significant than the boundaries of chronological time which people of the twentieth century assume to be the primary definition of reality.

Thus, in *The Bloodworth Orphans*, Forrest imagines the possibility that as the great historical tragedy of racial enslavement and exploitation takes its increasingly complex toll on succeeding generations, the world of Forest County (and of modern America) will enter into a period of social and spiritual breakdown in which the mythical patterns of recurrent sacrifice and suffering which Nathaniel dimly sensed in the nightmare visions of *There Is a Tree More Ancient than Eden* will become increasingly enacted in the world.

This is precisely the situation in which Nathaniel finds himself as the action of *The Bloodworth Orphans* spins toward its apocalyptic climax. At the very end of the novel, Nathaniel and his new spiritual guide, Noah Grandberry, leave their temporary refuge and find themselves "in the middle of a flooding, erupting black gang-war and police-fire and torches. And towards the entrance to the school, the burning body of the black mayor, with the head dismembered and spinning upon a twelve-foot pole, as if offered up in some mad ritual sacrifice. The field luminous with light, as if a star had fallen, shortly before dawn, and was burning at its zenith" (*Bloodworth* 382-83).

In this mythic world the two great spiritual antitheses of chaotic breakdown and recreation which Forrest sees as the primary creative and destructive rhythm of human life emerge in full view and confront the bewildered Nathaniel. Prostrated with grief and confusion by the terrible deaths of Rachel Flowers, Abraham Dolphin, and the three doomed siblings, Regal, La Donna and

Amos-Otis, Nathaniel receives a message from the mother of his childhood friend, Maxwell "Black-Ball" Saltport. "Black-Ball" has been converted to the Black Muslim faith and has risen rapidly in the church. Now, Nathaniel discovers that Saltport has been truly "black-balled." He has fallen from favor with the church leadership and is hiding out in a decaying tenement at the heart of the Forest country ghetto. Black-Ball's hideout is reminiscent of the ruined tenement where Bigger Thomas hides from the police and is also a Forrestian re-creation of a famous old South Side Chicago slum building which was ironically named the "Mecca." At the height of a wild conversation with Saltport, which shows Nathaniel that the Muslim power structure is just as prone to betrayal and the use of sacrificial scapegoats as the rest of the world, Nathaniel is caught in a police raid and taken for incarceration and examination to a large mental treatment facility, the Refuge Hospital, where he had come earlier with Regal Pettibone to hear the great music of Ironwood "Landlord" Rumble.

Chapter 11, which portrays Rumble's music, is one of the highpoints of the novel and an illustration of Forrest's incantatory jazz-driven style at its height. As we noted earlier, jazz is an undercurrent, a sort of basic riff, in much of Forrest's writing, but in this chapter he gives his feeling for the creative significance of African-American music, and particularly jazz, its full expression. The blind and spiritually wounded Ironwood Rumble is one of Forrest's primary symbols of the great spiritual force of re-creation and transformation. Like many great creators, Rumble seems to have paid for his gift with personal suffering and loss. In this sense, he is one of the avatars of the mythical figure of Orpheus, whose pattern of creation and crucifixion is reflected in a number of the major figures in *The Bloodworth Orphans*.[24] Even in the depths of the Refuge Hospital, the only place in the chaotic present where Rumble can be protected from victimization and enabled to express himself in his chosen art, the power of his vision is manifest. Rumble builds on the tragic experiences as well as the great inventors of the past and leads his hearers toward a vision of transcendence:

Rumble now plunged the patrons into the sacred pitfall fires of creation (making their faces as bloated sour roasting apples) down down down into the stormy vessels of terrors, and nightmare pits, at the banquet tables of isolation and the altar auction offerings, back back back into feverishly rooted connections. *Nobody knows. Motherless, fatherless.*

But Lord was he the promised Lucifer, Magna Cum Laude; or Christ on a vest-pocket watch chain, creation's dangling foundling, weeping and wailing in the wilderness? Or was he Long-Gone Faust with *Ax* and rags driven to hell and back? Or was he John Henry come back to life—with his hard clothes on? His nine-pound hammer miraculously turned into an alto saxophone, sculpting the train coaches into chariots which jigged, wing-bucked and praised the North Star. Or was he a conjure man dressed to kill? Or Lord Mephisto, the progressive pilgrim?

And into that kitchen, wizard-chef-warlock-high-priest-musician mixed trumpet, trombone, tenor sax, alto-sax, bagpipes, bass clarinet, flute, drums, violin, reinventing upwards a nourishing buried treasure of stormy cauldron served to the supping, sucking patrons, in their pitched nakedness, who sat upon orange crates, in tunics, looking as slaves, and oddly like choirboys, with scoops of ice in V-shaped paper cups over which they poured wine from the bottle nowcirculating about the L-shaped former surgery center.

Then he commenced to transport his homeless patrons on out of that cellar kitchen. (*Bloodworth* 294-95)

Nathaniel's encounter with the musical vision of Ironwood "Landlord" Rumble is paralleled by his meeting, also in the Refuge Hospital, with the man who becomes Nathaniel's spiritual mentor, Noah Ridgerook Grandberry. Grandberry is also a Bloodworth orphan and a half-brother to the tragic Bloodworth siblings. Thus, he is able to reveal the true background of Regal, La Donna, and Amos-Otis to Nathaniel. But Grandberry is also a Bloodworth orphan who has survived because he has encountered the force of chaos and deception and learned how to adapt to it. It is through Grandberry that Nathaniel is inducted into the mysterious and mythical history of Forrest's major symbol of spiritual chaos and destruction, the demon-trickster, Ford.[25]

In terms of sources, Ford is a mythical synthesis of the African trickster-god, the Judeo-Christian devil, and the Black Muslim messiah, W.A.D. Fard. Invoking the name of that historical figure of technological modernity, Henry Ford, Forrest's Ford is a masterful inventor of his own "tricknology." His characterization also draws on some of the more flamboyant African-American preachers, though the religion promulgated by Ford in his avatar as cult founder is closer to Dionysian mystery and pagan revelry than it is to all but the most extreme forms of protestant Christianity.

Ford makes his initial appearance in *The Bloodworth Orphans* through a series of mysterious allusions to what appear to be a number of different characters in the introductory "List of Characters." As the personal and social tragedies of the novel reach their culmination, Ford emerges from the shadows as a political crusader to whom Amos-Otis Thigpen has been donating some of the money he has extorted over the years from Abraham Dolphin. In addition, Ford offers support and protection to La Donna Scales after her discovery of the incestuous nature of the passionate love between herself and Regal Pettibone. One aspect of Ford's nature is that he feeds on human insecurity, unhappiness, and confusion. Therefore he is drawn, above all, to orphans and foundlings who have lost the basic security of knowing who they are and the nature of their heritage.

Grandberry reveals much more about Ford to Nathaniel: his seeming agelessness and his many different guises. Repeating ancient archetypes, Ford has also experienced the "serial hermaphroditism" ascribed by myth to the seer Tiresias; thus Ford has not only changed identities but genders. Nor is his racial identity any clearer. Ford is most often described as looking like a mulatto and his eyes, insofar as one can be sure of their color, suggest white ancestry:

But there was always something strangely attractive about this Ford. He always wears a cape, as green as a leaf, a broad white hat, with blue and red feathers in it. Although he walks with a slight limp, he is actually quite tall, handsome, high-yellow, yet livid-complexioned, with wildly greenish blue eyes, which I swear seem to change colors during the brief period when he looks your way, yet not shifty-eyed either, for when he does look you dead in the eyes, it's as penetrating as hell. He has dead-straight, almost Indian hair, though of a reddish color. He wears a neat Vandyke beard. He has a wonderful happy laugh, as if he understands all things, and knows all things. And the largest ears (a sign of generosity, they say!). You can imagine. And he often talks about building bridges between folks, by first of all giving folks bridges to build. (*Bloodworth* 242-43)

This bundle of contradictions and shifting shapes uses overt gestures toward generosity and unity in the service of destructiveness and chaos, showing his close kinship to the trickster figures of both African and Native American spiritual traditions. His is the omnipresent spirit of deception and ruin which always lurks beneath the surface of human affairs and which, in times of crisis and division, seems to emerge with renewed power. Noah Grandberry has spent much of his life in close relationship to Ford, and has come to know the trickster's tricknology as well as anyone. In fact, he finally reveals to Nathaniel that Ford is Grandberry's great-grandfather.

Noah Ridgerook Grandberry is a fascinating character in his own right, though his major role in the novel is to make Nathaniel his "rookie" or apprentice and to help the traumatized dropout commit himself to life in spite of the pervasiveness of evil and tragedy. Like his Biblical namesake, Noah is a perennial survivor of destruction who holds out to Nathaniel the hope of "finding a way out of noway" as Breedlove had instructed him he must do in *There Is a Tree*. As "Ridgerook" Noah also carries the heritage of the trickster and he has refined his own skills in tricknology through his long association and experience of many betrayals by Ford. Finally, as "Grandberry" Noah "bears" the "seeds" of a new and perhaps greater birth to arise out of the chaos of the present world. For, to quote one of Forrest's favorite lines from Nietzsche "only the man with chaos within him can give birth to a dancing star."

The final move of *The Bloodworth Orphans* is Nathaniel's own withdrawal and return. While in the Refuge Hospital, spurred on by the visionary music of Ironwood "Landlord" Rumble, Nathaniel studies the arts of survival and re-creation from Noah. After the two have learned how to use their refuge as a base for forays into the increasing chaos of the world outside, the two men decide that it is finally time to "stop sobbing over the past" and to embark again back into the chaos of the world outside. They descend from the Refuge Hospital into a city consumed by violent gang warfare and the total breakdown of civil order. However, as they run from the flames, Nathaniel almost trips over a boot box "with a screaming babe inside." Carrying this new foundling with them, Nathaniel and Noah make their escape from the city in a stolen police car. The final words of the novel are words of hope centered around the renewal of possibility exemplified in the rescued orphan: "They turned about and looked down upon the back seat in the boot box, at the little black baby's face—perhaps three months old, wailing with fear and life, its trembling little hands reaching upwards towards the two sad-faced sobbing men" (*Bloodworth* 383).

Divine Days

In *Divine Days*, his fourth novel, Forrest returned to the cosmic dialectic between chaos and re-creation which he had developed toward the end of *The Bloodworth Orphans*. In this case, however, he explored this antithesis on a scale that is at once more limited and specific, and more expansive and universal. *Divine Days* is an enormous comic epic of 1,135 pages in which the forces of creation and destruction are brought to bear on a brief but crucial period in the life of a new protagonist, Joubert Antoine Jones. This novel was also Forrest's first overall use of a first-person narrative structure.[26] *Divine Days* is presented in the form of a journal or diary written by Joubert during the week of his return to Forest County from army duty in Germany. The first section of this journal is entitled Wednesday, February 16, 1996, 6:00 a.m. The remaining 14 sections all are dated on the next seven days up to Wednesday, February 23, 10:00 a.m. These succeeding sections are not dated by year, partly because we assume they are part of the same week, but also in part to symbolize the archeypal and mythical character of this week. It is a week both in and out of time, and, as in *The Bloodworth Orphans*, mythic and historical time intersect in the course of the action.[27]

The idea of focusing an enormous narrative around a limited period of time is a frequent device of modern literature. The most famous literary 16th is that of James Joyce, who, in *Ulysses*, compressed his narrative of three lives and, by extension, the moral history of an entire culture, into the events of one day, June 16, 1904. William Faulkner framed the 100-year history of the Sutpen family and of the South within two tale-telling sessions in September and January of 1909-10. The use of a week also has other implications suggesting archetypal and recurrent patterns as in the holy week narratives of the New Testament.

The week of February 16, 1966, is a time of crucial transition for Forrest's protagonist and narrator. He returns from two years of service in the army in Germany and makes some crucial decisions about his future back in Forest County. Joubert Jones has some resemblance to Nathaniel Witherspoon, but is really quite different. Though close to the same age, Joubert is about five years younger than Nathaniel. They are both orphans and have a double Protestant-Catholic heritage. In fact, there is even a family connection in that Joubert's great aunt Lucasta is the birth mother of Nathaniel Witherspoon's father, Arthur. Despite such similarities, however, Joubert and Nathaniel are really quite different in situation, character, and heritage. Joubert is much more self-confident and sure of his trajectory in life than the perpetual dropout Nathaniel. Instead of the devoutly religious Sweetie Reed and Aunt Hattie Breedlove, Joubert has largely been raised by his elegant and sophistocated Aunt Eloise. A successful journalist and columnist, as well as part owner of Eloise's Night Life Lounge where Joubert was working when he entered the army, Aunt Eloise comes from a New Orleans Creole family and exemplifies the interest in art, literature, and gourmet living associated with this tradition. Largely through her influence, Joubert has a knowledge of cultural tradition and a broad awareness of the the history of civilization that enables him to take a very different perspective on the world around him than Nathaniel Witherspoon.

Such a family background, reinforced by his own determination to become a successful playwright, has led Joubert to encounter a much broader spectrum of African-American life than Nathaniel, particularly in the black middle class and in artistic and intellectual circles, though he also retains the same kind of connection with the life of the streets that we saw in Forrest's earlier novels. Through his earlier employment in a barber shop and his current work in his aunt's bar and liquor store, Joubert has contact with the seething diversity and variety of black life. It's surely no exaggeration to say that *Divine Days* is the most encyclopedic account yet created of the whole range of contemporary African-American urban culture.

February 16, 1966 is the beginning of a very busy week for Joubert Jones. He has barely returned to Forest County from his army service when he is immediately drawn back into the world of his family and of the culture represented by Aunt Eloise's Night Light Lounge. However, Joubert dreams of breaking free of the limits of this world and forging a career as a dramatist. In the course of his week of crisis and decision, Joubert has a number of experiences which force him to confront the meaning of his life as a gifted young African-American and to make some fundamental choices about his future direction.

Perhaps the most profound and universal of these experiences, and the one which most centrally shapes the overall narrative, is the struggle between between Sugar-Groove, the archetypal hipster, and W.A.D. Ford, the diabolical trickster, a conflict which deeply implicates Joubert, since he has been at various times a sort of disciple to both. Now he hopes to capitalize on his acquaintance with these remarkable characters by writing them into successful plays. However, Sugar-Groove and

Ford have both mysteriously disappeared before Joubert returns to Forest county from his army service. His investigations finally lead him to an already legendary account of an apocalyptic mountain-top confrontation between Ford and Sugar-Groove in which the demonic trickster finally blinds and mortally wounds his adversary, but not without being grievously and hilariously wounded himself. As the aging narrator of Sugar-Groove's last hours puts it, the doomed hipster on the mountaintop has managed to place "seven blazing shots in (Ford's) back sides; so that he'll have to stand up to shit from here to eternity" (*DD* 1068).

Ford, who we saw as a major player in *The Bloodworth Orphans*, was a significant part of the mythical world of Forest County almost from the beginning. In *Divine Days* Forrest further develops Ford as a cosmic symbol of the forces of chaos and disorder, which are dangerous and destructive to life, but also vital to the regeneration and re-creation of human meaning. Ford embodies the tendencies in African-American life which Forrest sees as most destructive—the chaos of drugs, gambling, promiscuous sex, despair, and violence which have turned our inner cities into infernos of misery and suffering. Ford also represents the "tricknology" of the successful criminals and cultish religious leaders who have manipulated and profited from this spreading scourge; in this sense, Ford is a further development of the force symbolized by Ellison's Rinehart. Yet, this is by no means the whole story. Significantly, Forrest draws much of the legend of Ford directly from Black Muslim mythology, for in Black Muslimism's founder, Elijah Muhammad, Forrest perceived the same combination of demonic trickster and spur to regeneration that he portrays in Ford. In fact, Forrest has said that whatever the ultimate shortcomings of the Black Muslim movement, Elijah Muhammad deserves to be remembered "for the lives he saved by dint of the obsessive faith he conjured and the self-help programs he developed. All of this must be placed into the equation" (*Relocations* 115).[28]

Ageless, many-sided, shape-shifting, and a serial hermaphrodite, Ford synthesizes important elements from many different religious traditions; he is somewhat like the Judeo-Christian Satan or devil in that his primary goal is to subvert God's creative order and reduce it to chaos. In this capacity he frequently appears as a cultish preacher, whose rites bizarrely parody Christian ceremonies and observances. There are also elements of Classical Greek myth and religion in Ford. His worship has a Dionysiac quality, while one of his major avatars as the "Seer" owes much, including his serial hermaphroditism, to the myth of Tiresias. But above all, Ford embodies the African (and Native American) tradition of the trickster god, who challenges humankind with deceptions and gifts, offering an inseparable mixture of benefits and sufferings. He is, one might say, the signifier of signifying.

The impact of Ford can be both creative and destructive, but the tranformative force inherent in Ford becomes manifest only when the trickster becomes involved with a creative human agency, an antagonist who can turn Ford's destructive power into positive human value. In *The Bloodworth Orphans*, Forrest had not yet imagined a sufficient antithesis to Ford, though he began to sketch one in the character of Noah Ridgerook Grandberry. In *Divine Days*, he creates a fully competent adversary in the figure of Sugar-Groove. For Forrest, Sugar-Groove symbolizes above all the transformative and re-creative power of the African-American or "Negro" cultural tradition. As Stanley Crouch indicates, he is the epitome of the "blues spirit." For Forrest, as for such earlier writers as Ralph Ellison and Albert Murray, the blues tradition is one of the great African-American creations. It grew out of the horrors of the middle passage, slavery and racism, re-creating out of this historic chaos the new and vital culture of black America. The wise elder who Joubert consults about the significance of Sugar-Groove's fate explains:

(The slaves') demonic mistreatment was more savagely fantastical than the testament of mayhem they had heard of, brought with them, survived coming here through, and were remaking orally, even as they were being transformed out of their skins, and blood, and souls, and eye-teeth, and backbone crack—into a new kind of people. Forged, fucked, and dislocated into a new race of people wherein anything human and inhumane could happen. . . . But our human rage was always to make a way out of noway. And to create a synthesis out of all nightmares that our experiences kept throwing up at us. That will to synthesize was what Du Bois never understood . . . to absorb and re-invent; to take it all in and to masticate it, and process it, and spew it back out, as lyrical and soaring as a riff by Father Louie. (*DD* 1048)[29]

Sugar-Groove is a Bloodworth Orphan like Noah Grandberry. However, he is a much more fully developed character, and his relationship to his white Bloodworth father[30] is an important theme of *Divine Days*. Wilfred Bloodworth deeply loves the African-

American woman with whom he created a child, and, in a roundabout and secretive way, tries to acknowledge that child and to pass an inheritance on to him. However, since he will not openly accept the boy as his son, Sugar-Groove is raised by an aunt and uncle who are both very dark and deeply involved in the African-American religious tradition. Sugar-Groove's terribly divided relationship with his white father symbolizes the complex interplay of black and white dependence and rejection, loyalty and betrayal, and love and hate, which shaped the development of African-American (and white) culture. In Sugar-Groove's case, his bitter involvement with his Bloodworth father reaches a climax when the two men violently quarrel over the memory of Sarah-Belle, the mother, and are only stopped from murdering each other by Sarah-Belle's spirit which appears and says to Bloodworth "how can you destroy what we created?" (*DD* 336).

Leaving his Southern origins behind, Sugar Groove, like so many of his African-American contemporaries, has migrated to the North where he has made a new life for himself. He becomes a legendary figure in Forest County, distinguised not only for his awesome success as an entrepreneur, a gambler, and a ladies man, but for his strange acts of charity. Even as a child Joubert was familiar with the legend of Sugar-Groove, which we first hear in the brilliant tall tale saga of Sugar-Groove in heaven narrated by Oscar (Williemain), the barber. He first meets the actual Sugar-Groove while working as a shoeshine boy in Williemain's barbershop, a wellspring of community history and legend in Forest County. While having Joubert shine his elegant and expensive "Alighieri" shoes, Sugar-Groove tells the boy the story of his Bloodworth past as a complex parable about the ambiguities of inheritance. From this point on Sugar-Groove becomes the young man's ideal, but Joubert is divided between his idolization of Sugar-Grove and his fascination with Ford.

Thoughout *Divine Days* Joubert attempts to resolve the conflict in his mind between Sugar-Groove and Ford, but it is not until he finally learns the truth about Sugar-Groove's final hours and his mountaintop struggle with Ford that he comes to realize that a choice between the two is not really possible. He understands at last that to truly celebrate the transformation and transcendence represented by Sugar-Groove he must also acknowledge and incorporate the chaotic energies embodied in Ford. In the course of the novel, Sugar-Groove is transformed from oral legend into historical allegory and finally into archetypal myth as Forrest seeks to represent in literary form the relationship of African-American culture to universal patterns of human experience.

However, the transcendent dialectic of chaos and re-creation represented by Ford and Sugar-Groove is only one of the many dimensions of *Divine Days*.[31] Another important theme of the book is the tragi-comic encounter between what Forrest sees as the mainstream of the African-American cultural tradition and the separatist and pan-African thrust of the Black Power-Black Arts movements so prevalent at the time of *Divine Days*. This impulse is represented in the tragic figure of Joubert Jones's primary romantic interest, the gifted woman artist and social worker DeLoretto/Imani. DeLoretto has desperately tried to transform herself into a true descendant of Africa by searching for what she believes to be her lost siblings; by lining her walls with fake African masks purveyed by the unscrupulous hustler and drug dealer Sambi!; by celebrating in her art the young gang leaders who are rapidly turning Forest County into an urban jungle; and finally by renaming herself and her son with symbolic African names derived from the synthetic ceremony of Kwaanza. Throughout the novel, DeLoretto keeps rejecting Joubert's amorous advances while urging him to become an *omowale* or "child who returns to the tribe," i.e., to the true African heritage. DeLoretto is tragically driven to suicide by a brutal encounter group session which destroys her increasingly fragile and ambiguous identity by exposing her dependence on such white persons as her wealthy patroness and her German lover. DeLoretto cannot acknowledge the contradiction between her quest for blackness and her dependence on the white establishment. For Forrest, however, the great strength of the African-American cultural tradition lies in its dynamic recreation of both African and European, black and white, traditions. In this sense he sees the "negro" tradition as the very heart of America itself, a key element in the complex dialectic between outcast peoples and traditions that constitutes the true America. DeLoretto's attempt to reject one side of her heritage leads her first to become the dupe of a charlatan like Sambi! and finally to lose herself altogether in her pursuit of the will-of-the-wisp of pure negritude.

The ultimate futility of the fad for Africanism, as Forrest sees it, is represented in the figure of Fulton Armstead who, in some strange inversion of the fanatical Puritans in *The Scarlet Letter*, goes around awarding a "double A" letter to black people he deems to be sufficiently pure in their blackness:

Fulton Armstead was quite clear—he was never seen without his dashiki. As the Civil Rights Movement commenced to fade and nationalist voices emerged these leaders termed Fulton's letters as symbolic of "linkage" between Africa and the Afro-American plight, trying desperately to keep up with the times and upstage the fledgling militants and claiming that the leader's letters stood for *Ancestral Art* or the *Ancestral Arc of Bones*. The significance and meaning of these letters—by simply uniting the double-A with the small "a" inside—came to take on a different meaning with each changing of the full moon, or so it appeared. Fulton's original meaning in all of this appeared more and more to be phased out, and blurred . . . as if some mad man had rammed all of the letters of the alphabet together into this brief triad. (*DD* 636-37)

In contrast to this portrayal of the futility of Africanism, Forrest richly celebrates the vitality of the African-American tradition with characters and scenes from a wide range of black life in America. The world of Eloise's Night Light Lounge with its uniquely individual barmaids and its regular cast of exuberant drunks is a vibrant new element in Forrest's fiction. Some of *Divine Days'* most hilarious moments are bar scenes, such as Daisy Dawes's attempt to shoot Joubert after he gets carried away by his signifying on her beloved preacher-man, the Rev. Honeywood "Sweet-Briar" Cox, or the gargantuan struggle to resurrect the "terrible tonnage" of McGovern McNabb from a drunken coma, an episode worthy of the great tradition of comic epics from *Gargantua* and *Don Quixote* to *Finnegan's Wake*. The barmaids, LaDorrestine Conway, Gracie Rae Gooden, and Estella by Starlight are richly realized characters as well. Each has her own style, her own story, and her own circle of admirers.

The bar is one center of action in *Divine Days*, but another is the barbershop where the brilliant oral historian and guardian of folklore, (Oscar) Willieman and the Shakespeare idolator Galloway Wheeler, preside. The barbershop plays a very important role in Joubert's life not only as his initial point of contact with Sugar-Groove, but as a repository of legend and folkloric tradition, exemplified by the dazzling tall-tale of Sugar-Groove in heaven which Williemain performs near the beginning of the novel and which becomes the theme on which Joubert rings the changes in his final valediction. The barbershop might be called the academy of the streets and Joubert feels that he has finally become a full-fledged member of the culture when he is inducted into Williemain's private club of storytelling and cultural commentary, the Royal Rites and Righteous Ramblings. Moreover, the barbershop is an important point of intersection between different layers and levels of African-American culture. It is there that the street meets the elite:

There were three major black professors who came into Williemain's and each held a place of respect and honor (and in Jamesway's case, reverence) accorded them absolutely nowhere else in the Negro Community. Of the three it was the Historian who was best known outside the barbershop. But Professor Jamesway was Williemain's favorite. I laughingly said one time that most probably Williemain would name one of the three barber chairs in Professor Jamesway's honor. The third Professor had the greatest vocabulary, it was rumored, in the Western World. He was in literature and religion. When he spoke even Galloway Wheeler shut up. Only these three professors could have corrected Williemain out loud in a barbershop full of people and not been referred to as a *louse*. (*DD* 844)[32]

While the oral culture of Williemain's barbershop evokes the richness of black folklore and oral history and the lively rhetoric of the street, Joubert's Aunt Eloise and her journalist colleagues, like the farcical C. Boone Lightboddie or the fascinating Warren Wilkerson, give us a sense of the importance of black newspapers in creating the modern African-American community. Joubert's Aunt Eloise is a particularly fascinating character. A woman of high sophistication and brilliant wit, Aunt Eloise has re-created the traditional art of tribal history into the terms of modern popular culture and media through her newspaper column, *Eloise Etches*, in the *Forest County Dispatch*. As part owner and namesake of Eloise's Night Light Lounge, she is also a patron goddess of the nightworld. As Joubert's aunt and stepmother, she is at once mentor, model and mother-figure to Joubert, the most important symbol to him of family, and the person with whom he must negotiate an amicable separation if he is ever to enter into his own creativity.

Aunt Eloise is the richest and most complex of a number of characters in Forrest's novels who represent the New Orleans Creole tradition. Joubert's affectionate, yet searching fictionalization of this great source of worldly sophistication and love of sensuality within the African-American heritage is a significant part of his (and Forrest's) struggle to understand the richness of the Negro culture without becoming ensnared by its overwhelming attachment to material and sensuous pleasures. Having heard the saga of Sugar-Grove scandalizing the heavenly angels with his high flying, Joubert imagines Aunt Eloise negotiating with St. Peter in an attempt to take it all with her:

Aunt Eloise is quite an expert on the layered cultural life that composes New Orleans' heritage—just as her Uncle Roderick Ledbetter Tobias is an authority about jazz. With the scores of possessions she had brought back from trips to the Crescent City (and old family attics) to North Africa, and Europe, Aunt Eloise might want to be buried with a bounty of her possessions like an ancient Egyptian (though in a rosewood coffin); she'll need a mausoleum. Certainly St. Peter has no place for all of Aunt Eloise's worldy estate, amid the many mansions and speciality shops of Paradise. Her cottage up at the Pier[33] is overstuffed; a non-heavenly, mini-mansion, made of hands and "surceased in a surfeit of curtains, sorrow and shit," as she whispered to me this morning, shortly before I went to bed, at 2:00, after too much Moet et Chandon and not enough of her famous variation on Creole Oysters Omelette. A corner lot in God's graceland. (*DD* 25)

As a counterpoint to the secular world of bar, barbershop and newspaper, *Divine Days* richly explores the range of African-American spirituality through a varied gallery of ministers, churches, and services. Through these portraits we see the authentic spirituality deeply embedded in African-American culture struggling to find expression through a screen of worldliness. Ministers often seem more powerfully motivated by their own egotism and love of the good life than they are by the struggle for transcedence, while many ritual practices smack more of Ford's "tricknology" than of genuine religious feeling. Yet, in spite of the many distortions he encounters, Joubert finds continual evidence of the quest for transcendence in his varied encounters with the personalities and institutions of African-American religion.

The preachers in *Divine Days* range from the corrupt, sensuous, and worldly Honeywood "Sweet-Briar" Cox to the bold and prideful Rev. Sheppard Tutwiler, who "always hounded his congregation about their morals, their lack of appetite for a tithing spirt, and their want of humility. . . . With his grandiose manners and his long greasy coat-tails, Elder Tutwiler was so bedeviling and taxing, that many of his congregation called him behind his back 'The Driver in grey tails,' or 'Elder T-for Terribleness sake'" (*DD* 471). The elegant and thoughtful Rev. Maruice Roper serves

Joubert a cup of "finely minted lemon tea," but seems different from many preachers in that "he didn't have any problems seeing the sacred and the profane, as blasting from the same backbone base of the human condition" (*DD* 446). Or we meet the patient and determined Rev. Wilbur "Spiffy" Lumpkins, "who worked as a red cap for years, to support his family, while he slowly and steadily built up his congregation on the week-ends from twenty-one souls to where he now claimed a membership of one-hundred twenty tithing hardies" (*DD* 446). In fact, *Divine Days* presents a virtual anatomy of the African-American religious life, including brief appearances by characters like Prayer Mother Rachel Carpenter Flowers who we have come to know from other installments of the Forest County saga.

These portrayals show that the religious life is as subject to the vagaries and follies of human beings as any other area of experience. Yet, underneath it all throbs the current of an authentic sprituality:

Deep within their voices I heard that old genesis grain—over, under, around, and through: in and out the window of the time—of the Negro singing voice: bone plucked, hardy, harp-haunted, accusational, grieving, roped off, roped in: fiddle-cracking, grief instructed; time-greased, woe-weary, wound-salted down, drum telegraphing, blues baked, hoe-cake fired, lightning mangled, fat-back foxy, bruised-blooded, merriment jangling; box-car coming, whistling and hushed over in Trouble. Then the whole note held in the expanse (as a hush over Jordan) with the shape of a noose. Now nearly all the train crooning sound, howling memories up of dispatching, feet-aching Negroes coming in great waves of sound from the Old Country to the Northern Kindom. (*DD* 476)

Here, in images strongly reminiscient of *There Is a Tree More Ancient than Eden*, Joubert evokes the terrible history which lies at the root of African-American religious feeling and which generates a deep and abiding hope for spiritual transcendence in spite of the wordly corruption of the institutions and leaders which claim to embody the world of Forest County. In the end, this impulse is most purely expressed not in the church, but in Sugar-Groove's climbing the mountain of illumination. However, Sugar-Grooves are as rare in their way as saints. The day-to-day preservation and nurturing of the hope for transcendence depends on the sustaining power of the African-American religious tradition, and, as Forrest presents that tradition, it is as important a force in the life of Forest County as the world of the streets.

Yet, despite the manifest richness and vibrancy of the African-American heritage of the churches and the streets, it's not clear whether this heritage will be sufficient in the face of the new chaos of the urban ghettos, of which we saw a prophetic glimpse in the apocalytic scene of urban riot and gang warfare at the end of *The Bloodworth Orphans*. Such an outcome seems even more foredoomed if young and gifted blacks turn their backs on the African-American tradition and become disciples of Ford or set out to pursue the will of the wisp of pure blackness and the African past. Joubert sees that the tragic DeLoretto/Imani died believing that:

salvation for the blacks . . . had come to mean a total eclipse of not simply the white man (although like the Black Muslims, Imani believed that the days of the white man were numbered, as the supreme power on this planet earth) but *all* that was both evil, and yes honorable too, in the Western experience; even as she Imani herself, epitomized so many of the material hungers and educational quests of the American Character. (*DD* 1022)

This passionate hatred of all things white drives Imani to mistakenly place her trust in the trickster Sambi!, a pimp turned huckster of fake African artifacts. In her art, Imani turns from portraits of spiritual leaders like Martin Luther King and Malcolm X to the heroic idealization of gang leaders—"certain desperadoes from the pits of the Vice Emperors, the Razor-back Cobras, and the Commencheroes . . . Zenith Zap, the Purple satisfier; Zodiac, the Space-Age Maniac; and Mad-Dog Dawkins, among their fitful number" (*DD* 116)—as Joubert describes them. Yet, this desperate attempt to embrace the new chaos of the inner city as a route to the destruction of the white man only drives the deeply divided Imani to destroy herself. When dealing with Ford, the promise of redemption leads only to chaos.

Toward the end of *Divine Days*, Joubert encounters one of the progeny of the inner city's underside, a confused and barely articulate thirteen year old girl, Iris "Cinderella" Lilybridge. Cinderella is pregnant—possibly by her own father—and lost. Joubert is deeply moved by her plight: "It was the anger and the hostility, coupled with the struggling and suffering soul of this child, this Cinderella, which also drove me to want to take this child up into my arms, suddenly, fearfully away from the desparate, no man's land—of suffer them unto me and harm them not—I had made of the Westside in my mind's eye (*DD* 678).[34] Joubert realizes that his attempts to help Cinderella can, at best, get her "off the streets and into a safe-house for the night" (*DD* 686). But this will not address the deeper problems of social and spiritual dislocation and despair that Cinderella represents. It would seem that neither the brilliance of a Professor Jamesway nor the "black is beautiful" ideology of a Fulton Armstead can offer a solution to the tragedy of the inner city:

What would Professor Allerton say about all this chaos in the whirlwind of a Forest County Winter's night? Cinderella on a short rope of existence . . . Rope twisted swing. How often had their clothing been hurled in and out of windows? . . . What significance would Fulton Armstead's double A with the little "a" inside have for these bombed out denizens of Forest County? (*DD* 686)

Yet even in the midst of this chaos there may be the seeds of a new transformation in the process of gestation, just as the unknown baby grows in Cinderella's womb. For even with her lack of education Cinderella has the urge to re-create. She is the author of a poem entitled "My Baby's Gospel Breath," which she has somehow written with the help of DeLoretto, who turns out to have been her social worker. Moreover, Cinderella and her mother insist that Joubert accompany them to the Rev. Roper's revival service, before they will go with him to the shelter. As he watches Cinderella awaken to the call of the service, he realizes that there is a force within her that is "loaded with the sweat-stilled-beaded ecstasy of life and the tear-stained hollowness of death, but not decay" (*DD* 707). As Cinderella's voice joins with that of the other worshippers, Joubert feels hope that even the lowliest of the underclass can rise to the great heritage of endurance and transcendence that African-American religion and music so profoundly expresses:

High-flying up that stage the voice of Cinderella is bolting space up this mountain, her feet don't touch down, as best I can tell, trying to keep up with her winged voice. Lightning never held a tongue to her (nor bell, book, or candle) . . . until she opened God's thundering mouth. Cinderella who spawned *My Baby's Gospel Breath*, amid all of the inharmonious upheaval and the general alarm of her chaos. This Cinderella with furious wings, as if lightning had a soul to sing, and hands to clap, and feet to fly, pouring up in a mound-making voice. Cinderella is setting this house on fire with her song. (*DD* 700)

His discovery of the drive toward re-creation even in the desperate and chaotic existence of Cinderella Lilybridge prepares Joubert for the final stage of his week of discovery and transformation. Toward the end of this week, late on Tuesday night, Joubert, himself, has a vision which sums up what he has learned and prepares him for his own task as an artist. In this dream-vision he sees Martin Luther King placing boxes containing the bones of the biblical Joseph, Frederick Douglass, and Sugar-Groove, high up on a mountain, and as he sees this scene he hears a voice speaking these words to him from what appears to be the face of the Rev. Maurice Roper:

"Young man, you'll have to take (the vision of these boxes of bones) with you the length of your days, as long as we as a people wander about in this land, and remain in a lost-found-lost condition. Until the spirit in these bones and within these boxes can come alive again, and then be transplanted into the bones and flesh of the new liberation, and then transformed again by the lyricism of the new covenant. The new Resurrection." (*DD* 976)

The last of Joubert's Divine Days, Wednesday, February 23, follows almost immediately upon this vision. On this day, Joubert prepares to leave the safe haven of Eloise's Night Light Lounge and his aunt's maternal care in order to launch forth on the seas of chaos in search of his own vision of order. Now, he is able to understand the significance of Sugar-Groove's transcendent fate which is finally narrated to him by the aging Warren Wilkerson, and to recognize the archetypal inevitability of the struggle between Sugar-Groove and Ford for his soul. He also summons the strength to come to terms with the tragic death of DeLoretto/Imani. Above all, these realizations and discoveries lead him to recognize that his task as an artist is to bear honest witness to both the chaos and the transcendence that have struggled for control throughout the history of the African-American soul. Only in this way can he carry out his mission of insuring that "the inner incandescence of Sugar-Groove's life will gain some species of permanency through my pen. Not everlasting life. No, not that . . . never that. Nothing is everlasting; but ever eternal, yes, because some of the divine and explosive life of Sugar-Groove's existence can give illumination to the proscenium of Heaven that is, or will be the kingdom of my stage" (*DD* 1133).

Notes

1. At the time of Forrest's birth the African-American population of Chicago was reaching toward 300,000.

2. Forrest refers to another movie theater located at the corner of 35th and Indiana: "the wonderful cowboy movies for thirty cents at the Joe Louis Theater on Saturdays" (47). Drake and Cayton in their *Black Metropolis*, the most important study of black Chicago at the time of Forrest's growing up, refer to 47th and South Parkway as "the center of the black belt" (379).

3. The complexity of this religious heritage is symbolized in *Two Wings*: "Nathaniel had a rosary in his pocket and a High-John the Conqueror leaf there and a prayer cloth Sister Rachel Flowers had given him (132). NOTE: All citations to *Tree*, *Bloodworth*, and *Two Wings* are to the Another Chicago Press editions. Citations to *Divine Days* are to the Norton edition.

4. The Pilgrim Baptist church at 33rd and Indiana, long one of the leading African-American churches in Chicago, is presided over by the legendary preaching dynasty of J.C. Austin. The building housing the church is a fascinating urban landmark, having been designed as a Jewish synagogue by the great architect Louis Sullivan for the congregation of his partner Dankmar Adler. Though never finished on the exterior, the interior is one of Sullivan's masterpieces. St. Elizabeth's is still a black inner city parish.

5. For an more detailed analysis of religious forms in Forrest's fiction see the essays by Danille Taylor-Guthrie and Bruce Rosenberg.

6. This article was reprinted as "A Conversation with Ralph Ellison" in *Relocations of the Spirit*.

7. Forrest's central theme of re-creation or the tranforming of chaos into order ("finding a way out of noway") is analyzed in A. Robert Lee's essay, "'Equilibrium out of their chaos': Ordered Unorder in the Witherspoon-Bloodworth Trilogy of Leon Forrest."

8. Toni Morrison gives naming a similar significance, though not as complex a treatment, in several of her novels. In *Song of Solomon*, for example, the naming of the Dead family by a drunken and confused Yankee soldier symbolizes the ambiguities of emancipation and the Northward migration of former slaves, while Pilate Dead's naming by her

father from the Bible, symbolizes the significance of religion as a transformative power in Black life. Forrest discusses Morrison's work and its treatment of the theme of reinvention in the essay "Morrison's Magic Lantern" in *Relocations*.

9. Forrest describes these women in his autobiographical essay "In the Light of the Likeness—-Transformed" reprinted in *Relocations* 15-16.

10. Nathaniel shares other characteristics with his creator, such as the double Catholic-Protestant religious heritage and literary aspirations. However, Nathaniel is no more Leon Forrest than Stephen Dedalus was James Joyce, Quentin Compson, William Faulkner, or the Invisible Man, Ralph Ellison. Other aspects of Forrest's character and life appear in his other major protagonist, Joubert Jones of *Divine Days*.

11. Written in 1945 for the *Viking Portable Faulkner*, the "Appendix" was printed at the beginning or the end of new editions of the 1929 novel until a new text was established in the 1980s. Since that time, the novel is usually printed without the "Appendix."

12. Our increasing knowledge of the traditional cultures of certain Native American tribes has made us newly aware of the profound significance of the dream-quest as a ritual of passage from childhood into maturity. Interestingly, accounts of dream visions like that in *Black Elk Speaks* also center around complex and shifting symbols in a way comparable to Forrest's use of the tree and the wagon in Nathaniel's nightmares and dreams.

13. This, for example, is the kind of sermon preached by the Rev. Shegog in Faulkner's *The Sound and the Fury*.

14. The idea of archetypal forms, one of the fundamental concepts of artistic modernism, had its roots in both the anthropological investigations growing out of Sir James Fraser's *The Golden Bough* and in the psychoanalytic explorations of Freud and Jung. Forrest drew even more extensively on this tradition in *The Bloodworth Orphans*, particuarly through his interest in the work of Lord Raglan, a follower of Frazer.

15. Nathaniel's association between history and nightmare may well reflect Joyce's Stephen Dedalus who says "History is a nightmare from which I am trying to escape" (*Ulysses* chap. 2, l. 377).

16. Forrest's vision of a crucifixion-lynching was also strongly influenced by Faulker's powerful account of the ritual sacrifice of Joe Christmas in *Light in August*, which Forrest was studying at the time.

17. Two other African-American writers seem to have had some direct influence on the themes and style of "Wakefulness," as well as a more general influence on *There Is a Tree* as a whole. One was Ralph Ellison whose prologue and epilogue to *Invisible Man* both stylistically and thematically anticipate "Wakefulness" and the other is James Bald-

win, who, in the final section of *Go Tell It on the Mountain*, makes a similar use of the rhythm of rising and falling.

18. As noted earlier, this section was added to the novel at the time
of its reissue by Another Chicago Press in 1988. Though a later addition,
Forrest clearly intends it to be part of the work and this is appropriate
enough in the light of Forrest's aesthetic of transformation and re-creation. In addition, "Transformation" adds another level of meaning to the
present and past explored in *There Is a Tree*, namely the perspective of
the future. It's interesting to compare "Transformations" with Faulkner's
"Appendix" to *The Sound and the Fury* also written at a later time and
carrying the Compson story further into the future. However, it's difficult
to say just how Faulkner intended the appendix to relate to the rest of
the work and contemporary editors are probably right in not including it
in new editions. However, it does shed a rather fascinating light on the
events and characters of *The Sound and the Fury* just as "Transformation" does for *There Is a Tree More Ancient than Eden*.

19. The "Epistle" was mostly written in 1984 shortly after Forrest published *Two Wings*.

20. Forrest uses this quotation from Nietzsche at the end of chapter
six of *Tree* (85) but it's a favorite of his and he uses it again in a prominent place in *Divine Days*. The whole quote is "only the man with chaos
within him can give birth to a dancing star."

21. The influence of Faulkner's *Absalom, Absalom!* is obvious here.
Faulkner's great novel gave Forrest an important model for the difficult
and complex probing of the Southern past and slavery through multiple
narrators. It's also clear that *Two Wings* is, in many ways, Forrest's
response to Haley's *Roots*. Like many African-American writers of the
1980s, Forrest felt it was time to tackle the subject of slavery. Another
powerful result of this impulse was Toni Morrison's *Beloved* (1987).

22. Reed's bird-like attributes and musical gifts not only link him to
the African past but also to the future. He is, we might say, a sort of
mythic forerunner of the great Yardbird, Charlie Parker, and a symbolic
prototype of the jazz musician whose art is vital to the culture and yet
relegated to its margins. Perhaps it's also significant that jazz became
one of the major cultural forms bringing together blacks and whites.

23. I.V. of course suggests "ivy" the clinging parasite, but may also
have the more modern implication of intravenous or connecting blood-
streams.

24. Like the mythical Orpheus, Regal Pettibone is torn to pieces by
outraged members of the River Rock of Eden Church who blame him for
the destruction of their church. Also like Orpheus, Abraham Dolphin symbolically returns from the dead when he escapes to the North in a

coffin, and when he dies his ashes are scattered down the Mississippi River. Ford demonically parodies this return from the dead in one of his bits of religious "tricknology," but Ironwood "Landlord" Rumble is the clearest avatar of the Orpheus myth.

25. Ford will become an even more important figure in Forrest's fourth novel, *Divine Days*, where the dialectic opposition between chaotic destruction and recreation are even more central to the novel's structure. In that novel, Ford's great antithesis is the saintly hustler, Sugar-Groove.

26. There were, of course, extended first person passages in *Two Wings to Veil My Face* (the narratives of Sweetie and I.V. Reed) and the internal monologues of Nathaniel Witherspoon which dominate *There Is a Tree* are a variety of first person presentation.

27. For the reader's convenience, I'm including here an outline of the dates (and page nos.) of the 15 sections of *Divine Days*:

Structure of *Divine Days*

1. Wednesday, February 16, 1966, 6:00 a.m. (9)
2. Thursday, February 17, 9:30 a.m. (83)
3. Thursday, February 17, 3:00 p.m. (97)
4. Friday, February 18, 10:00 a.m. (163)
5. Friday, February 18, 4:30 p.m. (209)
6. Friday, February 18, 6:30 p.m. (230)
7. Saturday, February 19, 7:00 a.m. (272)
8. Saturday, February 19, 5:00 p.m. (365)
9. Sunday, February 20, 10:45 a.m. (470)
10. Sunday, February 20, 1:15 p.m. (498)
11. Monday, February 21, 8:00 a.m. (594)
12. Monday, February 21, 7:15 p.m. (631)
13. Monday, February 21, 11:00 p.m. (644)
14. Tuesday, February 22, 9:30 p.m. (827)
15. Wednesday, February 23, 10:00 a.m. (987)

28. This is the conclusion of Forrest's essay on Elijah Muhammad in his recent collection of essays, published in hard cover as *Relocations of the Spirit*, and in line with Forrest's commitment to creative transformation, re-published in paperback as *The Furious Voice for Freedom*.

29. Of course, Wilkerson refers here to Louis Armstrong, often cited by Forrest as a symbol of the best in African-American re-creation.

30. Born as William or Billy Bloodworth, Sugar Groove is the son of Wilfred Bloodworth (possibly a brother of Arlington Bloodworth II) and the beautiful African-American woman Sarah-Belle (Gates).

31. The multiple meanings of the novel's title are one sign of its many dimensions. At various times "Divine Day" refers to the cult cre-

ated by Ford, the days of Joubert Jones's week in February 1966, the transcendent experiences of Sugar-Groove, the nights of exhuberantly comic celebration in Eloise's Night Light Lounge, etc.

32. Jamesway was loosely based on Forrest's own mentor, the black social psychologist and educator Allison Davis. This scene also pays tribute to two other important African-American scholars Forrest met at the University of Chicago, the historian John Hope Franklin and the literary critic Nathan Scott. Scenes of the mixed life that swirls around universities located in the inner city also play a significant role in *Divine Days*, while the character of Professor Allerton Jamesway is a fascinating portrait of the scholarly black intellectual.

33. Some well-to-do African-Americans had weekend cottages on Lake Michigan on the other side of the lake from Chicago (Forest County).

34. Chicago's West Side was an area of accelerating urban decay long occupied by other immigrant groups when African-Americans flooded into it not long before the time of *Divine Days*. The area was more rundown and lacked many of the more solid institutional traditions established on the South Side which had long been an African-American area.

Works Cited

Forrest, Leon. *The Bloodworth Orphans.* Chicago: Another Chicago Press, 1988.

——. *Divine Days.* New York: Norton, 1992.

——. *Relocations of the Spirit.* Mount Kisco, NY: Moyer-Bell, 1993.

——. *There Is a Tree More Ancient than Eden.* Chicago: Another Chicago Press, 1988.

——. *Two Wings to Veil My Face.* Chicago: Another Chicago Press, 1988.

The Mythic City:
An Interview With Leon Forrest

Kenneth W. Warren

This interview was conducted in Leon Forrest's Northwestern University office during the afternoon of December 3, 1992.

WARREN: Your most recent novel, *Divine Days*, entangles your reader in a web of family relations. Perhaps talking about your family might be a good place to begin. In an autobiographical essay you have written that you were "raised by a magical seamstress, a lady who was always transforming life: first, the cloth, now the body and then the very spirit of the recreated person before our eyes." Can you tell us a little more about being raised by your Aunt Lenora Bell and how it has shaped your approach to writing novels?

FORREST: She was actually a part of the extended family really. She wasn't related to us, but had raised my mother and was very instrumental in my raising and rearing. She was a complicated woman, a Republican—one of the very few Republicans around the neighborhood. She was also quite a good storyteller and would read to me a lot. And then, as I said in my article, she had all of these patterns in her room of works she was designing and dresses she was interested in making. So, it was very interesting for me to have a person who was not related in a direct way · and yet was very much interested in being a kind of matriarch, I suppose, in the family . . . and to have someone who was serious about reading to talk to in my formative years.

WARREN: So you say she was a storyteller. What kind of stories . . .?

FORREST: She would talk about growing up in Kentucky and her family. One brother had owned, as she says, a saloon (she was very refined), and the other brother died when he was quite young. And then her mother, who was a mulatto, was part of a group of teachers in Kentucky. So she was not that far really from slavery. And then my great-grandmother on my father's side—was born in 1875, and her mother had been in slavery. And so even though I was born in 1937, I wasn't that far from some of the stories that were either near slavery or at the frontier of it. And that's perhaps one of the reasons why I got interested in trying to write novels that had an historical sweep to them . . . but in a mythical sense . . . since I wasn't there nor were the people who I talked to really in the slave experience, but they knew of it.

WARREN: OK . . . so then, were there other storytellers? Your fiction is populated by people who are always somehow telling their narratives and interweaving their various stories.

FORREST: I mentioned, too, a great-uncle of mine who went to school with Louis Armstrong in New Orleans—George Dewey White who was quite a storyteller and a barber. And as you were sitting their getting your hair cut, he would tell you stories. He was always renaming people in the family. In families generally at this time, kids didn't talk very much. So you would just sit there and listen, you know, and you'd better not speak out too much. But it worked well because it allowed me to develop this layered sense of storytelling from various voices . . . and yet to keep them separate. My mother's side of the family was completely different from my father's side of the family. And then there was this Aunt Bell who was not related by blood but had raised my mother and me. And that was interesting just in terms of getting these separate sides of the family straight. Now I tried to incorporate in terms of my own fiction the sense of the diversity of the group. So that perhaps helped me a lot when I first started writing, to have that kind of background where these voices were very separate.

WARREN: Now the separate sides of the family . . . do they correspond to the differences, say, in the Catholicism on the one side and the Protestantism on the other?

FORREST: That's right.

WARREN: It's relatively unusual in the African-American experience that you get a representation of Catholicism as a force. Can you talk a little bit more about how Catholicism and African-American literature and life come together for you?

FORREST: Well, it was very hard because of the Catholic church at that time seemed to be so far from the ethos of African-Americans. Whereas if I was in Haiti, a Haitian writer, it would have been wonderful. Instead, it was just another way in which it seemed to me my own background was so splintered that I would never be able to write anything. A Catholic on one side . . . a Protestant on the other. And there are all kinds of other divsions within divisions. But reading Joyce and also later reading the Latin-American writers gave me a certain confidence in using the Catholic experience, simply because that was their experience—the Catholic Church—and they obviously wrote out of it with a certain strength and robustness. But it also gave me a confidence that I could use it in a way. And so that was one thing, but was a long time coming. I think I was more influenced by the ritual of the Catholic Church.

Then with the Protestants I was more influenced by the spirituals, in particular the gospels and preaching, because I didn't go to a Catholic school, which was different from all my cousins. They all went to Catholic school and were sufficiently indoctrinated. I had the blessing of going to a black school with some very powerful and prideful black teachers. So I learned some Negro history. And then we also sang spirituals and so on. From my father's side of the family I began to get a sense of the importance of the folk preacher. It seems to me that has saved my artistic life, really. I never would have made that discovery if I had only gone to the Catholic church—Catholic school.

WARREN: In what way did it save your artistic life?

FORREST: Because it gave me the voice into the conscience of the race. And I feel the preacher is really the bard of the race. And the church is also the place where the highest level of eloquence is projected—at least that was true when I was a kid. It's the place that even then made the connection between the spiritual and the secular experience . . . the spiritual and the political experience.

WARREN: So you see that the folk tradition as it came up from the South to the urban centers of the North managed to sustain itself and did not, as writers, say, from Jean Toomer and Richard Wright suggest, tend to die out because it didn't provide the kind of sustaining force that . . .

FORREST: Oh, yes, I think so. In Chicago and many other urban centers it still flourished. And witness even today the tremendous amount of powerful preaching in different black pulpits every Sunday in Chicago. And a lot of that is still southern preaching to a large degree—structurally and oratorically and so on. Now that also has to do with the fact that in my own fiction anyway there's a much more celebratory fervor, I think, than you get with some of the realism school.

WARREN: That's what's fascinating about your work. Chicago has certainly figured into American literature for well over a century now, but it seems to call forth a realistic ethos in writers whether you're talking about Theodore Dreiser, Frank Norris, or Richard Wright. Why does it strike a mythic chord in you?

FORREST: Well, mythic and comic in its resiliency. It's a city of a hustler. It's a city where you can get knocked down and smashed and make a comeback. I mean within the black community. Because it is a hustler's town and because it was said that if you came to Chicago you could get a job. In fact, these were the papers sent South—*The Defender, The Courier*—"Come to Chicago for a job!" And that kind of life, you know, was really the nourishing form in my own background coming up in the '40s and '50s. It was only later that a lot of that began to break down. But even then it was a city for the hustler. And that was the difference from many other cities—Cincinnati, Cleveland, different places—where if you were to get into public trouble or corruption you can't make a comeback. But in Chicago . . . just lay low awhile and you can come back.

WARREN: So does that explain why the folk preacher and the hustler are not so very far apart?

FORREST: Well, that's right . . . that's right. And of course the trickster of many kinds.

WARREN: Say more about the role of the trickster in your work.

FORREST: The trickster, to me, is the one who is not an agent of healing as it is in the African tradition where with the magical gods the story is ultimately worked out and harmony is brought forth. Rather a trickster is one who is always manipulating chaos for his own good and cunning, and there are all kinds. I mean there is the kind who is trickster as demon, that I deal with a little bit in *Divine Days*. And one of the things that I was trying to get at in *Divine Days* with the character Sugar-Groove, who is out of a trickster as hipster perhaps, is this other side of him that begins to turn a lot in the latter part of his life towards generous works and also apparently goes through some kind of spiritual metamorphosis.

WARREN: So this trickster, and we can keep Sugar-Groove in mind here, do you see it as specific to African-American literary tradition, or is he something like the conman that we see cropping up in most American literature?

FORREST: He would be both, of course. He is an American, so that is certainly part of the terrain. But it's increased for blacks because so much of what was available to make a living after the height of the job openings for blacks in the '40s and '50s and early '60s had to do with a kind of underground economy. And that underground economy sometimes was something like, for instance, a person who might be a numbers runner, or maybe an ambulance chaser, to someone on the other end of the spectrum who might be running drugs. But so much of what was available had to do with a coming up with a cunning hustle . . . a device . . . a certain kind of hustle to survive. And inherent in that was the role of the trickster.

WARREN: So does that describe the writer as well?

FORREST: The writer is taking a tremendous gamble in whatever he or she is working on. That it will all come out. And if you're ambitious enough you're rolling dice with some pretty rugged people who are no longer around, but their books are there to outwit.

WARREN: So those rugged people include Joyce, Faulkner, Ellison. Talk about how you see yourself in relation to any particular literary tradition.

FORREST: I see myself in line in at least three traditions. Once would be the very specific tradition of Langston Hughes and Sterling Brown—writers who used oral tradition and to a certain degree extended it a bit in their poetry. And then in a larger tradition with Ellison and Hayden—writers, I think, who took the oral tradition and recombined it with Western intellectual traditions, literary traditions, and placed yet a higher stamp upon their art. Then there was their connection with the larger American traditions of Poe and Faulkner and Melville and so on (the connections between Ellison and Melville, as you know, are very keen). That's another connection. And then ultimately, of course, the connection that we all have as American writers to the best achievements in the novel form of the 19th century as we've seen through European literature and Russian literature. So those are about three or four connections I like to make. I mean, I have been very much influenced by a lot of the writings later in Dostoevsky—in particular those wonderful monologues in *Crime and Punishment* and the *Brothers K.* and the investigation of this kind of tormented inner soul, and the idea that a guy can come in a tavern and tell you his story and that story in itself is an odyssey. Well, that's very different from what we had many hundreds of years ago where the only person who would have these extraordinary stories would be the world travelers. Here a person can live a life in a city and have an odyssey. And that connects us to, of course, obviously with both Dostoevsky, and of course, particularly with Joyce whom we were talking about.

WARREN: OK . . . this brings up a number of questions. One comes from the fact that along with writing you also teach literature, specifically, African-American literature. Do you find that students are receptive to the idea that they ought to have read Dostoevsky and Joyce in order to understand, say, what Ellison is up to and indeed, what you are up to—your fiction?

FORREST: No, because students, whether it's a literature class or a creative writing class, want to assume that literature is original in a way that nothing is original. I sometimes talk about all the influences in Morrison's work—and they're all over the place as they are with any first-rate writer—because she was very well read before she ever started thinking about writing. But students tend to feel that it dampers originality, the creativity of a writer, for you to point this out too much. Or others will feel rather intimidated by it.

WARREN: Do they respond differently if the influences you allude to are other African-American artists say, rather than Russian or Irish?

FORREST: Yes, somewhat. Then there's the question of gender, too, because if you mention some male figure—well, "Why not just other women?" I'm always anxious to point out, "Yes, but they're taking on men on what was supposedly only male grounds and in many cases outdoing them." But this gets into the ambitions of the writer. So unless it's an advanced class, it's like that wonderful Melville story—they "prefer not to."

WARREN: Well, you've mentioned the two words, tradition and then the ambitions of the writer, which suggests that one's attitude toward tradition is certainly not a matter of simple reverence. That is, when you sit down to write a novel, you're not approaching these great figures as simply icons; you're engaged in some sort of battle.

FORREST: The first expression is reverence, of course, when you read them when you're very young. The second is to think about, "Now, how can I cut my own path around this lion or lioness, or conversely, take him or her on in areas that they didn't know that well, but only suggested." That's certainly been my relationship with Faulkner about the folk preacher. Because I was very much taken with that wonderful little sermon of Reverend Shegog's in *The Sound and the Fury*, but I soon enough figured out that, hell, I'd know more about black sermons than Faulkner did. And why shouldn't I after all? I still salute him for doing that fine sermon and I wish others would have tried to do it. A lot of times a writer, an older writer, a prominent or famous writer, can suggest some clues for you to try to broaden or expand that he or she only touched upon.

WARREN: So then, in your attitude toward these older writers, two of the key words that come up again in your own discussions about your fiction and the discussion the critics are engaged in about your fiction are transformation and reinvention. Can you elaborate on these words?

FORREST: Transformation always refers to character and the idea that the kinds of black characters I'm interested in, the major ones anyway, are often going through several stages of psychological, spiritual, and political transformation. Sometimes in terms of strength and sometimes in terms of destruction, which is in *Divine Days* both with Sugar-Groove and also Imani. Reinvention seems to me so much a part of the black ethos, of taking some- thing that is available or maybe conversely, denied blacks and making it into something else for survival and then adding a kind of stamp and style and elegance. And it's all through African- American music and jazz and it's obviously all through sports of all kinds, and I think it's the link I have to Morrison and to Ellison. It's something a lot of the Afrocentric people haven't seen . . . that we're not simply a repository nor a reflection of the African experience, but that we're constantly remaking everything that was left over from Africa, everything that we got from the Euro- peans, into something completely new that both the Africans couldn't do and the Europeans couldn't do. Europeans didn't create jazz and neither did the Africans. Black Americans did that.

WARREN: How then do you account for the popularity of Afrocen- trism . . . ?

FORREST: It's part of our search—the African-American search—for wholeness and, also in some cases, for a purer answer.

WARREN: Now you're moving toward some of the more obvious, say, political import of reinvention in your works as well. Do you see that your work is engaging in contemporary political debate in any particular way?

FORREST: Maybe the last novel *Divine Days* does. But it seemed to me the way to approach that was through some satire and comedy in a way. Because one of the problems with much of the contemporary arts that I've seen is that they have these sort of easy pat answers. For instance, at the end of this play, between Malcolm X and Martin Luther King, there is this embrace, and now they're brothers, you know, which is really so much bullshit. Because what this resolution does is to narrow the toughness of the individual arguments that these men had with each other and about society. And this was serious business on the part of both men that they really believed in what they were doing and that the other fellow was going the wrong way. But I've noticed this with a number of recent, well-thought-of pieces, whether movies or novels in which some sort of easy embrace is forged and that in doing that it doesn't strengthen the group, but it suggests a kind of pabulum.

WARREN: Do you see that going on with students you're teaching here at Northwestern?

FORREST: Well, to the degree that they segregate themselves from the larger campus . . . yeah. This, of course, has to do with several reasons. One is that many come from the black middle and upper-middle class growing in the cities quite strong and very insular, with little experience of harmony with whites and little reason to feel that they would be integrated. The other part is the understandable pride of a people on the way up. And then, of course, all of the vicious racism that has been visited on these campuses in the last five years or so . . . so a lot of that has to do with this will to segregate.

WARREN: Well, it sounds like a climate where satire and parody would be a risky venture.

FORREST: Well, I haven't written any novels about Northwestern. . . .

WARREN: But if we take Northwestern as something of a microcosm . . . of a larger moment. . . .

FORREST: Well, there's a need for it, I think, because satire and comedy force you to divest yourself of your pomposity about your own demonically held vision, you know. And it also helps you laugh at yourself and it means that the individual has to come up with a tough-minded approach to life, so it can be very useful.

WARREN: I'm thinking here of the moment in *Divine Days* where Joubert Jones is speculating on the possibilities of dramatizing the outlandish exploits of the Black Muslim Leroy 5X Jones, and he ends up worrying on the one hand that he could be accused of being an Uncle Tom on the one hand and on the other an anti-Semite. . . .

FORREST: Oh, yes . . . that's a small scene. But what's happened is really like a fairy tale—a truck capsizes on the freeway, and all these pigs are running around. The Muslim, who's gone in and out of the Nation, grabs one and is barbecuing. Joubert is thinking about taking a creative writing class, and he says that maybe he might write about it, but then he would run into some of the problems, you know . . . as you're talking about, about how students would accept this guy eating pork—Muslim and Jewish kids—would not accept that. So it is a problem of how people will accept humor—if they will use it as a way of purgation and as a way of self-cleansing and coming clean with themselves and their society. But if you present these romantic images that are so false to human feeling and ideology, then you do literature and you do the group harm.

WARREN: Well, then what's interesting about the year 1992 is we have the publication of *Divine Days* and then, much later in the year, we have the release of Spike Lee's film on Malcolm X. Now, one might describe the film as a canonization of Malcolm X as a quintessential black male hero toward whom the ideal posture is one of reverence. And yet, you have a novel here that takes an irreverent stance towards heroism. One of the epigraphs with which you begin the text is a quote from Joyce in which he says the "whole structure of heroism is and always will be a damned lie." And later on you have a character who speaks very disparagingly of "Malcolm-mania." What are your feelings toward the contemporary reception of Malcolm X, either through Spike Lee's film or just a general attitude towards him as a historical figure?

FORREST: Well, I think that he is attractive because he represents opposite ends of the spectrum here. One, that he was such a consummate hustler and almost eventually as demon, but was successful in that world. Then he had the pins kicked out from under him and went through this spiritual metamorphosis in jail. And then he epitomized the other end of it, and that is the great potential of leadership. And that leadership represented the ability to tell whites off, and also to tell off the subservient black leadership. So all of that is quite attractive, and the odyssey of it is attractive. But what is missed here is any sort of criticism of Malcolm the person. The tendency is to deify two forms of figures, one, the underground hero, and then the hero who, when he was with the Muslims, even there he was a hero who was not accepted by the larger reaches of black society, nor whites. Though there's every reason for him to be the kind of yeasty mythical figure—you know, he's only been dead thirty years—that people would revere now, because he's almost like a grandfather figure to many of the young kids; it's almost been that far away from them. Then the other point is that you've got a lot of other people who would be in their mid-40s or maybe even older who are in important positions now, and for them Malcolm was an extraordinary hero when they were growing up. Now they're in the position of writing and expressing themselves, or in powerful situations, and they want a rethinking of Malcolm. Many of them have had the problem of running into what we would call, I guess, the glass ceiling in their own professional careers . . . and say, well, maybe Martin was wrong . . . maybe Malcolm was right . . . about the limits of society.

WARREN: Does his career still strike you as a career of possibility in terms of the present moment . . . and how one reinvents Malcolm X?

FORREST: Yes, but he is full of reinvention . . . I'm fearful that not enough is given to the process of that reinvention—that was my point—through the Muslims, for instance . . . that really made his life. And then, of course, there is all of the naivete of Malcolm, and the gullibility of him with *The Messenger*. I mean anybody who knows anything about preachers and is surprised that this preacher had an adulterous life has got to be pretty naive. But it's a fascinating story and it should be looked at more as a kind of saga as opposed to holding fast to everything that he said or did in his public life, because he was constantly making a lot of mistakes. He made mistakes in terms of his ability to access Elijah. He made mistakes certainly in his relationship with the civil rights movement . . . and he really apparently wanted in there. He certainly was a poor leader in terms of organizing people. What he could do was get a lot of people interested in what he was saying, but the kind of organization that you need to undergird a leader, that wasn't his strength. That was more of the precinct captain's strength that Elijah had.

WARREN: You said he made mistakes in regard to the Civil Rights Movement. Are you talking about his early uncompromising posture?

FORREST: I think he wanted the Muslims to move in that arena. Not only civil rights, but particularly the Freedom Movement aspect of the Civil Rights Movement . . . and the political arena . . . and he couldn't get them to do it.

WARREN: Well, your early career also includes a year as managing editor of *Muhammad Speaks*. How does that figure into your view, both of say, the Muslims or Malcolm X, or even your own work today?

FORREST: I thought quite highly of them on certain levels. One of them is the self-help business, which we still need. You look in the slums, there is a desperate need for some of these Mom and Pop stores, and even the Your Supermarkets. The racism in the faith was dangerous and unfortunate, although I must say that for the people they were dealing with, who were so dead spiritually, you needed something of a shock treatment, sort of an electric shock to awaken this dead man. And some of that shock had to be spiritual and nationalistic. Now, the problem is when the nationalism veers over into racism. Then when that happens obviously, it does all kinds of damage to the people who are on the way up. It cuts them off from the intellectual resources that they need. "Well, after all, whites are doing this, we don't need that; Asians are doing this, we don't need that." And after a while, you're into another kind of segregated hold.

WARREN: But is there something in nationalism that makes that kind of turn inevitable?

FORREST: Not necessarily at all. The Irish in Chicago, and in many places in this country really, the fervor that went into their political rise was nationalistic. But then you've got to turn the corner and let that nationalism and self-pride open you up to the larger resources of the outer society. It doesn't have to turn into racism. As a matter of fact, a lot of the people who are very popular or well-known—Powell for one and probably Mayor Washington— were initially nationalists, but along the way they are able to mix in other ingredients into their personality development. And one thing that can do that, of course, is to increase one's reading so that you're not just reading only *The Message to the Black Man* a hundred times, but you're reading a larger library and learning the techniques of political savvy that individuals from other groups have tried.

WARREN: Well it sounds, then, as if the Chicago political machine was one place in the past in which this kind of reinvention or crossing of boundaries actually took place . . . that you perceive something positive in that old. . . .

FORREST: Well, I see something positive in the sense that it gave people an experience. And a lot of people that broke with the machine initially were benefited by the machine in terms of learning politics. Then they had something to break with. But if you don't have anything to break with, then you don't have anything, you know. So that silent six or eight aldermen that Washington eventually had to fight with, too—even Washington himself—also came out of the machine at one time. But at least it gave people a grounding. The Muslims, of course, were enormously conservative. And still are. Malcolm was able to get himself together by going through this kind of conservative mode and then eventually making a kind of radical break with them.

WARREN: You also worked with community newspapers. How did that help shape your vision as a writer?

FORREST: I was with The Woodlawn Organization's newspaper, *The Observer*. I was editor there for a time. It was really good because it allowed me to get out a certain kind of first heat about the political situation—poverty and race and so on. And I could come to my fiction, when I would work on it in the evenings, looking at a literary life in a different way, in an imaginative way. Whereas I think what happened to a lot of people in the late '60s and early '70s is that they got their politics and ideology mixed up with their poverty and their fiction. So it was good in a cunning sense. It was also good training in terms of interviewing people, in terms of learning what could make a story, a certain compactness of language. And it also helped train me to write at the typewriter. So those years were very good. There was also something that got involved in my personality for a long time: the idea of having many different lives. So I guess I've always been attracted to people like that, and have tried to capture characters like that in my novels, who suffer from something more complicated than double-consciousness.

WARREN: Multi-voiced.

FORREST: Multi-souled.

WARREN: Which describes the plight of Joubert Jones in many respects.

FORREST: Yeah, I guess so.

WARREN: Who was also a journalist.

FORREST: He's a bartender, though.

WARREN: Now people have mentioned what they see as the auto-biographical aspects of *Divine Days*. Did you conceive this as an autobiographical novel?

FORREST: Well, no, I didn't. But my God . . . we're talking about a manuscript that was 1829 pages. I wouldn't have an autobiography that could go on that long. But on the other hand, I'll use anything I can get my hands on if I can use it in an imaginative way. And there are many things that have happened to me that I can't write about. They don't do anything for the imagination. But I might hear a story that you would tell me about something that happened to you that would just take me away, and the imagination would soar with it. So I'm always looking at the resources that can go into developing a rich inner life. And that hopefully enriched inner life can act as a springboard for the agency of my imagination. That's always what I'm looking at. Well, a lot of things that have happened are so intimate and I wouldn't mind writing about them, but I just don't seem to have any will over them, or power over them. I have encountered people in my life who were so powerful. I've tried to write about them, but I'm still overpowered by them.

WARREN: So you keep at that?

FORREST: Well, I don't because I go not to something or some-one that maybe I've only known quite peripherally but that encounter unleashed perhaps the characterological makeup within me of a certain character, a certain kind of character, who has been there for a long time, brooding.

WARREN: So clearly the novel is your preferred form, but Joubert is a would-be playwright. Why is he a playwright? Why are you a novelist? What effect does form have on vision?

FORREST: Well, we don't know if Joubert is ever able to find the form. He's writing out in longhand this story of Sugar-Groove, and he hopes to convert that into a play. And of course he has written a play on Ford. So it seems to me my distance in relation to Joubert is that I have published novels and I am writing this novel that was published in *Divine Days*, and he's at perhaps an earlier stage in his development let's say. So, that was one kind of thing. Some of the things he encounters I have encountered and others not. I certainly don't hear all these voices that he hears. He's always hearing voices.

WARREN: So were you attracted to other forms? I know you've written a libretto.

FORREST: I wanted to write poetry for a long time, but I couldn't get command of the eloquence of poetry and the form of it. I had all these poets that I admired so much, that were so grand and I couldn't equal that. But I kept some of that love of language alive, and also the idea of rewriting endlessly the way poets do. For a long time Dylan Thomas was a favorite of mine. Thomas had this method of working where he would change one word of a poem and then would rewrite in longhand the whole poem out . . . particularly the major poems like "Fern Hill" and "The Ballad of the Long-Legged Bait" and the sonnets. He left behind over 225 working papers. So some of that carried over into my obsessive rewriting of fiction. And obviously the love for language. But the discipline of poetry at its highest level seems to me still the consummate literary art.

WARREN: Do you think at some point you will go back?

FORREST: Occasionally, I'll write a little poem on a sort of ceremonial event. So many of the people in *Divine Days* are writers of one kind or another. Aunt Eloise is a newspaperwoman, and Joubert. And there's the guy that runs around the tavern all the time. . . Nightingale. Joubert's grand-uncle writes poetry. So there's some others searching for voices.

WARREN: Searching for forms as well.

FORREST: Imani has a brother who's a playwright.

WARREN: Now you suggested that for you one of the legacies of having been writing for community newspapers in the '60s was a discipline and an awareness of the need to distinguish what you were doing as a journalist and what you were doing as a novelist. But you also suggested that others weren't as successful as you at seeing the apparent pitfalls, as you say, of not being able to distinguish between the two. What do you feel is the legacy of the '60s in terms of African-American literary achievement today? Do you see something positive having come out of, say, the Black Arts Movement? The Black Aesthetic?

FORREST: Well, when you think about the writers who have really made the big thrust in African-American literature, they really start about 1970, I'd say, with *The Bluest Eye*. Beginning maybe with McPherson's stories in '69. McPherson, Wideman, Morrison, Walker—you can just go on and on—Gaines. These were writers who were really not touched directly by the Black Arts Movement. And that's sort of a story in itself. In fact, many of them wouldn't have been all that welcomed by the Black Arts Movement.

WARREN: But could one argue that the mere presence of the movement itself gave them something to work against? Or that the battle that those writers were fighting during the '60s somehow enabled the success that you begin to chart in the 1970s?

FORREST: Perhaps so. I mean, that would be the work of the scholar. But the published works of Gaines and Walker are really quite different from the Black Arts Movement. The works were so well-written that they were incorporated into magazines like *Negro Digest* and so on. But really they were doing something quite different. Toni, of course, would be old enough to certainly have witnessed the Black Arts Movement. But even then she was working on *The Bluest Eye*. But *The Bluest Eye* wouldn't have any place in the Black Arts Movement. You'd have to go down the line, I guess, and look at the particular writers and what they were publishing during that time and see how much of it was really, in fact, stuff out of the ideology of the Black Arts Movement. I certainly know that I can't think of one novel of any particular strength that emerged out of the Black Arts Movement.

WARREN: What about poetry?

FORREST: Poetry all over the place, and then the question is, "Well, how strong is the poetry?" There certainly was a lot of energy and there was also activity, to a degree, in the theater. But I think one of the legacies would be the energy that comes out of the Black Arts Movement, best revealed in poetry. Some poets have emerged. It seems to me you have to go in stages a little bit, like the Beat period. Well, who are the writers who emerged out of the Beat period? There aren't that many when you think about it. It was primarily a white movement with the exception of Baraka. So it isn't just putting a bad mouth on Black Arts, but just any movement. How many survive out of that? And there aren't that many given the great numbers who were involved in the Black Arts Movement. In Chicago, I think of Sterling Plumpp, but Sterling has gone on because he got reinvolved with the blues idiom, which has really saved him as a poet. And you know there are others who have been able to recombine the energy of the Black Arts Movement with the Women's Movement, for instance, like Sanchez and Evans and some of the others. But if these writers didn't recombine that energy with other energies then, by and large, they lost. They lost out because that was the first kind of feverish energy of a young creativity. And if that isn't recombined with other strengths either out of the culture or literary traditions, then the writers have fallen by the wayside. And that always happens.

WARREN: Now you chair the African-American Studies department here at Northwestern. Could one say that the true legacy of what was going on in the '60s with the Black Arts Movement was precisely the movement of African-American Studies into the academy and the institutionalization of African-American Studies? Does that strike you as accurate?

FORREST: It certainly had some impact, there's no doubt about that. First of all around maybe '66, '67, many schools started opening up a bit and then as you know, of course, after Dr. King's death there was a tremendous sense of guilt in all these universities about a lot of things. And the black students were able to say, "Well, you know, we're uncomfortable here and a lot of it has to do with the black or African experience." And so it had a kind of historical sweep to it. To bring in everything back from Martin Delany or, even before that, everything African in to the canon or into what was being taught. And they were probably energized a lot by what you're saying about reading Sanchez and many of the poets. But their great interest was to bring in the whole sweep of denied intellectual resources, I think. There's certainly a lot to what you're saying and a lot of their direct heroes would have been women and men who were in the Black Arts Movement. That's for sure.

WARREN: Do you think that the future—as an administrator of an African-American Studies program—do you think that the future of these programs is bright? Or dim?

FORREST: Well, I think it's going to be very useful for universities because of the demographics at the turn of the century where you have many more people of color in the university who want to go to the sources of ethnicity. On the other hand, most of our class is, 2/3 of the students who take our classes are white. So yeah, I think it's here to stay . . . and, of course, students generally want to take something about the black experience simply because you can't go through a three-month period without something extraordinary happening to black people in a large sense in this society, as revealed in the news. And people want to know about it, whether it's Rodney King one month and Malcolm X the next, you know. And so on. And students generally want to have some sense of what that means.

WARREN: Does that put pressure on the African-American courses to be. . . .

FORREST: Topical . . . yes. It sure does. And the problem is, as I was mentioning earlier, is to connect up with the larger historical background. So if you're going to talk about Malcolm, talk about Nationalism, and then you're back to Martin Delany, or you're going through Garvey and Delany and so on. But try to give them some sense of the sweep of everything that seems to be most immediate. If you're talking about Rodney King, well, that gets us back to Richard Wright, in the South, and to Faulkner and the writers who talked about the degradation of blacks through the police state. . . .

WARREN: Let's switch gears for a moment and go back to your career as a novelist. How would you describe your trajectory beginning with, say, There is a Tree, and ending up most recently with Divine Days. Do you see yourself charting a particular course as a writer or is it more serendipitous in terms of what comes next?

FORREST: It is open-ended in a sense of what might come next because I'm always working on little patches here and there. Little stories. I'll work on half-a-dozen pages or so and then I'll put them aside and come back and rewrite them endlessly and try to forget about them. So later I can come back to them with a certain tough, cold eye, let's say. I never know where things are going. I don't use much of an outline. I work from a very vague outline and I improvise that like a jazz musician over and over again. On the other hand, it is by now apparent to me that there is a little mythical kingdom (not an original thought) that I've been developing and so I am very much concerned with trying to bring certain areas into it that I haven't written about before.

WARREN: Do you see yourself staying in the boundaries of Forest County as you look forward to your next work?

FORREST: Yeah, I think so because I might as well. I don't have that much time left. So I, you know, better do what I can do the best. And there's so many things I can't do in terms of writing, and there are certain things I can do and so I suppose I'd best stick to what I can do.

WARREN: Would you want to talk a little about what you think is coming up next . . .?

FORREST: There was a lot left over from, believe it or not, *Divine Days*. There were about 150 pages cut from it and a long scene in there it seemed to me that I could just cut out and save. And that's a scene with Joubert in the army. I'm going to use that and that should be pretty interesting. And there were several sections of work that I wanted to use in *Divine Days*, and that might be another novel, a kind of sequel, but I never know if I can energize it. That's my problem.

WARREN: And how do you discover that moment when you energize it?

FORREST: Through hard work and rewriting over and over again. And you know, maybe I'll hit something that will just . . . the juice will shoot through it. And then I'm on the way to agony and ecstasy or something. But I don't know if that's going to happen. And then there's another one that would take up the life of

Nathaniel around the time he's 14. I have a lot of that manuscript, in fact. This was really a love story about a woman who commits suicide, and it's told in voices: several people trying to get a handle on why she commits suicide. I abandoned that because, at the time, I didn't think I had the power or control or whatever it takes to finish so then I got working upon the idea of *Two Wings to Veil My Face*.

WARREN: So this is something you've been thinking about coming back to then . . .?

FORREST: Yeah, that's right. So those are two kinds of projects. And then there's another one which might be a series of short stories. And so there are all these little dribbles and patches around. Maybe I can forge them into a story. I also have a collection of essays coming out next year, as you know.

WARREN: Coming out early next year?

FORREST: They'll be out in about May. One of them is a long essay on Billie Holiday . . . which, I think, is going to be in this special issue of *Callaloo*.

WARREN: Well, since you've brought up Billie Holiday . . . talk a little bit more about her as a major facet of your aesthetic . . . her voice is referred to often.

FORREST: I suppose she was more powerful than even I realized. My mother loved her a lot and really seemed to have understood her art quite a bit . . . used to play her songs a lot and would point to things that she thought she was doing. And she was about the same age (well, she was a bit older than my mother) but we used to listen to her all the time. I became intrigued more and more on my own with her because it seemed to me that she was a good example of the artist as thinker. And then all the problems of life that she had to contend with, she was able to turn them into this haunting artistic creation, you know. Although she was often wiped out personally by these problems. The other interesting thing to me was that Holiday was one of the very few major black singers who was not influenced directly by the church, and that allowed her to give voice to an urban song and heartache that was a combination of at least three things:

blues, and also the tradition of the cabaret singer, and the eloquence of jazz, particularly the jazz horn men. And she was fascinating for that. In other words, we were talking about a completely different voice . . . from Dinah Washington and from so
many of the black singers who were influenced directly by the
church, sang out in church, came out of the church. And so
we're talking about soul. She had soul. But it was a different kind
of soul. It allowed her, because she wasn't overwhelmed by the
simplicity of acceptance of faith inherent in the church, it
allowed her, perhaps even forced her, to think in a most savvy
and cunning way about these sentimental lyrics that she sang. So
Holiday also transcended the sort of tinpan alley Broadway song
she sang with something that's seasoned and sassy and evil and
lyrical quite all her own. So long before I ever thought about all
that, you know, there she was in my mind. So it's wonderful to
have some of this stuff in your background long before you start
to write or paint, to draw on. But again, the writer has to get that
kind of detachment to think in an analytical way about his or her
own sources . . . even as you are nourished by them in a sort of
natural way.

WARREN: Is that an ongoing process of detachment?

FORREST: Yes, and you have to have both . . . I'm often knocked
down by figures like Holiday. And then Charlie Parker . . . reading
certain writers. I have to sort of come back up again . . . But then
there's always the other side that says, "Well, wait a minute now.
I'd better try to think a minute about this."

WARREN: Take that into a reflection of literature, say, at the present
moment. Who are the writers who . . .?

FORREST: Knock me down? Probably the last would have been
Marquez, I guess.

WARREN: *One Hundred Years of Solitude*?

FORREST: *Autumn of the Patriarch*, too. There are writers out there,
but after a while, you know, you get so cold and you're sort of
reading a writer and asking, "Well, let me see what he's doing
technically." Well, another writer who fascinates me is Walcott.
But usually, I'm reading something I've read a long time ago,

over and over again, you know, to find some of these resources, any energizing resources in his or her work.

WARREN: Well, thanks a lot. I enjoyed this very much.

FORREST: Well thank *you*.

WARREN: We'll have to do it again.

"Equilibrium out of their chaos":
Ordered Unorder in the Witherspoon-Bloodworth Trilogy of Leon Forrest

A. Robert Lee

Descendancy: What's the score?
Leon Forrest: *Re-Creation*, A Verse Play set to Music by T.J. Anderson (1978)[1]

And what do I mean by re-creation and reinvention? I mean the powerful use of imagination to take a given form and make something that appears completely new of it—that creates within the reading or listening audience a sense of the magical meaning of life transformed. Leon Forrest: "In the light of the likeness—transformed." (*Contemporary Authors Autobiography Series*, Volume 7, 1988)[2]

One of the constants of Afro-American culture is the re-invention of life —or, the cultural attribute of black Americans is to take what is left over . . . and make it work for them, as a source of personal or group survival, and then to emboss, upon the basic form revised, a highly individualistic style, always spun of grace, and fabulous rhythms . . . a kind of magic realism. The improvisational genius of jazz is what I am getting at here. This is central to the art of Ellington, Armstrong, Lady Day, Sarah Vaughan, Ray Charles, Muddy Waters, Alberta Hunter; I could of course go on. . . . (Leon Forrest: "Faulkner/Reforestation," University of Mississippi, August 1988)[3]

"Word-possessed (and word-possessing)." Ralph Ellison's phrasing in his Foreword to *There Is a Tree More Ancient than Eden* (1973) does every justice.[4] For to enter Forest County, Leon Forrest's Chicago as a black city-within-a-city at once Northern yet shaped from the outset by a South of Mississippi and New Orleans, is also, and coevally, to enter a world conceived as if at an intervening remove. That is, recognizable as may be Cook County's South Side or black West Side, Forrest's language also indicates another kind of topography, displaced, shadowed

97

with memory and hallucination, and, often enough, apocalyptic.

His mythical kingdom thus inscribes a black "city" as much of the inner senses as, say, of the hardshell Chicago of Richard Wright's *Native Son* or, at a different reach, of the rambuntious Jewish-immigrant Chicago of Saul Bellow's *Augie March*. A Bigger Thomas, or a Bessie, may continue to exist, but as though in a kind of inward hyper-focus. A similar change of imagining holds for the black community at large with its street life, tenements and bars, its churches and pool-halls, blues and jazz.

It certainly does so for a population as diverse as the branded, ex-slave ancestor, Jericho Witherspoon; the supremely "black," adaptive jack-of-all-trades, Jamestown Fishbond; the eventually suicidal club-owner and abortionist, Abraham Dolphin M.D.; the genealogist, the Rev. Jonathan Bass; the ledger-keeping midwife, Lucia Rivers; a con-man as monstrous yet as fertile of invention as W.W.W. Ford; and of greatest relevance in Forest County, hornmen like Ironwood "Landlord" Rumble and protectresses like Hattie Breedlove Wordlaw and Great-Momma Sweetie Reed. Nor, too, can these be thought to belong other than to a black "Chicago" made the more nuanced by two Christianities, a Catholicism brought north from Creole Louisiana and a Bible Protestantism from Dixie's camp meetings and conversions.

If, then, a city of "the street," or of "the projects," with behind both always the indelible, haunting remembrance of slavery, Forrest's Chicago doubles as also a city of Lex. Like Joyce's Dublin, it almost consciously presses to be understood in terms of the language of myth (and the myth of language) as of any literal street-map, be the reference as it frequently is to the El, or to Dan Ryan Expressway, or to Lake Shore Drive.

For however striking the habitats and human repertoire of the novels, or indeed the sheer eventfulness of the lives depicted, Forrest's singularity lies, finally, in his style, his idiom, that which presumably more than anything else led Saul Bellow, in his turn, to speak of "a fiery writer . . . an original."[5] This reflexive bodying-out, or overall "naming," of Forest County as both a historic past and present and at the same time as the upshot of his own wheels of invention, amounts to nothing less than a textual drama in its own right. Little wonder that, alongside the dream-sequences, the genealogies, the folklore and fables of slave-legacy and tricksterism, it is the sermon, that acme of black signifying, which so often recurs as a centre-piece.

Even a first-time reader of *There Is a Tree*, or of the novels which follow, *The Bloodworth Orphans* (1977), *Two Wings to Veil My Face* (1984) and, now, the compendious *Divine Days* (1992) and his essay-volume, *Relocations of the Spirit* (1994), would be hard put not to recognize a writer for whom "the word" lies at the very center of all his endeavors.[6] Indeed "the word" might be said to be an energy in itself in all of Forrest, iconic, mosaic, and, however much to his own fashion, often ritualised as in exhortation or oral-formulaic. Only thereby, it would seem, can literary fiction for Forrest besiege, then re-cast and heal, the sumptous if broken reality which he has repeatedly claimed to be the ethnic-racial birthright of Afro-America.

Forrest insists, too, accordingly, that the best black art has always been one of "re-creation and reinvention," "individualistic style," "grace," "fabulous rhythms," in all, "a kind of magic realism." Such, at least, he has made no secret, has been the aspiration behind his own fiction. Skeptics, to be sure, have thought him sometimes prone to a disfiguring floridity, rhetoric simply too insistent or unremittingly biblical. In his concern to anatomize Afro-America's dispossession and survival, indeed to imply America-at-large as a cross-ply of miscegenated "orphans," Forrest overdetermines his novels. The upshot leaves the reader insufficient breathing time or space.

On this reckoning, his resort, especially, to one or another body of myth is thought too blatant, even unleavened. This means both the Judaeo-Christian and Hellenic constellations which recur, like Noah, Job, Odysseus, Oedipus, Tiresias and Eurydice, and the pan-African legacy, like Egypt's Isis-Osiris-Set triad, or Haiti's Vodun gods, or Afro-America's Brer Rabbit, Stagolee, High John The Conqueror and John Henry.

But if, as in the present argument, that view falls hopelessly short, then how indeed to arrive at the measure of a writer whose grand theme of a black America made subject to every kind of human unorder to which flesh is heir is subjected to an "ordering," a mythicization, imaginatively pitched to match? How to take hold of Forrest's at times quite dazzling "re-creation and reinvention"? Put yet another way, how to place his African-American modernism (and intimations of postmodernism) within, or alongside, a line of black literary innovation which includes, say, William Demby, William Melvin Kelley, John Wideman, Clarence Major, James Alan MacPherson, Toni Morrison and Ishmael Reed, and whose great tutelatory spirit for them as for Forrest has been Ralph Ellison?[8]

The Bible and folklore, then, *The Odyssey*, Dante, Bunyan, and, to cite from his 1975 interview with Maria Mootry, also "Joyce, Proust, Twain, Hawthorne, Melville, Faulkner (and) Dylan Thomas" provide some of the working touchstones.[9] As to African-American tradition, besides his admired Ellison he has often enough invoked as influences slave-narrators like Frederick Douglass and Harriet Jacobs, the Jean Toomer of *Cane*, the Baldwin of the historic essay-trilogy, *Notes of a Native Son*, *Nobody Knows My Name* and *The Fire Next Time*, and any and all of the contemporaries above. But Forrest speaks, too, in his interview with Maria Mootry, of his debt to "the Afro-American ranges of eloquence," from street talk and the dozens through to "the pulpit" and "the platter."[10] In the same register, if on a different occasion, he calls up "the Black Church, the Negro spiritual, gospel music, the blues and jazz" as, in a most engaging phrase, "the railroad tracks and wings for my imagination."[11]

Some of these sources have won due notice in the reviews. But rarely have they been seen as possessing a quite essential focus on his figure of the black musician. None stands out more than Ironwood "Landlord" Rumble, the blind jazz master and visionary so vital in the life of the ongoing persona of all the Forest County novels, Nathaniel Witherspoon. As Nathaniel dwells, intimately, even lovingly, upon the remembrance of Ironwood's art (in *The Bloodworth Orphans*), he at the same time refracts Forrest's own bid to make imaginative order of disorder, "magical meaning" where hitherto so much of black life and history has been denied the rights and means to determine its own fullest meaning.

Seeking entrance to Refuge Hospital, in which the jazzman has been incarcerated as a patient, Nathaniel calls to mind "ole Ironwood's boss-embossing music" and his response of being: "constantly astonished by the furious, heavenly design and the wreckage-resurrecting brilliance of Rumble's beauty blitz, his daredevil leaps, his mocking raps, his dazzling riff escapes, his one-butt shuffle scats, his signifying jagged tremelos, his soul chant crooning inventions." Memory, here, works doubly. Forrest's prose palpably re-enacts the finely contrived runs of improvisation played off a fixed rhythm inside any jazz or blues classic, be the model an Armstrong, an Ellington, or a Bird, to give three different but symptomatic Forrest favorites. And in the allusions to "furious . . . design," "raps," "dazzling riff escapes," "scats" and "jagged tremelos," it speaks, analogously, to Forrest's own narrative tactics, those of a daring, sometimes near pyrotechnic, effort to retrieve order from unorder—an effort, in his own phrase, indeed to be described as "wreckage-resurrecting."

On his way, a while later, to the apartment of the near-senile Bella Lenore, Nathaniel's mind again turns to Refuge Hospital: "where old Ironwood "Landlord" Rumble, the blind virtuoso of nine instruments, poured out a sad musical deluge—a free-flying blitzkrieg, unleasing a grand flood of underground, storehouse memories, signs, and wonders and miracles inside the inferno." As in the earlier passage, it would be hard not to recognize Forrest's transliteration of jazz idiom, each spontaneous improvisation from within a fixed meter or musical line. But this time, one also hears, if obliquely, the vocabulary of African-American history itself—the "grand flood of underground . . . miracles" with its implicit reference-back to slave-escape, or the imagery of citied subterraneanism in, among others, Richard Wright's "The Man Who Lived Underground," Ellison's *Invisible Man* or Jones/Baraka's *Dutchman*. "Storehouse memories," in fact, hold across the board. For a South, a black Dixie, one has the centennial voice of Ernest Gaines's narrator in *The Autobiography of Miss Jane Pittman* (1971). For a North, a Harlem, where better to turn than James Baldwin's essays or the south-to-north "prayers of the saints" of *Go Tell It on the Mountain* (1953)?

These collective African-American "memories," stretching from the earliest African diaspora through slavery-times and from abolition and the northward "Great Migration" into the cities, declare themselves in abundance in Forrest's fiction; their *locus* the human workings of "Forest County." History, as he seeks to render it, indeed operates as a storm against all the canons of order. His aspires to be a style in kind, myth-laden, "magic-realist" as only a black Chicagoan raised on two versions of fervent Christianity could conceive it, an idiom with the resolve to broach the *anagogia* invoked by Dante.

Forrest's own will to virtuosity, in other words, runs close to that which has brought on Ironwood's command of his nine instruments so admired by Nathaniel and which will so prevail in the great blues concert enacted towards the close of *The Bloodworth Orphans*. The ordering of unorder, for sure, might be thought the necessary remit of any writer worth his calling. But for a black American writer taken up, as, again, Ralph Ellison's Foreword to *There Is a Tree* puts it, with "those dilemmas bred of Christian faith and racial conflict, of social violence . . . and dreams of a peaceful kingdom," the task takes on a quite stir-ring impetus.

This may well explain why Forrest frequently resorts to hybrids of sacramental and vernacular style, skeins of word-play and echo (rarely more so than in the names of characters or churches), and, in *There Is a Tree* at least, a variety of italicized and other typographical layouts. He gives the impression of wanting to make the very language of his storytelling actually absorb, and pattern, as much as it can of the "chaos," the dev-astating human orphanage, of the world bequeathed by slav-ery—whether that points to a spirituality of conversions and redemptions or to the driving fevers of sex. At the same time, it is language which also incorporates those multiple strategies by which Afro-America *has* survived, be it through "putt'n on ole massa" or modern "jive," folk wisdom or the triumphs of black music and preaching.

Given the initial diaspora out of Africa and the Middle Pas-sage, the ensuing ranks of illegally fathered and mothered off-spring, and all the ancestral enigma, curses, and sexual bans and transgressions of color, which have passed riddlingly down through both black and white American history, perhaps no liter-ary form, finally, can ever pay anything like complete imagina-tive due. Forrest's "difficulty," his own circling style of modernism, nonetheless makes the attempt. Whatever else, Leon Forrest, or his fiction, cannot be faulted for lack of ambition.

For it is precisely the daring of his novels that (to call on Robert Frost) they seek to become stays against confusion, "orderings," paradoxically, of the calamitous human unorder inherent both in slavery itself, and then in its baleful, all too bit-terly enduring, aftermath. However Joyceanly fashioned, his fic-tion thus calls for, and itself creates, "order," out of America's reeling, often seemingly unorderable, racial inheritance. What, then, *is* the measure of Forrest's linked, unfolding, novels of Forest County, his own "musical deluge"?[12]

As Stephen Daedalus serves in relation to Joyce, so Nathaniel (or Nathan) Turner Witherspoon serves in relation to For-rest, and nowhere more so than in *There Is a Tree More Ancient than Eden*. Still the most intimate, and lyric, of the novels to date, it tells at a surface level the boy's rite of passage as a mourner of his recently dead mother. But when, in imagination, Nathan thinks back on black enslavement, its brandings and lynchings and, be it in the South or the northern cities, its residual workings in the historic color-line, a related but quite other emerging role becomes evident: that of a chronicler of Afro-America itself. Further, in discovering language for both ("I was always falling in love with the sounds and shapes of people and places," he confides at the outset), he also, and in the same discovery, embarks on the self-inscription which will make *There Is a Tree* his own *Portrait of the Artist*.

This creation of Nathan as first-person singular, a mulatto boy in his fifteenth year of both Catholic and Protestant roots and a prism both for the Witherspoon dynasty and that of a still wider, enclosing Afro-America, plays through all five of the unfolding acts—"The Lives," "The Nightmare," "The Dream," "The Vision" and "Wakefulness" (Forrest has added a sixth, "Transformation," in the 1987 re-issue). As in the schema Joyce had in mind for *Dubliners*, each tells a story as local space and time and yet as a history which enters the visionary and millenial. The upshot makes the intensely particular into the typological, a blues-like pilgrimage whose trajectory suggests a collective as much as a singular experience.

As, too, Nathan follows the hearse down the emblematic DuSable and Black Bottom Streets, on past "Abe Winestein's dog," the Joe Louis Theater and the Salem Cup-Overflowing Tabernacle, and comforted by Aunty Breedlove, his new motherlessness reflects both a self-emptying and a spur to self-plenishment. For out of her death comes his own "life," a flood of imaginative energy and consciousness about ancestors (his own grandfather and missing father especially), about race, religion, and the mixed-blood and all the south-to-north history which has contributed to the very making of him. Forrest so uses him as both subject and object, a consciousness at the very turning point of time-past and time-present.

First, in "The Lives," Forrest establishes his gallery, a "Chant of Saints" as it were—from the hideously martyred Master-of-Ceremonies Browne (beaten to death for his sexuality by his own father) to Maxwell "Black-Ball" Saltport, transformed after drugs and prison into the Black Muslim minister Maxwell 2X, from Jamestown and Madge Ann Fishbond, both so black, so feisty and individual, as to bring on the scorn of Nathan's own Dupont mulatto relatives (Nathan himself, in Jamestown's words, also "a little yellow boy"), to Louis Armstrong (of "towering and revolutionary power"), and from Frederick Douglass ("The North Star") and Harriet Tubman ("Breedlove's antecedent") to Abraham Lincoln (another "assassinated" father and "Christ-myth"). Each supplies a shaping presence, a voice of memory, for Nathan.

It is, however, his own voice which most presides, the agency by which is to be remembered his "human centerless family." This includes his defeated father, Arthur Witherspoon, and now his dead mother, but beyond them, and pre-eminently, Jericho Witherspoon ("succumbed" at 117 years of age and at one time a branded and escaped slave "Wanted Dead or Alive") and Hattie Breedlove Wordlaw, Dilsey-like, whose life he emblematizes in the single honorific, "Honor." Nathaniel posesses the "jagged-edged grain of . . . interior personality" through which the story will resonate. He makes no secret of his "fierce desire to mold and sculpt," likening himself, grandly, to Lucifer, as the artificer of "a world of his own within his loneliness." Who better, to cite *Moby-Dick* as a prior "dream" text, to be thought another Ishmael, another orphan-narrator, "escaped alone to tell thee"?

Nathan's imaginings, then, could not more be centrifugal, a gathering focus. In "The Nightmare" he moves out from "the street"—the Winestein grocery, The House of the Soul with its ribs and pork advertised through a blood-red pig, The House of the Brown-Skinned Goddess Salon where nappy hair is styled, The Music Conservatory where Taylor "Warm-Gravy" James plays blues, the Robert E. Lee High School, the Memphis Raven Snow funeral home, the Dupont residence, and more—into a vision of "flying," of terror, as brought on for Nathan by his mother's death with her hands so tightly bound with the rosary.

This "journey," "snaking and hissing" and variously likened to a bluesy train and the Mississippi, bespeaks guilt, terror, the boy's self-haunting projection of life's terminus. It plays, too, into "The Dream," Nathan's "funeral in my brain," his Bosch-like envisioning of Heaven and Hell in which "black skeletons appeared like orbit-lost suns" and "river-deep wounds" haunt his imagination like stigmata. "Light years from my home," subject to a "landlocked lostness," Nathan becomes the very sounding-board of black deracination. His own loss so plays into a sense of the larger community loss inaugurated by slavery.

"The Vision," its backdrop of a kind with the fanatic, inflamed Georgia of Jean Toomer (and, far from unrelatedly, of Flannery O'Connor), enacts the part-for-part dismemberment of a black slave Christ with "a band of blood-bruised angels" as chorus. This interplay of slavery and crucifixion, Dixie and Bethlehem, imagery as savagely baroque as any in the novel, typifies Forrest at his most "word-possessing," a rare, truly audacious, effort to "see" the monstrous spiritual essence of slavery.

In "Wakefulness" Nathan returns literally to the Fleetwood limousine and Breedy, but the journey home again gives way to that taking place in his feelings and brain. As the stream-of-consciousness last pages of the novel bear out, he has become immersed in the larger significations of all the "words" in his inheritance, a self now put to transpose them, too, into *imaginative* order. That order, cyclic, fabular, is to become, reflexively, nothing other than *There Is a Tree More Ancient than Eden.*

In adding to the Second Edition the two-part "Transformation," "The Epistle of Sweetie Reed" and "Oh Jeremiah of the Dreamers," Forrest fuses Nathan's boyhood visions into two historic later moments, Sweetie Reed's 1967 letter to LBJ on her 100th birthday as a bittersweet, half-comic "preachment" on the gains and limits of Civil Rights, and a later Nathan's witness in The Crossroads Rooster Tavern to the Rev. Pompey c.j. Browne's afterhours, "impromptu" sermon on the 12th Anniversary of Martin Luther King's assassination.

The one highlights Sweetie's memory of slavery, a story for her so personal and yet so shared. The other turns upon Browne's elision of a latest black crucifixion into the original. For nothing less is indicated by the compounding play of image and allusion in the "principal homily" he delivers, two slain messiahs, at any rate, two martyrdoms, and two matching sites of Golgotha and Memphis, Tennessee.

Such, to Nathan's ordering writer-artist's eye, also expresses America's unorder, in the words both of the sermon and yet of a far older biblical and African-American reference, that which has led as he says to "the ruins of the New Jerusalem."

This name of Bloodworth is not unknown to me. . . . I've heard of this infamous clan, all of my days, including a Hattie Breedlove Wordlaw, a dear woman, whom I always called "Aunt," even though she was not my blood aunt, but helped raise me and was like a second mother to me . . . the story recalls to me something of my own grandfather's saga. . . .

So, as *The Bloodworth Orphans* moves to its close, "Nathaniel" (or "Spoons" as he has become) links his own family to that of Noah Ridgerook Grandberry, last of the fated Bloodworths—kin, however, as a result not of "blood" but through the family's adoption of his father, Pourty Ford Bloodworth, himself doomed to kill, unknowingly, his own "father," Arlington Bloodworth II, and a vicious abuser of Noah's mother, Elaine Norwood. Argumentative, accusatory, ready always to seek out each further skein in the story, Nathaniel and Noah (no doubt, intertextually, out of Quentin and Shreve in Faulkner's *Absalom, Absalom!*) try to extract some guiding order from the cross-race, dynastic "chaos" (Nathaniel's repeated word) which has thrown them together. In the background a city riot threatens, yet another turbulence in lives already turbulent.

"This name Bloodworth," "this infamous clan," "my own grandfather's saga." These and like terms strike just the right note. For *The Bloodworth Orphans* marks Forrest's move into epic, the "genealogy" ranging across a century-and-a-half of a line begotten of the slave-owning patriarch, Arlington Bloodworth, Sr. (1817-1917), and whose members, white, black and virtually every mix of the two, have become the players in a downward black-white spiral. Forrest so unravels a story begun in ante-bellum plantation Mississippi, but whose racial legacy of blight, mendacity, human error and coincidence is lived through to its conclusion in the "present" of Forest County's post-war Chicago.

Given its intensely imagized styling, word-compounds, uses of memory, time-shifts and plays of biblical and black-folkloric archetypes, the novel quite evidently demands much of its first-time reader. The effect, even so, falls little short of the spectacular, Forrest's own *Book of Genesis*. Not the least of the ambitions is to make the Bloodworths a kind of ranking "house" of America, white, black, and a profoundest *mestazije* of both.

This, too, is a "genealogy" drawn from both scriptural and oral sources; Joyce, Faulkner or Ellison on the one hand, black oral and musical culture on the other. But in the gathering litany of slave-legacy, miscegenation, death, and the resort to trickster tactics for survival and power, each, even more, becomes subject to Nathaniel's authorial purview. He thus becomes as much participant-observer as observer, identifying his own Witherspoon clan with that of the Bloodworths. Each Bloodworth story, as it slowly unfolds before him, so builds into the next, a helix of dynastic overlap and cross-reference.

Part he extracts from the "Clearinghouse Book" of the midwife, Lucia Rivers, which he finds by accident with its "1000-page document-testament" of births and deaths, a kind of African-American pentateuch or archival naming of names. More comes his way through the "research" conducted by the Rev. Jonathan Bass which fatally reveals to Amos-Otis Thigpen the incest of his sibling Bloodworths, Regal Pettibone (adopted son and baritone accompanist to "Mother" Rachel at the River Rock of Eden Baptist Church) and La Donna Scales ("possessed by a terrible premonition: that she would ultimately be abandoned—eternally"), and which will lead directly, and grotesquely, by gun and then mob-attack, to their respective deaths. All three of the triplets, and their half-brother, Noah Ridgerook Grandberry, he learns, descend (of two mothers) from Pourty Bloodworth, just one of the many dynastic knots within the Bloodworth lineage. Even so, the Regal-La Donna relationship amounts to "a beautiful and terrible love-story" in Nathaniel's gloss, its "beauty" that of the heart's passion even as its "terror" lies in incest. It is his gloss, too, which links this fatal turn to the original slaveholding, human property as blight.

Nor do his Bloodworth lines of overlap and connection end there. There is Abraham Dolphin, bastard offspring of the relationship between William Bloodworth ("Body") and his half-sister Carrie Trout Picou, and whose contradictory role as successful club-owner of "The Eden Basement Lounge" and abortionist preshadows his despairing eventual suicide ("Burdened with rivers of guilt, Dr. Dolphin thought that perhaps his sonless condition was related to the vast numbers of formless and form-filled babies he had aborted"). There is Rachel Rebecca Carpenter Flowers, mother (by Arlington Bloodworth III) of Industrious Bowman and Carl-Rae Bowman (their surname taken from the "kindly Negro minister" who adopts them), the former killed in the Santa Fe Railroad Yards and the latter dead as a derelict in Memphis. Rachel, furthermore, who has been won over as a Christian convert by the Rev. Packwood, has married, self-punishingly, the obese, opera-obsessed Bee-More (MoneyCzar) Flowers, and dies brutally of cancer, Nathaniel recognizes perfectly for yet another Bloodworth Orphan.

Non-Bloodworths, equally, stir his imagining, foremost among them Maxwell (2X) Saltport, the betrayed Muslim minister; Jamestown Fishbond, Korea veteran, linguist, and friend, whose body is finally identified only by his dog-tag, having fought against the Portuguese for black African liberation in Angola; Bella-Lenore Boltwood, 89 years of age, close to senility, and who talks to Nathaniel of long-ago imagined loves and courtships; Master-of-Ceremonies Browne, whose singing attracts

Nathaniel and whose death at his reverend father's hands has already been told in *There Is a Tree*; and, his creative mentor, Ironwood "Landlord" Rumble, musical prodigy at three and suicide at 47.

Yet others come to him in hearsay and talk. He learns of, and then finds himself utterly held by, the William Body-Carrie Trout Picou liaison with its story of New Orleans prostitution, or the Body-Lavinia Masterson affair with its Algerian-French offshoot in Ahmed Picon. Each, for him becomes part of the web, the enclosing shadow of the Bloodworth patrimony. But above even these, there looms the great *eminence grise* of the novel, W.W.W. Ford, trickster supreme, so-called "serial hermaphrodite," and a kind of superlative if truly cynical African-American warlock in whom Ellison's Rinehart has become a near metaphysical trickster-god.[13] In his shifting guises as priest, drug-dealer, pimp, adopter of orphans, rhetorician, and Tiresian man-woman, Ford summons into being the very spirit of corrupt, extravagant survival.

For necessary as tricksterism, small and large, may have been to black survival, Nathaniel comes to recognize that such only in and of itself will not suffice. One aspect of his own need to seek the *ur*-story behind the Bloodworth spiral is the quest for some better moral principle to things, an altogether wiser, saner, American humanity. Even so, the dance continues, chaotically as ever, most evidently in his flight from the riot with Noah and with the black infant they encounter by chance, "its trembling little hands reaching upwards towards the two sad-faced sobbing men."

The "House of Refuge," the decaying, white penitentiary-asylum, in which the two find themselves held with Ironwood and from which they make their savvy forays for food and drink, acts as Forrest's image of this same "Bloodworth" America. It serves as the image of a detention-center in which, historically, blacks have been held, named and renamed, sexually and otherwise abused, in all made over into "selves" anything but of their own choosing. Noah, symptomatically, speaks of "chaos," "madness and constant troubled confusions." Nathaniel agrees, but, counteringly, invokes the music of Ironwood, the jazz and blues of the "wounded . . . blind bard warrior" as offering, momentarily or not, "black," spiritual harmonizations amid all the unorder. He also alludes to the "beautiful but tragic people" who have suffered the blight of the Bloodworths, the epilogue of a narrator-hero who even as he glimpses order finds himself obliged yet once again to take flight against "more chaos."

All of their respective commentary, in fact, applies. The Bloodworth genealogy implies an anything but linear history, rather a "chaos" writ large, and continuingly, through all American time and space. Nathaniel understands, even as he is appalled by, the evangelical wiles and tricksterism of a W.W.W. Ford, with his false church, staggering rip-offs and sales-pitches, and white girl accomplice in Gay-Rail (a variation of "Grail"). He also knows that the charade will continue as borne out in Ford's canny, duplicitous "adoption" ads which Nathaniel and Noah come across towards the end in the "Personals" column of the newspaper.

But the better resistance for him lies in the "re-creation and reinvention" of "what is left over." That he recognizes in the heroic musicianship of an Ironwood, the church singing of a Rachel Flowers or Regal Pettibone, the politics of a Jamestown Fishbond, or the sermons, well-meant or less so, of the likes of a Rev. Shelton Packwood or Rev. Jonathan Bass (preaching, too, to be compared with that of the Rev. Pompey c.j. Browne in *There Is a Tree* and *Two Wings to Veil My Face*). In their different ways, these each simultaneously resist *and* transform the chaos to hand. They offer, precisely, truly creative "recreations" of the nation's black history-within-a-history.

Above all, Forrest embodies this same process in Nathaniel himself. It falls to him, much as he professes himself unequal to the task, to make cohere, to "narratize," the Bloodworth story as a whole. Once again, though on a larger scale than *There Is a Tree*, the complication of an America self-enravelled in racial confusion actually gets taken into the very form of the novel—in the first instance in Nathaniel's effort against odds to discover and state the true, underlying "plot" of the Bloodworths, and behind that, in the orchestration of Forrest's own overall telling. No less, certainly, whether as "word," or as the "word" builds into a whole, as "story," can be said to have been in play throughout *The Bloodworth Orphans*.

Two Wings to Veil My Face opens with Nathaniel as amanuensis, the memorialist of a bed-ridden, weakening 91-year-old Great-Momma Sweetie Reed. In a room which, like that of Hawthorne's Customs House in *The Scarlet Letter*, might itself serve as an echo-chamber of past associations and remembrances, it falls to her student-aged kin, the rejected suitor of

Candy Cummings and self-confessed drop-out in his early 20s, to record upon a series of aptly named "legal" yellow pads the life of his own grandmother, or at least the paternal grandmother from whom he believes himself descended and to whom his devotion is total.

That life, begun in slavery, hard put to survive the Reconstruction years, and brought north to Chicago in the wake of her marriage to Nathaniel's grandfather, Jericho Witherspoon, he finds himself writing into being even as he listens, Great-Momma Reed's "reader" and "writer" at quite one and the same time, an inspired overlap which takes Forrest's "complication" into still newer reaches.

Sweetie's history in every way thus profoundly entwines with his own, another black genealogy, that of the Reeds and Witherspoons, again transposed into order out of the past's unorder by a Nathaniel Witherspoon quite literally called upon to set down "the word." In this, too, the novel offers one kind of "writer" as the secret sharer of another, Nathaniel in the role of Sweetie Reed's personal archivist foreshadowing Nathaniel as the eventual presiding story-teller. Reflexively, too, this "dual" Nathaniel does the even further duty of standing in for, but kept at a right distance from, Forrest himself, the Faulknerian "Sole Owner & Proprietor" of yet more Forest County.

Among latterday fictive accounts of the journey "up from slavery," Sweetie Reed's readily takes its place alongside that of the tough, enduring Jane Pittman in Ernest Gaines's novel or of the ghost-haunted Sethe in Toni Morrison's *Beloved*. Despite a specific departure-point, the ante-bellum Rollins Reed plantation of Mississippi, and a specific slave parentage, Reed's man-servant I.V. Reed and his wife Angelina, Sweetie's personal history also signals the enclosing larger black community history: witness at 7, in 1874, to the patroller's brutal rape and killing of her mother; the long-rankling marriage by arrangement at 15, in 1882, to a former escaped slave, the then 55-year-old Jericho Witherspoon; her traumatic parting of the ways from him in 1905; and her reluctant, half-delirious, attendance in 1944 at the memorial service for the 115-year-old "patriarch" in the Memphis Raven-Snow Funeral Home before an assembly of mourners which includes her diabetic, risingly hysterical "son," Arthur Witherspoon, Nathaniel's father.

These, and each further contributing tier of her life, she calls to mind before her rapt, impatient, grandson in a Chicago of

1958, a cycle of pasts relived as though a simultaneous and ongoing present. Told in slivers of recollection, voices-within-voices, pauses for enquiry and recapitulation, one time frame held in abeyance in order to complete the events of another, Great-Momma Sweetie Reed's story indeed could not more profoundly play into Nathaniel's own, her past deeded to his present as both deepest kinship and blood.

But this past is also a gift of language. The "word" she bequeaths literally becomes inscribed in his, a process once again involving its own "magic meaning," its own "reinvention." Whether, thereby, as interlocutor to Sweetie or eventual narrator, Nathaniel finds himself compelled to an ordering fusion of her tale inside his telling, or as he calls it, her "backwater time" and "storytelling powers and recollections" inside his "unfolding."

"Write it all down" the almost deaf Sweetie enjoins Nathaniel, as though fearful of losing her "other voices in other rooms." So, in obligation, he does, first the 19th century plantation-owner voices of her "blackbirding" white grandfather Rollins Reed and his deranged wife, Mistress Sylvia, caught up in her seven-mirrored mansion and her jewels as the war turns against the South. Across, and interplied with them, run the words of Sweetie's parents, I.V. and Angelina, of the conjure-woman Aunt Foisty ("a-huffing and a-chanting some of them broken-down African words"), of the slave-driver Reece Shank Haywood ("a big, muscle-flexing nigger" who near-strangles Rolley), of the mulatto Clea who helps Sweetie bury I.V., of the preacher whose name calls up a familiar other dynasty, the Rev. Stigwood Bloodworth, and of Wayland Woods, author of the near-illiterate but compelling letter long stored by Sweetie and written to Master Rollins demanding the return of his stolen "slave" daughter.

These, in their turn, echo down into the present century. First, Nathaniel hears Sweetie's invocations of Jericho Witherspoon, both his "talk" as he rises to prominence as a lawyer and politician in Chicago and his "lifelong journal" which reads "as if the very feel of history was ingrained in the texture of the pages." Nathaniel also discovers adjoining "texts" like the Reed-Witherspoon "freedom" papers and family ledgers (crucially that which contains a reference to 1905, and to Arthur Witherspoon, his name written with quotes around it). These, taken with Sweetie's "world of remembrances" as given in her "winging call-and-response manner," yield a world once "theirs" or "hers" but now also "his." To good purpose the novel says early on of Nathaniel:

"But now the young man . . . wondered if all the storytelling, the loving, the harsh disciplining, the praying and the direction had been a preparation for the day, *this* day, when he would have to take over her memories." But the most overwhelming of all these "memories" for Nathaniel, and which for him most "orders" all the contributing voices, lies inscribed upon Jericho Wither-spoon's back: the branded initials put there by his own white father to prevent escape. Seen through Nathaniel's child eyes at the burial, they become "memory" itself, or as the boy comes to think them, "memory wounds on fire." This "J.W. script," the "blis-ter-like italicized brand JW . . . vivid as a visitation," seizes him utterly. Sweetie's "Boswell," as he will at one point call himself, he discerns a whole composite Afro-America in this "birthmark" and in each further gathering sign—the "forged chain," the "rabbit's-foot bracelet" and the ever-present "shadow" of slavery.

For underlying the "multilayered collectivity of words" lies the stark, inerasable, eclipse of slavery. It is as if Forrest insists that from this slave-made African and American "scarlet letter," loaded up with black (and white) signification, there issues another enciphered, and truly momentous, challenge to interpre-tation. How, finally, ever to understand the slave nightmare, the historical "branding," from which the grandfather's "JW" derives?

Nathaniel Witherspoon may well solve the "riddle" of his immediate paternity, the mystery of the date "1905" in the Reed-Witherspoon ledger, and indeed Sweetie's own "blood" kinship with him. He may well, at Sweetie's prompting, begin to solve the mixed bloodlines of the Reeds, Witherspoons and the still further outlying "family" to which he is heir. He may even, as the novel's last paragraphs indicate, begin to recognize the complex, larger responsibilities of his own "signifying."

But "unorder," Nathaniel's own and that of the prevailing condition about him, and for which the "JW" acts as Forrest's hieroglyphic, continues to call out from him an ordering transfor-mation. Such, too, it may be said, holds for the boy who rides to his mother's funeral in *There Is a Tree*, or for the companion of Noah Grandberry who plunges into the riot of the closing chap-ter in *The Bloodworth Orphans*, or for the Nathaniel literally with the yellow-pad transcripts of Great-Momma Sweetie Reed's remembered history in his hands in *Two Wings to Veil My Face*.

As with its predecessors, and in whatever due complication, Nathaniel's "rendering" of genealogical unorder in *Two Wings* becomes a rare triumph of imaginative ordering; or, rather, the unorder becomes a triumph of Leon Forrest's ordering. For the achievement of all the fiction which makes up Forest County, with *Divine Days* there to further extend its reach, lies not only in the "thematics" of Afro-America or even the enclosing, larger America which across time and space brought it into being. It lies in Forrest's own making-over of "the word," the lavish imaginative workings of his "re-creation and reinvention."

Notes

1. Leon Forrest: *Re-Creation: A Liturgical Music-Drama*, Commissioned by Richard Hunt. Music by T.J. Anderson, words by Leon Forrest, 1978.

2. Leon Forrest: "In the light of the likeness—transformed," in *Contemporary Authors Autobiography*, ed. Mark Zadronzny (Detroit, Michigan: Gale Research, 1988), Vol. 7, 21-35.

3. Leon Forrest: "Faulkner/Reforestation," Lecture at annual "Yoknapatawpha Country" seminar, The University of Mississippi, August 1988. Reprinted in *Faulkner and Popular Culture: Faulkner and Yoknapatawpha*, ed. Doreen Fowler and Ann J. Abodie (Jackson, Mississippi and London: University Press of Mississippi, 1990), 207-13.

4. Leon Forrest: *There Is a Tree More Ancient than Eden* (New York: Random House, 1973), re-issued, Oak Park, Illinois: Another Chicago Press, 1987; *The Bloodworth Orphans* (New York: Random House, 1977); *Two Wings to Veil My Face* (New York: Random House, 1984); and *Divine Days* (Oak Park, Illinois: Another Chicago Press, 1992).

5. Dust-jacket comment, *There Is a Tree* (op. cit.).

6. Leon Forrest: *The Bloodworth Orphans* (New York: Random House, 1977). Re-issued, Another Chicago Press, 1988.

7. Leon Forrest: *Two Wings to Veil My Face* (New York: Random House, 1983). Re-issued, Another Chicago Press, 1988.

8. In response to the question "Do you consider yourself part of a "school" of black writing?" Forrest replied in 1978, "Well, McPherson, Morrison, Murray, Ellison, Wideman and I are all club-members you might say." See Maria Mootry: "If He Changed My Name": An Inverview with Leon Forrest, in *Chant of Saints: A Gathering of Afro-American Literature, Art and Scholarship*, ed. Michael S. Harper and Robert B. Stepto (Urbana, Illinois: University of Illinois Press, 1979), 146-57.

9. Mootry (op. cit.), 146.

10. Mootry (op. cit.), 150.

11. "In the light of the likeness—transformed" (op. cit.), 30.

12. The following criticism has played a part in the present consideration: ed. A. Robert Lee, *Black Fiction: New Studies in the Afro-American Novel* (London: Vision Press, 1980); A Robert Lee: *Black American Fiction Since Richard Wright* (British Association of American Studies Pamphlet, No.11, 1983); Keith E. Byerman: *Fingering The Jagged Grain: Tradition and Form in Recent American Fiction* (Athens, Georgia: University of Georgia Press, 1985); Bernard W. Bell: *The Afro-American Novel and Its Tradition* (Amherst, Massachusetts: The University of Massachusetts Press, 1987); and John F. Callahan: *In The Afro-American Grain: The Pursuit of Voice in Twentieth-Century Black Fiction* (Urbana, Illinois: University of Illinois Press, 1988).

13. For an excellent account of the trickster in Forrest, see H. Nigel Thomas: *From Folklore To Fiction: A Study of Folk Heroes and Rituals in the Black American Novel* (Westport, Connecticut: Greenwood Press, 1988), 103-08 and 158-73.

Leon Forrest and the African-American Folk Sermon

Bruce A. Rosenberg

Chicago-based novelist Leon Forrest is an experimental traditionalist. Like many of his contemporaries, his fiction verges on the metanarrative. His inventiveness lies in his language usage, a usage which foregrounds the word, which reminds the reader that he/she is reading a fiction, is reading words placed on a page by another human—though one with extraordinary talents. With Leon, that foregrounding involves echoing the style and tone of contemporary life. His novels are rife with the diction of jazz, street jive, and the language of "men" in ways undreamed of by Wordsworth, of inner-city black verbal codes. He almost always avoids the special narrative vocabulary, syntax, and verbal structures that signal that a formal fiction is in progress. Forrest recreates the world of his imagination in all its nuances of sound and sense, of tone and texture. Nothing in his experience is inappropriate; he wants us to experience life with the realization that he is recreating what is actually impossible to duplicate; so he makes us understand that his narrative is a constructed approximation. But what an approximation it is!

Forrest's strategy incorporates rap music, country-and-western lyrical echoes, street talk, and a constant reference to that most central element of the black experience, the folk sermon. In this respect he is a traditionalist. He is particularly sensitive to the sermons and the oratorical style of black preachers: the Reverends C.L. Franklin, Morris Harrison Tynes, Wilbur N. Daniel, Martin Luther King, Jr., Jesse Jackson. This recognition of the centrality of the African American sermon places him in the company of nearly every important black American writer of the past century: Zora Neale Hurston, James Baldwin (a preacher's son), Ralph Ellison, Langston Hughes, even Toni Morrison. The black sermon transforms the African American experience from a verbal code of song, narrative (usually exemplum), and symbol into an expressive system of communal values. Leon Forrest invokes this

115

expressively potent instrument as well as contemporary vernacular; actually, he invokes the sermon more frequently than any other form, and gives it greater weight. In the biographical sketch of him in *Contemporary Authors*, Forrest observed that "the black church, the Negro spiritual, gospel music, sermons, the blues, and jazz" were both "the railroad tracks and the wings for my imagination and the migrating train . . . of my sagas" ("In the Light" 30).

When sermons have been composed in past literature, they have usually been tangential to the main thrust of the narrative. This is the situation of Rev. Mapple's sermon in *Moby Dick*, and in *Portrait of the Artist as a Young Man*. Hurston, Baldwin, Ellison, and Forrest regard this genre more highly because the sermon is more expressively important in their culture. Probably the first serious "black" sermon in literature was that of Faulkner, the one preached by Rev. Shegog in *The Sound and the Fury*. It is a careful imitation of black spontaneously-composed preaching by an artist who listened carefully. Rev. Shegog's sermon is given prominence in the narrative's totality; but despite its relative centrality, it is an imitation by a white man. The sacred performance is set apart, stylistically, from the rest of Faulkner's prose, and the reader is conscious of reading a literary description of an oral performance that is quite distinct from, emotionally and stylistically—culturally—the voice and the presence of the character: it is the imaginative Rev. Shegog preaching. Faulkner, despite his efforts, is apart from, observing, his character.

The black folk sermon, as whites know it most commonly, is chanted rhythmically. Ellison's Rev. Barbee is stylistically typical:

> In the beginning . . .
> At the very start, they cried.
> . . .there was blackness . . .
> Preach it . . . (individual congregational response)
> . . . and the sun . . .
> The sun, Lawd . . .
> was bloody red . . .
> Red . . .
> Now black is . . . the preacher shouted.
> Bloody . . .

Faulkner's imitation sermon is a close copy of an actual performance. It is almost too good to be real. Rev. Jerry Lockett (whom I recorded on March 17, 1968) in Charlottesville, VA, was (is) real, and though the content differs, the similarity of style is unmistakable:

> This same Jesus
> On the third day in the mornin'
> We seen this same Jesus
> Oh Lord have mercy
> I tell you my Father
> Which art in heaven
> Gonna leave him now . . .
> Goin' down to Golgotha this Morning
> I seen Him there
> Oh yes He is. (Rosenberg *Bones* 294)

This preaching style, so widely practiced, and so widely imitated, is in a differently formatted form, a part of Forrest's arsenal. Like his models, Forrest begins in an Appollonian mode, and then incrementally escalates towards the Dionysian. The preacher becomes infected with the frenzy which his own performance has generated. Forrest-as-novelist does not indulge in this freedom of abandon; like all fiction writers, he must remain contemplative throughout, recollecting that great emotion in tranquillity. Only his diction and his characters' emotional state—thus described—may pass from pulpit oratory to chant, from the reasoned to the emotional, from the dispassionately logical to the engaged passionate. The preacher and many of his church will experience an altered (psychological? spiritual?) state. Thus the preacher reinvents life.

Forrest invokes the form and emotional drive of the African-American oral folk sermon within his narrative as a replication of the sermons of his preacher characters. He recreates the folk preaching ambiance, called by the ministers themselves the "spiritual sermon." In creating this experience Forrest borrows rhetorical apostrophes from the Rev. C.L. Franklin. *The Bloodworth Orphans* author has written to me that he was unashamedly influenced by the late Rev. Franklin—as have been so many preachers, whose style and individual exclamations he reproduces in his own fiction—ascribing it to a preacher of his imagination. Forrest thinks of it as being "quite close to the grain of oral tradition" (personal correspondence, 4/19/1991). Punctuating his *Bloodworth Orphans'* sermons in the style and with the language of

Rev. Franklin with his Detroit congregation, Forrest's preacher exclaims to his flock, "I don't believe you see what I'm talking about this night, Church" (30), or "I don't believe you see what I'm talking about" (32)—or its approximation, "I don't believe you see what I'm getting at" (33), and "Church, you ain't praying with me" (35), or "help me, Church, pray with me, if you please" (36).

The real Rev. Franklin's rhythmic delivery and mellifluous singing predominated (he was, after all, Aretha's father); his sonorous voice, the arresting rhythms of his oratory, gave immediacy and structure to his sermons—they captivated the congregation with their music. They gave a compelling aesthetic quality to his message. His audiences were involved passionately as well as rationally—such sermons are, after all, expressive of the black experience in America—captured by the magnetic compulsion of his voice. Daughter Aretha learned much from him; this family never wanted for musical expression.

In actual performance Rev. Franklin used these exclamations to enliven his audience and to stimulate their spirits—their spiritual enthusiasms—when they were waning, when they seemed in danger of losing contact with the Lord. These rhetorical strategies were meant to arouse them to further participation in the holy service (see Titon, 1989). Intensity was all. The African American folk preacher—the "spiritual preacher" as the men (and women) describe themselves, must quickly involve the congregation; he/she must gain the audience's assent, at the moment of performance, to be successful. "Success" means conveying to the congregation, instilling in them, the Spirit of the Lord. The performative situation is not that of a leader apart and distinct from those who are led; rather, the preacher attempts to achieve an intimate, simultaneous, symbiotic commitment with his flock to the Spirit. Is the singer distinct from his song? The preacher's ostensible purpose is to gain the congregation's willing commitment. He/she is God's spokesperson; it is through the Preacher's spiritual/rhetorical/histrionic guidance that the congregation achieves its union with the Divine. Analytically (psychologically) the congregation is not supposed to commit to the preacher, though he is at the moment of performance, God's agent. As many preachers have confided to me during out-of-church interviews (see *The Art of the American Folk Preacher*), while they are preaching they are lending their lips and their tongues and their throats (their organs of speech) to God. They are speaking God's words, and they aspire to do His will. He is speaking through them; they are at such moments merely His instruments.

Rev. Franklin often punctuated his sermons with these rhetorical appeals to his congregation to "pray with me," or he would chide them, conversely, for not "praying with me"; when his flock was listless he chastised them for not seeing (understanding) what he was talking about, or "getting at." For the preacher—Franklin and Forrest's imitation of him—these memorized and automatic exclamations are "pauses on the highway" (as Rev. Elihu Brown once described it to me); they give the minister/priest a moment's rest during which his/her thoughts can be marshaled to contemplate the lines to come. For the congregation these interruptions (such as "I don't think there's anybody praying with me") are not put-downs, but signals to them to get with it more closely, to become more involved in the service; they are incitements to the spiritually apathetic to embrace, immediately, deeper involvements.

Written and composed (presumably at leisure) literarily, Forrest's conscious recreation of these sacred performances gives his sermons a convincing virtual authenticity, appearing as though they were the verbatim records of actual oral, spontaneous performances. Forrest's Rev. Packwood adopts the rhythms and some of the actual rhetoric (and consequently much of the emotional muscle) of the Rev. C.L. Franklin. Forrest is the intermediary, transmuting—recreating—Franklin into Packwood. Forrest's prose sounds as though he were speaking to, not writing for, us, as if we were hearing the account of a story he was relating. Forrest's voice recreates the narrative for the reader.

"One of the literary constants of African American literature," he says in the *Contemporary Authors* biography, "is the reinvention of life" (31). His fiction expresses more than a simulation of the folk preacher in performance, more than the glorification of the oratorical skills of a gifted speaker. That has been done—by Faulkner, by Ellison, by Baldwin. Forrest recalls, in this capsule biography, that while still at the University of Chicago he perceived the black sermon "as a seminal source for his own fledgling art" (23).

At times Forrest's literary voice compels with the magnetism of the spoken word—at those moments when we are not consciously aware that he is literarily creating a fiction. The spoken word has its own power. When someone speaks to us, face-to-face, we are obliged to listen. The resonance of the voice is immediate and compelling, as the written word is not. It holistically surrounds us with the information that a human encounter is occurring. We rarely switch off another person's speech—not easily, in any event, not without offending the person whose extension the speech is—as we can turn off a radio or a TV. A phonograph record (or CD) can be interrupted by pressing a button or switch. But another human speaking cannot be so effortlessly and dispassionately silenced; and his/her address will insist upon a reply, eventually an interaction. Electric/electronic sound waves by themselves have no such force. We may not even want to brusquely terminate an unsolicited telemarketing message.

Canons of etiquette discourage us from hanging up on others; it is not polite. Hanging up (ringing off) before a conversation has been formally terminated is itself a meaningful statement. Another person, encountered live, merits a response on our part; the mechanically reproduced sound—such as voice mail—does not. Some people talk interactively at a movie screen, even a cathode ray tube, it is true, but that response is voluntary, does not rely on any protocol, and is, by the receiver, unrecorded. If a tree falls in a desolate forest, has a sound been made? In human interaction another human is present, speaking, demanding attention, demanding to be treated with the decorum that our mores require, and his/her words compel attention—and a response, however phatic. When we respond, we become more active participants in the communication transaction. No electronic voice simulation, however faithfully it reproduces the human voice, has this power.

Forrest's prose nearly has it. We can close his book, of course (as we can with any other) and terminate our transaction with him, but when his characters are "speaking," when he is "speaking," we are not so inclined. Rudeness, obviously, is not the point; we cannot so simply close off his character's conversation with us. We don't want to. When we read Forrest we will not likely terminate the story he is relating in its midst. We are being spoken to, we are interested to hear what is being said and what is going to be said (and happen). With most good fiction we suspend disbelief and persuade ourselves that we are experiencing history. Fiction has that quality. Forrest is able to win us over so that we willingly give him our assent, and in this manner he infuses his narrative with credibility. We follow.

The orally composed and spontaneously performed sermon is not limited to the repertoire of non-literates. In his demonstration of this fact Forrest is in the line of an extensive tradition. Chanted sermons by learned preachers illustrate ("demonstrate," to avoid the visual metaphor) that the same man can speak (preach?) in either style, that the use of either mode is dependent upon the "message," the situation, what metanarrative the preacher wants to communicate; it depends upon the preacher's will, the receptiveness of the audience, it is within the preacher's command. Notable examples: the Late Rev. Martin Luther King, Jr.'s Washington Monument exhortation, and his indoor auditorium speech on passive resistance; Rev. Jesse Jackson at the 1988 Democratic National Convention; and the Charlottesville, VA., preacher Jerry Lockett (who wrote out his sermon in prose, and several minutes into his performance began to chant—his natural mode of pulpit oratory. No matter how the performance is rendered, when transcribed on a page the prose is unmistakably prose; metrical traits are almost as obvious to the reader as to the listener (rhythmic performances do not reveal themselves in formatting)—this is a function of literacy, of the printed page.

The folk sermon—this form is folkloric as well as scriptural as preached in many black fundamentalist churches—has a structurally complex fluidity which helps make it emotionally moving. Forrest has heard many of them (many Catholic sermons also) and has reproduced them convincingly. "The structure of a black Baptist sermon is orchestrated, with highly associative links to group memory, the Bible, Afro-American folklore, Negro spirituals, secular blues phrases, politics, and personal testimonial" (Forrest, "In Chicago's Black Churches" 131). Thus Forrest taps into several high intensity veins: social, cultural, intellectual, religious, racial, ethnic, etc. The African American folk sermon conveys a holistic, unifying message, gaining strength from the union of its several components: "and then one night the Word of God came beautiful, flaming, chariot-swinging sweet and low unto her ears" (*Orphans* 34).

Forrest uses sermons in several ways: in the recorded utterances of preachers and of congregation's prayers and testimonies. Sermon oratory is also a part of the everyday speech of certain characters. He says as much in his condensed autobiography: "As a writer who comes out of a culture steeped in the eloquence of the oral tradition, I've come to see the Negro preacher as the bard of our race; and throughout my novels, that rich lodestone of eloquence has provided me with an important springboard" ("In the Light" 23).

These sermons have the power to effectively generate and invoke deeply felt emotions; they are guided by gradually intensifying rhythms—of the preacher's words, of the music, of the implicit rhythm in the congregation's reception of the sermon message. "It is the force of the music—the obsessive and repetitive rhythm—tied to lyrics suggesting a reordering out of chaos that leads from state of self-possession to a momentary state of blessed assurance, when you can 'take hold of your life throughout Jesus Christ" ("In the Light" 135). "The question at every turn in the service is how to keep the fire and zeal up-tempo, how to let neither the body nor soul cool off. The service is always bound up in a keening relationship between great solemnity and the furious rhythms of body and soul" ("In the Light" 130).

Rev. Packwood's sermon (*Orphans* 29-40) is, in its early moments, not consistently rhythmical, though the last portions of it are broken into tight metrical units (as printed on the page) divided by virgules (as was done in *The Art of the American Folk Preacher*). Rachel Flowers' response is similarly metrically regular:

I'm running on, I'm running on / I done left this world behind / I done crossed the separating line / I done left this world behind. (*Orphans* 39)

The exclamations of the congregation, an important part of the performance's dynamics, are not neglected. Rev. Packwood's sermon and Rachel Flowers' chanted prayer (*Orphans* 70-74) are punctuated with traditional exclamatory words and phrases: "Lord," "Lord what a garment—ain't He good?.," "Oh Holy God," "my God," "Witness," "church" (an apostrophe to the congregation), "stand by me"—Forrest listened carefully and closely when he went to church. Repetition is also in the form of metonymically related series: "her name, her honor, her honor, her stride, her station, her soul, her crown, her patched-up riddled wings, her gospel shoes filled with holes, her ashy long white robe" (*Orphans* 29-30); or semantically related nouns in sequence: "you moving like a tot through a half-mad train of thieves, gamblers, adulterers, liars, abominators, for your victory" (*Orphans* 37); or in apposition: "BE His floor mat, His watchwoman, His footstool, His Light-Bearer, His Messenger, His anchor to the world, His tambourine, His drum, His garment-servant, His body-servant, in the eternal clemency of the warning news about Salvation and Sacrifice" (*Orphans* 73). Images from the Bible are rendered metrically:

For my Father is a rainmaker. Didn't he arise in a Windstorm? And He's gonna return. Return in a storm. Gonna be royal and radiant with hair like lamb's wool: eyes like balls of fire. Gonna have a rainbow like a scarf about his shoulders. Gonna set upon a *Rock* and these here storms ain't gonna be able to move you . . . (*Orphans* 38; see comparable passage in Rev. Lacy's sermon, *Art* 124)

Forrest imitates Rev. C.L Franklin (below), whose recordings, at least, he admits to having heard. His Rev. Packwood, in an anaphoric passage, addresses his God with whom he is on intimate terms: "Why-er heard you promise Hosea you would ransom them from the grave; heard you, Father, promise Moses you would stand by your people in the rages of their bondage; heard you reveal the meaning of the ladder to Jacob of a soul-collecting Nation; heard you stir the intelligence and faith to Ezekiel's tongue to know that dry bones can live" (*Orphans* 39).

The preacher, the man of words, is a potent presence in black society. Hurston thought so, Ellison thought so, as did Baldwin. Forrest called the Rev. Wilbur N. Daniel "an awesome anchor" to his people. Words—particularly the preacher's words—have the power to move and to persuade people, to induce the Holy Ghost to work on the earth, to walk on the earth. The Rev. Morris Harrison Tynes once told Leon,

I think that each man's historical perspective determines his response to this divine encounter. There is something in his life that exalts him to great inspiration. Take Handel writing the *Messiah* in less than thirty days. He must have ascended to heaven! . . . . I think the same thing happens in preaching at its zenith; and, yes, I do think it is the moment of a miracle. ("In the Light" 131)

Forrest invests his characters—especially his preachers—with this power; he energizes his novels by making them more dynamic, more vivid. *The preached folk sermon is a potent moving force on others than African Americans.* Rev. King at the Washington monument and/or Rev. Jackson at the Democratic convention speak to this point. Both men (as have thousands of other preachers) gradually engaged their audiences/congregations, heightening their involvement on an emotional as well as rational level, gradually turning up the intensity (identifiable by altered decibel level, change in vocal pitch, etc.) until the audience was "theirs," rocking to their rhythm, all the while being increasingly won over by their message. The last, dying words of M.C. Browne—by Forrest's intention a "sermonette"—begin with, "I done found jesus *ohohoh*, at *last* . . . at last, amen this morning i come to *know* Him, mother-dear, and grandma dear-dear and little nathan, I found our jesus, youall, this morning on the altar of my heart. . . ." (*Tree* 11). In "The Dream" chapter, Nathaniel cries out to Aunt Breedlove, "Oh but auntie breedy how can I be a prophet in a strange land, where we've been stripped to the bone?" (*Tree* 87). In that part of *There Is a Tree* ("The Vision" 115-48) the visionary sees the crucifixion in terms of gospel song/vernacular/alliterative: "and I could see the man upon the slab of the tree quaking, his mouth trembling and quivering (although he did not utter a mumbling word) as this soldier (bent now over the man's right hand with the same kind of precision, his liquid eyes sparkling like those of a jeweler inspecting the fairest pearl of his horde of preciously purloined gems, now hammering the nail into the unshaken right hand" (*Tree* 19-20).

In what Forrest called "a literary sermon as eulogy" (personal correspondence, April 19, 1991), Rev. Pompey c.j. Brown remembers and laments Rev. Martin Luther King, Jr., at The Crossroads Rooster Tavern in a verbally pyrotechnic declamation, drawing from street slang, history, the Bible and literature, described by the author as "something of a transformation of Adam Clayton Powell, Martin Luther King, Leon Sullivan, and Richard Prior" (*Tree* 205):

And Mister Jefferson, that juggler sucks slave's breast (the declaration up his snuff-box); enlightened when in the course of Pandora's box: a test case for Nigger's apartheid, shake that chain and drop your ass. To perish out of this world backwards: Lords of the land, tongues coiling, counselled by Lucifer's fruit. Fear is shot through the eye-teeth of men's rage as an inherited whirlwind. Oh the bugger-baron snorts on his rip van winkling Twilight manufactured FABULOUS behind the sanctuary chariot cadillac like a circus clown with a monkey on his back. (*Tree* 208)

Faulkner and Melville, amongst others, incorporated preacher's sermons as distinct and discrete narrative entities within their fictions, apart from the voice of the narrator. Forrest's characters preach, his narrative persona preaches; oratorical strength is not only that of the characters, but of the narrator himself. Faulkner's Rev. Shegog was a man of (moving) words; Leon Forrest's voice—not merely those of his characters—is also; consequently his story, his narrative, gains strength and emotive compulsion. Not that the entire economy of Forrest's novels is sermons: only where the dramatic situation requires it. Preachers are important in black culture; their influence is highlighted and thus magnified in the novels of Forrest (as with others). The voice of Leon's narrator is often that of a verbally talented folk preacher, a man with the gift of words (a black Thomas Pynchon or even a James Joyce). But Forrest is no mere player of word games; though he can pun with anyone writing today and has mastered the allusions technique, these trivial pursuits are not really what his novels are, at bottom, about.

The comparison with Joyce is obvious, and has already been made; it is implicit (sometimes even explicit) in some of Forrest's prose:

and now the young man Nathaniel felt in his pocket for the prayer cloth, that the blind singing-choir directress and prophetess Sister Rachel had given him; still carrying it, starched now, in his pocket and thinking suddenly how a simple prayer cloth could be turned into a snot rag (ah, mighty Joyce); or to drive the Moor mad; or to cover the hand in the basket Aunty Foisty; or dipped in Lamb's blood, or used to wipe the face of the bedraggled, falling and rising Redeemer's face of glory to the world, forever and ever; or to wipe the tears and then the blood from His feet. (*Two Wings* 32)

His popular/folk/colloquial/learned/loutish/high-serious/casual register style evokes comparison with contemporaries Pynchon and Barth, Hawkes and Coover, and Kathy Acker (deleting much of the profanity), with Vonnegut, and in Europe, Grass. Yet, despite Forrest's humor, despite his careful attention to the word as it is spoken, he has not been found to be as accessible as they, perhaps because of his virtuosity which greatly complicates and thickens his prose. He has taken folklore and popular modes and genres seriously. And he has become one of those writers who has enlarged our concept of what is "mainstream." He is, of course, a "black writer." But he is more than that, as Graham Greene was more than a "Catholic writer." Partly by his own talents, Forrest has widened the currents so that they can now include his writing. As he said at one point, "I wanted to be a singer of the language—in the tradition of her majestic self

(Mahalia Jackson) and the Negro preacher" (*In the Light* 34). Singer he is, because he has been an astute listener. Like Faulkner, he has a great ear for people's speech. Like August Wilson, like Gloria Naylor, Forrest listened to the words of his contemporaries until he got it right, listened hard enough until it flowed from his pen with authenticity. He is an extraordinary reader of his own writing, which he performs with a preacher's histrionic skill: intonation, gesture, expression, and eye contact are all active. His own sensibility is extraordinarily complex, loaded with allusions to literature, to the Bible, and to contemporary culture; often expressed in a religious mode, an intricate exploitation of his language's semantic and phonological complexity in his Chicago-educated elegant, formal style, and a whimsical playfulness blended in. Forrest's awareness and recording of contemporary life is encyclopedic. Like Mahalia's, Leon's song is intricate in its surface texture; and like hers too, his performances are ultimately rewarding.

Works Consulted

Forrest, Leon. *The Bloodworth Orphans*. Chicago: Another Chicago Press, 1987.

——. "In Chicago's Black Churches, There Is a Place for the Commingling of the Spiritual and the Physical, for Eloquent Oratory, for Humor and Humility." *Chicago Magazine* (1985): 129-35, 148.

——. "In the Light of the Likness—Transformed." *Contemporary Authors-Autobiography Series* (1987) 7: 21-35.

——. *There Is a Tree More Ancient than Eden*. Chicago: Another Chicago Press, 1988.

——. *Two Wings to Veil My Face*. Chicago: Another Chicago Press, 1988.

——. Personal correspondence with the author, 1991.

Hubbard, Dolan. *The Sermon and the African American Literary Imagination*. Columbia, MO: University of Missouri Press, 1994.

Lawless, Elaine J. *God's Peculiar People: Women's Voices and Folk Tradition in a Pentecostal Church*. Lexington, KY: University Press of Kentucky, 1988.

Rosenberg, Bruce A. *The Art of the American Folk Preacher*. New York: Oxford University Press, 1970.

——. *Can These Bones Live?* Champaign: University of Illinois Press, 1987.

Titon, Jeff Todd. *Give Me This Mountain*. Champaign: University of Illinois Press, 1989.

Leon Forrest and the AACM:
The Jazz Impulse and the Legacy
of the Chicago Renaissance

Craig Werner

Leon Forrest's hometown of Chicago is in many ways the most paradoxical of American cities. By many measures the most segregated major American city, Chicago nonetheless nurtured some of the most challenging, multiculturally inclusive black artists of the 1960s, 1970s and 1980s. Influenced by the interracial political and cultural exchanges of what Robert Bone has labelled the "Chicago Renaissance" (1935-1950), Chicago-based writers and musicians have felt little sense of contradiction between the vernacular and "high art" traditions of European- and African-American culture. Like Gwendolyn Brooks—whose life and work represent crucial links between the Chicago Renaissance and the generation of black Chicago artists who began working in the 1960s and 1970s—Forrest and contemporaries such as Clarence Major draw much of their power from the juxtaposition of European-American modernist and African-American musical traditions. Like founder and spiritual leader Muhal Richard Abrams, musicians affiliated with the Association for the Advancement of Creative Musicians (Anthony Braxton, Roscoe Mitchell, Amina Claudine Myers) combine European modernist approaches to composition with their multi-faceted African-American musical heritage to transcend limiting categorizations based on race or genre.

Theoretically engaging and emotionally compelling, their works offer crucial insights into the relationship between culture and liberation, understood in psychological, spiritual, or institutional terms. Brooks' dedication to community-based arts programs, particularly following her "conversion" to a black nationalist perspective during the 1960s, made her one of the South Side's best-loved elders. Similarly, the AACM drew inspiration from, and shaped its agenda in response to, the community activism centered on the Coordinating Council of Community

Organizations (Radano). Although Forrest was never a member of the Nation of Islam, he worked on the staff of the Nation's newspaper *Muhummad Speaks* from 1969 through 1973. Sharing the fundamental African-American sense of art as a "functional" aspect of everyday life, post-Renaissance Chicago artists consistently resist the academic tendency to divorce cultural production from political or spiritual awareness.

Outside of relatively small communities of intellectuals and artists, however, neither the writers nor the musicians have attained widespread recognition. Despite its marvelous live performances and fascinating revoicings of "accessible" classics such as Bob Marley's "No Woman No Cry" and Jimi Hendrix's "Purple Haze," the Art Ensemble of Chicago (whose members include AACM members Mitchell, Lester Bowie, Malachi Favors, and Joseph Jarman) receives much less attention (and sells many fewer albums) than Ornette Coleman or the World Saxophone Quartet, who share many AACM concerns. Although he shares both thematic and stylistic concerns with successful black novelists such as John Wideman or his former editor Toni Morrison, Forrest's work remains relatively unknown. In the context of American cultural economics, this lack of popular recognition perpetuates itself. Many of the best AACM recordings—including the vast majority of those produced prior to Abrams' move to New York in 1976—remain unavailable. Despite the support of Morrison and Saul Bellow, who wrote a glowing statement for the cover of *There Is a Tree More Ancient Than Eden*, Forrest's original publisher, Random House, allowed all three of his novels to go out of print prior to their reissue by Another Chicago Press in the late 1980s. Only an historically significant "rescue" by Norton, which has no realistic hope of short-term financial gain, kept Forrest's Joycean (in both size and, in numerous passages, brilliance) *Divine Days* from going out of print when original publisher *Another Chicago Press* encountered paralyzing difficulties.

In the remainder of this chapter, I will argue that the art and experience of Leon Forrest and the AACM musicians highlights the difficulties faced by artists responding to W.E.B. DuBois's call for African-Americans to merge the fragments of their "double consciousness" into "a better and truer self" incorporating African and European traditions. After surveying the main currents of the Chicago Renaissance as they provided the setting in which Forrest and the AACM began to work, I will delineate some of the connections between the explicitly multicultural "jazz impulse" (which parallels important currents of European-American modernism) and the specifically black (and implicitly Afrocentric) "gospel impulse" in African-American culture. Finally, I shall provide a brief demonstration of how the jazz/modernism/ gospel nexus comes together in Forrest's powerful narrative voice which—like Abrams' "Levels and Degrees of Light," Mitchell's "Noonah," or Myers' "African Blues"—clearly deserves a stronger response than it has yet received.

The Chicago Renaissance

One of the most important revisions of 20th Century Afro-American cultural history focuses on the significance of Chicago between the mid-1930s and the mid-1950s. Prior to the publication of Robert Bone's germinal essay "Richard Wright and the Chicago Renaissance" (1986), constructions of Afro-American literary history typically identified the Harlem Renaissance of the 1920s and the Black Arts Movement of the 1960s as primary points of reference. Whether phrased in terms of the "School of Wright" or of "protest literature," criticism of the intervening decades focused almost obsessively on Richard Wright. In turn, criticism of Afro-American literature of the 1950s frequently posited a simple reaction against Wright. In such frameworks, Wright becomes a writer of sociology, a naturalist with leftist inflections; Baldwin and Ellison appear as champions of a non-racial "universalism;" black women writers are marginalized (Hurston) or distorted (Ann Petry as naturalist, the early Brooks as universalist). Perhaps the most important implication of Bones' revision concerns the long-term influence of this simplifying critical discourse. The "sociological" approach to Afro-American literature, like its deracinated "universalist" double, established an interpretive framework—reflected in both academic criticism and the mass media—which continues to undervalue the work of artists who cannot be reduced to familiar categories.

Providing an alternative to such narrow constructions, Bone's identification of a Chicago Renaissance contributes to the construction of a cultural history in which the synthetic sensibilities and reception difficulties of Forrest and the AACM are at least comprehensible. Bone asserts that between 1935 and 1950 Chicago had all of the elements of the Harlem Renaissance with the exception of an effective publicist such as Alain Locke. Listing the Chicago-based writers (Wright, Brooks, Margaret Walker, Frank Marshall Davis, William Attaway, Theodore Ward, Arna Bontemps, Marita Bonner) who created a body of work as rich as that emanating from Harlem in the 1920s, Bone details the importance of migration, patronage, academic institutions, and publishing outlets. In exploring the significance of the Chicago Renaissance, it is useful, if somewhat artificial, to focus first on developments within the African-American community and then on the interaction of this community with white Chicago.

The Chicago Renaissance originated in the massive migration of Afro-Americans from the rural South to Chicago that began during World War I and continued throughout the 1930s and 1940s. Inspired in part by the crusading journalism of Robert Abbot in the *Chicago Defender* (which also published the work of black writers such as Langston Hughes who did not participate directly in the Renaissance), the migration was significant in economic, political, and cultural terms. Black workers moving to the South Side brought with them cultural traditions that shaped some of the most important subsequent developments in American vernacular culture. Transplanted from Mississippi and Arkansas by Muddy Waters, Howlin' Wolf and others, the Delta blues strongly influenced black secular music and rock and roll, which was in its inception interracial, but rapidly came to be marketed primarily by and for whites. Similarly, the sacred traditions of the southern black church rapidly developed into the polished gospel music of Clara Ward, Roberta Martin, and Mahalia Jackson, which in turn contributed to the vocal styles fundamental to 1950s rhythm and blues and 1960s soul music. Alongside these musical developments arose literary organizations exemplified by the South Side Writers group which the Mississippi-born Wright helped organize in 1936 (Fabre 128). As interracial cultural contact declined during the 1950s and 1960s, these specifically African-American cultural resources provided a supportive context for the development of second generation Chicago artists such as Forrest, whose family came to Chicago from Mississippi (the paternal side) and New Orleans (the maternal side).

Several significant forums for interracial cultural and political interaction complemented these developments within the black community. As Berndt Ostendorf and William Howland Kenney note in their investigations of Chicago jazz of the 1920s, pre-Renaissance Chicago had provided a setting in which white musicians could absorb at least the superficial aspects of Afro-American musical aesthetics. Of greater lasting importance, however, was the patronage provided black artists and intellectuals by the Julius Rosenwald Fund. Noting the shift away from the individual patronage characteristic of the Harlem Renaissance, Bone details the importance of the Fund as a source of economic support for black writers and scholars, especially after Edwin Embree assumed its directorship in 1928. Relying on the advice of an interracial board of trustees including Charles S. Johnson, Embree used the Fund's fellowships program to support Wright, Bontemps, Attaway, Walker, Horace Cayton, St. Clair Drake, E. Franklin Frazier, and Katherine Dunham. The Fund's support of non-Chicago writers such as Ralph Ellison, Zora Neale Hurston, Langston Hughes, Robert Hayden, and, later, James Baldwin underscores the significance of the Chicago Renaissance in the general development of Afro-American culture of the 1930s and 1940s.

Most of the writers supported by the Rosenwald Fund were directly involved in organizations that encouraged interracial contact. Wright viewed the John Reed Clubs, sponsored by the Communist Party of the United States, as a vital source of support for black writers attempting to overcome their cultural isolation. The Illinois branch of the Federal Writers' Project provided both financial support and a forum for contact between black and white writers. While a great deal of the interracial cultural activity took place on the political left, even relatively conservative cultural organizations supported interracial communication during the Renaissance. Based in Chicago, Harriet Monroe's influential *Poetry* magazine published the work of black poets, most notably Langston Hughes, alongside that of T.S. Eliot and Carl Sandburg. One of *Poetry*'s patrons and a prominent member of Chicago's social scene, Inez Cunningham Stark conducted a poetry workshop for aspiring South Side poets, which culminated in a competition won by the young Gwendolyn Brooks.

The most significant institutional interaction between black and white intellectuals during the Renaissance, however, centered on the University of Chicago Sociology Department. Developed under the guidance of Robert Park, the "Chicago School" of sociology viewed cities as settings for the development of new, more advanced forms of culture. Delineating a race relations cycle progressing from contact and conflict to accommodation and assimilation, Park envisioned America as a "melting pot" which would eventually generate a "raceless" society (Matthews; Ross; Bone 455-56). Part of Park's attempt to realize this vision involved direct support for black intellectuals, most importantly Charles Johnson, St. Clair Drake and Horace Cayton (Ross 439). As Chair of the Sociology Department at Fisk University, Johnson extended the influence of his former teacher into the Afro-American academic world. Equally significant, however, was the research carried out by Cayton and Drake as graduate students at Chicago. Investigating the South Side from a Parkian perspective, Cayton and Drake published their findings as *Black Metropolis*, which includes an important preface by Wright.

Reflecting the interaction of sociological and cultural perspectives, *Black Metropolis* and Wright's novel *Native Son* played crucial roles in encouraging sociological approaches to Afro-American culture. Focused on the broad social significance rather than the individual nuances of Afro-American experience, the sociological approach encouraged interpretations of black culture as "protests" intended to engage and rectify social "problems." Despite the Parkian commitment to increased interracial contact, the widespread acceptance of such approaches (which were rarely applied to white artists) ironically contributed to the growing intellectual and social segregation that helped bring the Chicago Renaissance to an end in the 1950s. Despite the use of quantitative evidence generated by Chicago school researchers in support of liberal policy agendas beginning in the 1940s, the application of sociological methods to cultural criticism allowed white readers and critics to underestimate both the individuality and the complexity of Afro-American cultural expression. Neither Forrest's fiction nor the AACM's music responds well to interpretations emphasizing "problem" or "protest."

The legacy of the Chicago Renaissance, then, is mixed. On the one hand, it encouraged an explosion of creative and intellectual activity by Afro-Americans that has few parallels. For young blacks such as Brooks, Forrest, Abrams, and Mitchell, the Renaissance provided a stimulating environment which allowed them to respond with equal intensity to the black community as a distinct reality and to the surrounding white community. At the same time, however, the Chicago Renaissance established the sociological premises that would discourage the development of an interracial audience willing to engage the full complexity of the resulting work.

After the Renaissance

By the middle of the 1950s, the Chicago Renaissance had clearly come to an end. Whatever the critical misapprehensions of their work, Ellison and Baldwin signalled new concerns in Afro-American literature. Afro-American music was entering a period of rapid transition. Influenced strongly by the electric blues emanating from Chicago's Chess studios, rock and roll emerged as a focal point of American popular music. Transforming American musical traditions without regard to racial or generic distinctions, Ray Charles, Sam Cooke, and others created the blues/gospel hybrid that would eventually be labelled "soul." Most directly relevant to the development of the AACM, early 1950s jazz underscores the cultural dilemma facing post-Renaissance Chicago artists. Long perceived as an example of white exploitation of black musical forms, big band jazz attracted few young black musicians during the 1940s, although several, including Charlie Parker, served apprenticeships with big bands. Developed as a radical alternative to white jazz, be-bop was increasingly perceived as an African-American "art" music requiring great technical virtuosity and theoretical knowledge, but no longer deeply embedded in the life of the black community. In response, jazz musicians such as Miles Davis, Ornette Coleman and John Coltrane established the contours of the multi-faceted "free jazz" movement, which includes most AACM work.

Politically, several significant national developments deeply influenced Chicago's young black artists. The Southern Civil Rights Movement created a new sense of optimism regarding the possibility of racial progress. Whether viewed in terms of *desegregation*—the removal of barriers excluding blacks from full participation in public life—or of *integration*—the realization of a Parkian vision of assimilation—the Movement encouraged community-based political activity. Ronald Radano has demonstrated convincingly that the AACM drew its inspiration and institutional structure directly from community organizations founded in Chicago during the late 1950s and early 1960s: the Coordinating Council of Community Organizations, the Chicago Freedom Movement, Operation Breadbasket, People United to Save Humanity, and the local offices of the Student Non-Violent Coordinating Committee and the Southern Christian Leadership Conference.

Despite the general optimism, however, several cross-currents anticipated the de facto cultural segregation that undercut the development of an audience prepared to respond to the new generation of musicians and writers. Under the guidance of Elijah Muhammad, the Nation of Islam articulated its black separatist agenda from a South Side base. Particularly after the emergence of New York-based Malcolm X as a charismatic national leader, the Nation exerted a strong influence not just on its members but on the growing number of young northern blacks for whom the promise of the Civil Rights Movement increasingly appeared to be a lie. Although Forrest never seriously considered joining the Nation (which did not require the staff of *Muhammad Speaks* to be members), he was obviously aware of its mythology and agenda. Equally important was a shift in tone within the Civil Rights Movement during the mid-1960s. Black liberation theologian James Cone describes Malcolm's perspective during the 1950s and early 1960s as a vision of America as "nightmare" in contrast to Martin Luther King, Jr.'s vision of the American "dream." Extending his analysis to the mid-1960s, Cone emphasizes the increasing similarity between Malcolm and Martin's visions. After his journey to Mecca, Malcolm returned with a much broader vision of the possibility of human community. Confronting Vietnam and the spectre of domestic violence, King increasingly emphasized the nightmarish reality rather than the visionary possibilities.

Nowhere was the connection between these visions clearer than in Chicago. King's experience in Chicago—specifically his unsuccessful campaign to desegregate housing—marks a major turning point in the Civil Rights Movement. The shift of attention from the south to the urban north—which brought the movement to the communities of the northern liberals who had supported the earlier stages—brought the reality of northern segregation (both physical and cultural/intellectual) into sharp focus. When the residents of the white working class suburb of Cicero met King's march with taunts and violence, it became clear to many young blacks—especially in Chicago—that the dream was far from realization. The increasing prominence of black militant organizations in the community both reflected and contributed to the growing separation between black and white communities, especially outside the middle classes.

So, although their visions of human and artistic possibility had been shaped in a world where interracial communication seemed a possibility if not yet a reality, black Chicago artists who began work during the 1960s found themselves in an almost entirely African-American context. Although the members of the AACM were highly aware of the works of European and European-American composers such as Stravinsky, Bartok, Dvorak,

Stockhausen and Cage, they had almost no direct contact with white composers in the Chicago area. As Radano and John Litweiler observe, their activities were based almost exclusively on the South Side. The most important academic institution for the younger generation was not the University of Chicago but Wilson Junior College where Forrest and musicians such as Mitchell, Jarman, Favors, Henry Threadgill and Anthony Braxton studied between 1955 and the founding of the AACM in 1965.

Despite these tensions, neither the AACM musicians nor Forrest express any sense of contradiction regarding their use of European- and African-American cultural traditions. In large part, this reflects their understanding of the relationship between the modernist and traditionalist currents of European-American aesthetics. Avant-garde composers such as Schoenberg, Webern, and Cage interest Abrams, Jarman and Mitchell in large part because they reject 19th century compositional practices. Much modernist composition reflects a widespread dissatisfaction with the hierarchical implications of harmonic structure, which (at least in the new constructions of musical history) required that all musical elements be subordinated to a tonal center, conceived in terms of "tonic" and "dominant" elements. The serial composers' rebellion against traditional harmony paralleled Miles Davis's movement away from scale-based bebop improvisation to the melodic emphasis of modal jazz. Similarly, explorations of "folk" music as the base of "high art" composition conducted by Stravinsky, Bartok, and Ives could be seen as analogous to the African-American composers' revoicings of blues and gospel. Significantly, each of these composers evinced a serious interest in African-American music, both as vernacular "material" and as a source of insight into the relationship between compositional structure and improvisational freedom. Rather than representing an antagonistic alien influence, then, European-American modernism provided many AACM musicians with access to alternative perspectives on shared aesthetic problems.

Similarly, as his incisive comments on William Faulkner, Ralph Ellison and James Joyce indicate, Forrest draws freely on European, European-American, and African-American cultural resources. Honoring the memory of Lucille Montgomery, a black teacher who encouraged his development by insisting that Forrest read Langston Hughes and DuBois alongside the European-American classics, Forrest asserts a "complex, varied, Black/white" perspective as the foundation necessary to respond to the "ancestral imperative" and to "forge the intellectual tools to free our people" ("Light" 29). This sense of a shared cultural project was of immense importance to post-Renaissance Chicago writers and musicians. Performing under various names including Abrams' germinal Experimental Band and the Art Ensemble of Chicago, AACM members have made major contributions to the American compositional and improvisational traditions. Among the musicians who have contributed to what Art Ensemble of Chicago member Joseph Jarman (echoing New England Conservatory faculty member and influential jazz critic Gunther Schuller) called "third stream music with a heavy jazz bias" (Litweiler 173) are Roscoe Mitchell, Lester Bowie, Malachi Favors (all of the Art Ensemble), Henry Threadgill, Amina Claudine Myers, and Anthony Braxton. Movements associated either directly or indirectly with the AACM developed in St. Louis (the Black Arts Group), Detroit (Strata), New York (Collective Black Artists), and, more recently, New Haven, where composer-pianist Anthony Davis occupies a position in some ways analogous to Abrams' in Chicago (Giddins, *Riding* 193). Significantly, each of these cities also supported the work of broadly conscious writers including Eugene Redmond and Henry Dumas (St. Louis) and Robert Hayden (Detroit).

In addition to their interest in European-American modernism, most of the musicians affiliated with these groups resist attempts to draw distinctions between forms of black music. Articulating the sensibility behind the Art Ensemble's use of the phrase "Great Black Music Ancient to Future," Mitchell observes that when he was growing up in Chicago "music wasn't divided into categories the way it is now, with one age group listening to this and the next age group listening to that, and so on. I liked what my parents liked—Nat Cole and other pop singers, as well as Charlie Parker and Lester Young. You were exposed to all kinds of music on the radio in those days, and when you became a musician, it was just a matter of deciding what kind of music you wanted to play" (Davis 180). Recalling his early career as a writer, Forrest emphasizes a similar access to multiple sources of inspiration: "I listened almost religiously to all kinds of Black music, while I was writing and incorporating every sound I could set my ear to into my fiction (including of course the spiritual incantation of 'A Love Supreme' by 'Trane" ("Light" 31).

Critical descriptions of both AACM music and Forrest's fiction tend to foreground the modernist, rather than the vernacular, dimensions of the work. Perhaps the best musicological analysis of the AACM (and free jazz generally) is that of Ekkehard Jost, who describes "a movement in all directions, toward all aspects of world music. This could become possible only when the formal, tonal and rhythmic canons of traditional jazz were overthrown, and it has led not only to incorporating musical elements of the Third World, but equally to adapting the materials and creative ideas of the European avant garde" (175). Attributing the distinctiveness of the AACM specifically to "geographical location" (163), Jost identifies a number of specific concerns involving the fundamental elements and relationships of the art form, which are analogous to those explored in Forrest's fiction. Jost specifies the AACM concern with the relationship between individual (solo) voice and its collective setting (168); a tendency to emphasize the texture or tone color of local events (168); and the belief that each of these events assumes meaning "not as an isolated occurrence sufficient unto itself" but from "a dialectical relationship to the music around it" (171).

Similarly, John Litweiler frames his discussion of the AACM in terms that recall Forrest's investigation of the fundamental mystery of the artist's voice. For Litweiler, the most intriguing dimension of AACM music is "the tension of sounds in the free space of silence" (176). Identifying the underlying aesthetic assumptions of the Art Ensemble of Chicago as an outgrowth of "modern American selectivism," Gary Giddins sees the core of the group's structural practice in "contrasting tableaux or accumulated details assembled around a single motif; in each case, a large-scale work is constructed of fragments" (*Rhythm-a-ning* 196). Jost sounds a similar theme when he describes several of the most important AACM works as "multi-thematic suites, or pieces in which one or more melodic models serve as the contents of a collective or 'group memory' improvisation" (171). No literary critic has provided a better description of the structures of *There Is a Tree More Ancient Than Eden*, *The Bloodworth Orphans*, or *Two Wings to Veil My Face*.

Jazz, Afrocentric Spirituality and the Gospel Impulse

What distinguishes both Forrest's fiction and the AACM's music most clearly from European-American modernism is their underlying spiritual vision. Where many AACM members articulate their spirituality in Afrocentric and/or mystical terms, however, Forrest draws his vocabulary directly from the gospel church. The difference is more apparent than real. Many AACM members trace their musical roots directly to the gospel church: Braxton sang in a gospel chorus; Leroy Jenkins learned to play violin in church; Malachi Favors is the son of a preacher. Similarly, Forrest's perspective on the gospel church, particularly as it involves the black preacher, clearly emphasizes an encompassing spiritual vision that moves far beyond the confines of most European-American popular religion.

For the AACM, as Radano suggests, modernism (understood as a reaction against hierarchical aesthetics), rhythm-centered experimental technique (understood as a reaction against the tyranny of harmony), and a serious interest in spirituality express the same basic concern. Mitchell makes the connection between technique and spiritual vision explicit when he says "Cats that play bop are more concerned with things like chords and changes rather than spirits . . . in free music you are dependent on the spirits because you don't want to fool with those chords" (Radano). Similarly, Abrams explains the AACM emphasis on process in spiritual terms: "Change is synonymous with any conception of the deity" (Litweiler 198). In an often-cited comment on the impact of the AACM on his own life, Art Ensemble member Joseph Jarman describes what amounts to a conversion: "Until I had the first meeting with Richard Abrams, I was like all the rest of the hip ghetto niggers; I was cool, I took dope, I smoked pot, etc. I did not *care* for the life that I had been given. In having the chance to work in the Experimental Band with Richard and the other musicians there, I found the first something with meaning/reason for doing. That band and the people there was the *most* important thing that ever happened to me" (Jost 164). AACM member Alvin Fielder echoes Jarman when he comments simply that the AACM "was like a church—it *was* my church" (Radano).

Generally recognized as the spiritual center of the AACM, Abrams sums up the communal function of the organization: "if the AACM is anything, it's a very excellent idea. It's not so much what is or isn't done, it's the idea and what it could mean to different groups, depending on their energy. The idea: to pool our energies to a common cause" (Litweiler 196). It is hardly surprising that some of the most powerful AACM music—Abrams' *Levels and Degrees of Light* and Myers' gospel-inflected "African Blues" from *Amina Claudine Myers Salutes Bessie Smith*—expresses spiritual experience. In contrast to this spiritual emphasis, European-American modernism, as Timothy Reiss observes, has been predicated largely on a repudiation of theological, essentialist, or transcendental ideas. This characteristic divergence of European- and African-American world views may well account for the difficulties both the AACM and Forrest have experienced in obtaining a serious hearing from the white avant-garde in spite of large areas of shared concern.

These issues coalesce around the changing significance of the "jazz impulse" in African-American aesthetics. Ralph Ellison, the most insightful and influential theorist of the relationship between African-American music and literature, defines the jazz impulse as a way of defining/creating the self in relationship to community and tradition. Applicable to any form of cultural expression, jazz provides a way for new ideas, new *vision*, to enter the tradition. As many artists and critics have observed, almost all successful jazz is grounded in what Ellison calls the "blues impulse." Before one can hope to create a meaningful new vision of individual or communal identity, the artist must acknowledge the full complexity of his/her experience. Although the blues impulse is based on intensely individual feelings, these feelings, for most blues artists, can be traced in part to the brutal racist context experienced in some form by almost all blacks. Substituting the less "philosophical" term "affirmation" for what Ellison calls the "transcendence" derived from the blues confrontation, Albert Murray emphasizes that, especially when his/her call elicits a response from a community that confirms a shared experience, the blues artist becomes "an agent of affirmation and continuity in the face of adversity" (38). Both the individual expression and the affirmative, and self-affirming, response of the community are crucial to the blues dynamic. Seen in relation to the blues impulse, the jazz impulse provides a way of exploring implications, of realizing the relational possibilities of the self, and of expanding consciousness (of self and community) through a process of continual improvisation.

What has been less clearly recognized in discussions of African-American aesthetics is that both the blues and jazz impulses are grounded in the "gospel impulse" (see chapter nine). The foundations of African-American cultural expression lie in the call and response forms of the sacred tradition; in the 20th century, the gospel church provides the institutional setting for the communal affirmation of individual experience. As Amiri Baraka notes in *Blues People*, both the call and response structure of the secular work songs and the AAB form of the classic blues can be traced to sacred forms which encode West African understandings of self, community, and spiritual energy. If the blues impulse can be described as a three-stage secular process—1) brutal experience; 2) lyrical expression; 3) affirmation—, then the gospel impulse can be described in parallel terms derived from the sacred vocabularies of the African-American church: 1) the burden; 2) bearing witness; 3) the vision of (universal) salvation. Bearing witness to his/her experience of the "burden," the gospel artist—possessed by a "Spirit" transcending human categorization— communicates a vision affirming the possibility of salvation for any person willing, as Forrest phrases it, to "change their name." Whether phrased as "burden" or "brutal experience," as "near-tragic, near-comic lyricism" or as "bearing witness," as existential "affirmation" or spiritual "vision," the blues/gospel process provides a foundation for the jazz artist's exploration of new possibilities for self and community.

The relationship of blues and gospel is not simply formal, however. As Greil Marcus notes in his discussion of Robert Johnson, most black blues artists bear witness to their brutal experience in a vocabulary derived from the black religious community, from which they feel excluded. Contrasting sharply with European-American modernist expressions of a world in which religion has been reduced to comforting delusion or oppressive institution, Johnson's songs express a theologically resonant *damnation*, not simply alienation. Many of his most powerful blues have explicitly religious titles: "Hellhound on My Trail;" "Me and the Devil Blues;" "Stones in My Passway;" "If I Had Possession Over Judgement Day."

Both the relational sense of self and the refusal to separate secular and sacred experience reflect what V.Y. Mudimbe refers to as West African *gnosis*. In traditional West African thought, as Robert Farris Thompson demonstrates, human beings stand continually at the crossroads, negotiating the exchange of energies between spiritual and material spheres, between ancestors and descendants. Organizing this *gnosis* around the "orisha"—spirits associated with overlapping and interrelated energies that can be summoned in response to ever-changing circumstances—this Afrocentric sensibility contrasts sharply with Judeo-Christian traditions emphasizing the battle between God and Devil (seen as profoundly *different*, essentially binary, forms of energy) for possession of the *individual* human soul. Described in detail by Mudimbe, Thompson, bell hooks and Patricia Hill Collins (who emphasizes the connections between Afrocentric and feminist epistomologies), this type of Afrocentrism also differs from the Nile Valley (priestly and at least implicitly patriarchal) Afrocentrism of Molefi Kete Asante, which frequently inverts existing binary structures to assert a relatively static vision of "African" civilization. Recognizing the Afrocentric dimensions of the gospel impulse is important for several reasons. Although some black religious singers—notably Bessie Jones and Bernice Johnson Reagon—are conscious of the African roots of the gospel tradition, many church members continue to view Africa through the European-American dichotomy of "pagan" and "Christian," thus creating the seeming paradox of a profoundly Afrocentric institution that openly repudiates Afrocentric phrasing.

Recognizing the underlying connection helps clarify the relationship of Forrest's aesthetics to those of the AACM. In part because of their emphasis on rhythm, AACM members frequently express the spiritual core of their vision in (West) Afrocentric terms. Perhaps because of the Nation of Islam's association of Africa with a binary mythology of black Gods and white devils, Forrest emphasizes the specifically American practices of the gospel church. Like the early James Baldwin, who critiques binary myth-making (whether Christian or Muslim) in *The Fire Next Time*, Forrest articulates a profoundly Afrocentric cultural sensibility in a voice that insists on the "jazz" complexity of African-American experience. Commenting on the significance of Africa in the contemporary black church in Chicago, Forrest emphasizes the actual distance between American blacks and (one of) their ancestral homeland(s): "Yet how much the congregation knows of Africa is worthy of contemplation. More than likely, the thinking would go something like this: There are oppressed poverty-stricken people over there; they are black and we are black; they have been oppressed and so have we. Wherever the black man is in the world, he is catching hell. We came from Africa; therefore, we must help them. And it is in this sense that the black man here identifies with the heartaches over there" ("Souls" 133). However useful as a source of political or cultural motivation, this type of identification remains far too abstract to provide a base for the type of *transforming* voice Forrest seeks to create in his fiction.

Leon Forrest and Transformation
One of the most frequently used terms in Forrest's non-fiction, *transformation* is crucial to the jazz, blues and gospel dimensions

of his vision. In an important autobiographical essay titled "In the Light of the Likeness—Transformed," Forrest associates the "improvisational genius" of jazz with the "magical realism" of Latin American writers such as Gabriel Garcia Marquez and Isabel Allende. Commenting on his own multi-cultural heritage, Forrest emphasizes black music as a "source of personal or group survival" that enables African-Americans "to place a stamp of elegance and elan upon the reinvented mode." "*Reinvention*," for Forrest, "has been the basic hallmark of the transformation" of black fiction exemplified by Ellison and Toni Morrison (31-32).

Although his own work is obviously oriented toward modernism and the jazz impulse, Forrest acknowledges its base in blues and gospel. He agrees with Ellison and Murray that a direct apprehension (rather than theoretically mediated interpretation) of experience defines the blues impulse: "For the blues singer, personal, existential experience always outweighs handed-down wisdom" (33). Echoing Murray's observation that the purpose of the blues is to allow the singer to survive long enough to get the blues again, Forrest observes: "the worst thing that can happen to you, if you are a blues believer, is the loss of the blues. It is an eternal education. You lose the blues at the risk of losing your hold on existence" (33). Responding to Big Bill Broonzy's music as a process in which "each new carving (is) connected to the theme of the larger blues he's creating," Forrest emphasizes the jazz implications of the blues impulse, describing Broonzy's "shape-singing of his character's personae; transformed into something heightened and different" (22).

One of the most significant aspects of Forrest's perspective concerns his awareness of gospel, which has received little attention as a source of literary inspiration. Commenting on the "transformations" of Thomas A. Dorsey, widely recognized as the "father of gospel music," Forrest celebrates the former blues pianist's ability to "transform the refinements of the spiritual into a music that fitted the more angular needs of an awakening people, hungry-hearted for a dialogue in song which captured both their secular and their spiritual sense of life as agony and wonder" (26). In his discussion of call and response in Chicago's black churches, Forrest again emphasizes the irrelevance of binary constructions: "There is a place here for the commingling of the sexual and the spiritual" ("Souls" 130). Forrest describes the sermon form in terms paralleling AACM musical structures: "The structure of a black Baptist sermon is orchestrated, with highly associative links to group memory, the Bible, Afro-American folk-lore, Negro spirituals, secular blues phrases, politics, and personal testimonial" (131). Highlighting the jazz implications of such complex structures, Forrest celebrates the sermon as "the very source for reinvention and transformation of the self" ("Light" 23).

Describing his vocation as a writer, Forrest images the African-American novelist as a kind of jazz preacher: "he can go on to transform life into new life, even as he is transformed by his creation, as a preacher is transformed, as he seeks a collective transcendence" ("Light" 24). Forrest connects this vision directly with his own career when he describes how a visitation from the spirit of Mahalia Jackson helped him find his voice during a period when few of his "intellectual friends . . . cared for the life of the spirit" (33-34). Mahalia's presence helped focus Forrest's desire "to be a singer of the language—in the tradition of her majestic self and the Negro Preacher" (34). Turning his attention to his fiction, Forrest identifies the "Black church, the Negro spiritual, gospel music, sermons, the blues and jazz" as "both the railroad tracks and the wings for my imagination" (30).

However compelling this conceptual framework, Forrest has encountered many of the difficulties faced by the AACM in calling forth a broad-based response to his vision. On one level, this is an economic problem. Gary Giddins has detailed the problems faced by AACM members trying to make a living from their music (*Riding* 190-91). Lester Bowie recalls the early days of the AACM: "I and other players . . . enjoyed playing in free form, free fashion, but we would always play it for ourselves and never thought seriously about performing it in front of an audience. We knew that it was impossible to get hired at a club doing that" (Litweiler 186). Such real and pressing economic concerns reflect a related problem in contemporary African-American culture. As Forrest observes, the power of call and response aesthetics derives precisely from their realization in a communal context. The affirmations (and dissents) of the congregation—which in turn call forth responses from the preacher—express the dialectical relationship between improvisational vision and individual experience. Forrest describes the ideal: "A sermon is open-ended, allowing a preacher to expand new ideas or to cut out sections if they aren't working. The role of the congregation during a sermon is similar to that of a good audience at a jazz set—driving, responding, adding to the ever-rising level of emotion and intelligence. Ultimately, the preacher and the congregation reach one purifying moment and a furious catharsis is fulfilled" ("Souls" 131).

If this dynamic interaction is available to preachers and jazz musicians, it remains relatively abstract for novelists, who rarely engage in a direct call and response with an audience. Observing the reluctance of some middle-class blacks to accept the "marriage of blues and spiritual" ("Light" 26), Forrest questions whether call and response aesthetics are still capable of organizing the "cosmic consciousness of the race:" "If the preacher stood as the linkage and the oracle from Mississippi to St. Louis to Chicago, let us say, how much does the substance of his sermon now renew the sons and daughters of the great migrations—now unto the fifth and sixth generations" ("Light" 32). This troubled awareness of the changes experienced by the black community in northern cities—the fragmented urban world familiar to European-American modernism—lies behind Forrest's understanding of contemporary alienation (whether phrased in blues or existential terms) in relation to a spiritually resonant heritage that at times seems to be slipping away. However difficult it may be to elicit an affirmative response (and the absence of the response, as numerous jazz musicians and modernist writers have learned at great cost, may result in madness, addiction, or death), only a complex, realistic call offers any hope for meaningful transformation.

I would like to conclude by suggesting several approaches to Forrest's work in relation to the jazz impulse. Gayl Jones provides a valuable overview of the ways African-American novelists translate jazz into written forms:

In literature jazz can affect the subject matter—the conceptual and symbolic functions of a text, translate directly into the jazz hero, or have stylistic implications. The writer's attempt to imply or reproduce musical rhythms can take the form of jazz-like flexibility and fluidity in prose rhythms (words, lines, paragraphs, the whole text), such as nonchronological syncopated order, pacing, or tempo. A sense of jazz—the jam session—can also emerge from an interplay of voices improvising on the basic themes or motifs of the text, in key words and phrases. Often seemingly nonlogical and associational, the jazz text is generally more complex and sophisticated than the blues text in its harmonies, rhythms, and surface structures.

In addition to using many of these devices, Forrest draws on jazz by treating the literary text as a form subject to revision in the manner of a jazz composition, and mythology as a reflection of cultural psychology rather than a repository of universally applicable values. It should be emphasized that these approaches are analytical conventions; the real jazz richness of Forrest's voice is best experienced through direct response to the many passages in his novels that resemble the contextualized solos of AACM music. Among the most powerful of these are Nathaniel's meditation on the nightmare of history in chapter four of *There Is a Tree More Ancient than Eden* and Ironwood "Landlord" Rumble's solo (along with Nathaniel and Noah Grandberry's responses) in chapter eleven of *The Bloodworth Orphans*.

One of the major problems facing Forrest as a jazz writer involves the relatively "fixed" form of the literary text. Where musicians can vary their call in response to the changing contexts of performance, writers are usually limited to the original form of publication. This problem parallels that faced by jazz musicians who record their music, thereby transforming a single version of a piece into a "standard" point of reference. Although some musicians address this problem by recording multiple versions of the same song over an extended period of time, Langston Hughes' term "disc-tortion" (*Reader* 89) applies to both recorded music and literary forms. Highly aware of this problem, Hughes suggested one response when he published distinct versions of his modernist epic "Montage of a Dream Deferred." The version published in the 1958 *Langston Hughes Reader* is divided into five distinct sections while the version published in *Selected Poems* the following year treats the entire poem as one large movement. In addition, the later version reorganizes smaller sections. For example, Hughes breaks the poem "Jam Session" (*Reader* 107-08) into three distinct lyrics, "Jam Session," "Be-Bop Boys," and "Tag" (*Selected* 246-47).

Adapting this approach to the novel form, Forrest significantly altered the 1973 text of *There Is a Tree More Ancient than Eden* when it was republished by Another Chicago Press in 1988. Published during a period when some of the most influential black writers—notably Baraka—were asserting relatively closed ideological visions that simplified cross-cultural experience, the first version of the novel concludes with an image of ongoing process that cannot be easily reduced to a political formulation: "i crumbled upon the floor rising and falling rising and falling and rising and falling" (163). Published during the later years of the Reagan presidency, the later version concludes with a new section, "Transformation," that places the first version's theme of ongoing process in an explicitly political context. An implicit response to the increasingly desperate realities of the black community, Pompey c.j. Browne's sermon in the final chapter of "Transformation" calls for a renewed response to Martin Luther King's vision. Listening to Rev. Browne at "The Crossroads Rooster Tavern," whose name combines African, blues and gospel imagery, Nathaniel Witherspoon meditates on the preacher as a figure who "over the years, has himself become something of a transformation of Adam Clayton Powell, Martin Luther King, Leon Sullivan and Richard Pryor" (205). Rev. Browne sounds a necessary challenge to the community which is literally and figuratively at the crossroads: "Yet I hear Martin's voice still to fight on, crying forth in the wilderness; we feel like-a-shouting marching out of the wilderness demanding of the Lord remembrance: Honor, Honor unto the Dying Lamb of our learning lanterns—the frontier of the shrouded dream. Thank God Almighty I'm free at last; but free to uncover what freedom beyond the mountain top's metamorphosis? Is paradise without politics?" (213-14). As contextually aware jazz artist, Forrest knows that the question demands a much different response in 1988 than it would have in 1973.

Forrest's treatment of myth also reflects his commitment to envisioning new possibilities. In his influential essay on *Ulysses*, T.S. Eliot defined the "mythical method" as "a way of controlling, of ordering, of giving a shape and significance to the immense panorama of futility and anarchy which is contemporary history" (177). Resisting Eliot's elevation of myth over experience, both leftist (Bertolt Brecht) and Afro-American modernists (Zora Neale Hurston) view myth as a *part* of the perceptual system operating *within* the world. The shift in emphasis encourages a dialectical understanding of how experience leads to changes in the understanding of particular myths and of how choosing new myths for inspiration can change experience. Hurston's *Moses, Man of the Mountain* exemplifies the process. Although she acknowledges both the Judeo-Christian and Freudian interpretations of Moses, Hurston emphasizes his role as African conjure man, thereby encouraging black readers to develop a higher awareness of their African cultural heritage.

Reflecting Hurston's work in comparative anthropology with Franz Boas and Ruth Benedict at Columbia University which culminated in her writings on African religions in Haiti (*Tell My Horse*) and New Orleans (*Mules and Men*), Moses is part political leader

and part conjure man. Revoicing a familiar image from the spirituals, which frequently parallel the situation of the slaves with that
of the Hebrews in Egypt, Hurston presents a Moses who experiences deep frustrations while attempting to shape an oppressed
and demoralized people into a powerful, self-reliant nation.
Unlike the Biblical Moses, however, Hurston's Moses is not by birth
a member of the community he leads out of bondage. Rather,
he is a member of the Egyptian nobility who is transformed first
into a Hebrew and then into a Hebrew leader by the mythmaking powers of Miriam and Jethro. The phrase "I AM WHAT I AM"
reveals the importance of Hurston's confrontation with the inher-
ently ambiguous substructure of cultural mythology. Drawing on
his profound knowledge of he natural and supernatural forces—
from a West African spiritual perspective there is no fundamental
difference—Moses uses beliefs, as much as material forces, to
restructure political reality.

Anticipating Hurston's political positions of the 1950s—which
superficially appear "conservative"—*Moses, Man of the Mountain*
suggests that the key to meaningful progress for African-Americans lies in a belief in their own myth-making power rather than
in protesting their political situation. Sounding the jazz/modernist
theme of the isolation of the artist who redefines the mythology,
and therefore the reality, of a community, Hurston summons the
rhythms of the gospel preacher in her description of Moses as an
artist who gradually assumes power over and responsibility for his
own mythology. As Moses contemplates the beauty and terror of
self-creation, of transformation, Hurston describes his situation in
terms that would certainly be recognizable to Forrest and the
musicians of the AACM:

Moses had crossed over. He was not in Egypt. He had crossed over and
now he was not an Egyptian. He had crossed over. The short sword at his
thigh had a jewelled hilt but he had crossed over and so it was no
longer the sign of high birth and power. He had crossed over, so he sat
down on a rock near the seashore to rest himself. He had crossed over
so he was not of the house of Pharaoh. He did not own a palace
because he had crossed over. He did not have an Ethiopian Princess for
a wife. He had crossed over. . . . The sun who was his friend and ancestor in Egypt was arrogant and bitter in Asia. he had crossed over. He felt
as empty as a post hole for he was none of the things he once had
been. He was a man sitting on a rock. He had crossed over. (104)

Forrest uses a similar mythic method in his treatment of Wallace D. Fard, who is described in *The Autobiography of Malcolm X* as the messenger who "had given to Elijah Muhammad Allah's message for the black people who were the Lost-Found Nation of Islam here in this wilderness North America" (161; for background on Fard, see Lincoln). Associating Fard with the organizing theme of the lost child, Forrest approaches the "source" of the Nation of Islam's binary mythology in a way that underscores his determination to decenter simplifying myths.

Throughout *The Bloodworth Orphans*, Fard appears in myriad forms, most of them associated with the African-American search for origins. From his initial appearance in the "List of Characters" where he places newspaper advertisements in hopes of obtaining unwanted babies, Fard—under numerous names—is frequently mentioned but never unambiguously present. Forrest's treatment of Fard as a trickster figure in the tradition of Brer Rabbit or Rinehart from Ellison's *Invisible Man* emphasizes the inadequacy of any identity or spiritual vision based on an unambiguous myth of origins. Present only as a linguistic construct, the Fard of *The Bloodworth Orphans* can be called on to authorize any belief system. In the final chapter of *The Bloodworth Orphans*, Noah Grandberry describes Fard—transformed into Ford, perhaps in reference to one of the founders of white America's economic mythology—as an animal trapper, a curve-ball pitcher, and a conjure man who, in the tradition of Hurston's Moses, eludes all definition: "But I have never known anyone in my long life to eat one of those graveyarders and live to tell it (yet FORD, why old *Ford*, old centerpiece W.W.W., or W.F., could)" (322). Referring to the "character" explicitly as "mythical," Grandberry interprets "Ford's" association with the snake in accord with both the Christian myth of the snake as a sign of the devil and the West African myth of the snake as an emblem of the orisha Shango (himself a figure for the conjure man): "Oh, I've seen some wear the skin of that snake around their waists to conquer their foes. I remember when I met our foe, and particularly Your Foe, for the Second time, the mythical Reverend W.W.W. (or as I used to call him, upon a sterling occasion, W.A.D.) Ford, as he was then known, *why*, he was wearing one of *those* snakes about his waist" (322). Resolution of these meanings lies entirely in the responses of Grandberry's and Forrest's audiences. In contrast to both Eliot and the Nation of Islam, myth for Forrest represents a way of meditating on origins rather than a fixed point of reference for judging the chaos of contemporary experience.

The most rewarding experience of Forrest's fiction, however, is to be derived not from a general set of guidelines for reading, but from the reader's open response to passages such as Rumble's solo, which revoices motifs from the spirituals (the motherless child), the *Odyssey* (the lost son), the Nation of Islam (the Lost-Found people), *Invisible Man* (the hospital setting as the equivalent of the Golden Day), Afro-American folklore (John Henry) and countless other sources. Like the musicians of the AACM, Forrest consistently strives to realize the underlying imperatives of the jazz, blues and gospel impulses: to acknowledge the complexity of experience in a way that enables the individual and the community to realize change in accord with an encompassing spiritual vision. I would hope that by suggesting appropriate contexts for the reading of Forrest's fiction, this chapter will encourage the development of an audience willing to provide an affirmative response contributing to the release of the potentially liberating energies of our African- and European-American ancestors.

Works Cited

Asante, Molefi Kete. *Kemet, Afrocentricity and Knowledge*. Trenton, N.J.: Africa World Press, 1990.

Bone, Robert. "Richard Wright and the Chicago Renaissance." *Callaloo* 28 (Summer 1986): 446-68.

Collins, Patricia Hill. *Black Feminist Thought*. Boston: Unwin Hyman, 1990.

Cone, James. *Malcolm, Martin, and America*. Maryknoll, N.Y.: Orbis, 1991.

Davis, Francis. *In the Moment: Jazz in the 1980s*. New York: Oxford University Press, 1986.

DuBois, W.E.B. *Writings*. New York: Library of America, 1986.

Eliot, T.S. *Selected Prose of T.S. Eliot*. New York: Harcourt Brace Jovanovich, 1975.

Ellison, Ralph. *Shadow and Act*. New York: Vintage, 1972.

Fabre, Michel. *The Unfinished Quest of Richard Wright*. New York: William Morrow, 1973.

Forrest, Leon. *The Bloodworth Orphans*. Chicago: Another Chicago Press, 1987.

——. "In the Light of the Likeness—Transformed" in *Contemporary Authors Autobiography Series* 7: 21-35.

——. "Souls in Motion." *Chicago* July 1985: 128-35, 148.

——. *There Is a Tree More Ancient than Eden.* Chicago: Another Chicago Press, 1988.

——. *Two Wings To Veil My Face.* Chicago: Another Chicago Press, 1988.

Giddins, Gary. *Rhythm-a-ning: Jazz Tradition and Innovation in the 80's.* New York: Oxford University Press, 1985.

——. *Riding on a Blue Note: Jazz & American Pop.* New York: Oxford University Press, 1981.

Grimes, Johanna L. "Leon Forrest." In *Afro-American Fiction Writers After 1955: Dictionary of Literary Biography,* vol. 33. Edited by Thadious M. Davis and Trudier Harris. Detroit: Bruccoli Clark, 1984.

hooks, bell, *Yearning: Race, Gender, and Cultural Politics.* Boston: South End Press, 1990.

Hughes, Langston. *The Langston Hughes Reader.* New York: Braziller, 1958.

——. *Selected Poems.* New York: Vintage, 1974.

Hurston, Zora Neale. *Moses, Man of the Mountain.* 1939. Urbana: University of Illinois Press, 1984.

Jones, Gayl. *Liberating Voices: Oral Traditon in African-American Literature.* Cambridge: Harvard University Press, 1991.

Jones, Leroi (Amiri Baraka). *Blues People.* New York: William Morrow, 1963.

Jost, Ekkehard. *Free Jazz.* Vienna: Universal Edition, 1974.

Kenney, William Howland. *Chicago Jazz: A Cultural History, 1904-1930.* New York: Oxford University Press, 1993.

Lincoln, C. Eric. *The Black Muslims in America.* Boston: Beacon, 1973.

Litweiler, John. *The Freedom Principle: Jazz after 1958.* New York: Quill, 1984.

Malcolm X, with Alex Haley. *The Autobiography of Malcolm X.* New York: Grove, 1965.

Marcus, Greil. *Mystery Train: Images of America in Rock 'n' Roll Music.* New York: E.P. Dutton, 1982.

Matthews, Fred. *Quest for an American Sociology: Robert Park and the Chicago School.* Montreal: McGill-Queen's University Press, 1977.

Mudimbe, V.Y. *The Invention of Africa: Gnosis, Philosophy, and the Order of Knowledge.* Bloomington: Indiana University Press, 1988.

Murray, Albert. *Stomping the Blues.* New York: Vintage, 1976.

Ostendorf, Berndt. *Black Literature in White America.* Totowa, N.J.: Barnes & Noble, 1982.

Radano, Ronald M. "Jazzin' The Classics: The AACM's Challenge to Mainstream Aesthetics." Forthcoming in *Black Music Research Journal* (Spring 1992).

Reiss, Timothy. *The Discourse of Modernism*. Ithaca, N.Y.: Cornell University Press, 1982.

Ross, Dorothy. *The Origins of American Social Science*. New York: Cambridge University Press, 1991.

Thompson, Robert Farris. *Flash of the Spirit*. New York: Random House, 1983.

Toomer, Jean. *Cane*. New York: Liveright, 1975.

Wilson, William Julius. *The Truly Disadvantaged*. Chicago: University of Chicago Press, 1987.

Thinking Beyond the Catastrophe:
Leon Forrest's *There Is a Tree More Ancient Than Eden*

Kenneth W. Warren

> As flowers turn toward the sun, by dint of a secret heliotropism the past strives to turn toward that sun which is rising in the sky of history. A historical materialist must be aware of the most inconspicuous of all transformations.
>
> Walter Benjamin, *Illuminations*

The "Transformation" section which Leon Forrest appended to the 1988 edition of *There Is a Tree More Ancient Than Eden* opens with the bold anachronism of "The Epistle of Sweetie Reed," a letter to President Lyndon B. Johnson, dated May 7, 1967. Written in reply to a congratulatory note from the President on the occasion of Sweetie Reed's one hundredth birthday, the epistle's title and its rhetorical style recall the New Testament epistles, specifically St. Paul's letters to Timothy. The interweaving of spiritual and homely advice that characterizes Paul's more personal letters reappears in Sweetie Reed's words to the president: The apostle's urging that Timothy "give up drinking only water and have a little wine for the sake of your digestion" (1 Timothy 23) is echoed by Sweetie Reed's injunction that Johnson "Avoid all strong drink. (Except hot tea.) . . . (and) drink one glass of boiling hot water before breakfast each and every morning."[1] And like the first epistle to Timothy, which warns of scandal, corruption, and profiteering within the Christian community, Sweetie Reed's letter stands before the reader of Forrest's novel as a warning and an exhortation—a belated commentary on Johnson's Great Society Programs, his war on poverty, and on the growing rifts within the Civil Rights movements as well.

In the novel, the epistle's belatedness is part of its point. It is a warning that knows, even as it is being written, that it will go unheeded and ignored. Sweetie Reed's letter necessarily reaches the reader too late to avert the catastrophes it was written to avert: the election of Richard Nixon, the "failure" of the Great Society, and the violence of the summers of 1967 and 1968. In one instance, she cautions Johnson to "have only indirect telephone conversations with a man known to us all by the name of richard millhouse nixon; but do everything humanely possible to keep him out of the White House—and by whatever means necessary, if you have to stand in the door of the White House and block his way, personally" (176-77), giving the president a warning that rolls into itself an anachronistic "prescience" of Watergate and the White House tapes. And such a belated prescience makes the *Transformation* section and the novel itself an object lesson in thinking beyond the catastrophe, a discussion of what to do when "the worst" has come to pass—the "worst" in the case of the *Transformation* section centering in the assassination of Martin Luther King, Jr., whose death lies twelve years in the past by the time the novel concludes. As regards the novel as a whole, however, the "worst" is nothing less than history itself. And the process of thinking beyond the catastrophe might be described as thinking simultaneously both through and against history.

In explicating the first edition of *There Is a Tree*, which ended with a segment entitled "Wakefulness," Keith Byerman has effectively illuminated the way that the novel "deals with the personal and private rather than the social condition of orphanhood."[2] Acknowledging the way in which the novel attempts to "give a full inventory of the cultural resources of even a young, innocent black man," Byerman's reading focuses on the "isolation of Nathaniel Witherspoon."[3] The addition of *Transformation* to the novel calls for a reassessment.

In adding this section to the novel Forrest sought, in his own words, to make explicit a process of "transformation in which the writer takes the body of his character materials up to the high place."[4] The apotheosis that he describes derives from a variety of sources: the Roman Catholic celebration of the Eucharist; the transport to which a folk preacher is subject at the height of his sermon; and the high literary appropriations of these materials in the works of James Joyce and Ralph Ellison, respectively. Like Ellison and other African-American writers, Forrest strives to show that the materials and practices of black folk culture burgeon with aesthetic possibilities. In giving artistic notice to folk culture the writer pays homage to traditional forms and ancestral figures. For Forrest, however, this homage is tinged with irreverence. In designating the significance of his sources such that they become answerable not to a past that preexisted them but to the past that appears only at the moment of its reconfiguration. The past is not merely the sequence of events that has made the present possible; rather the past as a possibility depends entirely on the present.

This historical attitude has powerful ramifications at the level of form. Charles Johnson, among others, has lamented the difficulty of reading Forrest's work. Proceeding from an assumption that the drama as a form provides a model for determining a successful shaping of fiction, Johnson faults Forrest's novels for their lack of "conventional dramatization."[5] While Forrest's emphasis on voice and on dramatic and interior monologue might indicate the appropriateness of the dramatic analogy that Johnson wishes to draw, a more helpful means of getting at what is going on in *There Is a Tree* would be to see it in terms of the cinema. The seamless juxtaposition of dream, reality, history, and prophecy is precisely the world of the motion picture, so it is no surprise that the world around Nathaniel Turner Witherspoon often reminds him of "the wonderful cowboy movies for thirty cents at the Joe Louis Theater on Saturdays" (47) or "the movies at George Washington Theater at Downtown" (50). In seeking to find his voice and create his life, Nathaniel must not only contend with the historical distortions and mythmaking of a cinema that can create "blue-eyed Indians." He must also accept the logic of cinematic syntax in trying to shape his own self out of the material that the past makes available. More specifically, in order to come to terms with his mother's death, Nathaniel must take the assemblage of biographical fragments about relatives, acquaintances, ancestors, historical personages, and himself— fragments that make up the novel's first section, "The Lives"—and edit them into a coherent, historicized, and sustainable vision of himself. He is at once the audience and editor of his own history, the consumer and producer of the story of his life.

Nathaniel's approach to the lives of others is laid out explicitly in his first meditation. After acknowledging the extent to which he had "depended so much upon the people closest to me to give definitions to my life" and his sense that this dependence was giving way to a "fierce desire to mold and sculpt out of my dreams, a world in flight" (50), Nathaniel delineates a method for his self construction:

I found myself revering certain fragments of personalities, which were glorious or demonic, but always grand, yet I would never take the total garment of any soul, never the resonance. . . . Often fiercely rejecting certain aspects of all of my heroes, even as I paid sacred homage to other segments of their personality. (5)

Each life is presented not as a whole but as footage to be trimmed—some aspects of it to be revered, other parts to be placed aside for possible future use: "I always found myself discarding segments of new heroes—returning to them later only to bonepick" (6). Responding to films, books, and his elders with the same desire to emulate and appropriate, Nathaniel plays and replays himself and the life of others, hardly distinguishing lived event from reproduced image, becoming in this way a figure for a moment of crisis when history could either confirm its propensity for destruction and violence or redeem itself, and, in the words of Hattie Breedlove, "lead us forward and remake the world for us in this dungeon" (91).

The seemingly disproportionate weight that the novel places on Nathaniel is justified by the central role that he plays in *There Is a Tree*, and the other two novels from Forest County (Forrest's fictional geography), *Two Wings to Veil My Face* and *The Bloodworth Orphans*. In John Cawelti's words, "Nathaniel's discoveries, experiences, dreams and visions, as he undergoes such crucial episodes in his life as the death of his mother, his grandmother's narrative of his family history, and the tragedy of the Bloodworth family, are the narrative center of Forest County."[6] The center, here, however, is not a fixed point. As Nathaniel's chronic self doubt reveals, the center is a point of risk. "You are potentially a prophet," Hattie Breedlove tells him, but then quickly adds, "which means that i have to understand that you can also be dangerous, and if you are not smart—or i am not wise—you could be easily used against us by the enemy" (70). The power of the chronicler and the prophet is at once the power of good and evil, the power to liberate and the power to oppress. To prophesy is not to predict the future but to make the future as one is remaking the past. The novel, somewhat paradoxically, suggests Nathaniel's singularity and his typicality in this regard. He is, in a sense, "chosen," to prophesy by virtue of his alienation from others: "For even then I knew that I would always be a minority member of any and all situations—fascinated by many kinds of scenes, yet never at home at any way stations" (6). But he is also chosen by virtue of his typicality. He is not at all unusual. For by definition, no one is at home at a "way station." Nathaniel embodies the rootlessness of an entire people stolen into slavery, and as a youth, Nathaniel may be no more than (which is to say a great deal) a figure for the present, and the site for articulating, what Benjamin terms the past's "claim" on the present "generation."[7] He is the moment when both amnesia and memory are possible.

During a visionary dialogue towards the end of "The Dream," a dialogue to which Nathaniel is characteristically a spectator, Nathaniel's grandfather, Jericho Witherspoon, tells Jamestown Fishbond that there is reason to believe in the capacity of the young man to "draw his own conclusions" (108). "Jamestown, I say let's take a chance on this youth," Witherspoon suggests. Jamestown is less sanguine. His name signifies his historical and spiritual dimensions (the year 1619 when the first Africans were introduced to the settlement at Jamestown is, along with 1776 and 1877, one of the "lucky" numbers in the book). He is therefore marked by the horrors and hopes of history, and his response to Jericho Witherspoon is ambivalent: "Oh, I am quite prepared to have faith in him, but I cannot afford to take a chance on history, for I know too much about amnesia; I can't afford to leave our survival to seasonal chance, and other barometers of history . . . (109). What Jamestown wants is some recompense for the horrors of the American past. He wants payment: "for they shall pay for the loss of memory. . . . Generations have to pay for the bloodshed, avarice and madness of their forefathers" (111). By contrast, Witherspoon, the almost white, former escaped slave, who lives to be 117 years old, stresses the universality of evil and the ability of African Americans to transcend and transform the evils of the past. He tells Jamestown that the "historical laundry list of abuses is as deep as the ocean in every land, and the savagery practiced here has its historical roots and ancestors' memory even upon the continent, from whence we all did perhaps spring" (110). He then reminds Jamestown, and Nathaniel, that "you come from a people who have a history of never currying favor but rather making do out of the dust, transforming the most rudimentary thing into utilitarian survival kits of usefulness. . . . Only a Black man could have turned a peanut into a star, making survival units for the commonweal" (110). But Jamestown's bitterness seems unquenchable, and Nathaniel's fascination with Jamestown suggests that this bitterness is the cup from which Nathaniel will most likely drink.

Jamestown's biographical fragment, one of the longest in "The Lives," reveals him to be a protean figure—"ebony-black" but later in his life suffering from vitiligo that is turning him white *"about the ankles, throat and hands"* (17). He is a wanted felon, travelling under a variety of aliases, a genius or a dolt depending on which of his IQ scores one consults, a polyglot, an artist, a jazz buff, and a revolutionary. The bulk of his biographical fragment recounts a severe beating and near drowning he is subjected to when, dressed as a Catholic priest, he is pulled from a train in the South. With the threat of castration and lynching—Billie Holiday's "Strange Fruit" provides the refrain for the segment—hovering in his consciousness, Jamestown recovers from the near death experience of drowning, with a desire to "bury his combatant" (23), but with a feeling that such a desire is beyond fulfillment.

In the third segment of "The Nightmare," Jamestown becomes a central figure in rejecting another form, a false form, of transformation, i.e., the rejection of blackness by those blacks who are almost white in appearance. The segment is structured around Nathaniel's reminiscence of one of his birthday parties when his Uncle DuPont, who sometimes passed for white, barred Jamestown from attending because he felt the young boy was too black. In presenting images out of sequence, flashbacks, and close-ups. Nathaniel is at once spectator and participant—camera eye and actor during the sequence. Although he is playing catch with a sixteen-inch softball with his uncle and a friend named Black-Ball, Nathaniel, at the outset, describes the scene almost panoramically, seeing Mr. Dickson's red wagon, which is being driven by Jamestown as he peddles watermelons, "a milk-white Cadillac (that) shot past the rattling-along wagon" (48), sundry other comings and goings, and the new buildings surrounding the neighborhood. And while the central action of this scene has Jamestown, presumably recalling DuPont's earlier slight, rising from the wagon and hurling a cantaloupe at the older man's head, narrowly missing contact. Forrest cuts abruptly from this scene to earlier scenes where Jamestown in the company of his stepfather Dickson is selling produce aboard the same wagon. In these earlier scenes, both men are "riding cool (like cowboys on the white bearded screen at the Joe Louis Theater—only all the cowboys were white)" (50), and when Jamestown rises, it is merely to call out "PUT DOWN THIRTY PIECES OF BREAD AND GET YOUR REEEEEEED-RIPE WATERMELONS-TOOOOOOODAAAA" (52).

By juxtaposing what usually happened with what happened *that* time, Forrest underscores the shock and surprise of Nathaniel and Uncle DuPont when Jamestown's act of memory and vengeance transforms the everyday into a "state of emergency."[8]

Immediately following the flashback to the party from which Jamestown was barred, Forrest gives us a close-up of the cantaloupe hitting the wall: "It smashed, like a mirror going in thirty pieces, against the wall milk-white, crashing through our laughing" (54). It is only after this close-up that we are allowed to see the delivery and the flight of the "cantaloupe hurling through the summer air with the fantastic precision of a fastball by old Satchel Paige at the Black-Ball All-Star game" and to hear Nathaniel's screamed warning, "Look out, Uncle DuPont" (55). And just as quickly Forrest takes us back to the past when Jamestown won a painting contest, for "*a painting he didn't really like or want to paint . . . a painting of Lincoln with his arms around the shoulders of a Negro slave*" (55). Feeling himself an "Uncle Tom" for submitting to his teacher's desire that he paint the American allegory of liberation, Jamestown atones by creating and submitting directly to the school superintendent another painting, which none of the other boys get to see, called "Fear No More the Stench of the Dying Sun, for Heaven Is a Reefer and Salvation a Lost Bottle of Wine, Worth a Wee Bit More than Thirty Pieces off the Eagle's Ass." Its title bespeaks the painting's irreverence. For his trouble, Jamestown is promptly expelled from school.

This flashback works to establish Nathaniel's fascination with Jamestown and the craziness and vengeance he represents, so that by the time Uncle DuPont responds to Jamestown's assault by running up the stairs, retrieving his .45, and firing down the street at Jamestown, Nathaniel is not in the position of a partisan but is part of the film audience, watching as

the old horse carried the rider like the Lone Ranger into the setting sun—looking frantically for Tonto, or for any ally for that matter—on the screen at the Joe Louis Theater. . . .

It was like the movies, all right. Just like the Saturday triple feature of cowboys and Indians (and the cartoons). . . . But at the movies you knew who to pull for, although Black-Ball always pulled for the Indians. But Uncle DuPont firing with all his skill and aim, even though his glasses had smashed against the white wall, real live bullets down DuSable

Street—well, anyway, just who was the bad guy and who was the good guy? (59)

It is this final troubling question that Nathaniel is forced to confront. That evening, after DuPont and Jamestown have played out his scene from the wild west on the streets of Chicago, DuPont verbally circles the wagon of skin color—"You see we're in an extraordinary danger. . . . We mulatto men must stick together at all costs" (59), telling Nathaniel where he must stand. DuPont's words, however, are not the last ones on the meaning of the incident. Jamestown's act of vengeance, as a result of Forrest's editing, has taken on more than a personal dimension. It is at once the anger of a great pitcher barred from the major leagues during his prime because of racism, the frustration of an artist forced to toe the line of convention rather than follow his heart, the bravado of the cowboy film star, and the hurt of a boy barred from a party because his skin is too dark. The layered texture of this incident becomes mesmerizing to Nathaniel, who watches Jamestown's getaway, until the little red wagon has long disappeared.

Marked on one side by technologies of mechanical reproduction and on the other by the "figural interpretation" characteristic of the Pauline epistles, tradition in *There Is a Tree* is not defined by the continuity of everyday practices stretching back beyond memory but by the ongoing necessity to break the continuity the past has bequeathed to us in order to make a future possible. The genius of Forrest's novel is not so much that it applies the strategies of film to its presentation of African American history and its use of Biblical interpretation, but that it sees the affinity "already" present in all three. In his cut-and-paste operation on the figures from his past and present, Nathaniel (and Forrest) are not behaving irreverently towards tradition as much as they are behaving traditionally irreverent in service of a new vision. The heavily symbolic and allusive "Vision" section of *There Is a Tree*, for example, superimposes crucifixion, lynching, apostolic martyrdom and a host of other Old Testament, Egyptian, and Hellenic allusions into a drama that plays itself out surreally on the screen of Nathaniel's consciousness. The audacity of the section is to suggest that the "whole" of this cultural past must be confronted and reconfigured if Nathaniel is to transcend his past and transform himself. H. Nigel Thomas, writing in regard to *The Bloodworth Orphans*, makes an observation that is applicable here. In Forrest's view, according to Thomas, "all Afro-American rituals are shown to be inadequate to meet the needs that created them in the first place—unless one has the power to manipulate those rituals."[9] Rituals, in essence, require their future manipulation in a context different from the point of origin. They only serve their purpose when they are given a different reading.

But Forrest's technique is not so much an innovation as a rediscovery. In *Mimesis* Erich Auerbach writes,

Paul and the Church Fathers reinterpreted the entire Jewish tradition as a succession of figures prognosticating the appearance of Christ, and assigned the Roman Empire its proper place in the divine plan of salvation. Thus while, on the one hand, the reality of the Old Testament presents itself as complete truth with a claim to sole authority, on the other hand that very claim forces it to a constant interpretive change in its own content; for millennia it undergoes an incessant and active development with the life of man in Europe.[10]

Forrest, of course, would add Africa and America to the last sentence, but the method Auerbach describes would receive an endorsement. Exercising control over experience, tradition nonetheless becomes responsive to change and development in human affairs. The desire of tradition to remain authoritative requires that it take cognizance of experience. This notice, however, is taken in a characteristic way. Rather than making possible "a presentation which carefully . . . respected temporal and causal sequence, (and) remained within the domain of the earthly foreground," figural interpretation of history dictated "a fragmentary presentation, constantly seeking an interpretation from above."[11] A text written in this vein favors the "interpretive" over the "causal," "parataxis" over "hypotaxis," as well as the word "and" over the word "meanwhile." Looking back over *There Is a Tree*, especially the third chapter of "The Nightmare" and "The Vision," the reader cannot help but be struck by the preponderance of coordinating conjunctions.

Moreover, figural interpretation's "fragmentary presentation, constantly seeking an interpretation from above, is in accord with Walter Benjamin's description of the picture of reality made possible by film. The order at work in the process of making a film is not the order of sequential experience, but an act of editing that comes from above, as it were, in order to give shape to the discontinuities in time and space that may have been involved in the actual shooting. The motion picture consists of "multiple fragments which are assembled under a new law."[12]

And by virtue of the horrors of the middle passage and slavery, during which, to quote Jamestown Fishbond, "a people's total soul has been ripped off, whored upon, misused, wracked, raped, ruptured, and mangled" (109), the African American experience is also fragmented and discontinuous. As a result, as Hattie Breedlove reminds Nathaniel, this earthly fragmentation requires God's "world-holding power" to give it meaning (89). Underscoring her interpretation is the fact that she coaxes the naked Nathaniel from under his mother's death bed at the end of "Wakefulness."

By making tradition and experience more a matter of interpretive prowess than everyday practices, Forrest's novels confront the crisis of the contemporary novel, African American or otherwise. One feels almost embarrassed to speak of a crisis that has been long rumored but is now, more often than not, deprecated. Among other things, the popular success of some serious novelists—particularly African American women—has testified to the form's extraordinary adaptability and staying power. Hortense Spillers points out that:

only in some communities are "the people" not reading novels any more since novels abandoned "plain-speaking," bound for *explication de text*, about sixty years ago. It appears that women's fictional work maintains, as a general rule, not only an allegiance to "power to the people," but also "talking" to "the people" in the now-familiar accents of representation and mimesis. The work of black women writers is specifically notable in this regard.[13]

Like the mythic gray goose in *There Is a Tree*, the novel can be killed, mangled, and mutilated, but when all is said and done, still manage to be seen somewhere else, hale and hearty. Accordingly, the crisis in mind here is not so much a matter of the imminent disappearance of the form or of a loss of all its popular resonance. Rather, the crisis lies in what might be the price exacted from the novel for its continued viability—the displacement of the history it wishes to commemorate.

For all its mimicry of cinematic and Pauline strategies of interpretation and composition, *There Is a Tree* refuses to make the final move of "putting it all together." The reasons are clear. On the one hand, the success of figural interpretation depends on the interpreter's certainty about the presence of Divine Providence and the inevitability of the redemption of the saved. Remove this certainly of heavenly redaction and the concatenation of historical events becomes unreadable. In Forrest's novel, the "whole" that ought to orchestrate the fragments is a redeemed, transformed Nathaniel—a Nathaniel ready to step forward and prophesy. This figure, however, remains outside of the frame of the novel. Nathaniel's successful self-creation remains in doubt, even in the appended "Transformation" section, which finds Nathaniel, on the twelfth anniversary of Martin Luther King, Jr.'s birthday, seated in *The Crossroads Rooster Tavern*. He has obviously made something of a successful passage into manhood, but the jeremiad which Pompey c.j. Browne delivers to close the novel defines Nathaniel's world as one in which the outcome is still in doubt. "Is that Tomorrow grieving and slouching in a Windstorm?" (214), Brown asks ominously. And in answer, his conclusion is a warning: "For still our ancient enemy employs his woe; his craft and power are great, and mighty with avenging hate, on earth is not his equal for menace without mercy, for sabbath without soul, for fire without warmth" (214). At best, Nathaniel's odyssey ends here only to begin anew against forces equally implacable as those he has already confronted.

In terms of the novel's refusal to provide a cinematic "final cut," the resistance may be foreordained by an absolute difference in media. The acceleration of cinematic technology has more efficiently shrunk the ambit of the novel than expanded it. Auerbach warns that the "concentration of space and time such as can be achieved by film . . . can never be within the reach of the spoken or written word" and that "by virtue of the film's existence, the novel has come to be more clearly aware than ever before of the limitations in space and time imposed upon it by its instrument, language."[14] Seemingly more elastic of resources, language emerges as a somewhat unexpected barrier. As novelistic experiments attempt to set before the reader an array of new experiences, the technician is brought up short. In the midst of the novel's most artful of artifices the scaffolding of language remains visible. The reader is always brought back, however, subtly to the process of production. The check stands in marked contrast to film where, despite its greater dependence on technological apparatus, "an equipment-free aspect of reality" becomes possible. "In the studio," Benjamin elaborates, "the mechanical equipment has penetrated so deeply into reality that its pure aspect (is) freed from the foreign substance of equipment . . . the sight of immediate reality has become an orchid in the land of technology."[15]

And yet Benjamin could not fully absorb how quickly "immediate reality" would be able to extend its reach over the scene of production, exploiting the "exhibition value" of "such extraneous accessories as camera equipment, lighting machinery, staff assistants" in producing, as a satellite to the feature film, the experience of the making of the feature film. The production of films whose titles begin with "The Making of . . ." could, of course open up the door of infinite regress—all films, even those about the making of other films, could become subjects of the camera eye—but the process "naturally" arrests itself. The extraneous accessories, including the director, who become the "stars" of "The Making of . . ." derive their significance, like frames in a film, from a sequence that is determined by the new law of the feature film as cultural event. The history of the feature film, even when that film attempts to represent "history," is its own making which may be so elaborate an undertaking that, in terms of its logistics and budget, may indeed rival or outstrip the "original" event being commemorated. The film can thus lay legitimate claim to its own documentation, can indeed demand its own history, by virtue of its own status as a significant event.[16]

A contrast with an earlier point may be helpful here. While the editing of a film imposes a new law on the historical sequence of images it has before it, that editing works for the most part directly on the "material" of that sequence. Strikingly independent of the sequence of events required to shoot the film, the editor is nonetheless dependent on the material produced by the history of the shoot. On the other hand, as the motion picture addresses the history of the event it wishes to represent, it finds itself astonished at the immateriality of the past it wishes to document. The "stuff" of that past—chronicles, photographs, memoirs, oral testimony, etc.—seem to have a flimsiness that gives way to the slightest of pushes. The event to which they point is beyond the reach of our experience, even when that experience lies within memory. The filmmaker cannot help but feel that within the grasp is the possibility of making a history more real than history itself.

Read against this background the course taken by *There Is a Tree* yields up a grim and hard-eyed logic. While it inaugurates a process of cinematic composition, the novel halts well short of completing for the reader and for Nathaniel the process it sets in motion. We never see the final product, nor do we create it as we read. What Forrest's novel gives us through the vehicle of Nathaniel Witherspoon is partial access to the making of an experience we would have had if that experience had ever gotten made in the first place—the access is partial because the scene of the novel's composition with author and writing instruments is not represented. Throughout Nathaniel's turmoil the immediate reality of his anguish is never transmitted to the reader. Inasmuch as Nathaniel often seems outside his own life (to the extent that he can treat his autobiographical fragment in the same way he treats the biographies of the other characters) his life is not felt but is rather made available for interpretive reconstruction. We see a great deal of the novel's extraneous apparatus, but without our having direct experience of the representation of Nathaniel's transformation, this apparatus is never locked into a scheme of significance. And in the scheme of things, it shouldn't be. the scaffolding and set remain intransigently visible as if we had come upon a project abandoned part way through because of tragedy or bankruptcy. One can wander about, looking for clues and guidepost as to the "original" plan, but the best one can do is to construct possibilities that remain unverifiable. The feature film was never shot. Thus if one thinks of "The Making of" as an assurance of the commemoration of the event, *There Is a Tree* can only be the fragmented memorialization of the event or events that did not happen—the birthdays that did not happen, the celebrations that did not take place, the still awaited redemption of the history of the oppressed. To be sure, the novel's grimness is not a capitulation to despair—no one is counseled to give up. It is, however, a recognition that the proper monuments to the past can only be created by a future that we have not yet known.

Notes

1. Leon Forrest, *There Is a Tree More Ancient Than Eden* Chicago: Another Chicago Press, 1988), 175. Subsequent references appear parenthetically in the text.

2. Keith E. Byerman, *Fingering the Jagged Grain: Tradition and Form in Recent Black Fiction* (Athens: University of Georgia Press, 1985), 240.

3. Byerman, 249.

4. Leon Forrest, "In the Light of the Likeness—Transformed," *Contemporary Authors Autobiography Series*, vol. 7 (Detroit: Gale Press, 1987), 24.

5. Charles Johnson, *Being and Race: Black Writing Since 1970* (Bloomington: Indiana University Press, 1988), 72.

6. John G. Cawelti, "Introduction," to *The Bloodworth Orphans* (Chicago: Another Chicago Press, 1987), xvi.

7. Walter Benjamin, *Illuminations*, ed. Hannah Arendt (New York: Schoken Books, 1968), 254.

8. Benjamin, 257.

9. H. Nigel Thomas, *From Folklore to Fiction: A Study of Folk Rituals in the Black American Novel*, Contributions in Afro-American and African Studies, Number 118 (New York: Greenwood Press, 1988), 159.

10. Erich Auerbach, *Mimesis: The Representation of Reality in Western Literature*, trans. Willard R. Trask (Princeton: Princeton University Press), 16.

11. Auerbach, 74.

12. Benjamin, 234.

13. Hortense Spillers, "Afterword" to *Conjuring: Black Women, Fiction, and Literary Tradition*, ed. Marjorie Pryse and Hortense J. Spillers (Bloomington: Indiana University Press, 1985), 259.

14. Auerbach, 546.

15. Benjamin, 233.

16. My thinking on these matters has been greatly aided by Fredric Jameson's *Postmodernism or, The Cultural Logic of Late Capitalism* (Durham: Duke University Press, 1991); see especially 1-31.

Blood Bastards:
The Bloodworth Orphans
and the Psychology of Form

Jeffrey Renard Allen

"(A) nigger is . . . a form of behavior, a sort of obverse reflection of the white people he lives among."

—Quentin Compson in *The Sound and the Fury*

"We don't die.
We multiply."

—Black street expression

I. Space

Recently, I taught a course in the African-American novel whose goal was to examine the question, what does it mean for a black novel to have a black voice? My students enjoyed the novels overall but felt disgust and hatred for Leon Forrest's *The Bloodworth Orphans*. We had discussed again and again Larry Neal's dictum that the black writer must think black, write black and teach black values to a black audience. However, my students saw no black aesthetic at work in Forrest's novel. "Why he don't write black. Why you choose this novel? It ain't got no story. It's all in pieces. It ain't realistic. Why he write so crazy? Who he writing for? English teachers?" One student pointed to the author's photograph on the novel's rear cover that showed a lightskinned man with wavy hair. "You sure he ain't white?"

I remained tight-lipped. "Keep reading."

Admittedly, my student's objections raise crucial questions about Forrest's implied audience. One interviewer asks Forrest, "Do you write for a particular audience?" Forrest responds, "No. I only write for people who are interested in serious literature" (Harper and Stepto 149). We should always take a writer's pronouncements with a grain of salt. Indeed, I find Forrest's response an interesting bit of signifying. *The Bloodworth Orphans* is "serious literature," but this tells us little. By way of a definition, I believe

Forrest writes for a dual audience. The text itself, the story and intertextual references, are for followers of "literature." The style—structure and language, the texture of the novel— weaves a net that unconsciously draws in those who live the very *flow* of black culture itself.

To understand the implied audience(s) of Forrest's novel, we must first examine the novel's two main concerns, the divided self and the double self. Metaphorically, the novel represents these issues as a conflict between vision and voice, sight and sound.

II. Vision/Sight

Where James Joyce figured the white artist as explorer, as Ulysses, Jean Toomer re-figures the black artist as Cain, as the cursed wanderer, that Ulysses who says, "Noman is my name." Like all the principal male characters in *Cane*, Ralph Kabnis, the Northern artist/intellectual is divided between reason and soul, mind and body, passion and control, and art and life, symbolized by his inability to identify with black folk life in the South. Expressed in his very name, Kabnis believes his black blood is a cane, a crutch—and not a very firm one at that, soft like the sugar inside a canestalk. Toomer's metaphor for integrity is the circle. *Cane* presents a circular structure—opening in the South, moving to the North, then closing in the South—figured by the fragmented moons which precede each section of the novel. Further, Toomer figures the black artist as the tragic mulatto of plantation literature, a man torn by two ways of thinking, a man at home nowhere. As the fractured circle prefacing "Kabnis" illustrates, *Cane* has no closure, for Kabnis's (Toomer's) dilemma remains unresolved.

In *Light in August*, William Faulkner revises Toomer's mulatto by a visual symbol, invisibility. Essentially, he erases Toomer's circle altogether. The novel centers on the issue of blood as origin; Faulkner shows the dangers of emphasizing bloodline as the source of identity. Blood in the body is invisible to the eye, and invisible blood is, literally, black. Joe Christmas plunges into black life with women in the North, "trying to breathe into himself. .the dark and inscrutable thinking and being of negroes . . . (and) expel from himself the white blood" (212). When Christmas is castrated, we *see* his blood for the first time, this "pent black blood" that rushed from his loins "like a released breath" (440).

Christmas is a very divided man. Note the DuBoisian veil in the following passage: "None of them knew . . . where Christmas lived and what he was actually doing behind the veil, the screen of the negro's job" (312). Christmas does not know who he is, but searching for integrity, he *decides* he is a mulatto and acts out the racial stereotype of the tragic mulatto. As well, he is doomed to play the role of sacrificial Christ of his *given* last name. Joe Christmas is a man in search of wholeness, and redemption, but unlike Eliot's Hanged Man in *The Waste Land*, he can never transcend his life, rise about his immediate circumstances to see how he might rise above his dilemma.

Faulkner mirrors this division in the very structure of the novel itself. It has two main narrative strains, one involving Joe Christmas—as translated, interpreted through the consciousness of several characters—and the other, Lena Grove. The two stories are kept separate; Joe and Lena never meet. Joe never finds the pastoral groves, the Eden suggested in Lena's last name; instead, he is lured and eventually snared by the symbolic lynch (lench) rope implied in her first name. (It is no accident that, like Christ, Christmas is thirty-three.) Faulkner's point, the "blood" of origin is a sacrificial cross, the burden of a false identity. And Christianity seems incapable of crossing all the boundaries that separate people, as true identity must always be defined in the self's relation to other selves (people). Christ as love remains invisible to our eyes. Further, this love is always connected to chaos and violence, Christmas's blood is spilled into "peaceful valleys" but he finds no peace from chaos (439-40). In short, like Toomer in *Cane*, Faulkner breaks down the purity of narrative coherence for what we might call a *mixed blood narrative*. Faulkner's novel is about the dangers of origins, not knowing who you are or where you belong, where to rest the hat of home. Put differently, Faulkner's novel is about the failure of *sight* to determine identity. After all, Lucas Burch, Christmas's "double," is darker than Christmas but no white person labels him a Negro. At bottom, Faulkner questions the notion of "blood-consciousness," a fundamental tenet of Modernism.

Many critics have noted how Ralph Ellison defines black invisibility as possibility. I don't want to restate the issue here. But we should note that Ellison makes no separation between sight and sound. "It was a strangely satisfying experience for an invisible man to hear the silence of sound" (Ellison 13). And later, "I play the invisible music of my isolation" (13). Ultimately, Ellison suggests that black wholeness and identity is a question of recognizing the relationship between sight and sound, how one sees you and how you see yourself, how one wants you to speak, and how you decide to speak. Such is the message of the famous battle royal episode. Viewed from above, the white canvas of a boxing ring is identical to the white cloth of a blank movie screen or a blank sheet of paper. In this instance, the audience is white and what plays on the screen is a fiction created by whites. As well, the canvas is roped. Offering us these symbolic lynch ropes, Ellison uses the battle royal as a symbol of white control and manipulation of the black voice. After the fiasco, the narrator wants to give his speech but is unable to because his mouth is clogged with *blood*. He fails to see that the white audience has no genuine interest in his voice. The suffocation of voice clarifies the importance of the narrator's symbolic death: voice and identity involve blood. The road to home/identity is in the tongue. Black blood/identity is defined in how we speak. Later, the invisible man's submersion into self occurs fast on the heels of the spear he throws through Ras's mouth— his cutting off a language dangerous to the self. And the submersion itself develops the relation between black speaking and writing.

Still, there is one dangerous voice that the protagonist never shuts up, his own. Ellison's man underground posits the notion that the enlightened black artist is the "unconscious" mind of America: "Who knows but that, on the lower frequencies, I speak for you?" (568). Ellison rejects one essentialist concept—race or blood consciousness—only to embrace another. The problem lies in Ellison's notion of language and action. His narrator never moves beyond being America's confessor. As one passage in *The Bloodworth Orphans* makes clear, the confessional is not a mode that allows for participation, movement, action, collective improvisation: "Dolphin knows . . . that confessions are safest that tell everything apparently (or nothing in terms of personal indictment) to a trusted ear—that only reveal a fragment of what really happened, amid the ceremoniously detailed telling of every evading discussion. . . . As long as this exists, then a fragmentary telling . . . doesn't overextend the good listener into the role of 'activist'" (Forrest 146).

III. Voice/Sound

In *Absalom, Absalom!* Faulkner embodies the issue of history and race in the process of the novel, in the very action of its language. Offering us a modified stream of consciousness, Faulkner uses ironies, memories, indirection, and family histories to destroy narrative coherence—Cain as wandering language. As well, the long Faulkernian sentence permits contradiction, debate, dialogue, or in short, call-and-response. The novel masquerades as a third person narration, centered on a dialogue between Shreve and Quentin Compson, the two of them retelling what has been told to them, and speculating about conclusions. However, there is one organizing voice in the novel, one central consciousness. Every character speaks the same. The third person narrator masks the first person voice of Quentin Compson, for at heart, the novel is about his refusal to come to terms with the race issue. As the language races along, we begin to understand that race literally becomes inseparable from the telling. Race is subjective perception. As Quentin Compson tries to knit together the story of the Sutpen family, his voice constantly plays on the relationship between objectivity ("facts") and the unknown, sound and silence. All of consequence in the novel lies in what is *not* said. The reader must fill in the textual gaps. Silence acts as an invisible presence in this novel, centering on the question of race. In one scene, Sutpen cannot recognize his first wife once he discovers she has black blood. Quentin's silences suggest an unwillingness to apply the implications of race to his own process, as in his refusal in the last lines of the novel to say/admit that he hates the South, a refusal that he states *twice*.

The double is another central idea in the novel. The title is a double. There are two Quentins, the Quentin in the past (with Henry Sutpen and Charles Bon, who are themselves doubles), and the one in the present with Shreve at Harvard. Shreve and Quentin are also doubles; it is *voice* that makes them mirrors of each other: "They stared-glared-at one another, their voices (it was Shreve speaking, though save for the slight difference which the intervening degrees of latitude . . . both thinking as one, the voice which happened to be speaking the thought only the thinking become audible, vocal' (378). Like the *Waste Land*, *Absalom. Absalom!* incorporates a multiple consciousness in a single voice, a disintegrating consciousness that mirrors a disintegrating culture. Both texts share the problem of bringing diverse cultural contexts into satisfactory relationship. Unlike Eliot, Faulkner offers a partial solution to the dilemma. In this double portrait of the artist as a young man, he gives us a *double language* as a strategy for attacking the singularity of white discourse and for moving beyond the limitations of the mixed blood narrative. Still, Faulkner does not explore the full implications of his novel: the white voice must actively participate in dialogue with the black voice. Faulkner refuses to speak with two tongues, to let blacks (and women, for that matter) speak for themselves.

IV. Habitation and the Seeing Voice

The Bloodworth Orphans provides the recollections and meditations of its central character, Nathaniel Witherspoon, a man who resembles Leon Forrest in appearance, age,—he is thirty-three in 1970, Christ's awakening age, as Forrest would have been—hometown (Chicago), and profession (writer). Hence, Nathaniel is the author's fictional double, as well as the novel's central consciousness; as such, he gives the novel its *form*.

Nathaniel is like one of Faulkner's fragmented selves, torn by Catholicism and his mixed racial past. The Bloodworth family mirrors/doubles this fragmentation. As we shall see, the Bloodworths and Nathaniel must learn to re-make and re-assemble the self at the level of language and form. Forrest's concern is orphanage at the linguistic level. Orphan is a derivation of Orpheus, the poet of Greek myth who was ripped apart but whose voice found a new life in nature and objects. African-Americans are orphans, America's bastard children, culturally dismembered by slavery.

One of the most dangerous consequences of this fracture was the white imposition of Christianity, a masking strategy that concealed the true purpose of slavery (the acquisition of money) while justifying its existence. Money was the "absent cause" (Jameson 35). Similarly, the Church tried to mask its origins, built its foundation over pagan roots. Time and again, Forrest shows how Christianity tries to contain the pagan, be it African or Greek. But this pagan element constantly ruptures traditional belief and practice, such as in the following scene, a symbolic play on the primal Dionysian forest in Euripides's *Bacchae*: "The advent of Rachel, when she was struck down dead to life in those . . . terrible woods . . . while the 'blood swam in her head' and streaked down her legs . . . in the mud, and she was lifted up and long and away upon wings of fire . . . by the moon-witnessing campground preacher, Packwood" (28). Packwood was "once upon a time a Blues-prince . . . struck down in the woods . . . ten years before" (29). We recall that for Christianity Satan embodies all that is pagan, and that many black church folk saw the blues as satanic, "the devil's music." Packwood had once made a pact with the devil, a familiar archetype in the iconology of the blues. Of course, European folktales often had such Faustian pacts occur in the primal forrest. The passage contains numerous other primal/pagan images—moon, fire, blood (menstrual)—that interpenetrate the mud of Christian creation.

Of course, survival dictated that African-Americans don the mask of Christianity, but they did so by constructing a new mask, a syncretic face, African and American, pagan and Christian. Chapter two of the novel, Rachel's conversion, mirrors the testifying and conversion scenes in James Baldwin's *Go Tell It On the Mountain*. Both involve preacher/congregation interaction, call-and-response, the very heart of African-American improvisation. In both novels, spiritual conversion builds to a sexual frenzy, spiritual passion becomes earthly desire, leading to an orgasmic release: "And as the church stormed back against the night with handclapping and tambourines ablaze, crying and shouting and weeping and whispering, trembling, shuttering and wailing; they all heard her (Rachel) cry upon the wings of the storm, her body shuddering like a leaf upon the tree" (40). The point, Africanisms surface in the music, language and dance of the black church.

Still, Christianity cannot unify the divided black self, provide a hiding place from the cycles of brutality that black Americans have endured: "The church supplied her (La Donna Scales) with a history, a myth, a mind, a home, . . . a sense of direction, a faith. . . . (But) amid La Donna's sense of calling into the world of salvation, she was also charged with the feeling that she would be cast out ultimately" (113).

Does Islam offer an alternative? The novel's villain is W.W.W. Ford, a symbolic representation of W.D. Fard, counselor to Elijah Muhummad (founder of the Nation of Islam), the man who Muhummad believed was God in the flesh. Ford makes his first appearance in the novel as the Methodist deacon, Dallas "Wizard" Ford, "retired colonel; member of the ancient free and accepted masons," who has sold playboy preacher Regal Pettibone a Lincoln. The luxury car underlines the materialist foundations of The Nation of Islam. The Nation of Islam rejects any belief in a spiritual universe (Muhummad 1). But there is another textual "silence" here. Elijah Muhummad was the great whore of Babylon, with his pot of gold and his harems. Islam is the flipside of the Christian coin. Indeed, we see why Nathaniel reflects on the "convolutions of Pettibone's masks" (4). Both Pettibone and Ford wear the mask of religion to hide carnal greed. In this supposedly "scientific" religion, Ford mechanizes religion, robs it of the blood of passion/spirit, very much like Henry Ford, the Jew-hating capitalist who mechanized automobile production and dulled the worker's mind and spirit. So, While Fard, Muhummad and the Nation of Islam preached the superior quality of black blood, the issue they masked was one of blood money, their exploitation of fellow blacks. In one scene, right after he has "made a killing," Dolphin spots another manifestation of Ford, Norbert Peabody Ford, a former boxer known for his "killer instinct" (174): "Dolphin despised the abundance of money . . . tumbling down upon him, like a wizard of the stock exchange. . . . Yet always cursed to think back upon that money and the resources from whence his first stake in the world originally came: human flesh. . . . Blood money from the blood of his own" (174).

Elijah Muhummad's emphasis on black blood led to radical revisions of the Bible and a total rejection of Hebrew beliefs. His anti-Semitism entailed a rejection of black American folk culture, as we blacks saw the biblical, Jewish struggle for freedom as one mirroring our own. The problem, black survival means cultural survival.

Another manifestation of the Satanic villain is L. Ralston Ford, a chauffeur. Ralston is name-play on Ellison's Ras the Destroyer. We recall that Ellison's character often attempted to inspire riot (chaos and doom) through his voice. Ralston and Ras are both false prophets; though he is a chauffeur, W.W.W. is like a double road, a forked path. Ralston can offer us no true direction: "*was he a long-lost rhapsodist, whose gig was up, whose policy had lapsed: Ole Ulysses Driftwood, axed by the dozens playing Gods, wandering the monstrous rails without a key to the city*" (82).

How can the Afro-American resolve the numerous contradictions of her/his historical self? Through the *psychology of form*, a negotiation between language and the cultural self. In *Counter-Statement*, Kenneth Burke argues that form is the psychology of the audience, the "creation of an appetite in the mind of the auditor (reader), and the adequate satisfying of that appetite" by the author (Burke 31). Burke calls this the *psychology of form*. Certainly, a writer who sets out to upset the reader's expectations is similarly interested in psychology. The writer provides food that is hard to digest, and even harder to swallow. But the pill may be for the moral and mental health of both author and reader.

With his phrase the *sociology of form*, Raymond Williams historicizes structural issues. All forms carry certain ideological assumptions. A relation of structure, "can show us the organizing principles by which a particular view of the world, and from that coherence of the social group which maintains it . . . operates in consciousness" (Dexter and Fisher 67). Jazz offers such a structure. It is a structure of emotion, a structure of mind, a structure of rhythm, and most of all, a structure of *language*. Jazz is a merging of context (the political unconscious) and text (the sociology of form), to construct the form of forms, the *psychology of form*, a *process* that uses deconstruction and fragmentation in a search for integrity, both textual and authorial. Call-and-response give art its full resonance. In accordance with the participatory nature of black folk culture, the artist provides a call; and the audience must respond. Artist and audience collaborate to produce meaning and coherence. Linguistically, the reader must join the hermeneutic circle in the *creation* of meaning, become a creator, and hopefully, s/he will *think* newly as a result.

Forrest voices his novel as the implied authorial body, a vessel worried with holes, gaps and spaces. His concern, the possibilities of jazz as a language to fill these gaps and create a whole self and identity. After all, orphanhood is a lack. As readers, we must all parent the black text. Let us not miss the important role that naming plays in the formation of Afro-American identity. Certainly, naming for us has its roots in the ancestral language. In many African cultures, the naming of something is the designation of being, be it the designation of a human being, images or even gods (Jahn 125). In this Forrest novel, the reader must *name* the text of blackness.

Henry Louis Gates argues that blackness is a text (Gates xxviii) and that whites have always tried to suppress this text, specifically the black voice; but in the text of blackness, the language is the "return of the repressed" (xxviii). Like Gates, Forrest posits no simple correlation between the fictional text and the "real" world. Gates says "the House of Black Fiction has many windows, but many are cracked and jagged. . . . It is a house of tatters, created by novelists who fail to realize that by the very act of writing—the language of which is not reality but a system of signs—they commit themselves to the construction of coherent, symbolic worlds related to but never relegated to be merely plausible reproductions of the real world, not even the nightmare land of the inner city" (46).

If psychology corresponds to the inner city, then Forrest's world is the outer city, the psychology of language, the cultural mind, not the Freudian or Jungian psyche. Put differently, Forrest privileges language, *music*, over character. Hence, though he relies heavily on stream of consciousness, any attempt to decipher the various hallucinations, dreams, nightmares, visions, fantasies, sermons, and testimonials of the characters would be to lose oneself in chaos, to highlight the personal unconscious, and miss the political unconscious. We must not fall victim to western "tricknology," an unfathomable labyrinth of deception and depression. It is enough to understand we are the victims of Western constructions about religion, myth, sexuality, family, psychology, race, gender and, especially, origins, that form the *histoire* (history and story, or his-*story*), the master text of the West. Hence, we must problematize notions of interpretation; Forrest deconstructs both the notion of blood (race) consciousness and the collective unconscious. Both theories are ahistorical and apolitical. Language is the answer.

Obviously, *chaos* is a Greek word, the etymology being of crucial importance to black culture, for it implies that orphanage is a cultural condition; culture is social as language is social; it figures that orphanage surfaces in the very language of the black text. Since the African-American has a dual heritage, her/his language is shaped by two traditions. Coherence of the fragmented self involves a negotiation between the two traditions.

Blues and the spirituals share the *feelings* but they differ lyrically. The blues offer a tragic and often, tragi-comic view of life, while the spirituals are fundamentally optimistic. These are the conflicting twins of black culture. What might link them? Jazz, Forrest suggests. That is, jazz as jive, hep, *double talk*. The novel's crucial scene of understanding takes place in an insane asylum —that home of mental breakdown—and involves a dialogue between Nathaniel and Noah Grandberry, with the music of the great jazz musician Ironwood "Landlord" Rumble, acting as a chorus. Where Ellison's Louis Armstrong has "made poetry out of being invisible . . . because . . . he's unaware that he is invisible" (Ellison 8), Rumble is fully aware of his invisible status in white America. Ellison tells us about the strength of Armstrong's voice but Armstrong never speaks *himself*. He is a signifying genius, aware of the power of language, and the regenerative powers of humor. "*Once upon a time, the goose drank wine, the monkey chewed tobacco on the streetcar line. . . . The monkey broke, the streetcar choke. . . . They all went to heaven on a billy goat*" (83). Ironwood would have no problem understanding the full significance of the "Blackness of Blackness." Faulkner had dissected the racial discourse, laid bare the skeleton. But, we ask, how can these bones live? What would constitute a constructive racial dialogue? Language. Black language is the storehouse of black life. The blues is such a language. Ironwood's band plays a jazz blues, "St. James Infirmary," a song that Armstrong made famous. Then Noah speaks with hep perfection, re-creating a myth about the origins of evil and orphanhood that incorporates both the religious and the secular, and that improvises on both white and black beliefs: "Out of this *World*, Nathaniel, beyond *All* reason, and back over there behind your head, young rookie—out of this heaven-high, storm-blasted Refuge Hospital window, across the railroad tracks, over the river and down through the looking-glass woods of life's constantly reflective journey. . . . Ah yes, there was the Paradise, where the snake dwelt in the graveyard" (318).

The other quality of heptalk is its use of nonsense. Heptalk is the play of language itself, a mode of improvisation concerned more often with sound than sense. The language of nonsense creates a certain silence. But Forrest doesn't concede to negation, to silence. Heptalk is a play between sense and nonsense, sound and silence. Noah's singing, his "somnambulist 'improvisations' . . . (are) representations . . . of the no man's land of transition" (Soyinka 148). As well, it is a play between the serious and the comic, between tragedy and comedy. Jazz is a double language. This is why jazz instrumentalists strive for a human "voice," while jazz singers imitate instruments.

As Langston Hughes points out, *all* black music is jazz, for all black music is ultimately geared to black survival, continuing the deferred dream. "Jism" is one derivative of the word, the sperm of creation; and "to jazz" means to fuck, express life as sexual passion. Further, black music is a play on fragmentation, a dismissal of essentialist notions of a unified self, for in racist America blacks must constantly shift and change the self. For Forrest, Afro-American life is the blues life, the jazz life, a circle of language, style and sound, movement and change. Chaos confronts harmony. Noah says, "(T)he only way I've found to stop the bounding voices, even the hunting corpse of my mother's body—slung over my shoulders, eternally—which racks me day and night, is through Action. *And* we've got to move forward now (382).

The insane asylum becomes a new church for Noah's testifying and Ironwood's music, where Nathaniel can find his own bench of participation in Nietzsche's Dionysus-Apollo brotherhood. Indeed, Rumble is a "Landlord" because he keeps and guards the music. Where Ford, the Mason, offers us the voice of deceit and entrapment, a voice gleaming with the glue of a false Egyptian cement, Noah constructs an ark, that home built to withstand all floods, with the waters of his voice. Like that other greater signifier, Louis Jordan, he carries the river in his voice.

Noah doubles for the Yoruba god, Ogun, artist, explorer, the knowledge-seeking instinct, "protector of orphans," "roof over the homeless," poet, the essence of creativity (Soyinka 26-30). Like Cain, Ogun is associated with blood since he spilt the blood of his kin (157). Hence, he is associated with destruction. According to the Yoruba, tragedy originated when a slave rolled a boulder down the back of the godhead and shattered him into a thousand pieces, multiplied the godhead. Ogun is tragic art itself, as his poetry and music play on the theme of dissolution and re-integration. Through this process he lessens the gulf of communal separation, appeases the abyss, provides a measure of harmony to chaos, and strengthens the communal psyche. Through word-play both Noah/Ogun destroy logic, coherence, to recreate a passion play of language rather than blood. Jazz is a *language of transition*. As Wole Soyinka notes, "It is 'unmusical' to separate Yoruba form from myth and poetry" (147). He continues, "Ogun's identification with the innate mythopoeia of music (is not merely) fortuitous. Music is the language of transition and its communicant means, the catalyst and solvent of its regenerative hoard" (36).

Noah and Ironwood teach Nathaniel the true meaning of "poetry," that word that Ellison so favors. Ellison's definition of poetry as it relates to the work of Romare Bearden is equally applicable to Nathaniel Witherspoon/Leon Forrest: "Where any number of painters have tried to project the 'prose' of Harlem—a task performed more successfully by photographers—Bearden has concentrated upon releasing its poetry, its abiding rituals and ceremonies of affirmation. . . . Bearden's meaning is identical with his method. His combination of technique is eloquent in the sharp breaks, leaps in consciousness, distortions, paradoxes, reversals, telescoping of time, and surreal blending of styles, values, hopes and dreams which characterize most of Negro American history" (Harper and Stepto 165).

Both Regal and Nathaniel are preacher/poets. Where Regal is dismembered, his voice scattered in Orpheus fashion, Nathaniel learns to collect the fragmented strands of his personal voice. Ellison used the first person narrator to attack the notion that blacks speak in a single voice. His emphasis is individualism. The individual voice renders the cultural voice invisible. This narrator is not as sensitive as he would have us believe, for sensitivity must be tested in practice, in action. Ellison's narrator is as static as Joe Christmas. Locked in the double role of crazed nigger and sacrificial Christ, Joe Christmas can run no further than the cross of the lynch rope. The singular voice allows the invisible man to mistake his grave for a womb.

Interestingly enough, Joe Christmas often misperceives both sight and sound. His foster mother puts "into the can beneath his round grave eyes coins whose value he did not even recognize" (158); and in one scene Max and Mame hold a conversation, but "it was as if they talked at and because of him (Joe Christmas), in a language which he did not understand" (182-83). Where the biblical Christ is sensitive, Joe Christmas is dead to the senses. He is incapable of interpreting the data that enters his body. The invisible man and Joe Christmas both repress rather than express their true selves.

In one scene of *Light in August*, Joe Christmas reads a book and finds himself distanced from the materiality of the words on the page, his thoughts frozen on. "He would not move, . . . his whole being suspended by the single trivial combination of letters in quiet and sunny space, so hanging motionless and without physical weight" (104). In this parody of ascension and knowledge (light), the page might as well be invisible. Forrest suggests that words, language, can fill up the space of invisibility. Forrest's third person omniscient narrator reinstates the idea of a collective voice, the nexus that draws together the numerous strands of black oral culture. Despite the chaos of subterfuge, indirection, and wandering, Nathaniel maintains a coherent voice. Forrest makes no distinction between physis, external physical space, and psyche, internal psychological space. Home is the space of language, the habitation of voice. Forrest revoices certain Faulknerian themes. Where the invisible man must hibernate underground, and where Joe Christmas finds the ascension of the hangman's rope, Nathaniel Witherspoon sails off in full verbal flight, and the novel is his sailing, his journey.

The chaotic end of the novel takes nothing away from this sense of affirmation. Essentially, the end is a fictional play on real events in Chicago history. The gang battle with cops symbolizes the West Side riots that followed the assassination of Martin Luther

King, as well as the Black Arts Movement's advocacy of revolutionary violence. The lynching and burning of the mayor express the hatred that many blacks felt about Mayor Richard J. Daley, especially after he called in the National Guard to quell the fiery rioters. Both the gang battles and the lynching will backfire against the black community. Fire has a double meaning. It is the hell-fire of chaos, but also the fire of liberation, Ogun's fire, the fusion of self and community. Nathaniel, Noah, the infant and the reader all join lives. Forrest is telling us that the ultimate defiance of white power is the Promethean birth of a black child. As Joe Christmas discovered, blood-craving, blood-obsession will only lead to blood violence. The gangs are obsessed with blood. Forrest alludes to the infamous gang battles of the late sixties and early seventies between two Chicago street gangs, the Blackstone Rangers and the Disciples. The Rangers identified themselves with the colors black and blue, and the Disciples, red and black: "Hundreds of erupting youths, in red jackets and tams, were fighting scores of ungovernable youths in black jackets" (383). Gang members often called themselves "Bloods." The whole context of these riotous gangsters serves as a "silence" in the text. The sound of silence. But where Ellison's invisible man believes he is the invisible voice, the underground psyche, the very unconscious of America,—Forrest suggests that this voice is inactive. The invisible man promises to become active, argues he is in a state of hibernation, but like Dante's Satan, he is a frozen man. His voice never moves. Ellison's protagonist is the isolated, existential hero. He never acts or involves himself in black communalism.

In contrast to this immobile man in a self-created womb, Forrest gives us a real, mobile baby in a symbolic womb, "its trembling little hands reaching towards the two sad-faced sobbing men" (383) in the car. Nathaniel, Noah and all of us must respond to the call of the baby's gesture. None of us know this child's biological parents. We must create a "lie," an exaggeration of parentage that can nurture future black generations. Forrest stresses fiction as creation, not blood as creation. Imagination is the only road to mental wholeness and health. The car shows us that change and movement is necessary for black survival. The tenor of the metaphor must find its vehicle in *movement*.

Indeed, the novel both opens and closes with images of vehicles and movement, Pettibone's Lincoln and the infant's shoebox. Where the Lincoln is a mask for materialism, the shoebox is a true womb for growth. About his great jazz poem *Montage* of *A Dream Deferred*, Langston Hughes writes the following, "Now, to wind it all up, with you in the middle—jazz is only what you (the reader) . . . get out of it. . . . A great big dream—yet to come—and always yet—to become ultimately and finally true. . . . That future is what you call pregnant. . . . The Papa and The Mamma . . . are anonymous. But the child will communicate. Jazz is a heartbeat—its heartbeat is yours" (Hughes 494). In other words, jazz involves the reader/listener in a circle of sound and vision. Both participate in the act of creation. A newborn baby must be named. Naming gives identity; the reader must participate in the naming of the text; s/he does so by making the word flesh, translating the spirit of the text into material existence of his/her own dual positionality. And here lies the significance of one of Forrest's epigraphs from a black spiritual, "Jesus told me that the world would hate me, if he changed my name . . . changed my name." Self-hate involves letting others name you. Jesus can change my name, change my name, as long as I can change his.

Toomer and Ellison represent failures of the imagination. Toomer's mistake was his connection between blood and identity, and Ellison's, the connection between the unconscious and identity. As Forrest shows, One must define oneself culturally, linguistically. The question of his novel might be stated thus: What is the worth of blood in determining identity? The answer, blood has little value. Unlike Ralph Kabnis, Nathaniel Witherspoon learns to move in a world that is fluid and energetic. Where Kabnis is imprisoned in a static circle, Witherspoon flows in accordance with African notions of time, a synchronic and cyclical waxing and waning of reoccurrence and repetition; this sea of movement keeps one in the community of ancestors and instills a sense of direction.

Forrest questions the notion that blackness and identity can be solely defined in terms of biological parentage. Just as it is speculation about his unknown parentage that drives Joe Christmas to self-destruction, it is such speculation that causes nearly every tragic episode in Forrest's novel. Amos-Otis Thigpen's revelations—words from Amos, a would-be prophet—about the incestuous love affair between LaDonna Scales and Regal Pettibone leads to the death of both Scales and Thigpen. The congregation of the River Rock of Eden Baptist Church blames the destruction of their church on the incestous love between their pastor

(Regal) and LaDonna. Regal is literally ripped apart by his female congregation of Maenads. Because he cannot parent a son, Abraham Dolphin blows his brains out: "How can a man live out the length of his fiery days without a vision-prize? A legend-bearing son, carrying on to uplift the stalking saga of father's tribunal" (195). Only the physical *sight* of a son would confirm Abraham's existence. Like Regal, he too is torn apart: (the) plane scattered the physician's ashes down the Mississippi River" (195). Unlike the narrator of Langston Hughes's poem "The Negro Speaks of Rivers," Dolphin fails to understand that the African legacy is "more ancient than the blood that flows in human veins." Language precedes blood. Hughes's narrator "heard the singing of the Mississippi when Abe Lincoln/went down to New Orleans," the birthplace of jazz; and such knowledge allows him to grow deep as the rivers. But Dolphin, this would-be Christ, finds only dissolution, not salvation and knowledge.

Similarly, Noah Grandberry recognizes that blood is not thicker than water. He experiences no mental dissolution after learning he is a Bloodworth orphan. The mouthpiece of the gods, he reveals his origins to Nathaniel, purges them by slipping the yoke and turning it into a joke: "FOOL! Don't worry, young rookie, 'cause he was bawn and bred in a brier patch, weaned on trouble, and naturalized upon the dungeon riff of bad times" (314). Noah finds solace in the oral tradition, the folktales, the woofing, the riffs. Noah teaches Nathaniel that the ark of black survival is the voice. In the opening pages of the novel Nathaniel rides "shotgun" to Pettibone in the preacher's Lincoln "chariot," suggesting that Pettibone is the lead to Dolphin's suicide. And because Pettibone is a earth-shaker and hell-raiser, Nathaniel thinks him a "Poseidon commanding the waters" (5). By the novel's close, Nathaniel knows that Pettibone was a false God, prophet and saviour. The Lincoln is no chariot, but a symbol of Pettibone's narcissism and materialism. Indeed, one scene suggests that an obsession with blood origin is the origin of narcissism itself: "And now observing Money-Czar Flowers (Regal's stepfather) watching himself in the floor-length mirror, or the portrait of himself in his early twenties, stationed so that he could see its reflection on the opposite wall in the mirror, Nathaniel thought, Perhaps that's the nature of all vanity, to return to the source of its bloated vision pictured upon the flooding waters of Memory— drowning, trying to retrieve the sweet, innocent Genesis reflection" (69-70).

If the waters of Noah's voice are the source for direction, then Nathaniel must absorb this voice. That is, Noah has already experienced immersion in the pool of mythopoeic forces; now it is Nathaniel's turn. Here lies the meaning of his name. In the vernacular sense, Nathaniel is "With er spoon" ("Has a spoon"). The spoon is an instrument that must be submerged in liquid; the spoon then carries the liquid into the mouth. Noah teaches Nathaniel that the black voice must not be allowed to "wither," to dry up, to be rendered speechless.

The Jewish, Christian, and Muslim symbolism clue us to the meaning of Nathaniel's first name. Of course, Nathaniel refers to Nat Turner, the prophet, preacher and liberator. But it also refers to *Nathan the Wise*, the Lessing drama. The titular protagonist is a Jewish Trader. A Christian knight and a Muslim sultan fall in love with his daughter. Hence, all three faiths are brought in close contact. The triangle turns out to be a "blood" relationship, a symbol of the unity of the three religions, for the knight and the daughter are actually brother and sister and both are children of the sultan's brother. The blood revelation leads to harmony rather than chaos. In Forrest's novel, the three religions represent the tripartite selves of black cultural identity. Interestingly enough, Elijah Muhummad believed that a biological mulatto would bring the lost black sheep into the fold (Muhummad 19-20). However, he failed to realize that the true black prophet is a *cultural* mulatto. Nathaniel is this prophet. Again, Forrest revises certain Black Muslim beliefs without rejecting them all together. The baby stays in the bathwater.

The passage from *Light in August* that serves as an epigraph to the novel defines orphanhood as a lack of name: "'He will eat my bread and he will observe my religion,' the stranger said. 'Why should he not bear my name?'" *Light in August*, *Invisible Man*, and *The Bloodworth Orphans* all end with an actual or symbolic birth. Fathered by the dark Lucas Burch, Lena Grove's child may possibly be another "mulatto" of uncertain progeny. The Invisible Man hibernates in his symbolic womb, but the reader has no sense of how to resolve the conflict between American individualism and African American communalism, has no sense of what form his rebirth will take. But Nathaniel Witherspoon is *in* the tradition, and moves in the tradition. To truly understand Forrest's novel, we need only finger its narrative pulse. One of my students summed it up best, "After a while, I stopped trying to understand it (the novel). I just followed wherever it took me." Forrest's voice forces us to focus less on the text of black life than on its texture. As the student said, "Got to move, so the white man can't catch you. Got to go crazy, act crazy, talk crazy so he leave you alone."

Works Cited

Burke, Kenneth. *Counter-Statement*. Berkeley: University of California Press, 1939.

Ellison, Ralph. *Invisible Man*. New York: Vintage Books, 1982. (Originally published in 1952).

Faulkner, William. *Absalom, Absalom!* New York: Random House, 1987. (Originally published in 1936).

——. *Light in August*. New York: Random House, 1972. (Originally published in 1932).

Fisher, Dexter, and Stepto, Robert, eds. *Afro-American Literature: The Reconstruction of Instruction*. New York: Modern Language Association, 1978.

Forrest, Leon. *The Bloodworth Orphans*. New York: Random House, 1977.

——. "'If He Changed My Name': An Interview with Leon Forrest." *Chant of Saints*. Ed. Michael Harper and Robert Stepto. Urbana: University of Illinois Press, 1979, 146-58.

Gates, Henry Louis. *Figures in Black*. New York: Oxford University Press, 1987.

——. "Preface to Blackness: Text and Pretext." *Afro-American Literature: The Reconstruction of Instruction*. Ed. Dexter Fisher and Robert Stepto. 44-71.

Hughes, Langston. "Jazz as Communication." In *The Langston Hughes Reader*. New York: George Braziller, Inc., 1958.

Jahn, Janheinz. *Muntu: African Culture and the Western World*. New York: Faber and Faber, 1961.

Muhummad, Elijah. *Message to a Blackman*. Newport News, Virginia: United Brothers Communications Systems, 1965.

Soyinka, Wole. *Myth, Literature and the African World*. Cambridge: Cambridge University Press, 1976.

Toomer, Jean. *Cane*. New York: Boni and Liveright, 1923.

Circle of Safety, Circle of Entrapment: Women's Languages of Self-Invention in Toni Morrison's *Beloved* and Leon Forrest's *The Bloodworth Orphans*

Veena Deo

The language is born in the body's middle parts
A rumbling conceived by joy or rage
Rises to the tongue and sets it free
The language comes bursting forth
Spewed from the mouth like angry spittle
Flung on listening ears as one would hose
Unsuspecting dry grass

The language leaves the speaker breathless and satisfied
Knowing that the Holy Words have been spoken

Pausing in the afterglow
Looking for a twinkle of comprehension
Looking for a nod of approval
I realize I have been speaking in tongues[1]

In her talk "Language and Resistance: Disrupting Words," bell hooks spoke very powerfully about how the African-American experience in this white, capitalist, racist patriarchy (as she put it) has left blacks in general, and black women in particular, wounded severely "at the place where language occurs,"[2] thereby hindering articulation of extremely painful experiences. Women writers, she said, feel the pain of this experience even more sharply, since what they say often becomes socially isolating for them and difficult to live with. Articulation draws attention to the articulator, and what becomes intensely alive in writing by being identified and named may conversely cause destruction for the writer in reality. For articulation is a struggle within and without. As examples, hooks spoke of many young women who abdicated their lives as writers at the very point when they were most intensely creative—Sylvia Plath, Anne Sexton, Lorraine Hansberry, Bessie Head and Zora Neale Hurston. hooks' assertion that writing is a very difficult and painful act of creation which has direct personal and political ramifications and is open to appropriation, misrepresentation and exploitation by being used out of context very significantly speaks of the women characters who use creative expression and language to articulate their selves and their lives in both Toni Morrison's and Leon Forrest's works.

For the purposes of this paper, my focus is restricted to Morrison's *Beloved* and Forrest's *The Bloodworth Orphans*. These works highlight African-American experience as being "orphaned" literally as well as metaphorically. Forrest's characters are real orphans abandoned by their parents by intention or by death (as in the case of Nathaniel Turner Witherspoon—the central consciousness of his novel). They agonize over their personal, unknown past as well as point to the parallel mythical story of Oedipus as a basis for a philosophical consideration of the difficulty of establishing knowledge of one's parentage. Morrison's characters are orphaned because of their experiences with the condition of slavery in their recent past where the slaveholders played with their lives as if they were pieces in a checkers' game, as Baby Suggs, the wise matriarch of the story thinks of it. Their orphaned condition necessitates self-invention in various ways. As writers, both Morrison and Forrest, therefore, address issues of self-invention, creativity, language, history and memory. Self-invention or definition is never possible in a social and cultural vacuum, hence both investigate a variety of resources available to their characters. Morrison's Sethe attempts to invent herself by decoding a lost language and culture she remembers very vaguely through a few images from the past when her mother and her caregiver, Nan, spoke an African language. Sethe is closer in time to the memory of her mother's Africa and is not entirely socialized into Christianity. Forrest's characters, clearly in limbo because they are inheritors of both African and European cultures, seek to name themselves through their mixed heritage. The role of Christianity is all powerful and dominating, at once enabling and inhibiting self-definition. Both try to find language(s) that will bear the burden of their characters' unique experiences.

As a woman writer, Morrison's ideas of her own creative processes are closely related to those of her women characters. On the other hand, Forrest, as a male writer, provides us with a close but outside view of the creative processes his female characters employ. Both, however, focus on the disrupted lives of African-American women and men in this country whose personal histories are often missing and/or painful and who re-invent themselves through various creative processes—whether language itself, or song. Both writers create "motherless" orphans, symbolically representing the historically violent displacement of African-Americans during slavery and through its attendant uprooting vices of miscegenation, separations and other forms of exploitation. Both writers testify to their characters' need for what Morrison has called in her interviews after *Beloved* "an enormous hunger for love" and desire for the sense of being worthy of love rather than hatred and abandonment. Both writers show their characters seeking love which has complicated physical, psychological and spiritual dimensions that blend together in intricate ways.

Beloved is the story of a daughter who returns to Sethe's house "124" as a grown up version or the "ghost" of her daughter she killed in order to save her from slavery. Not only is the ghost back to claim her share of love and security, she also has a role in the lives of the survivors in the house, Sethe and her other daughter Denver, by helping them cope with their difficult past and continue to live in the future. To think of a mother's killing of her child as an extreme form of motherlove replete with enormous guilt and pain is a remarkable statement in itself; to find the language to speak about the reappearance of this daughter in adult form as a necessary device of exorcism and the future survival of the family members without trivializing the subject at hand is even more remarkable. Morrison finds the language and brilliantly executes the task.

Our initial perception of Sethe and Denver's world clearly suggests a world locked in silence and isolation and inhabited by strange spirits. We learn that in the process of "beating back the past" which encroaches on the present, Sethe has decided to "just talk" rather than to pray, thereby seeking forms of articulation outside of organized religion and community (35). Sethe's talk is an intensely personal technique for survival. Her peculiar isolation from her own community is as much a result of her independent spirit as it is a result of the deliberate withdrawal of the community from her affairs. She has to learn through Paul D, Beloved, and Denver that she will need to emerge from this isolation and confront the past for future survival. With Paul D's arrival and a promise of a future together, Sethe's resolve to confront the past weakens, making Beloved's arrival almost necessary and appropriate.

Beloved's devouring passion for Sethe's company and her possessiveness is often re-created as an incestuous passion. Beloved is described as being unable to take "her eyes off Sethe." No matter what Sethe was doing she "was licked, tasted, eaten by Beloved's eyes" (57). Her all-consuming passion is destructive in its very realization and articulation. Yet there is something rather immensely complex in Beloved's single-minded pursuit of and claiming of Sethe's affection. She is devious, manipulative, sensuous, and even seductive with Paul D in order to gradually isolate Sethe into a state of total dependency on her. Beloved's language, Morrison has acknowledged in her interview with A.S. Byatt, was the hardest to work with. She endows her with language that is pure images and pictures with a sense of immediacy. The subject-object dichotomy is absent. Her perceptions are concrete, immediate and always present, a testimony to the ever present and disruptive nature of images from the past. These images one needs to acknowledge, interpret, and in some ways re-order so as to live. Stylistically, Morrison represents Beloved's language without punctuation to suggest her disruptive, unruly character. Beloved carries through her language the whole weight of African-American experience of the Middle Passage, and of the vulnerability of women to sexual exploitation and their yearning for love and security amidst so much dislocation. As such, her arrival amidst Sethe and Denver ties her to more than their specific past. Morrison attempts to compress in images what could take volumes to write (the horror of the middle passage, for instance). She demonstrates that the process of recovery is really the act of appropriating and manipulating language to suit one's unique situation and needs; ultimately, an attempt to live through language is pure pictures at first, but transforms to something more musical as the women find a language for their desire.

All the characters in *Beloved*, male and female, who have experienced slavery have realized that they needed "permission for desire" and if they could love anything they chose, then that was "freedom" (162). Sethe too, as a motherless child who tries to re-invent herself, needs to find a different language to do that. Sometimes she has to delve back into images that reappear in her mind at crucial moments in her life. These images are from a lost African culture that she needs to decode without access to the language. She remembers the people from "the time before Sweet Home" who sang and "danced the antelope." Sethe recalls, "They shifted shapes and became something other. Some unchained, demanding other whose feet knew her pulse better than she did" (31). This reference to the "other" as the point of location from which to view herself is also a reference to Sethe's affirmation of her self-worth and her desire to survive. The antelope, which is a significant religious symbol in some African tribal rituals, is a glimpse, however fleeting, into selfhood. It is the image of the antelope in relationship to Denver in her womb that pulls her through a difficult and brutal time when she is a runaway, and almost entirely hopeless.

Language in the form of images that return, get named and identified then provides the necessary will to survive. Sethe knows that the mind is a devious thing and very selective in its ability to remember. Although nothing from the past dies and anyone can imagine it, as Sethe believes, pictures from the past cannot be controlled. She remembers the location of her most humiliating experience, "Sweet Home," also as a place of beauty and life. "Boys hanging from the most beautiful sycamores in the world. It shamed her—remembering the wonderful soughing trees rather than the boys" (6). The very act of recovery of the past involves creation that is at once beautiful and terrible. If she focused only on the terrible, she would not be able to survive it.

Morrison's attempt to make the language do the work for her is especially evident in the chapter where language breaks all formal categories of expression and genre and attains a heightened and unique form of threnody where Denver, Sethe and Beloved feel their way through their lives together (215-17). Stylistically, Morrison represents the three voices intermingling a sense of yearning, love, and accusation in a togetherness which marks a complete circle, seeming closed and satisfying. Women needing and finding a "safe" place such as this closed circle to express themselves in without feeling threatened to restrict their self-expression and desire is also commensurate with what bell hooks spoke of in her lecture mentioned earlier. Their language of short assertive sentences, questions/answers collectively approximate poetry, harmony, and connectedness. Morrison also provides an outside, male perspective to this closed circle of voices through Stamp Paid, who hesitates, guilty yet proud, in front of Sethe's door as he tries to make sense of what he hears.

What he heard . . . (was) a conflagration of hasty voices—loud, urgent, all speaking at once so he could not make out what they were talking about or to whom. The speech wasn't nonsensical exactly, nor was it in tongues. But something was wrong with the order of the words and he could not describe or cipher it to save his life. All he could make out was the word *mine*. The rest of it stayed outside his mind's reach. (172)

The emphasis here on "mine" shows clearly that the women had finally expressed their desire for love, thereby also expressing their claim to be loved rather than simply be used, and that a sympathetic outsider, like Paid, had understood this. Morrison feels the need to deny the possible perception that the three women's language is irrational and nonsensical rather than affirming and relevant to self-recovery.

Language, then, has to be found to name Beloved's and Sethe's experience that in some ways symbolically represents the collective black experience of slavery (where considerable repression of humiliating experiences occurred) before Sethe can hope to survive. Sethe herself struggles with the fear of being abandoned by her mother, one of the reasons why she attempted to protect her own child by killing her and putting her beyond the suffering of this world. She finds out through Beloved's accusations about being abandoned that she couldn't save life by destroying it and its attendant suffering; that life is precious, no matter how problematic it is for the individual, thereby affirming the value of life.

Leon Forrest's *The Bloodworth Orphans* interweaves several narratives of African-American men and women who share a feature of experience—unknown origins or lack of parental presence in their lives. They fear eternal abandonment and are on a spiritual quest to find personal history and redemptive love through religion and music. Forrest's work appeals to the reader at multiple levels of meaning as he orchestrates the stories of different experiences in the contemporaneous urban setting of Forest County, drawing on the entire African-American experience in the South and its connections to world mythology (particularly Greek and Egyptian), thereby using a wide range of literary devices from both African-American and Western cultural traditions.

All of the characters have disrupted, difficult lives and even those who seem to be financially or professionally successful are emotionally insecure and yearn for knowledge of and connection with their past as much as with their fellow human beings. Forrest's central narrative consciousness is Nathaniel Turner Witherspoon, through whose eyes we perceive many lives. Because of Forrest's narrative focus on the development of Nathaniel Witherspoon, we are brought very close to the consciousness of women, but we remain aware of Nathaniel Witherspoon's presence as a filter through which we access the women's consciousness. Forrest uses direct speech reported through Witherspoon—sermons, spirituals, jazz, dreams, nightmares, fantasies, and visions—a wide variety of languages to help us understand the women in his narrative.

Women in *The Bloodworth Orphans* have a significant cultural role as mothers and bearers of cultural knowledge. The emphasis on the old spiritual "Sometimes I Feel Like A Motherless Child," with its evocation of dislocation and trauma of cultural and real separations through the experience of slavery, suggests their thematic importance. In three of Forrest's works, we see Nathaniel Witherspoon seeking stabilizing influences through many mother-like women he knows. They are storytellers with memory of the past and interpretive skills of historians, as seen in Sweetie Reed, his grandmother in *Two Wings to Veil My Face* (1983); they are women of intense spirituality and commitment who know suffering, as seen in Hattie Breedlove Wordlaw and Madge Ann Fishbond in *There Is a Tree More Ancient than Eden* (1973) or in Rachel Flowers, Bella-Lenore Boltwood and La Donna Scales in *The Bloodworth Orphans* (1977). Nathaniel Witherspoon does not know Aunty Foisty of *Two Wings* directly, but finds out about this wonderful, powerful, wise, ancestral, witch-like character through Sweetie Reed's narrative-giving testimony to the strength, love, and support he seeks from these women.

Forrest is also interested in the fatherless condition of his orphan characters, thereby poignantly locating the African-American experience in a liminal space—neither in Africa nor completely assimilated in America. This location is replete with endless problems. It is not freely suspended between two worlds as one might think. Nor does it allow its African-American residents real freedom to define their lives as they wish even though America has always been a place for many to start their lives over again. Social, cultural, and religious institutions of the dominating culture define the parameters of their lives in ways so that self-definition away from this language of domination is almost impossible.

Yet, Forrest's characters continuously search for means of self-invention. For them, language which is fraught with contradictions is often inadequate to express intense emotional experiences and yearnings. Approximating music is one way; yet even the best of the jazz players, Ironwood "Landlord" Rumble, finds safety only in an insane asylum. We hear Reverend Bass, who helps unravel the many genealogical mysteries, tell Amos Otis Thigpen: "Remember, now, Father Armstrong's words: 'You can say anything you want on a slide trombone, but you've got to be careful what you say with those words'" (154). The idea of being able to "say anything you want" in jazz improvisations somehow deceptively suggests that one will always know what one wants to say. As a matter of fact, memory often has to face stern repressive forces that make it very difficult to appear. Reverend Bass himself understood that.

. . . there are stories that no card, epistle or slanting memoir (world or heartbeat) can unburden or carry, the minister reflected. Bass's congregation never confessed these larger-than-life tragedies—not to him, in private, nor to anyone else, for that matter. If they were on the brink of utter chaos, they sought a great solace in the bottle. (146)

Bass finds that confessions only "tell everything apparently" and "only reveal a fragment of what really happened, amid the ceremoniously detailed telling of every evading discussion" (146). Morrison's *Beloved* is testimony to this same difficulty of evasive memory when Sethe tries to explain to Paul D her past act of attempting to kill her children to save them. Her narration becomes circuitous and she is frustrated at the realization that Paul D would have to understand it either instinctively or not at all. Forrest's use of language seems conscious of this difficulty and attempts to approximate the cascading and disrupting experiences with intensity and finesse. Descriptions of the blind Ironwood "Landlord" Rumble's one man jazz band improvisations in the insane asylum—Refuge Hospital—where he is institutionalized; portrayals of Rumble's own painful experiences through his music evoking a blues-like power to transcend pain by "finger-(ing) its jagged grain," as Ralph Ellison has defined the blues; and images of the rejuvenating or cleansing effects of his music on Nathaniel Witherspoon are testimony to the fact that Forrest also attempts to approximate Rumble's intensity through his style (78). It is pertinent here to quote an entire paragraph and a listener's response to Rumble to see the power of the prose that describes the music and its personal and collective significance:

Bathing, baptizing, purifying Sound into the shape of the softly jangling tambourine in his left hand—washed pure in the Cross—fretful, blissful innocence, lamblike on the skins of baying tide-tossed Sound, as the three bags of wool, winning-ballooning, kiting into nine circles, encompassing the voice of Styx and Niobe and now with bellowing steel-making resonance of a nine-pound hammer; lining track out the projected Soul, Ironwood flourished inside of an invisible moldering, of a stirring wakefulness, as the rib of Adam dancing into new singing shape riffed from his image-spieling, reshaped out of the valley of dry bones: humbled by the glorious harvest of her fire-scarred fingers upon the ladder fire escape, touching back into his essence . . . *a long way from home.*

　'Oh Lord, a motherless child, and a long ways from home—don't I know about it,' cried out Victory. (297)

Hence, it is the language of music—sound, voice, and rhythm creating fleeting images—that seems attractive and useful. Rumble obviously conveys his meaning through sound, riffs, repetition of key thematic phrases, and worrying of certain notes and so on very successfully. Women in this book don't have access to this language except perhaps Rachel, who uses her voice effectively.

　Rachel Rebecca Carpenter Flowers, the intensely religious, blind, but all-seeing Mother-Witness of the River Rock of Eden Church, often resorts to Biblical quotations and cliches; however, her intense character can only be captured through the effect her singing or evangelical preaching has on others. The quality of her voice is remarkable and influential. Sisters of her church jealously remark that she would use her voice "when she replaces Gabriel one day." Nathaniel recalls how listeners were both "petrified" and "awestruck" when Regal, her adopted son, and Rachel sang together: "As if the door indeed was open and a surreptitious voice was calling them on a delicate lyre, a voice along the grapevine from a cellar door leading back to the well of origins" (11). Another of his remarks establishes Rachel as at once strong and vulnerable:

He thought about Rachel's weeping countenance (God, what vision was she seeing then?) which reminded him of a fossilized vegetable with that wonderfully flowered, protuberance of a nose when she (with Regal) was captured wild in song-flight and soul-flowering ecstasy (her fingers intertwined with Regal's like a holy serpent of ancient times weaving about a tree) in her blindness upon the day of resurrection. (14)

Unlike Morrison's compression in stark sentences, Forrest captures complex experience that breaks boundaries of time and place in a language that cascades with a sweeping evangelical force filled with emotional urgency. The quote above is a long breathless sentence that gives us a glimpse at Rachel's emotional intensity, her old, withered, not-so-attractive facial characteristics juxtaposed to her ecstatic singing. Her posture of holding Regal's hand evokes at once their mutual desire for return to the Edenic past, foreshadows awareness of sin and the Fall, and suggests her acute consciousness of the burden and guilt of incest which causes her so much pain and makes her intensely desirous of redemptive love through self-sacrifice. Her good works and social commitments, her leadership role in the church and outside the black community, and her musical talent all help to give her the status of a saint or the elect in God's Kingdom. Christianity, which provides her an avenue for redemption, also gives her a language of scapegoating. She uses her husband, Money Czar's deterioration as a reminder to herself of the paradigm of Lucifer's life as well as her own holiness. Her intense suffering on the death bed where she struggles with her own pride testifies to her personal agony and guilt. Relinquishing hold on life becomes so difficult for her that as she strains to do her last penance, we as onlookers along with La Donna, Regal, Nathaniel and others wish her agony to stop.

Forrest writes here as though every sentence needs to urgently capture every facet of an individual or an experience. Language pours over boundaries with energy and force throughout the book and reminds one continually that the lives re-created in this book are chaotic rather than orderly. They cross many boundaries of kinship limits too, even if it is unwittingly at times—as in the case of the Regal Pettibone and La Donna Scales relationship. All this is a part of their donnee of life as African- Americans.

La Donna Scales is a good example of someone inescapably trapped in socio-cultural structures and relations. La Donna is also an orphan, brought up by nuns and placed in different foster homes. The ideas that dominate her existence are those of romantic love, physical beauty, guilt about her sexuality, fear of eternal abandonment, incest and visions of self-sacrifice as a means of redemption. The Catholic church, fairy tales (particularly those of Snow White and Cinderella), the Maypole, and the circus-carnival are some of the more prominent backdrops of her nightmare visions. She seeks answers for why she was abandoned by her parents in the first place and blames her birthmark on her temple as a sign of evil. She is said to be partial to Maypoles, which become her imaginary location for her sexual awakening as well as a contrary awakening to the horror of Original Sin. The Maypole also symbolizes her sense of being suspended and spun around endlessly through life with controls in the hands of "some invisible demon" (106).

Jesus, her Savior, and his representative, the church Father, become objects of intense spiritual and sexual desire. On the one hand she dreams of a life with her parents in an Edenic setting with no shame attached to physical love; on the other hand, she is horrified to find that it is a nun and a priest who have consummated their love physically. Here it is important to mention Marc Shell's study *The End of Kinship* where in the context of Shakespeare's *Measure for Measure* he has examined at length the challenges to the taboo of incest provided by "major religious and philosophical traditions of the West, which have sought, by practicing Universal Siblinghood, to transcend altogether the distinction between kin and nonkin, thus between chastity and incest" (4). Ideas of democracy and Christianity have all envisioned Universal Siblinghood, thereby raising the specter of incest without really addressing it.[3] For the church it is still very much a sin. The irony for La Donna is that she sees spiritual incest acted out in the physical consummation of love in her nightmare vision between the brother and sister in Christ, but does not see this as a contradiction within the philosophy of the church (although she is aware of the corruption in the church and is veering away from it). Ironically, this also becomes a foreshadowing of her own relationship to her "Brother-man" Regal who turns out to be her sibling. The torment of her spirit is marked by her loss of speech. She is said to wither up

into a curled state of smoking fury; her plagued voice, coming in gasps like blood clots. Her inner voice climbing, careening, ruptured, lost then found. Rasping and babbling and vomiting for days, fearing that even the bed she now slept upon was rotten, as the bed she had been con-

ceived in, born in, and now fouled in was the portrait of her abandoned, rockpile lot. (230)

Katie-Mae Gentry, with whom she lives after her incestuous relationship is revealed, tries to help her out of her condition by
saying that she didn't bring "new news into this world—Lawd
today," but La Donna cannot forgive herself.

She only gradually finds her voice like a babbling child; more
than that she goes to work for the dubious character W.W. Ford
who seems to be Satan himself and whom she has seen before
in the guises of the juggler in the circus-carnival and the syphilitic
nun who promises to transform her into a beautiful "lily-like milk-
maid" (123) as she struggles to get free from her Cinderella-like
role "down on all fours, by the fireplace" (121). These references
to fairy tales are also in the context of her trying to compete with
the mother/nun for the love and attention of the father/priest in
her visions. The fear she faces in this nightmare is that the priest
does not see her transformation and recognizes her only by the
color of her birthmark. La Donna's fear of invisibility is clearly
linked to her difference as a black woman in the white Catholic
world. All her nightmare images seem to come back full circle to
her own life because the language of her spiritual well-being she
has learned from the Church (which she says has given her
"direction" and "faith" as well as "a history, a myth, a mind") is
also the one that condemns her (113). Toni Morrison's narrative
comments about "romantic love" and "physical beauty" as "the
most destructive ideas in the history of human thought. Both originated in envy, thrived in insecurity, and ended in disillusion" gain
a clear significance in our understanding of La Donna's life as a
black woman (*The Bluest Eye* 97). La Donna's end is finally violent, but gives her tormented spirit a respite. She has envisioned
the Oedipus-like ritual sacrifice as "wrenching and affirming,
fruition-bearing and stigma-purging" often enough in her life to
think of herself as a sacrificial lamb whose life's meaning is in the
sacrifice (107). She cannot think of herself as worthy of love or
life.

She describes her first encounters with Ford in a diary, so we
learn about this form of expression she uses. However, for the
most part we only see her through her nightmares that mark a
circle around her and out of which she cannot escape. Her life
and Regal's end violently and tragically, re-creating fully the
myths of both Oedipus and Osiris. These mythical cycles that pro-

vide meaning to their lives are ironically the cause of their torment as well. It is life in cultural limbo that creates these horrors for them.

Bella Lenore Boltwood, another old, nurturing aunt to Nathaniel, was so haunted by the loss of her brother in the war that she was unable to develop any love relationship with any man all her life. She is another romanticist struggling with incestuous love and its attendant agony. She fed her fantasies with romantic stories of unrequited love by reading *Romeo and Juliet* and *Wuthering Heights*. When we see her for the first and the last time, she is found dying yearning to be loved. The language of her disarray is particularly poignant since all her sewing, her books and belongings that reflect her creativity are simply abandoned and strewn everywhere.

Two very different African-American writers, Toni Morrison and Leon Forrest, concerned about issues of self-invention, African-American history, and language find different linguistic avenues to articulate experiences that are enormously debilitating and disrupting. The language found for such expression threatens to break linguistic boundaries in ways the experience itself does social boundaries. Morrison's women learn to survive in language and affirm life in a closed circle of voices; Forrest's survive in song and acts of penitence that become important examples to his central Odysseus-like figure, Nathaniel Witherspoon. Women in *The Bloodworth Orphans* do not hope to survive in language in their specific reality as La Donna finds out that naming her reality simply provides turbulence and loss of words; but Sethe and Denver find language more empowering in *Beloved*. Both books end without complete closure and may be interpreted as reflecting some hope for women in *Beloved* and for the newfound baby in *The Bloodworth Orphans* and the compassionate caregivers Nathaniel and Noah, who have learned much about the painful experiences of foundlings. Yet, Forrest's *The Bloodworth Orphans*, by emphasizing mythic cycles and paradigms, leaves one with a greater sense of foreboding—that life will follow these heart-wrenching patterns eternally—than Morrison's *Beloved* does.

One cannot help but recall Morrison's observations on the difference in thinking between black male and female writers as a final thought in this discussion. In her article "A Slow Walk of Trees (As Grandmother Would Say) Hopeless (As Grandfather Would Say)," she explains from experience what she sees as the difference between the way black men and women think about their condition in this country. Both her grandfather and her father seemed to her to be pessimistic or cynical, whereas her grandmother and mother tended to maintain some faith in the improvement in black people's situation. Of her grandmother she says:

One sees signs of her vision and the fruits of her prophecy in spite of the dread-lock statistics. The trees *are* walking, (Morrison's metaphor for black progress) albeit slowly and quietly and without fanfare of a cross-country run. (160)

Of her grandfather, she believes that despite his pessimism he too would be glad to see some changes because, "After all, he did hold on to his violin" (164). Forrest's Nathaniel Witherspoon also seeks out Rumble's music as perhaps the one way to articulate the chaos around him. Morrison's Sethe and Denver instead seek the safety of their closed circle.

Notes

1. This is an unpublished poem titled "Speaking in Tongues" by Elaine Shelly, writer and performance artist now living in St. Paul, MN. "The Years In Between" are her journal writings recently published in Patricia Bell-Scott (ed.) *Life Notes* (New York: Norton, 1994).

2. bell hooks' lecture was held at the Walker Art Center at Minneapolis on October 8, 1991, as part of a lecture series titled "Word Power."

3. It is pertinent here to mention again briefly Marc Shell's study referred to in the paper as a good source of discussion of ideas picked up by nineteenth-century English Romanticists and French Republicans such as the Marquis de Sade regarding the notion of the Siblinghood of mankind and its effect on kinship boundaries and the issue of incest. If Christianity is located historically as a revolutionary ideology, its link with Romanticism becomes apparent. The contradiction within Romanticism, where on the one hand it challenges the taboo of incest and on the other hand condemns it, is reflected in the discussions that Coleridge had about his utopian society envisioned at the banks of the Susquehanna, but which was later abandoned. The philosophical problems thus located are even more problematic in the African- American community in Forrest's novel, since the orphans have been abandoned liter-

ally and metaphorically by their African and European parents to find "a way out of no way" and live with dignity.

Works Cited

Ellison, Ralph. "Richard Wright's Blues." *Shadow and Act.* New York: Vintage Books, 1972. 77-94.

Forrest, Leon. *The Bloodworth Orphans.* 1977. Chicago: Another Chicago Press, 1987.

——. *There Is a Tree More Ancient than Eden.* 1973. Chicago: Another Chicago Press, 1988.

——. *Two Wings to Veil My Face.* 1983. Chicago: Another Chicago Press, 1988.

hooks, bell. "Language and Resistance: Disrupting Words." Lecture Series. Walker Art Center. Minneapolis, 8 Oct. 1991.

Morrison, Toni. *Beloved.* New York: Alfred A. Knopf, 1987.

——. *The Bluest Eye.* 1970. New York: Washington Square Press, 1972.

——. Byatt, A.S. Interviewer. Writer's Talk Series. Roland Collection on Videotape.

——. "A Slow Walk of Trees (As Grandmother Would Say), Hopeless (As Grandfather Would Say)." *New York Times Magazine* 4 July 1976: 104ff.

Shell, Marc. *The End of Kinship.* Stanford: Stanford University Press, 1988.

Shelly, Elaine. "Speaking in Tongues." Unpublished poem, Feb. 1985.

The Flesh Made Word:
Family Narrative in
Two Wings to Veil My Face

Keith Byerman

Leon Forrest's first two novels, *There Is a Tree More Ancient Than Eden* (1973) and *The Bloodworth Orphans* (1977), have as their central figure Nathaniel Witherspoon, but they use him primarily as a vehicle for presenting the black community, both in the immediate and geographical sense and in the larger historical sense. *Two Wings to Veil My Face* (1983), the third of the Forest County works, focuses more directly on Nathaniel's personal and familial concerns. As in the earlier books, this character's consciousness is the means by which Forrest explores the complexity of the African-American experience; in this novel, however, that is done through the stories of the Witherspoon and Reed families. Moreover, story-telling itself becomes a central issue in the narrative. Readers are asked to consider the relationship of the teller to the truth of the tale, the possibility of truth itself when both speaker and listener have important interests at stake, and the relationship of gender to the narrative of family history.

In a sense, *Two Wings to Veil My Face* is a traditional patriarchal narrative. It is a quest for fathers, with an underlying assumption that the identification and understanding of fathers provides the key to the identities of the children. Thus, Sweetie Reed, the principal narrator, tells Nathaniel the stories of her father, I.V. Reed; her grandfather, the slaveholder Rollins Reed; and her husband and Nathaniel's grandfather, Jericho Witherspoon. She does this to make him understand her eccentric behavior the day of Jericho's funeral several years before the narrative's present time. Moreover, the story becomes Nathaniel's patrimony, told to him after he turns twenty-one and directly concerned with his spiritual and material heritage. In this sense, Forrest, though from Chicago, follows in the Southern tradition of William Faulkner and Robert Penn Warren both in tracing Southern patriarchy and in creating a complex pattern of story-telling that

problematizes history even as it records it. The past is not a finished product of agreed-upon data, but a struggle for coherence in a field of competing voices, of myths, of conflicting
facts, of divergent interests, of lacunae and silences, of distortion
and lies, and of prejudices, needs, and desires that constantly
shape and reshape the story. To this modernist narrative process,
Forrest adds the complicating factors of race and gender, not
merely as themes but as perspectives to be accommodated
within the telling.

The story that Sweetie tells Nathaniel appears to go far
beyond her declared purpose. She claims to want to explain to
him why, fourteen years before, she had refused to attend the
funeral of her estranged husband. Though they had been separated for many years, her refusal came as a shock to the family.
At the time of the telling, Sweetie is in her nineties and apparently
near death. She feels compelled not merely to relate the story
but to have Nathaniel record it in longhand. She rejects his offer
to tape-record it, demanding instead that he actively participate
by serving as amanuensis. In addition, she does not present any
immediate explanation for her behavior. Early in the narrative,
Nathaniel remembers the time of the funeral, but Sweetie does
not speak of it in terms of justification until some two hundred
pages later. Instead, she tells of a much earlier time when she
returned to the deathbed of her father to hear *his* explanation of
his behavior, both before and after her birth. Roughly half of the
novel is taken up with I.V.'s story of slavery and the immediate
post-bellum period. Only near the end and after considerable
prodding from Nathaniel does she explain that her separation
from Jericho was not only because of his lack of religious faith
but, more importantly, because her son Arthur (Nathaniel's father)
was in fact the product of a liaison between Jericho and another
woman. Thus, the completion of the quest deconstructs that very
patriarchal order that motivated it. The story of the father is the
story of the violation of law and morality. The characterization of
Jericho as heroic by both Arthur and Nathaniel throughout the
novel only strengthens the ironic force of the revelation.

The conclusion also serves, on the surface at least, to validate the telling of I.V. Reed's story. If the tale of Jericho Witherspoon is the narrative of a flawed hero, that of Reed is one of a
cringing anti-hero. Sweetie describes her father as one "*whose
body had been touched to the wishbone of the master; a
tongue flapped backwards and pressed to the sole of the foot-*

less shoe" (6). He slept under Rollins Reed's bed, even after the emancipation, so that he would always be available to meet the white man's needs. He was generally despised by the other slaves because of his obsequious nature. Thus, he seems to serve as the counterpoint to Jericho Witherspoon; they are a fictional version of the dichotomies so often found in black history: field/house slave, Booker T. Washington/W.E.B. Du Bois, Martin Luther King/Malcolm X, Ralph Ellison and James Baldwin/LeRoi Jones. Such a pairing suggests that Forrest is voicing his variation on a black "master narrative."

But I.V.'s story subverts such a narrative in both detail and structure. Sweetie clearly expresses her contempt for her father both because of specific actions and because of his character. And he himself expresses the self-interest motivating the tale:

Auntie Foisty told me before she passed, slaves would see me as a bloodhound all my days yet they would never tell on me—but would whisper my name in their heart of hearts and never trust me. The sole way I could ever hope for salvation was to tell the whole story out loud before I died to each of my children and each of their children's children unto my last dying gasp. . . . Me personal, not through any hired third hand, but by my very own lapping tongue. (139)

Confession becomes the means of salvation, though not through a priest or other religious authority, but through family history. The narrative, then, is sanctioned, not by law and patriarchal order, but by responsibility to the personal and familial past and future. Significantly, the authorizing figure is Aunt Foisty, who, as shall be seen, acts simultaneously as the representative of God and the black experience.

I.V. speaks to save himself; whether he in fact speaks the truth is constantly being brought into doubt by Sweetie, both as audience for his tale and teller of her own. She sarcastically refers to him as "honest Ivy," the name given him by the plantation owners. A key question, given her skepticism, is why she is so obsessed with his story. She has little interest in his salvation, since she seems to consider him doomed from the beginning. Despite this, she needs from him recognition:

I had not seen him since I left that plantation, twenty-four years before. Maybe I wanted to hear him say just simply *I tried to love you, Sweetie;* discover those old tongues of feeling, as a water-pump rod to the well water, covered and gutted by tons of leaves and old shoes, soles and tongues and lapsed life insurance policies, and free papers, discarded there as a refuse dump in the well of time and memory. But I thought those old tongues would fly up in his face as a plague of stinging bees if he ever opened himself up that much, I said in my spitefulness. Yet I knew his word would be a foundling lie, so maybe not even that; but to give me a portion of recognition as his child, that never sprang from his tongue while I was there. (45)

In effect, she seeks from a man of lies the truth of herself. Such desperate effort is necessary because her life has been one of negation. The defining experience of her childhood was the kidnapping of her and her mother by white men determined to enslave them even though the War had been over for several years. Rollins Reed and I.V. arrange a ransom payment, but only Sweetie is returned; Angelina had already been raped and murdered. The reuniting of father and daughter is in fact a profound separation:

And when that patroller man plunked me down on Rollins Reed's knee and you stood there looking down at me from behind that screen door and scratched on it when I lifted my arms out to you, up to you; and I wondered what does my daddy have to say to me with my arms lifted out to you. You kept on scratching on that screen door with your long fingernails as if to scratch out my eyes for an apology, reappearing in your life as the vision of your wife's life taken from you. Blaming me because you dared not blame them. And I wondered what was wrong with me that you did not want to take me up into your arms; you who had not seen me since I was four and they had taken me and your wife off to another slavery. (152)

Sweetie's perspective makes I.V. the patriarchal villain of the narrative of *her* suffering. And this coheres with her description of the violence inflicted on her mother and her own participation in burying Angelina with the aid of the other "slaves." Her emphasis is on what I.V. should do as father; because he fails to meet this standard, she is negated as his child and must define herself in part through her hatred of him. The story of racial violence is intensified by the episode of the black father's callousness. The narrative becomes one of the victimization of black women.

But the image of I.V. scratching on the screen opens up family history in a way that questions the message of Sweetie's tale. I.V. is as much a figure of suffering in that scene as his daughter if we see him in human rather than demonic terms. Sweetie is not only the returned loved one, but even more deeply the emblem of what I.V. has lost. She is a constant reminder of the loss of Angelina and a constant stimulus of the intolerable pain of that loss. What he seeks to scratch out is not the child but the pain; unfortunately for Sweetie the two are inseparable for her father.

Importantly, in his deathbed confession, he resists speaking of this moment that is in fact the whole story as far as Sweetie is concerned. In this refusal, he replicates her own narrative to Nathaniel years later. Both stories then have an absence at their centers; in fact, the narratives exist precisely as the avoidance on the part of the teller of the key element for the audience. They insist on telling the truth "slant," in the mode of indirection so often found in the African-American narrative tradition (See Byerman, 4-8; Levine, passim; and Mitchell-Kernan). What I.V. puts in the place of direct representation of that experience is the story of his own destiny; in the process he forces a reconsideration of the thesis of female victimization.

The central tale he tells seems only tangentially related to Sweetie's life. It occurs before she was born and involves people she never knew. It takes the form of a morality play in which an apparently minor act of spite is shown to have vast and fatal consequences. At the age of thirteen, I.V. becomes angry at Reece Shank Haywood, the plantation's black driver, because Haywood has taken I.V.'s girlfriend. In retaliation the boy tells the driver one night that Rollins is in the cabin of Jubell, a woman Haywood desires for himself. What I.V. hopes for is some impetuous act that would lead to a whipping for his rival. In this, I.V. plays the role of the Signifying Monkey, the folk figure who provokes trouble between others but remains safely outside the action himself. But Haywood, rather than merely confronting the master, tries to kill him. While I.V. has no love for Rollins, he had intended only conflict, not murder. To stop the killing, he slings a stone that strikes Haywood on the temple; he drops Rollins and runs away. I.V. resuscitates the master somewhat and drags him to the Praise Shack before seeking help from Aunt Foisty, the plantation conjure woman and healer.

The ambiguous meaning of this drama is revealed in the two directions the story now takes. On the one hand, Haywood's escape attempt ultimately fails because the stone I.V. used to stop his violence made him deaf and thus unable to hear and avoid the bloodhounds put on his trail. In this ironic version of a Biblical story, David tries to save Goliath by using his slingshot, but instead insures his death by the accuracy of his aim. Haywood is captured and punished by being given the "water cure" on the orders of the mistress Miss Sylvia. He dies from this torture. The interwoven tales of scripture and African-American oral tradition—David and the Signifying Monkey—produce a parable with the clear moral message that even small wrongful acts can produce dire consequences.

But the other direction the story takes subverts this homily. If Haywood is doomed by I.V.'s act, Rollins is saved by it. For after dragging him to the Praise Shack, I.V. seeks help, not from Sylvia, but from Foisty. This is partly from fear for himself, but also to give Haywood more time to escape. The result is that the master is profoundly changed by the ministrations of the conjure woman. This part of the narrative follows the form of the Pygmalian story, with, as shall be seen, important racial implications. The Rollins Reed who is carried into the shack is the archetype of the evil master:

My remembrance is back to when Master Reed was an unleashed bloodhound to his niggers. I recollect when he'd whip them soon up in the morning till nightfall can't stand moonlight's shadow; he'd shake down hot red peppers into their wound lashes; other times drop hot wax from candles into their bleeding sores and scabs, left there from the master's earlier lashes. . . . Love to go cutting after slave women. . . .— From the soles of his feet to the temple of his crown Rollins Reed was baptized in pure meanness and cruelty. (86)

Foisty acts to save this moral monster, not because she is a version of the stereotypical mammy who feels compelled to aid white folks, but precisely because the situation gives her the opportunity to change the nature of power on the plantation. She brings him back from the verge of death, but in the process seeks to cleanse him of his evil nature. "Come down to me as I peeked in on her the last day—Auntie Foisty making herself a man" (126). The man she makes is one within her power:

Sur-ren-der to me, Sur-ren-der to Him. . . . He is you Rock! I am you Rock! Sur-ren-der to the Rock, the Cross, the Lad-der. He you Rock, Roddy. I you Sur-ren-der. . . . Give It Up! Sur-ren-der. . . . Angel got two wings to fly

you a-way. . . . See the chariot, feel the fire, know the suffering. . . . Sur-
ren-der to the Rock, Roddy. (126)

The equation of herself with God is a self-authorizing act that
inverts the traditional plantation pattern. Normally it is the master
who creates the slave—designating a role, naming, holding the
power of life and death—in part on the basis on religious authority. The slave woman here invokes the divine patriarch in order to
subvert Rollins' patriarchal position. In doing so, she raises herself
to the position of author and creator.

Her authority as a maker of men is not merely self- pro-
claimed. She is in fact both the embodiment and the keeper of
black history. She came over on a slave ship and, according to
I.V., was midwife to half the slaves on the plantation as well as
wetnurse for both Rollins and his father. Moreover, she is the true
memory of all their experiences:

Then, too, Auntie Foisty's mind seems to get sharper, more supple,
deeper with each fork-turning in the long woods of her days; so much
so, Master Rollins himself bends to her for recollecting 'bout the rightness
of Old Master's records on the crop books unto the peculiar weather
bend of each stripped-down branch and blade of grass of the seasons,
what his pappy, Old Man Rollins Reed, kept fifty-odd years before, in the
beginning time. Those books partly burned in a fire, so who do they turn
on, Auntie Foisty, who can't read or write; even asking her what each
slave was sold for, hour, day and year of the auction. Most of the time
she ain't for sure about the money part of it; but knows where each and
every one of 'em was sold off to. *So here she is called on to correct
them books*, where the fire burnt off the face of the blue-black ink to
curling ash, or give the justice to the pages and the ledger where the
sheets burnt out. But seasons, crops and slaves she remembers whole;
when each slave was sold out this plantation; when they come into this
world and how they went out: backwards or forwards. (111-12; emphasis
added)

Foisty's power is human history; her memory supersedes the
white written word. She recalls not what is most important to the
master—the monetary side of the ledger—but the human side
which the numbers effectively erase. She knows, not the puta-
tively neutral record of the ink marks, but the human traces
behind those marks. She knows *how* slaves died rather than just
when. She knows the story *whole*, instead of merely its economic

significance. Moreover, as the repeated emphasis on burning suggests, whites have in fact made themselves vulnerable by reliance on the written word. The story of their mastery is dependent on black oral history, on the memory of one who both is and tells of the flesh in the word, the human suffering that is the truth of slavery.

Thus, when Foisty speaks to Rollins in the Praise Shack, when she tells him that he has brought "woe" to the slaves, there is no denying her. She baptizes him in mud, urging his conversion each time she lowers him into the grave-like hole and draws him up again. The allusions to Biblical creation—the mud, the six-day process—imply the profound evil of the slave master. It took God the same time to create the entire universe as for Foisty, who identifies with the Creator, to make a decent man out of a slave holder. The end result is mixed. Rollins acknowledges his evil past, the power of Foisty, and the need for greater humanity toward blacks, but he retains the title and role of master. One crucial twist to the narrative is Foisty's demand that I.V. become Rollins' personal servant and sleep beneath his bed. While she intends this as I.V.'s punishment for what happened, she also wishes to provide Rollins a constant reminder of the experience he has been through. Thus, she who defines the past also shapes the future. Further, she pushes her influence into later generations by compelling I.V. to pass his story down to his children and grandchildren.

This command guarantees that he himself will be read by Sweetie and, in the present time of the narrative, by Nathaniel, as the villain of the Reed-Witherspoon saga. But he seeks to counter this interpretation and thus disrupt the simple text that Sweetie wishes to create. He reminds Sweetie repeatedly that he is her father and Rollins her grandfather and that her own faith requires a degree of respect for him; moreover, such paternity means that part of what she is came from them.

Nathaniel, I guess that's when I could see the evil of spite-work upon not only I.V. Reed's soul, but how it had come to transform my soul whenever I was away from my church and my God. I thought upon I.V. Reed's presence in my life or faced the shadow of his life, upon my very life, across it, me his only blood, marking he had ever existed. (153)

She is the trace of his being beyond his mortal life, but he is her connection with the past, with that sense of family she so deeply desires. He has survived all those more powerful or more honorable than himself: Rollins, Sylvia, Reece, Foisty, Angelina. This in itself suggests to Sweetie a puzzle of history:

For when I thought about it I.V. Reed was the only one who had survived this place, from the old days, the beginning time, though the plantation itself seemed about to collapse upon him. Maybe it had something to do with a combination as mysterious as a conjurer's mix of *his* stubbornness and *his* willfulness on the one hand...and his terribleness of bending to anything, as a branch in a windstorm; all made manifest by his reverence for the master's will and his silver supper tin, while licking the platter—to suck it down as an odd way of conquering, and conjuring. (156)

Such insight does not keep Sweetie from reading I.V. Reed as demonic; she persists in calling him a liar and child of Satan though she needs his story for her meaning. Even when he reveals the tragic fact that the stone he flung both saved and doomed Reece and that this circumstance has literally haunted him since then, she still verbally assaults him. She only stops when he comes to her part in the narrative.

This episode comes to the very heart of the story she tells Nathaniel, for it is the introduction of Jericho Witherspoon into the Reed family history. This is part of the history she thought she knew, the part that begins her explanation for her attitude toward her husband. She had always assumed that, for reasons unclear to her, Witherspoon and her father and grandfather (Rollins) had arranged her marriage. What I.V. explains is that it was Jericho who paid her ransom, though he thought he was purchasing Angelina's freedom. Sweetie is offered to him, though she is forty years younger, when he learns that Angelina was murdered. Thus, Sweetie is doubly negated; she was freed with money intended for her mother, and she is married as a surrogate for Angelina. The three men against whom she has defined her life—Rollins, I.V., Jericho—in fact are the ones that made her life possible. Her father's narrative reshapes the meaning of her existence. The story she had constructed placed her heroically in the center against male antagonists whom she both demonized and monumentalized. The history she learns is of her own insignificance except as a signifier of her mother's absence. She was not valued or scorned for herself, but because she was the trace of Angelina. The mother is the center of the tale, but her role decenters rather than affirms the place of the daughter. Sweetie's meaning then is a lack rather than a fullness; in place of the morality play that had been her life, she now has a human tragedy in which she was merely an understudy. All of the men acted out of love rather than hate or disdain, but it was not love of her. She is the sign of loss rather than desire. She becomes, in effect, one of the orphans so common to Forrest's fiction.

The story that Nathaniel has been waiting for ultimately brings the notion of orphanhood full circle. Just as Sweetie is deprived by I.V.'s narrative of her place in family history, so Nathaniel has his taken by Sweetie. One function of the structure of the text now becomes clear. Sweetie's narration of her father's story and her own alternates with Nathaniel's memories of his childhood, including his grandfather's death and funeral and his father's responses to both Sweetie and Jericho. Just as she demonizes I.V. in her voicing of his experience, so Nathaniel, through his own and his father's memories, monumentalizes Jericho. Arthur says, "'No one can call this man down, to heel; who carried our hopes and outrages upon his shoulders, as the natural garment of his burdens, for over a century; not to speak of the seal of history upon his branded back'" (197). Nathaniel himself thinks of Jericho as a king (29).

The effect of Sweetie's tale, like that of I.V., is to demystify those made extrahuman by their descendants. Sweetie begins the process by apparently confirming Jericho's strength:

And though he was very good to me, I was a child in his eyes, partially because I was a woman and partially because I was in fact a child bride, though that was nothing unusual, I had never had a proper growing up. So he educated me. I became the child we seemed not to be able to keep alive. But I was dissatisfied, I wanted to do something with the mind I was developing and he wanted me to have his child and see it grow up, though he drew pleasure transforming me into a brilliant student of his teachings. I was as the mustard seed before his mighty sun. (263)

She offers another Pygmalian tale, this one a more classical transformation than the story of Foisty and Rollins. Here an ignorant girl is made into an articulate woman; the imagery of adult-child and seed-sun suggests the natural and beneficent effects of this patriarchal relationship.

But in the very process of affirming Jericho's power, Sweetie questions it. The training of her mind creates a desire to use it for purposes of her own. Her husband seems to see her education as a constructive way to bide time until she enters her proper role as mother to his heir, but it creates in her a desire for self-expression. Despite his "pleasure" in the cultivation of her mind, she remains for him largely a nullity as a person, just as she was for I.V. She observes that the inability to produce a healthy child was assumed by him and the community to be her failing, not his. Her social-welfare work, her devotion to education, and her morality counted for nothing next to her "deficiency" in maternity. Her turn to religion and deep commitment to God can be seen as a quest for empowerment in circumstances which suppressed any authentic self-realization.

The secret of the text goes to the heart of patriarchal power. Sweetie reveals to Nathaniel that his father was illegitimate. Because Jericho requires an heir in order to perpetuate himself and because Sweetie cannot produce one, he goes outside the marriage to find a woman who can meet this need. When the child is two months old, he brings it to Sweetie to raise as his son. She is torn between desire to protect a motherless child and shame and anger at her husband's behavior. She is again the displaced woman, and this time she is old enough to be aware of the public humiliation the situation creates for her. She offers to allow Jericho and the baby to stay "until other arrangements are made," but the husband-father refuses to negotiate. The man who carries the literal brand of slavery on his back, risked his life for freedom, and purchased hers will not compromise: "'Sweetie, if I stayed, that would simply be a call to your spite-work. I would never know an hour of peace and solitude. I'll not allow you to bargain over my freedom'" (282).

But of course he is perfectly willing to bargain Sweetie's. He exercises the patriarchal prerogative of imposing a role and burden on her while he evades confrontation with her moral indignation. The acquisition of an heir transcends moral boundaries; his freedom has expanded from the right to control his own life to controlling those of others. In this context the advice of Lovelady Breedlove, Sweetie's friend and spiritual advisor, seems curiously like that of accommodating slaves such as I.V.:

"But, Miz Love, this is too much."
"Ain't nothing too much. . . . You suppose to hold on and ask for more, more burden. You holding on to the kitchen (where they provide food for the poor), helping out in a wonderful way, but that's for them what drops in."

"But isn't that enough?"

"Not if more is your portion; then that kitchen ain't but a molehill to a mountain." (283)

Faith requires accepting whatever portion is given; the point is to see it as possibility rather than misery. Such an attitude in effect validates the patriarchal perspective. Men act according to rules that benefit themselves; women must bear the cost of such behavior. Jericho in this instance seems to fall in that line going back to Rollins and I.V. that makes orphans of children.

Lovelady's reference to the kitchen, however, suggests in fact the possibility contained in the condition of loss. If the patriarchs paradoxically generate orphanhood in their pursuit of family lines, then it is up to the women and children to nurture and embrace each other. The kitchen set up by Lovelady and inherited by Sweetie provides for all the motherless (and fatherless) children, of whatever age. Lovelady and Sweetie required of all the "guests" that they leave as payment whatever they could, and, if they had nothing, to "make a mark of it when you get home on your own books":

Often nothing at all was left; but Sweetie Reed's remarks were intended to assist the dignity and the challenge to try and not accept charity. It occurred to him (Nathaniel) now that the charity of the kitchen and the insistence upon a gift from the guests was to set up a counter-weight relationship, so that eventually the kitchen would no longer exist but the idea of charity at both ends would remain within the scope and vision of living no matter where you found them, and no matter who you might be. (281)

What the kitchen creates is a new kind of family, in which the dignity of the individual is intimately tied to responsibilities to the group. "Counter-weight" implies the balancing and sharing of power rather than the hierarchal structure that allows Jericho to compel Sweetie to accept the baby and then to leave. Everyone in the kitchen is recognized as needy—as a motherless child—and as giving. Sweetie points out to Nathaniel that such an arrangement is essential for human dignity,

because it seems like it's such a hard thing for one person to give to the brethren without feeling sorry for that soul to a point of despising him or her for their poverty of bread, meat of knowledge, and particularly thinking that somewhere down deep in the castaway (runaway Jerry made me aware of this) that there is something lacking in that lost soul, fundamentally. (281)

Unlike Jericho, who demands something specific (a baby) from his wife in exchange for her life, Lovelady and Sweetie accept whatever can be offered and thus can give the "lost soul" a measure of freedom as well as dignity.

It is in this light that the one additional voice of the text must be read. On the surface, it too seems to validate a modified patriarchy since it is the words of a father seeking control over his daughters. It seems an apparent contradiction of I.V.'s indifference to the child Sweetie in an assertion of the fatherly role. But the letter of Wayland Woods, a runaway slave serving in the Union army, in fact repudiates the established order. Having left a fugitive, he promises his return as an avenging angel. His anger is directed, not merely at Rollins as the master, but at Sylvia as well for her self-righteous assumption of superiority as a slaveholder. His address to "the Dearest Mistress Sylvia" parodies social convention:

I remembers rite well Mistress Sylvia your breathing lips as pouting hot coals spatting heat up from hell as licking tongues and backing it all off with a soul sweet as a dove-cooing voice at the redeeming fount. Master Satan is your soul mate and you is Master Satan's soul property unto the shadow of winging down Death. . . . You may hum them hymns of over the sea in a warm quail, but spite is the lead voice in the Sabbath song of your cold-blooded, jack 'o lantern face for a soul. (287)

He signifies on the idea of mastery by making her the mistress of evil rather than divine authority. He renames her out of his experience, reversing the process of verbal control. He claims for himself, as Foisty did, divine authority for his words and actions and in the process inverts the structure of power:

But be of one true faith, scarecrow woman, bout your faithfulness servant Wayland Woods, if it cost me the breath of my soul, I'll purchase my daughters out the bondage-pit of slavery's blood—not with silver or gold—but with a swoop and a grasp with the last leap of my blood and raising up of the sword and breath as wings to the morning. Here my hand be lift to this Almighty God given to me by your words and Him to strike down by your words and hand, eyes, and feet, hipbone and tongues, and backbone, specially as sword to dove's tender-bride's neck. (287)

He rejects the notion of human beings as property; his daughters will not be gotten with money. Rather, he plays on the word "purchase" to turn it from a monetary to a religious meaning. He will take hold of them in his role as protective angel, while in the same action making the slaveholders "pay" for their evil. Like Foisty, he claims for himself a dual role as embodiment of mercy *and* justice. He seeks not to possess but to free the enslaved; he seeks not to displace but to destroy the enslaver.

If Sylvia represents to him the patriarchal order's view of persons as property, Rollins represents its claims of *seigneur droit*. Woods requires evidence that his daughters have not been violated by the master, not because, as their father, he wishes to maintain their exchange value, but rather because the protection of their virginity denies the owner his claims of full mastery. Moreover, he trusts the word of his own wife and not that of Rollins in ascertaining the truth of the matter. Woods again plays with language to create an inversion of roles:

For be it known this high noon I'm gonna have my woman peak my daughters loins to see and if they ain't yet virgins down to a natchile bloody cloth—then know its the wrong tyme of month for you by the moonlight's set to masking up a jack muh lanterns smile over your natchile grave, if them gals ain't still virgins by lanterns. If your hands trembling with these words set down by me and Yankees and my words to them so they know how to write in a proper-tongue way, then think how many messages I've sit down to my daughters in blue-black ink and if they ain't receive them all don't mean a second I ain't rite even more in my hart of harts. These daughters they be my bond and my balm. (288)

Woods asserts not only the power of his language to intimidate Rollins and instruct his own wife and daughters, but he also uses it to invert gender roles. It will be the "wrong tyme of the month" for the master if he is found to have violated the girls. He, rather than women, must be concerned with the power of the moon. He must hope for the evidence of menstrual flow; if that "natchile" blood does not come, he will be in his "natchile" grave. Female blood is both sign and ink that will write Rollins's fate. Masculine authority must submit itself to female truth.

Woods reshapes the notion of mastery as well by his play with the word "bond." While he had used it earlier to refer to slavery, in this passage it takes on a more affirmative quality. His family is his tie to the plantation; they "bond" him to it in his desire to restore and create a natural order of blood rather than power. Moreover, the bodies of his daughters are the source of his promise (his "bond") that he will return. Their flesh is his word. Unlike Rollins, who enslaves his daughter Angelina, and I.V., who binds Sweetie into self-abnegation, and Jericho, who views the absence of a child as a broken promise between husband and wife, Wayland Woods' bond is both a "balm" and a liberation. His claim to his daughters is that of a free man, who desires neither exploitation nor domination; he wishes only to protect and nurture them in cooperation with their mother.

It is noteworthy that Woods' message is written in more than one hand. This statement of freedom, dignity, and family is itself the product of cooperation between profoundly different men. Sweetie says of the white Yankee soldier who assisted Woods:

And how this letter, shaped by more than one hand, could give me some revealing power to stay me in my lostness . . . even as it was also scrawled out by one who no doubt laughed in the misspellings even as he was swept up, no doubt, in the courageous outrage of this riddle of a freedom-driven man before him, because of the learning he as slave had received from the mistress who damned him. (290; ellipses in original)

The motherless sons of war come together to create the text of black family, a text which both deconstructs the patriarchal order of slavery and generates the family of black freedom. Both writers are essential to the creation of such a text. The Yankee gives it its "proper-tongue" structure necessary for an address to a white audience. But Woods' semiliterate expression gives it authenticity; his diction and style leave no doubt that these are his words and his beliefs. The veracity of the letter lies precisely in the irony of his gaining partial literacy from the woman he repudiates through his words.

Nathaniel thinks again that he has arrived at a still center of moral certainty. Here is a black truth that cannot be compromised. But Sweetie again disrupts his monumentalizing by reminding him both that "destruction is part of the redemption" (291) and that his own history lay elsewhere. It is not Wayland Woods,

Aunt Foisty, or Shank Haywood that Nathaniel must accept, but rather I.V. Reed and Lucasta Jones, his biological grandmother. If he is going to acknowledge Sweetie's role in his life, which he wishes to do, then, she insists, he must acknowledge I.V. And if he is going to face the truth of family history, then he must face Lucasta. So Sweetie offers him his inheritance: in her safe, he finds a tintype of Lucasta and, hidden in I.V.'s shoes, diamonds that belonged to Sylvia. The sign of patriarchal order—inheritance—is embodied here by emblems of illegitimacy and orphanhood. Nathaniel is the doubly illegitimate heir to the diamonds: they come through Rollins' illegitimate daughter Angelina to Jericho's bastard's son. Lucasta, of course, is one source of that bastardy.

It is an inheritance fraught with ambiguity. The diamonds were originally bought with wealth obtained from brutal slave labor, but they now financially liberate one of the families originally enslaved. Nathaniel sees in the tintype not only his biological grandmother but also the image of the saintly Angelina and finally that of his own dead mother. His reading of the visual text disrupts not only his notions of good and evil, but also those of Sweetie. She persists in hating Lucasta even as she compels Nathaniel to accept her. She had told her story in part to get from him sympathy for her years of emotional logic, but instead he performs for her the troubling function she saw as her own:

I do love the truth of Justice, no matter where the beacon's taper light falls, Mother Sweetie Witherspoon Reed. . . . But can you recognize Lucasta from Angelina? Oh, you never lied, most sacred liar prophetess. I do. I do love within my/our loathsome inheritance. . . . But do I only love the enlightened cause of Justice? Oh no way out but to burn out the alabaster blight of this blindness; oh, light of the body is luminously of the eye. . . . No two wings to hide the riddled features upon my fated American face. (294; ellipses in original)

The end is not resolution but the tension and conflict that love generates. The polyglossic tale that is black history is not necessarily harmonious, but neither is it easily dichotomous. To insist on either is to descend into sentimentality and self-righteousness. Lucasta and Angelina, I.V. and Wayland Woods have their part in the story, and they cannot be reduced to each other nor tidily divided into absolutes. Each has a voice, irreducible and articulate. Sweetie Reed's telling of their tales does not turn them into a monologue. Each voice demands to be heard; she and then Nathaniel resist their speaking, but cannot finally silence it. The truth is not in resolution, but in the multiplicity of voices. All the orphans produced by all the different fathers (who are themselves motherless) have gifts to bring and stories to tell. Nathaniel's true inheritance then is not some tidy patrimony but all the voices in the wind of all the mothers and fathers. And his gift to them is the recording of their words; he creates, in effect, their testament. They made him an orphan; he gives them a family history.

Sermons, Testifying, and Prayers: Looking Beneath the Wings in Leon Forrest's *Two Wings to Veil My Face*

Danille Taylor-Guthrie

Leon Forrest's *Two Wings to Veil My Face* is an incantatory novel which derives its rhythms from the powerful oral traditions of African-American spiritual life. In this novel the young man Nathaniel Turner Witherspoon comes to understand the words of his grandfather, Jericho Witherspoon, "trouble, remember, and reveal." Like Ralph Ellison's Invisible Man, the young hero is haunted by his grandfather's words of advice. Jericho Witherspoon's advice differs from that given by the Invisible Man's grandfather, advice to mask and use trickery. Jericho, however, counsels that one must know oneself or become one's own worse enemy. These forefathers born in slavery perceived the battlegrounds of life differently and therefore passed on different strategies for survival. The character Jericho is more like a Biblical patriarch living to be one hundred and seventeen years old, and anointing not his son Arthur, but his grandson Nathaniel. Jericho is not the only grandparent who has something to bequeath to Nathaniel. The matriarch Sweetie Reed, his grandmother, is a prophetess who possesses the history and stories he must confront to go beyond revealing to believing; a belief in and acceptance of self no matter what the ties of bloodlines are.

Though the narrative of the novel is not action-orientated, the power of ritual and performance propel the novel as Nathaniel, the protagonist, listens to the stories of Sweetie Reed, his grandmother. Thus, within an oral tradition similar to that of a griot, Nathaniel must transcribe his family's history and hence in part make it his own in what becomes a ritualistic process where he is transformed into full manhood.

Two Wings opens with Nathaniel, now twenty-one, having been called to his grandmother's bedside. While listening to Sweetie Reed fourteen years after the death of his grandfather,

Jericho Witherspoon, he remembers time spent listening to Jericho read to him from his journal. The dichotomy between the oral, Sweetie's stories, and the written, Jericho's pages, is established early here. Sweetie has chosen to clarify several things that have always mystified him: why she would not attend officially Jericho's funeral and why she stopped using her married name, Witherspoon. She reveals the intimacies and complexities of her life so that he might better understand his own. Nathaniel is a man without direction and commitment, something of which his grandparents had plenty; Sweetie is a helper and feeder of the needy, and Jericho is a man of action and law. The revelations of the past are troubling for Nathaniel, especially the tales of his great-grandfather I.V. Reed. I.V. is a trickster who deceived Aunt Foisty into reviving their slavemaster, Rollins Reed, yet he helped Jericho escape from slavery. He is a devoted body servant, yet he retains the sounds of Africa. I.V. is the link between conterminous and autonomous African-American slave and Euro-American slave-holding cultures. The other significant ancestor that Sweetie tells Nathaniel about is her mother, Angelina Reed. Angelina is the child of Rollins Reed and the slave woman Jubell whose rape Reece Haywood tried to avenge. There are many other colorful characters in the novel, ranging from relatives to undertakers and from preachers to heroic slaves. Their names provide symbolic access to their roles and meaning in the larger text. Characterization provides a richness and color, and frequently humor to the novel. This is a story of currents of experiences in which Nathaniel must learn to swim or drown. He must write himself into being, as a man of the flesh and of the spirit, understanding the past in order to have a future.

Two Wings to Veil My Face expresses the author's own belief in the artistry of African-American survival in the "Babylon" of America. Jericho and Sweetie are ex-slaves who knew intimately the "beginning times," the "backwaters" of time. These are the dark days of slavery. This is the book of Genesis for the people known as African-Americans and it is this legacy, this story, that they both must give to Nathaniel. They cannot pass their inheritance on to Arthur, Nathaniel's father and Jericho's son, because he is of the generation after slavery which wanted to forget the old times, and not "trouble the waters" of memory. It was not important to Arthur and his peers that they keep alive memories of the past because the past was still living in the generation of their parents. Arthur and his ilk attempted to establish a false kingdom in a dream world, a Camelot, whose values would not be molded upon the experiences of the past.

The lessons of life that Nathaniel learned from his father, Arthur, and from his Uncle Hampton and Aunt Genevieve were as illusionary as the magic of Merlin Spotswood, the free black magician of old. Uncle Hampton advised him to only marry a woman he cared for, not loved. This is the kind of advice one might get from the lyrics of a blues song or jazz rendition where the vulnerable heart of a man must be protected behind the bravado of control and "coolness." His Aunt Genevieve would recite to him tales of her days as a madam in a whorehouse of madness in New Orleans, whereas the bookish Arthur would never broach the subject of male sexuality or intimacy with his son. All three believed that experience was the best teacher. Their lives of lovelessness, debauchery and illness would ensure genocide if repeated. Arthur's alcoholism manifests his weakness. His body recorded every nuance of his life and emotions, but he did not "believe" in the power of the spiritual; therefore he could not heal his body or rest his soul. He would satisfy his physical cravings with a "sugar tit" but would not face the curse his diabetes symbolized. Nathaniel is about to fall victim to the same malady, as his engagement to Candy Cummings reveals. Candy is a superficial progressive at best, who is unworthy of receiving the mantle of the fighting foremothers she hopes will be bestowed upon her at Sweetie's bedside (altar and stage). She is unable to sing their music and has delegated the spirit songs to the quaintness of folk music. It is Sweetie who saves Nathaniel, though she is unable to save his father. Arthur's unhealthy condition, that she is only able to feed and not cure, reflects her prideful charity as Jericho calls it. Charity must be more than nourishment; it should feed *and* trouble so that her "guests" may carry on the fight—her bread must strengthen, not poison. Thus Nathaniel's memories of his grandmother are filled with the smells of food that had fed him well, but now she takes Jericho's advice to heart and troubles the "backwaters" to turn him into the "spiritual" revolutionary of his namesake.

Sweetie Reed's lessons for living are not easy to understand or accept for either Nathaniel or herself. She waits until he is twenty-one to "school" him. This is only one set of the sevens that amplify throughout the novel. Sweetie witnessed her mother's rape and murder, and was returned to her father when she was seven years old. Nathaniel is seven when his grandfather Jericho dies and is told by Sweetie upon reaching his "majority" she would explain all to him. Sweetie is seventy-seven years old when her husband Jericho dies, and he in turn is one hundred and seventeen years old. Jericho was born in 1827, a slave and child of his white master. In African-American folk-beliefs the number seven is an important prime number which is empowered with magical properties. To be the seventh son of a seventh son connoted a particularly powerful ability to have second sight or be a conjure man. The seventh son makes an excellent doctor and has the ability to see spirits.[1] In *Two Wings* this is the "second" mind that is repeatedly mentioned, a spiritual (for good or evil) voice that speaks to the conscious mind. Jericho, as Rev. Browne testifies, has his own prophetic vision of African-American life.

Forrest filters these and other folk beliefs through his imagination and incorporates them into his literary style. His goal is not only to capture the rhythms of African-American oral culture but to infuse these sounds with folk and intellectual traditions of African-American culture. Thus, his fiction is operatic. The ideas and emotions of a people are "staged," and meaning is conveyed via drama. A sense of ritual and performance are thus fused in the novel. They become vehicles for reflexive moments, as Victor Turner would define them, where the culture, and thus potentially the reader, becomes fully conscious of itself.[2] Nathaniel is a liminal character whose rite of passage through the chaotic tunnel of history we follow.

One important aspect of the cultural context from which the ideas and aesthetics of the novel are derived is African-American spiritual culture. This culture is multidimensional, not being merely one denomination, religion or even one set of folk beliefs. In this folk system it is believed that the world is infused with spirituality to which those with special gifts have access and can see/read. The spiritual condition of a person is often more important than physical health. Sweetie is forever saying, "one must get right on the inside before you can be right on the outside." These beliefs derive from a syncretized African culture whose "waters run deep," and which still operates as a matrix within African-American life. African metaphysics combined with Christian rituals and theology are central here. But African-American Christian beliefs are not monolithic. Nathaniel is exposed to Catholicism by his mother's people—the Du Ponts—and Protestantism by his father's side: "Nathaniel has a rosary, a High-John the Conqueror leaf and a prayer cloth Sister Rachel Flowers had given him" in his pocket.³ Nathaniel encounters many of the formal and informal traditions that have become part of the African-American arsenal for survival. Forrest even utilizes the impact of Islam, not only as a twentieth century phenomena but also evoking memories of those Africans who were Muslim before they came to America, as documented by Alex Haley with his forefather Kunte Kinte.

Rituals have the power to renew and transform. Specifically, the ritual of communion with the priestly traditions of the Catholic church reverberates throughout the book. The wafer, as the flesh of Jesus Christ, is echoed in Sweetie as a baker of bread who offers it in an attempt to nourish poor blacks physically and spiritually. It is to her altar that she beckons Nathaniel, the same altar she was unable to make Jericho kneel at until *after* his death. Sweetie does not stoically mumble blessings as she dispenses bread; she can preach, too, and when she does, no one can stop her—not Arthur, the wounded king and her son, nor Rev. C.J. Browne, the powerful and dramatic minister, nor Raven Memphis Snow, the undertaker and ferryman of the living to the land of the dead. Communion, however, is a reciprocal act of sharing and fellowship. Sweetie gives lessons and food, yet her guests are expected to give whatever they can in return. When Nathaniel and Sweetie drink from the same cup, a new fellowship has been established at the end of the novel: "Now Nathaniel touched his lips to the cup of Remy Martin, doused over the sassafras leaves; it was bitter to his palate, but his throat was dry as a hollow cough . . ." (267). Nathaniel now believes, swallowing the bitter history told by Sweetie, and he can then move from marginality to responsible manhood.

Baptism, the "outward sign of inward grace,"⁴ is the other significant ritual used repeatedly. Baptism ritualistically washes away sin to reconnect and initiate a person into the community of faith. Without baptism one can not take communion. Water as a symbol of cleansing, renewal and death is powerfully used by Forrest. Sweetie brings these elements together in her sermon at Jericho's funeral. She defines what baptism means to her: "But now I was saying to him: 'This very moment of the bathing of sorrow and baptism must be sewed to the drowning and the dunking of the body so as you come up against it again; that your body is being washed away in the waters broadcast, away into the tide'" (210). Sweetie had never been able to convince Jericho that he should submit himself to Jesus the Christ thereby acknowledging him as his "Lord and Master." Sweetie, in her revelations about her encounter with Jericho in death, describes being surrounded by water while she baths and anoints his body. Sweetie believes that baptism is more than a mere cleansing. It is an immersion up to the precipice of self annihilation. It is easy to understand why Jericho, who had himself been a slave in the house of his blood relatives, would find it difficult to submit to another master. Jericho does not understand how he can leave his body and self behind, but to Sweetie these waters also have the potential to bestow life and are the same waters from which life evolves. All must pass through the waters to be born, and then pass back through them in death.

As they struggle to live, characters are referred to as swimmers and often there are casualties. As they sink beneath the waters, their bodies are lost to the living; but if one throws the clothes of the drowned man into the river they will clothe his soul (213). Thus, it is ironic that, for Sweetie, spiritual rebirth is an experience close to death. Whether souls live or die or make the necessary transformation is based on faith and submission. Forrest reinforces this idea by repeatedly referring to sleeves, be they full of holes, silk or those of a straight jacket. These characters are frequently described as being lost in the wilderness where the type of sleeve they wear reflects the state of their souls. Thus, Jericho and Sweetie are totally naked as they wrestle and baptize each other. When they are free of the sleeves of their worldly concerns and points of contention, they can be born again in a state of harmony that allows them to finally be the bride and groom of the spirit and of the flesh.

Layered on top of these ideas are the images and stories of the Hebrews found in the Old Testament. I.V. Reed is a David figure when he fells the stronger Reece Hayward. He is also a musician and poet like King David who frequently felt persecuted. Other Biblical images are connected directly to Jericho. Jericho's name is not derived form a Biblical hero but from a place, the city of the first victory of the Hebrews in the land of Canaan after they had wandered in the wilderness for forty years. Canaan was the promised land in the covenant between the Hebrews and God. Arthur and Sweetie are territorial in their battle over Jericho as if he were a thing to be possessed. In addition, Jericho is unlike the patriarch Abraham, being more like Issac, his son, in two respects. First, Issac trustingly follows his father to the top of the mountain where Abraham has been instructed to offer the boy up as a sacrifice to God. God intervenes before the sacrifice is made, being pleased by Abraham's obedience and faith. Jericho, in turn, is called by his father, his white slave-master, and is not rescued from his sacrifice to the false faith of inferiority and obedience by blacks, held by the slaveholding South. He is branded with the initials J.W. on his left shoulder so that he will never forget his station in life: to always be a slave. It is this journey to the mountain top that makes Jericho deter-mined to prove his father wrong. He escapes from slavery despite rewards offered by his uncle. Jericho lived a successful life as a judge and leader of his race but had no heirs until the age of seventy-eight. And secondly, he, like Issac, bestows his blessings not on his first born but on his "Short Ribs," Nathaniel, his grand-son. Like Issac, Jericho loved meat, his favorite being goat. Nathaniel would ritualistically serve him platters of goat. These times are fondly remembered by Nathaniel, who recollects serv-ing his grandfather and reading from his journal. Jericho's journal was his holy book in which could be found the testimony of his life. At other times Jericho would raise Nathaniel high on his shoulders, above the limits of gravity and society. Nathaniel agreed with his grandmother's description of Jericho as "a wizard, a worker, and a warrior" (192). When Sweetie first met him after arriving north, he seemed to be her "savior."

African-American spirituality is complex with many forms of expression: preaching, praying and testifying. These forms are brought to Nathaniel's conscious mind as he sits beside his ninety-one-year old grandmother who recounts history within states of religious revelry as she rises and falls in and out of con-sciousness. His own memories are filled with the testimonies of Sweetie to the wonders worked by God witnessed in her life. There are also prayers, the most significant being Nathaniel's own at the end of the novel when he is forced to reconcile history with his knowledge and experience. The sermons of Rev. Pompey C.J. Browne, on the other hand, are very theatrical, grounded in the performance tradition of the culture. Browne's sermons include not only call and response patterns between speaker and audience but are staged. At an Easter service Browne and his other performers (ushers, choir and deacons) wear costumes in what might be termed religious theater. Browne goes so far as to transform himself into the resurrected "character" Jesus in a drama where he becomes god. This is a corruption, using the transformative powers of the sermon for self aggrandizement and show. There is further elaboration of the dark side of secularized spirituality in the novel and in the character I.V. Reed.

I.V. Reed is Nathaniel's great-grandfather and Sweetie's father. He is a trickster whose relationship to his slavemaster, Rollins Reed, is diabolical in contrast to Sweetie's ties with the Master of her soul, Jesus. His story begins with his confession on his deathbed to his daughter. I.V. is seventy-nine, the same age of Rollins at his death. The year is 1904, Sweetie is thirty-nine, and it has been twenty-four years since she has last seen her father when he and Rollins sent her north to marry Jericho. Both father and grandfather participated in the "sale" of Sweetie to Jericho.

I.V. is not a father nor great-grandfather one can readily be proud of. But I.V. is the father and patriarch of their lineage which both Sweetie and Nathaniel must understand and accept. He is part of the dark portion of their "beginning times." I.V. is like an i.v., intravenous tube, which can nourish, medicate or poison the body. He plays the mouth harp, from which he creates the Pan-like music of his impish character. These are his reeds. Reeds have historical importance in African-American music. I.V. always sits up in the trees when he plays for slave gatherings and thus an association with a "Bird" (Charlie Parker's nickname) might be made. Parker made the music fly, but he was also plagued by a heroin addiction, ingested intravenously. The paradoxical way that death and poisoning can co-exist or result in life and creativity is implicit in the I.V. character and the institution of slavery.

I.V.'s slavery entailed his being the servant to the body of Rollins Reed. Rollins orphaned, beat and salted I.V.'s wounds, forcing him to keep his eyes not on the sparrow but on his gleaming shoes he polished relentlessly. Their surface could reflect one's image; thus, when Rollins and I.V. gazed into them, they saw the refracted reflection of their own faces. Rollins possessed a masquerade mask that had a black face on one side and a white on the other, and when he would dance twirling to the music, they blended together into a black/white whole. This blending of identities signifies the psychological dependence on I.V. in Rollins. I.V.'s wings having been clipped early by Rollins, he is never able to soar above his bondage. Salted birds do not fly.

I.V. was not a totally isolated character; his musical talents made him acceptable to both the white and black communities. For field slaves, he was a repository of the old sounds and rhythms of African culture. He would play at their gatherings perched in a tree, enhancing the music's ethereal qualities. He would also play for them music he learned from white culture and transform it for his black audience. In turn, he would take the sounds and dances of African-American culture back to his white audiences. I.V. possessed perfect pitch and could imitate any sound, yet he was more than a mimic for he would imprint his own style on any performance in true artistic form, thereby creating a new aesthetics that bridged both cultures. I.V. (ivy) could be a clinging parasite attached to a host as he was to Rollins, and yet he could be the wily trickster whose actions could result in good or bad. An encounter with I.V. places one at the crossroads unsure of which road to take. The wrong choice for Nathaniel could make him very much like his great-grandfather who led a life of deceit and cowardice.

Sweetie only remembers I.V. as a vine attached to Rollins. Even their feet were the same size; consequently, I.V. wore Rollins' cast off shoes. Sweetie did not know that there was another body that had shaped her father—Aunt Foisty, the African midwife, healer and converted Christian. It was her curse upon him that made him sleep under Rollins' bed and wear his shoes. This curse was his punishment for the death of the slave-driver Reece Shank Haywood. Sweetie learns about these events as she sits by her father's deathbed. His confession is constantly interrupted by Sweetie until it turns into a dialogue. This conversation becomes a stylized ritual of name calling and mutual damnation; they sound like riffs between competing instruments on a bandstand. I.V. is a formidable talker more experienced in the verbal arts, and he "blows" Sweetie off the bandstand, regaining control of his story. This is difficult for Sweetie because she is seeking truth—her real history—while he feels no compunction about magnifying the past through his imagination. The entire process is maddening for Sweetie, who must discern the truth as best she can.

I.V.'s power to deceive others with his silvery tongue is legendary. Reece and Foisty were both taken in by him. Reece did not perceive I.V.'s jealousy and vengeful motivation when I.V. told him that Rollins was "blackbirding" with his woman, Jubell. Rollins' "blackbirding" is the raping of his slave women to satisfy his sexual appetite and assert his dominance over slave men. Thus the concept of rape and it's connection to Nathaniel, male sexuality, and the "truth" is rendered in several ways in the novel. Nathaniel never has rape explained to him by his parents, but he overhears an account of an African-American woman's rape and murder, which was witnessed by her husband, and perpetrated by a group of whites. The husband likewise is murdered. This horrendous crime ignites Nathaniel's imagination and only Sweetie will give him any factual information to ground him. Sweetie gives him the context to understand that this is a crime of violence and an assertion of power as whites assault the woman in front of her stripped down husband. Because he is unable to protect or rescue her, the violations are compounded in their nightmarish qualities. Perhaps Nathaniel's parents are unwilling to talk about this because they harbor the fear that at any time they to could become victims. Nathaniel, the child, is also made aware of the fact that this is a crime that is committed by males on females and sometimes even males. Though the act of this violation is committed on the body and soul of a woman, its effects are felt also in the psyche of their men: husbands, fathers, brothers and sons.

Nathaniel finds as he grows up that black men interact callously with women. Uncle Hampton freely advises him never to marry the woman *he* loves. Would the pain of witnessing the rape of his wife be less if she were not the wife of his heart? What does it mean to be an African-American male if one can not protect one's woman from the most base assaults and in turn have her witness his castration? The church offers the message of chastity which he finds useless. He learns no wisdom from his father while his peers are forever encouraging him to seduce as many women as possible. Nathaniel himself is "raped" when "friends" put a listening device in his car, brutally intruding into what should be a private and intimate moment with his girlfriend. When he does not "perform" up to their standards of male sexual exploitive prowess, they ridicule and mock him; his manliness is questioned. He is forced to stay off the "scene" for quite a while, unable to live down the reputation of being a talker and not a doer. Nathaniel seeks a mental as well as a physical marriage, not easy to come by in this life, having only been achieved by his grandparents in the troubled waters of death.

I.V. is haunted by Jubell's rape and Reece's murder for the remainder of his life. Reece attempted to defend Jubell despite the consequences. Even though he is a slave-driver, there is a limit to his complicity in the institution of slavery. He will not be a slave at the cost of his manhood. It is Reece's spontaneous urge to avenge and protect an African-American woman that makes him a hero in the slave community. He should have been

Angelina's father. While Reece sought to protect Jubell, I.V. acts to protect Rollins. He feels responsible for the Reece attack because of the various "roots" or spells he attempted to "fix" on Rollins. In trying to kill Rollins, I.V. has unleashed forces that have the potential to boomerang on him. The most powerful hex he attempted was when he encased Rollins' shoeprint within a shell sealed by wax and then buried it by the river. Upon going back to look for it, he discovered the shell had been smashed as if a whirlwind, the voice of God, had seized it. He thought the spell had not worked, but unknown to him the agent sent to carry out his wishes is Reece. Reece has choked Rollins to the point where he appears more dead than alive. I.V. rescues him with a sling-shot like the young David. I.V., despite all the pain and humiliation he has been made to suffer because of Rollins, can not imagine his life without him. His bonds are mental, the most complete form of slavery, and he is therefore unable to seize freedom when it presents itself. Neither Jubell's rape nor that of any other slave woman, including Angelina, is worth risking his life for.

Not only does I.V. rescue Rollins but he deceives Foisty into healing him. Foisty is another of Forrest's memorable characters. She is an African who remembers the middle passage and a time before slavery. The story of her arrival to America makes her a figure of respect and fear for both blacks and whites:

Then I remember one of the stories 'bout Auntie Foisty, up from the white folks, how she was so powerful cunning and touched. She cut a trap-door in the hole of slave ship on the way over with her long nails, sealed it back up with her lips so as no one could tell and then outswam the sharks, the slavers and Satan—but thought she was on her way back to Africa—when low and behold if she ain't delivered up in a storm to the arms of a missionary off the coast of Virginia, who saw her terrible vision in the face of a huge, smooth-faced rock, while out fishing; thought she was a bastard angel, whose wings got shattered by a streak of lightening—its light brought low as one of them lost, shooting stars, from worlds, eyeballs beyond this one. (124-25)

She is a direct link between two continents; and though she converts to Christianity, it is interwoven with her traditional belief system. Foisty, ignorant of Jubell's rape and the wounding of Reece, sets out to make a different kind of white man. In the Praise Shack, Foisty works on Rollins for six days, reshaping and molding not only his body but his soul as well. She mixes concoctions and recites incantations to make him a less harsh master and she succeeds in this. Any humanity he displays from that point in time on is attributed to Foisty's hand. She encases him in clay, birthing him from the earth. She is not merely healing Rollins but literally reaching into the bowels of hell to bring Rollins' body back—but she is not a god, so his spirit is lost. Rollins is one of the walking dead, a soulless man. And it is to a similar state of soul-lessness that Foisty condemns I.V. to. He must not only sleep beneath the bed of his master, but he must also wear his shoes. Sweetie accuses her father of being heartless in his relationship with her, and she is correct because he is heartless (deadmen have no hearts) and soulless.

I.V. denies he is incapable of love, asserting his undying love for Angelina. Angelina was the living proof of Rollins' crime against Jubell. I.V. and Sylvia Reed, Rollins' wife, are co-conspirators of Rollins. Sylvia's symbols are the mirrors and diamonds she surrounds herself with. She constantly gazes upon her reflection in seven mirrors, especially when she is dressing for her masquerade balls. These mirrors are dangerous because they distort one's self-perceptions and have the capacity to steal one's soul. Not only is Angelina confused by these weapons of deception, but Sweetie is nearly killed by them when the mirrors fall on her and shatter like diamonds. Sweetie loses her hearing in the accident, like Reece, which makes her wonder if she is not the heir to Foisty's curse on I.V. However, Sylvia is a witch in her own right. She attempted to poison Foisty and exerted her power by killing Reece with the water-cure. Foisty births, Sylvia kills. Sweetie's deafness is more the result of Sylvia's witchcraft than Foisty's root-work.

Sylvia ignores Rollins' transgressions, being content to embrace her diamonds, the sign of their wealth. She converts to such tangible objects derived from the labor of slaves and from their sale, even those that are Rollins' children. Yet, rather than sell Angelina and add her to the stockpile of diamonds, she decides to mold and play with her like a doll. Angelina, though beautiful and free of the drudgery and sweat of fieldwork, is a victim of slavery's mental tortures. Yet she truly is an "angel" in the beauty of her form and spirit. Though schooled by Sylvia in letters and manners, she remakes this knowledge and grows in grace beyond her teacher. She is wedded to the despicable I.V., who tries to keep her isolated from other slaves, but she feels a deep loyalty and commitment to them, and does all that is in her power to assist them. She is forced to live with her father without his open acknowledgement of his paternity until he has lost all of his material goods and is left with only this evidence of the darkest side of his life. Sweetie believes deeply in the power of the divine to recreate goodness from evil of which her mother is living proof. She knew her mother's beauty and loved her deeply. Angelina was the one who gave her the most enduring lessons in survival, not her father, I.V., nor her husband, Jericho. Again I.V. is witness to a rape and murder, and again he fails to accept his responsibility. He blames Sweetie for her mother's death and failure to return to him. She was a wife he coveted for sexual pleasure, not accepting the fact of fatherhood which logically follows sexual activity. To him her pregnancies had nothing to do with him other than denying him access to her body. If I.V. had created a home for his wife and child, as a husband should, they would never have been kidnapped by the patrollers and Angelina subsequently slain.

The rituals of baptism, confession and communion, along with the social realities of rape, love and identity, are interwoven throughout this novel in the stories that seem to Nathaniel to be mythic in the amplifications of the imagination, or legendary in their historical dimensions. The sermons of *Two Wings*, however, pull together the concepts of sacred and profane within the sphere of African-American cultural expressive forms. Two sermons are presented side by side at the funeral of Jericho, one by Rev. Pompey C.J. Browne and the other by Sweetie. Long before this incident Sweetie had ceased being a member of any church, nor was she preaching in public. She was disillusioned with the organized church's concern with materialism and its corruption of sacred rituals. For her the church, illustrated by the Easter service in Rev. Browne's church, had become too theatrical. However, Rev. Browne's sermon at Jericho's funeral does not contain any theatrics. Both sermons eulogize Jericho but in two different ways, reflecting the differences between public versus private performance. African-American dance and music have been part of American public performance where the distinctiveness and resourcefulness of this culture have been exposed. However, as part of American popular culture, they have been denigrated as illustrated in the ugly contours of the minstrel tradition. The church and its rituals have housed African-American "public-private" performances. The first churches were held in the "hush arbors" hidden away from the eyes and ears of any white audience. As these gatherings became more formal they were housed in "praise shacks" where African-American Christianity was born. There praises could be shouted to the Lord in celebrations that were public to a black audience but unknown to whites. Their very existence was illegal, but slaves' faith made them unfearful of white laws or punishments, for they obeyed Divine Law. Camp meetings and revivals where evangelical ministers preached to mixed audiences were where the practice of African-American religious celebration became more public. Sweetie believes that these more public forums of worship have been corrupted by avarice and a new focus on performance as entertainment instead of praise. When the African-American church moved into their own edifices, some of this pollution was still evident. This move did, however, protect the public rituals of baptism, marriage and death from hostile eyes, making them private again. Ironically, Sweetie's sermon goes beyond the private decorum of private-public behavior, unveiling the hot intimacy of her faith in Jesus and love for Jericho. The gawkers are removed from the church by Memphis Snow the undertaker.

Rev. Browne delivers a eulogy that addresses the heroic and noble image of the public man, Jericho Witherspoon. The Rev. Browne sometimes seems to be the epitome of corruption and decadence in the black church. His name is an example of the absurd classical names, in this instance a Roman general and politician, frequently given slaves as a joke—"a nigger joke" as Morrison puts it in *Sula*. His service at Easter is closer to a James Brown performance than a religious observance. He is resurrected not as Christ, J.C., but like J.B., who in a seeming fit of exhaustion is covered by a cape only to throw it aside in a renewed outburst of energy. This act could be judged, as Sweetie does, as profaning the sacred; but it is also evidence of the thin line that exists between the scared and secular in African-American culture—The Blues/Gospel dialectic where ecstasy, confession and rebirth are taken from the confines of sacred private space to public theater and in this case returned to the church infused and there remolded into forever changing modes and forms of African-American interpretation of the Holy.

Rev. Browne's Jericho sermon begins with a testimony to the lessons his grandmother Browne taught him; how she had lived a life of subterfuge, cooking in the big house in return for a black schoolhouse; how she understood the dangers of the education provided for African-Americans by whites who sought to lock them into lives of ignorance and servitude. She did not believe in the divinity of the word as given to her by her master, and she taught her pupils the truth beneath the veil of color in an old abandoned outhouse. Like Mother Browne, Jericho knew never to show his complete hand to Euro-American society. If his own uncle and father could not be trusted, then how could strangers? All he need do was to touch his back to feel the scars of this lesson. Jericho specifically taught Rev. Browne to be wary of the idolatry of materialism that possesses the soul of America:

My beloved mourners, when that happens to us, Jericho Witherspoon taught me, then we have become stone cold dead in the market-place. Learn not to nourish your souls, nor incorporate your spirits in symbols of quicksand, as the very visage of God's manifest to mankind, reflected in stone polluted and corrupted soul as those ancients who thought they worshipped God's house when they worshipped the sun in reverence. . . . But, mourners, you are backing right up to the auction block; feeling up the chains that bind and declaring, in the chambers of our blindness: Lock me up, with or without a gravestone for dead to the heart in the chamber door of idolatry. But rather do something about human existence, within the society of man's convict ways; strip the foreskin of your heart, look deeply into the mirroring images there, as you accuse your neighbor of desiring the worldly goods of your chamber door. Do something about human existence, Jericho Witherspoon preached; don't mirror God to God just because He made you in His image; He wants more out of you than simply a carbon copy. And so, in this context, I believe that Jericho Witherspoon's spirit must be rekindled in the darkness. (187-88)

Rev. Browne has learned well from his male and female progenitors and should be taken seriously. His sermon ends with the sounds of music melding with the language of his speech to convey the spirit of his message.

An analysis of the sermon highlights ideas and features that exist in the novel. One aspect of Forrest's style is to repeat an idea or word again and again, playing variations on their meaning which amplify the reader's understanding of larger issues. The reader must soar bird-like as if one were listening to a jazz solo in a large orchestrated work. Browne lambastes his people's worship of material things and castigates them for having lost sight of more substantial values. Jericho taught him, and he in turn must instruct others. Cars are not the mustard seeds that Jesus sought to sow, nor will they serve as their chariots to heaven. They will not be able to clean up their souls with vacuum cleaners nor wash them in a machine. God does not speak through a radio, and his brilliance makes diamonds pale in comparison. No drug or incantation can be as powerful or fulfilling as the Word of God. Fancy furs will not hide an impoverished spirit. When African-Americans become idol worshippers, then they are slaves again. The diamonds and lessons of a Sylvia Reed cause blindness and bondage of the spirit such as I.V. suffered from, making him chained to his white master's spirit. Jericho calls for African-Americans to make a new covenant not with the scars of blood-letting (circumcision) but made with the heart and sealed in actions. God does not want seven images distorting his image back to him. Such reflecting is immobilizing. It is a self absorption that is deadly. God would not have given humans free will and imagination if he had wanted "carbon copies" of himself. Rev. Browne wants all to remember Jericho as a lighthouse guiding those lost in the darkness.

Sweetie's sermon, on the other hand, is more intimate but it confirms the message of Rev. Browne. She unveils the hidden, divulges the proximity of the dead to the living in an African ontological system. Nathaniel fuses the Christian with the African after the unraveling of Sweetie's narrative. He shares communion with his grandmother, throwing him to the "threshing floor" where he must pass from his liminal state to the community of belief. Belief in the past without which he can make no future.

The circle of the novel is closed in a final ritual which is not normally associated with religion—writing. Nathaniel has been instructed to write out in long hand, with blue-black ink, on legal pad, what Sweetie narrates to him. Writing and texts have always been important to him but he has up to this point been unclear how this interest can become a vocation. Journalism's superficial reporting of facts was uninspirational, especially when compared to the texts of Jericho's journal and the Bible he read so often as a child. The year is 1958 when the Civil Rights movement is moving on its own momentum, thrusting a new generation of leaders in more revolutionary directions. Will Nathaniel have a role to play?

The epistle of Wayland Woods gives him the final direction and hope he needs. This letter reveals the power of the written word, and the possibilities of love and courage that African-Americans possess. The historical models of how to be a husband

and father available to him are not only I.V. Reed but also slave-men like Shorty George, who was willing to face death to be reunited with his black love. Wayland's letter gives the articulation of African-American manhood a literary voice. His letter to the Reeds protects his family still held in servitude. Nathaniel converts to the possibilities of strength and goodness in the past despite the treachery and violence that exists there, too. His present and future can be one where the body and soul can be nourished and co-exist harmoniously. He is the heir to both his grandparents as a doer—he will write. Nathaniel in *Two Wings to Veil My Face* travels the backwaters of time and survives; he successfully passes into manhood. His safe passage has assured his spiritual and physical selves, affirming the male and female dichotomies of himself and life. He is thus reborn as a man capable of loving, dying, and most important, living for what he believes.

Notes

1. Newbell Puckett, *Folk Beliefs of the Southern Negro* (Montclair, N.J.: Patterson Smith, 1968).

2. Victor Turner, "Are There Universals of Performance in Myth, Ritual and Drama?" *By Means of Performance*, ed. Richard Schechner & Willa Appel (New York: Cambridge University Press, 1990) 9.

3. Leon Forrest, *Two Wings to Veil My Face* (Chicago: Another Chicago Press, 1988) 132.

4. *Dictionary of the Bible*, ed. James Hastings. revised ed., Frederick Grant & H.H. Rowley (New York: Charles Scribner's, 1963) 87.

Earthly Thoughts on *Divine Days*

John G. Cawelti

Only the man with chaos within him can give birth to a dancing star. . . .
  Nietzsche, as quoted in *There Is a Tree More Ancient Than Eden*

   Leon Forrest's novel, *Divine Days,* was published in the Spring
of 1992. It was his fourth novel and both a considerable departure from, and, to use one of Forrest's own favorite terms and
themes, a *reinvention* of his previous work. It is much longer than
his first three novels and has a very different range of episodes
and characters, but it is also a "reinvention" of Forest county[1]
and presents new insights into a variety of characters who have
appeared in earlier Forrest novels. Its central figure, the aspiring
young dramatist Joubert Antoine Jones is similar in many ways to
Nathaniel Witherspoon, the protagonist of Forrest's first three
novels, but he is also significantly different in his character, in his
life situation, and in the ways Forrest uses him as a narrator. He is,
for one thing, much more sophisticated, reflective and self-aware
than Nathaniel. In form, *Divine Days* is also very different from the
earlier works. *There Is a Tree* was a highly lyrical and experimental
novel in which Forrest used several different kinds of internal
monologue to represent the complex layers of consciousness—
individual, cultural, and historical—which flow through Nathaniel
Witherspoon's mind. The novel centered around key events in
Nathaniel's life, but it also delved into more dreamlike and visionary realms of consciousness, recreating Nathaniel's cultural and
spiritual heritage as a young African-American male. *The Bloodworth Orphans* made Nathaniel a witness and participant in the
tragic story of the black descendants of the Southern white
Bloodworth family, while in *Two Wings to Veil My Face,* Nathaniel
became even more a character to whom stories of the past
were told. Here he is not so much a witness as a scribe, writing
down his grandmother Sweetie Reed's account of her life and
that of her slave father as she remembers his telling it to her. In
Bloodworth the internal monologues and visionary-dream land-

233

scapes of *There Is a Tree* are replaced by a brilliant use of the sermon and analogues to other African-American forms such as that of the jazz improvisation as well as a complex use of mythical archetypes which reflect the heights and depths of the African-American experience, and tie this great historical tragedy to some of the most profound myths of Western Civilization, particularly those of Oedipus, Orpheus and Osiris. *Two Wings* adds to this a use of historical, documentary and folklore materials to evoke the world of the Southern slave plantation.

In *Divine Days*, Forrest creates a novelistic form which, through the creation of a more complexly self-reflective central character, develops a greater philosophical depth and awareness.

Divine Days represents a specific week and a day in the life of Joubert Antoine Jones, from Wednesday February 16 to Wednesday February 23, 1966. These days are presented to us in 15 different sections headed with specific days and times and narrated by Joubert. This week is a turning point in Joubert's life. He is twenty-nine and has just returned to Forest County after a stint in the army, where, like Forrest himself, he served in Germany as a public information specialist. Now he must put his life back together after this time away from Forest County.

Joubert, like so many of Forrest's characters, is an orphan, whose father and mother have been killed in separate accidents, one in a car and the other in a plane. He also comes from a richly cultivated and intellectual background. Since his mother's death, Joubert has been virtually raised by his aunt Eloise, who had married his father and then, after his death remarried a man named Hickles. A remarkably lively, witty and determined women, Aunt Eloise combines a career as a journalist—she writes a widely-read and influential column for the *Forest County Dispatch*—with the operation of a liquor store and bar, *Eloise's Night Light Lounge*. She is a very well-educated and sophisticated woman whose columns are "an amalgam of Noel Coward, Langston Hughes, Claudia Cassidy, and Alberta Hunter."[3] She also has a profoundly maternal feeling for Joubert whom she views as her own "Baby Bear" not quite ready to launch out into the world on his own. She supports Joubert's aspirations as a writer, but is trying to steer him toward a career as a successful journalist, though Joubert's real desire is to become a dramatist.

On his return from the army, Aunt Eloise wants Joubert to live at home, and work at *Eloise's Night Light Lounge* while he furthers his journalistic career by free-lancing for the *Dispatch*. One of Joubert's problems is how to detach himself from the overpowering influence of Aunt Eloise without bringing deep hurt to the person he is closest to.

Aunt Eloise comes from a highly talented Creole family, the Tobiases, whose ups and downs and whose quirky legacies are one of the important secondary elements of the novel. She is "quite an expert on the layered cultural life that composes the New Orleans' heritage. . . . Her cottage up at the Pier is overstuffed: a non-heavenly mini-mansion made of hands and 'surceased in a surfeit of curtains, sorrow, and shit,' as she whispered to me this morning, shortly before I went to bed, at 2:00, after too much Moet Champagne and not enough of her famous variation on Creole Oysters Omelette." Yet in spite of her dedication to material things Aunt Eloise has a serious spiritual side: "She desires a spiritual glow to her existence—but she wants it all on her own terms" and is also quite knowledgeable about contemporary literature, loving to quote from Frost and Yeats on appropriate occasions.

Joubert, himself, has finished high school and has, before his departure for the army, taken some college courses and become involved with various people at the university. He has directed and acted in several plays and has written some himself, most importantly a play based on his brief acquaintance with one W.A.D. Ford, a notorious preacher and cult leader. Joubert completed this play during his first year in the army and sent it to a producer, but it has mysteriously disappeared. Above all, Joubert is characterized by an obsessive and almost visionary ability to hear voices:

I have an awful memory for faces, but an excellent one for voices. . . . I'm too hypersensitively attuned to the sound of voices, babblings, otherworldly and worldly tongues. I never forget the nuances of sounds within voices. . . . The plague of inner voices so riddled me—because you see I have no control over those moments when those voices, or a specific voice might hit me. . . . For when a voice hits me, I'm like a man caught up in a shooting gallery.

In addition to his formal education, Joubert has encountered the African-American oral legacy in the tales and verbal games he has encountered on the streets, especially in the precincts of the local barbershop where, during his early teens, he shined shoes to make a little extra money. Here he becomes a kind of apprentice to the head barber, (Oscar) Williemain who is a classic tale teller and local historian in the oral mode. One of *Divine Day*'s great set pieces is a tale of the legendary character Sugar-Groove in heaven told by Williemain. But the barbershop heritage is still more complex, for another barber, Galloway Wheeler, is a passionate lover of Shakespeare who quotes the bard on every occasion and "who can look into a glass of sour-mash and hear the voice of the Bard, as he calls forth Hamlet's speech." The complex interplay between Williemain's oral heritage and Galloway Wheeler's idolatry of the white dramatist Shakespeare can be seen as one emblem of African-American culture, as Forrest sees it. The problem is not cultural deprivation, but a confusing surfeit or plethora of cultural legacies, and the solution, as Forrest suggests both in his fiction and in his essays, is not the discovery of some mythical African heritage, but the reinvention or recreation of the diverse heritage of black Americans which synthesizes the rich complexity of many different cultural strands. As an aspiring playwright, Joubert himself faces this problem of the artistic reinvention of his heritage. This crucial week in his life brings him to a new level of understanding of his mission as an African-American writer through his meditations on three important characters whose fates are unfolded to him in the course of this week. Joubert's attempts to understand the truth behind the disappearance of the mysterious W.A.D. Ford, the death of his former mentor, the legendary hipster Sugar-Groove, and the life and tragic suicide of De Loretto Holloday, a black woman artist and social worker to whom Joubert has been strongly attracted, provide the chief unifying threads which tie together the complex events of Joubert's week.

II

W.A.D. Ford, a character of many names and legends sometimes known as W.W.W. Ford, and, in an earlier avatar as "The Seer," is one of Forrest's most distinctive creations and a long-time resident of Forest County, if such a legendary and shape-shifting figure can be said to reside anywhere. He plays a prominent role in *The Bloodworth Orphans*, where Noah Ridgerook Grandberry, the survivor of the four tragic Bloodworth orphans, tells Nathaniel about his own period of discipleship to Ford when the latter was operating one of his many religious sects. In typical Ford fashion this sect's practices involved wildly erotic ceremonies which hint of archetypal fertility and resurrection rituals. In one episode, Ford begins a forty-day fast in a golden coffin, announcing to a press conference that "he would stay perched in the golden gobbler coffin—like a burnished golden Easter egg—and arise on Easter Sunday morning." When the police arrived they found that "a golden blond, not a golden egg, was now dancing "the dance of seven veils with a wine-drugged Egyptian cobra snake about her throat" (*Bloodworth* 327). This blonde, Ford's white mistress, comes from a very powerful Jewish family and is known to Ford's disciples as Euphrates or the Gay-Rail (grail).

Though, as revealed in *Divine Days* Ford disappears from Forest County in the early 1960s, his track can still be found in the early 1970s when Nathaniel and Noah run across classified ads in the paper placed by Whitehurst Barns Ford (D.D. and L.L.D) and by Franklin Ford "travelling market research analysis, with world-wide contacts and credentials." It is clear that, whatever else he may be, Ford has a kind of immortality in his continual shape-shifting.

We find out much more about Ford in *Divine Days*, though it is characteristic of such a figure that there is nothing certain that can be pinned down; Ford remains more myth and legend than actual character. We learn that before he went into the army Joubert spent seven weeks with Ford in order to gather material for a play based on Ford's Forest County cult which was known to "The Fatha's" followers as DIVINE DAYS, presumably in reference to its ecstatic religious experiences. Among the central symbols of Ford's cult are a monstrous dog, ALL SOULS, which Ford keeps in the basement of his church to frighten his followers into line, and a balefully blazing star which adorns the walls of Ford's storefront church. Joubert also discovers that Ford keeps his disciples under control through sadistic confessional rituals which involve running fearful lizards over their bodies. An inner corps of Ford followers, the Effete Elite, also help maintain order within the flock, a satirical jab at the Black Muslim Fruit of Islam.

Significantly, the premises which Ford occupied with his DIVINE DAYS sect for seven weeks before mysteriously disappearing "immediately after sundown on the Saturday before Easter, leaving no forwarding address" are those which Joubert's aunt and uncle have leased, renovated and *reinvented* as Eloise's Night Light Lounge. Many of the episodes which take place between the regular customers and the barmaids of the Night Light

Lounge are as bizarre and wild as the cultic rites of Ford's DIVINE DAYS, and are brilliantly hilarious comic episodes unlike anything in Forrest's earlier fiction.

When he disappeared, Ford left behind him two things which symbolically preside over the action at Eloise's Lounge: a gigantic turd and a balefully dazzling star, which no one has been able to turn off or take down. One of Joubert's important tasks in the course of the novel is to invent a name (a meaning) for Ford's star.

Though his mysterious disappearance has occurred long before the beginning of the novel, Ford continues to haunt Joubert's thoughts, just as his spirit seems to preside over the scene in the form of the DIVINE DAYS star. In addition, Joubert's play about Ford mysteriously turns up, having been discovered in the dead letter office by a friend who works for the Post Office. There's some suggestion that the ms. may have been seized by the FBI seeking information about Ford. Joubert also remembers that his idol and mentor Sugar-Groove had told him about an ill-fated encounter with Ford many years before, when Ford, in an earlier identity as "The Seer," had deceitfully promised Sugar-Groove a chance to speak with his dead mother. Finally, at the end of Joubert's week and a day, Ford reappears before disappearing once again. Joubert receives news of a violent confrontation in the mountains between Ford and Sugar-Groove, a clash which results in the death of Sugar-Groove. Joubert's attempt to understand the meaning of Sugar-Groove's last days and of his final encounter with Ford are among the climactic events of *Divine Days*.

Other revelations about Ford turn up in the course of *Divine Days*: he has had many avatars including, the "serial hermaphrodite" experience of both male and female existences; he is probably immortal, his name Wizard (or Wondrous) Alpha Decathlon Ford, suggesting magic and myth, an existence from the beginning (from Alpha to Omega) and multiple guises and talents like some Olympic champion of evil. In addition, Ford's own explanation of his surname invokes a bizarre parody of the incarnation. Ford's divine father, seeking a truly virginal receptacle for his seed could find such purity only in the distant mountains where he discovered a filthy wild girl, who he washed off and then

"forded over swamps and floods, rugged quarries, through savage thunder and furious lightning through tribes of cannibals and suffering pits of slavish humanity, with my mother high upon his shoulders in order to bring that gentle goddess to safe, high, dry grounds for the delivery of the promised one, on the other side of the 1500 mile river." Apparently Ford's old man had impregnated her high in the mountain range, between a rock and a hard place, by the light of a burning bush, watched over by a peculiar star. Billions of beatitudes were sparked in eternal space, worthy to match (let Ford tell it) the miracle of the Virgin Mary's conception and the Assumption of Mary, to say nothing of the immemorial night a star stood still over a stable. "And when she beheld me in her arms, and looked upon my face," the teary-eyed Ford confided to his congregation in all humility, his voice barely above a trembling whisper, "She *then* looked into the Heavens, and she heard a voice, schooling her, this lamb-meek, gentle maiden, as it acclaimed, the birth of her son to be recorded now, and forever more, *The Divine Day*.[4]

His many identities give Ford a wide range of symbolic meanings and, in fact, one of the central themes of *Divine Days* is a probing of the complex mystery of Ford's significance. As the passage just quoted indicates, there's a basic level of symbolism in which Ford is a fallen angel, diabolical, an anti-Christ figure, a Mephistopheles. But this demonic character is further complicated by Ford's connection with African trickster gods and the classical seer of Greek myth, the blind Tiresias, also a serial hermaphrodite, who represent divine forces of more ambiguous, if not more positive, energies. In more contemporary terms, critics have associated Ford with W D. Fard, the mysterious Black Muslim angel messenger who gave the Word to Elijah Muhammad, with Ralph Ellison's shape-shifting con-man hustler Rinehart, and with Henry Ford, the symbolic founder-spirit of modern industrialism. Perhaps all these are in some sense avatars of Ford because they also manifest two complex and somewhat contradictory attributes. On the one hand, Ford clearly represents the dark and manipulative side of human creativity in religion, power and art. As he explains to Joubert during their brief association:

The constant problem for every great leader, my young friend, is to keep his flock convinced through cycles of new horror and ecstasy, that they are parts of a new covenant with God. But *you* spin this new covenant out of some old myths. *You* invert, convert, the meanings of these myths. The people . . . come to believe that it is you who've righteously come to actually save those old, so-called truths; when really you're spinning out a new fantasy, in accordance with your own high sense of drama, your interpretation. So you've spun them into a faith based on the dire need to sacrifice more and more, until any fragment of a gift you give the faithful makes them feel joyous—even when you abuse them. Abuse is very important, for it is linked to their sense of sacrifice, and their need for sacrifice.

Of course, this is not totally dissimilar from Forrest's own theme of *reinvention*, but in Ford's case the recreation is for purposes of control, manipulation and abuse, which for Forrest, is always a danger in those who have the power to create. But even if there is this demonic or fallen side of Ford, he has another attribute which indicates that, however much we rightly fear the dangers of Ford's demonic power, we cannot do without him. In his shape-shifting demonism Ford also exemplifies the primal energy of chaos, the basic material of creation. Ford is the world without vision or transcendence, but as Sugar-Groove realizes in the final revelation he passes along to Joubert, there can be no light without darkness, no creation without chaos. Ford is both shit and star and we must understand this double relic-message to understand Ford's true significance.

"Ah yes, but there must always be chaos; this, too, has been my brief—but surely not remarkable discovery in the Light of the lyricism transformed . . . Chaos, world without end, Amen, which nourishes the Light of Radiance, and which the Light of Radiance (magic, terror, beauty, wisdom, experiment) transforms . . . This little light of mine will go howling down into the night; this conscience . . . and maybe, must maybe" . . . Ah and then I understood what Sugar-Groove had seen upon that mountain, in the nick of time, and its burning and its turning.

III

Look, Joubert, there is a river of time more ancient than Eden, where every form of waste and wonder has been discarded, past all parchments of recorded time; you enter, or I should say you are tossed adrift or hurled asunder, into those babbling, turbulent waters to make a way out of noway, even out of nothingness. Tossed off. Told to swim. Sail even. Get lost. Or die. You have to teach yourself to swim through all this ahistorical garbage, ecstasy foul, fair weather, remake yourself against the temperament of even the wrinkled, rowdy river; occasionally you happen upon a divine spring of renewal, but don't count on many of 'em. You didn't ask for any of this—but you get all of it—more waste than wonder. Always another agony bed in the river to bridge, to cross. (Sugar-Groove to Joubert)

Ford just is and perhaps for this reason he is both constantly changing and immortal, embodying the essential chaos of matter. Sugar-Groove is the *reinvention* of Ford into a seeker. He, too, is a hustler, something of a trickster and an operator though his skills are more often used to save others than to manipulate or exploit them. Above all, he is characterized by a kind of style: elegance, beauty, gracefulness. And though he has been given many names, he remains fundamentally the same. Though he is seventy years old at the time of the novel, he still possesses the haunting grace of the mysterious youth in his favorite song, "Nature Boy." Women fall passionately in love with him and are transfixed by his hypnotic grey eyes. His reputation for grace is such that after he dies, he gains a kind of immortality when this quality is transformed into a marvelous folk legend dealing with Sugar-Groove's heroic exploits in heaven.

Sugar-Groove is also a Bloodworth orphan and thus carries in his self the divided and ambiguous heritage of the American Negro. He is the unacknowledged son of a wealthy Southern white man, Wilfred Bloodworth, and his black mistress Sarah-Belle. In some ways he resembles the brilliant Regal Pettibone of *The Bloodworth Orphans*, but Regal meets a tragic fate, torn apart through the operation of the terrible curse of the Bloodworth line, when, ignorant of his true heritage, he falls into a passionate and incestuous affair with his sister. Sugar-Groove is consciously aware of who he is and is able to avoid the Bloodworth doom to pursue his own quest for illumination.

With his multifarious operations and his dashing style and grace, Sugar-Groove is already a Forest County legend when Joubert, at age thirteen, is shining shoes in Williemain's Barber Shop. Sugar-Groove, as the possessor of many pairs of fancy imported shoes, is one of Joubert's regular customers. One evening when Joubert has been left alone in the barbershop, Sugar-Groove appears with two pairs of his Alighieri shoes to be shined and this Dantesque footgear provides an appropriate introduction for a journey into the *Inferno* of Sugar-Groove's Southern past.

Prompted by Joubert's questions about the Tobias family and its own strange heritage, Sugar-Groove decides to tell Joubert about his own early life down in Sugar-Ditch, Mississippi. It was well-known in this area that Sugar-Groove was the son of the wealthy and powerful white landowner Wilfred Bloodworth and his beloved black mistress, Sarah-Belle. Sugar-Groove's mother had died in childbirth, apparently choosing to give birth to her baby at the cost of her own life. However, Bloodworth has never acknowledged his son, who is thus, like Joubert, an orphan. Also like Joubert, Sugar-Groove has been raised by his aunt Gracie Mae Gates and his Uncle Ice. When he is twelve, his white father, Wilfred Bloodworth, begins to give him a monthly, but irregular allowance. Bloodworth still will not openly acknowledge Sugar-Groove as a son, and the boy must come at night to the back door of the big house in order to receive his dole. This continues until the boy is seventeen, when he has the opportunity to go away to college. Though both his father and his aunt and uncle want him to attend Tuskeegee Institute, Sugar-Groove chooses instead to attend a Negro college in the West which, under the influence of W.E.B. DuBois, seeks to teach the liberal arts to young blacks. When he returns home two years later, he is told that he will receive the final portion of his inheritance in installments. On his way one dark night to receive the first of these installments, Sugar-Groove stumbles across the murdered body of his beloved white half-sister Roxanne, who has always been kind and loving to him, having among other things first taught him to read.

Later, it is revealed that Roxanne's own white brother Paxton, driven in some way by the Bloodworth curse and its urge toward incest, was the actual murderer. However, Sugar-Groove realizes that if he is found with the body he will be lynched. After telling his father of his discovery, he flees with his baby daughter Bella-Belle to the north, where he eventually *reinvents* himself from William Bloodworth through Billy Blood or Worthy to a man of many names:

There was Sugar-Ditch for his home town, but the only others that I was aware of (Sugar-Dripper, Sugar-Dipper, Sugar-Groove, Sugar-Grove, Sugar-Spook, Sugar-Goose, Sugar-Sack, Sugar-Shank, Sugar-Swift, Sugar-Alley, Fountain-Head Sugar, Sugar-Stoker, Sugar-Stroke, Sugar-Splib, Sugar-Stagger, Sugar-Saint, Sugar-Spine, Sugar-Dick, Sugar-Stud, Sugar-Loaf, Sugar-Smoke, Sugar-Shit, Sugar-Eyes, and Sugar-Shark) referred to various tributes paid to his revealed sexual merriment and moxie and prowess; or his cunning at dice, cards, gambling tables and other games of chance. (Oscar [Williemain's] Sugar-Groove Saga)

This gothic allegory of the historical transition from Southern slavery to the life of a Northern "hustler and drifter" reflects the basic pattern of African-American story from slave narratives to Ralph Ellison's *Invisible Man*. However, Forrest's own distinctive recreation of this pattern centers around two key episodes in Sugar-Groove's early life which took place when he was fourteen and still involved in his ambiguous relationship with his father, Wilfred Bloodworth. These episodes have a profound influence on Sugar-Groove and play an important role not only in shaping the rest of his life, but in making it possible for him to experience the final illumination that he is able to pass on to Joubert.

The first of these episodes occurs when the fourteen-year-old William Bloodworth goes to the Bloodworth mansion one evening to pick up his allowance. Though he is often not allowed to enter the house, on this evening his father lets him into the library., where, curious what his father is reading, he opens a large bible and finds a photograph of his mother dressed very scantily, symbolizing Bloodworth's possession of his mother's sexuality. The young Sugar-Groove is enraged at this picture and tries to tear it up. A violent fight breaks out when Bloodworth tries to stop him. Bloodworth's mature strength prevails and he is about to kill Sugar-Groove, when father and son suddenly become aware of the presence of Sarah-Belle and her spirit crying out "*How can you destroy what we created.*" Sarah-Belle's voice stops the fight, though Sugar-Groove's rage at Bloodworth remains and he later tells Joubert of a dream in which he castrated his father to punish him for this sexual exploitation of the mother.

There are many complications to this episode through which Forrest explores the terrible sexual ambiguities created by the heritage of slavery and racism and the sexual exploitation of black women by white men. The episode also enables Forrest to develop a related theme, which is basic to his fiction: the archetypal experience of the loss of the mother and the father's lack of acknowledgment which creates the spiritual condition of the orphan, a state which Forrest views as fundamental to the experience of African-Americans.

The second major episode of Sugar-Groove's story occurs shortly after the discovery of his mother's picture and the ensuing struggle with his father. Desperate to reestablish some contact with his dead mother, Sugar-Groove begins to visit a man in neighboring Forrest County who claims to be a seer, and who, Joubert and Sugar-Groove later realize, is one of the avatars of

W.A.D. Ford. The seer promises to help Sugar-Groove speak with the spirit of his mother, but first insists on telling him the terrible story of P. F. Bloodworth, progenitor of the mixed Bloodworth line, whose tragic fate Forrest narrated in *The Bloodworth Orphans*. Forrest's reinvention of certain parts of the Bloodworth story sheds some interesting new light on that tragic saga, but within the context of *Divine Days*, it makes Sugar-Groove aware of the Bloodworth curse of family incest and determines his separation from his own daughter out of fear of that curse. In addition, the Seer brutally tricks Sugar-Groove into entering a graveyard promising him that he will be able to speak with the spirit of his mother. Instead, Sugar-Groove is confronted with a hanged scarecrow, symbolizing the futility and danger inherent in the attempt to regain possession of the lost mother.

By this time, it is evident that Sugar-Groove is, among other things, a *reinvention* of Oedipus in terms of African-American history and that, on this symbolic level, Ford, the Seer, is his Tiresias. Just as Tiresias' gift for prophecy was associated with his hermaphroditism and his blindness, the truths about the underside of human nature which Ford reveals are connected to his demonism and his role as a trickster. Ford's burial alive parodies the human desire for immortality, his rope-trick the dream of transcendence, and his graveyard game with Sugar-Groove the need to possess the lost mother. Sugar-Groove as Oedipus must learn not to let himself be destroyed by his father's betrayal and the absence of his mother. Or, in terms of Forest County, he must *reinvent* his condition as an American Negro into a special state of grace:

Sugar-Groove had spent his life in submission to experiences of all kinds. Had surrendered something of his soul in order to know . . . to be . . . mainly too, because his life as a black man had been one of denial . . . an attempt to deny in him, his individualism. Sugar-Groove had railed and raged to break taboos in defiance. Living outside the bourgeois entrapments of the Negro world; Sugar-Groove had lived by his wits; his outlawish celebration of his own deviance, his marginality; submitting to no other gods before him, save his own inner vision; and yet there had always been that yeasty energy which threatened to explode within him for spiritual ascendancy.

On the last day of his week and a day, Joubert goes to a nursing home to interview old Warren Wilkerson, a retired journalist, about the last days of Sugar-Groove. Wilkerson, another shape-shifter who has often passed for white in order to discover the secret plans of racist groups[5] knows the truth about Sugar-Groove's death and has come into possession of a diary in which the dying Sugar-Groove recorded his final thoughts. He tells Joubert that, sensing his death approaching, the seventy year old Sugar-Groove had gone up into the mountains seeking, like Oedipus at Colonus, to purify himself for some final illumination, or, like an American-Indian Warrior, to set out on his final vision quest. On the top of this mountain, Sugar-Groove has his final confrontation with Ford. Appropriately enough, Sugar-Groove's magical seven hours of mythical illumination culminate in a moment of rollicking mythical comedy. Sugar-Groove's vision is interrupted by a bolt of lightning which announces Ford's appearance with a rifle. When the trickster has emptied that rifle at Sugar-Groove without hitting him, Wilkerson reports to Joubert that "The demon, the Seer Ford awakened the dormant survival hunger in Sugar-Groove; the force that also was and is the fundamental force of the Universe . . . the explosion to resist. The thrusting thirst to project one's survival." Fortunately, Sugar-Groove had kept his own rifle with him and

when Ford did an about face, and scurried back to get more ammunition, Sugar-Groove came up firing from his sheltered spot where he was scribbling on his diary, concerning the ongoing action and rifle fire of the demonic Ford. Placed perfect fire in the hound-dog's ass. Seven blazing shots in the Seer's backsides; so that he'll have to stand up to shit from here to eternity.

Ford is, of course, ultimately victorious and his second volley fatally wounds Sugar-Groove. In his final assault on Sugar-Groove's dying body, Ford commands his eagle, a bird version of the demonic canine ALL SOULS to rip out Sugar-Groove's eyes. This blinding not only establishes the final mythical identification between Sugar-Groove and the apotheosized Oedipus, it also gives Sugar-Groove a final illumination:

in this triumph of evil over all that Sugar-Groove thought he was coming to see of the resplendency of radiance, Sugar-Groove now was into the total rage, terror, and dangerous fear within the loathsome monster's eyes: the jails, butchery, and savagery locked away there, the heinous Herod, the heil Hitler, and the slaver's vows . . . all of which commenced with the very last stages of the lamps of his own eyes, their last flickering, as they fell upon the demonic Seer's heinous Hitlerian, slaver's orbit, within his eyes. Seconds before the Seer's murderous breath spewed forth: *Then put out the Light* of Sugar-Groove's eyes, which was the commandment given to the abominable eagle. But now Sugar-Groove took all this inward, these final stages of Light most terrible, from within the monstrous Evil One, which lies within us all, Brer Bear Jones, at its most rank, and savage extreme, world without end.

It is this realization of evil as well as good in man that gives an inward illumination to Sugar-Groove enabling him to unite at last in spirit with his lost mother:

For Sugar-Groove's last words scrawled out in his thrust to affirm life in death and even over the demon—were the words, I heard you report to me, a while back there from the ghost of Sugar-Groove's mother's lips. Written out just before . . . as he turned away from the pen to the rifle: 'How can you destroy what we created.'

Sugar-Groove and Ford represent many things, but in the most abstract sense they divide between them the primal moral potential of human beings: to give in to the chaos of reality and become an agent of the demonic or to seek to rise through suffering to grace and transcendence. Yet, though these energies are fundamentally opposed (indeed their clash is for Forrest the essential source of myth—Satan vs. Christ; Fate vs. Oedipus; Angels vs. Demons) they cannot exist without each other. This may be why the trickster-God of Africa is so fascinating because he/she seems to embody both darkness and light in one figure. Perhaps because their historic fate has been so shaped by the diabolical African-Americans have shown an extraordinary moral and artistic potential for renewal. In a key passage toward the end of *Divine Days,* wise and wily old Warren Wilkerson explains to Joubert his view of the meaning of Negro culture in America:

Some West Africans used to believe—before the white Christians snatched them up body and soul—that the souls of the dead were reincarnated in human or animal mode. Faith spun of a concept that the world of spirits was really inhabited by souls of dead human beings. Spirits haunted the air; resided in trees, woods, forests, caves. Yorubas believed animals possessed souls and not unlike the souls of human kind—and that they too went to the land of the profoundly dead. Then when you recombine all of that with what the slaves ran into from their master's world, which was flood-gate with ghosts, over-run with bogey men, demonic spirits, bad-ass goblins; and wild fairy tales (and don't even start to talk about the mythologies of the Old Testament; and the miracles in the New), you commence to glean a fragment of the spooked-out world of the slaves. Now as to the real world a-borning, why shit their demonic mistreatment was more savagely fantastical than the testament of mayhem they had heard of, brought with them, survived coming here through, and were remaking orally, even as they were being transformed out of their skins, and blood, and soul, and eye-teeth and backbone crack—into a new kind of people. Forged, fucked and dislocated into a new race of people wherein anything human and inhumane could happen. . . . But our human rage was always to make a way out of noway. And to create a synthesis out of all nightmare that our experience kept throwing up at us. That will to synthesize was what Du Bois never understood . . . to absorb and reinvent; to take it all in and to masticate it, and process it, and spew it back out, as lyrical and soaring as a riff by Father Louie.

It is this kind of synthesis and *reinvention*, the bringing together of the potential cultural and human energies symbolized by both Sugar-Groove and Ford that Joubert comes to understand as his essential task as a writer.

IV

Yet, before Joubert can come to his culminating realization of the complex and interrelated significance of Sugar-Groove and Ford, he must also experience in a personal way the suicidal futility of the wrong kind of attempt to reclaim a lost heritage, to return to one's roots, to repossess the lost mother. In the midst of various affairs and romances, Joubert had been especially attracted before he left for Germany to a talented young black woman artist, De Loretto Holloday. De Loretto's life is full of contradictions. She has increasingly turned for the subjects of her painting to portraits of ghetto gang chieftains whom she idealizes as leaders of the people. Yet she lives the life of a middle class professional, residing in a lakefront highrise apartment, mostly inhabited by whites, from which she watches the ghetto through a pair of binoculars. Though she hopes to make her art a force in the struggle for black liberation, her most important patrons are white. In addition she earns her living as a social worker and thus, as a member of the middle class white bureaucracy. De Loretto is increasingly torn apart by these contradictions in her life. To overcome them she has plunged into a search for an idealized lost family inspired by visions of her dead mother. In addition, she has tried to rename herself Imani[6] and to surround herself with what she imagines to be the artifacts of her African heritage. Ironically, these consist of a collection of masks—fake masks at that—supplied by the crooked huckster Sambi!, a former pimp who has become a promoter of spurious African artifacts and ideologies to cover his actual operations as a drug dealer.

However, De Loretto's attempt to repossess her lost mother is fatally self-destructive and, late on Tuesday night, Joubert learns that she has committed suicide by taking an overdose of sleeping pills. The immediate cause of De Loretto's suicide was, he is told, her violently self-destructive reaction to a retreat she had attended where, in an encounter group-like session a circle of militant blacks had pointed out to her the gaping contradiction between her desire to identify herself with her African heritage and the reality of her middle-class way of life. Unlike Sugar-Groove, who has learned that one must create out of chaos, by "making a way out of noway" De Loretto/Imani finally cannot tolerate the contradictions of her situation and kills herself. One of Joubert's sad tasks on the last day of his week and a day is to sort through De Loretto/Imani's belongings and try to plan an appropriate funeral ceremony.

Joubert finds Imani's diary and, as he reads it and remembers some of his own earlier conversations with her, he thinks of his futile attempts to persuade her that her desperate quest for her lost family and for a return to African values were a waste of time; in her conversation with him a week earlier, he remembers how she had tried to convert him to the idea of *omowale*, a Yoruba word for "child who has come back home." Joubert, of course, was "less interested in omowale, *Cane,* and Toomer, than I was in the new glow of deepened warmth and attraction for De Loretto, which came over me as a sudden, warm breeze on a chilly February day." By reading Imani's diary on this last day Joubert begins to understand how De Loretto/Imani's very beauty had made her the object of sexual exploitation by both black and white males. Tyrannized by a harsh stepfather and raped by her stepbrother as a young girl, De Loretto/Imani has constructed an elaborate fantasy of a lost family around what she remembers as her mother's dying wish that she seek out her lost siblings. This search for the idealized lost family becomes

mixed up with her interest in African roots. Yet Imani is also fascinated by power and easily deceived by its appearance. She has
always been particularly interested in Joubert's tales of Ford; she
now cultivates the local gang leaders, believing them to epito-
mize tribal values, and she has even had a white Nazi lover who
continues to have a strong hold over her, actually helping push
Imani over the brink by demanding a sexual encounter with her
on the night she kills herself. Significantly, as he reads further, Joubert discovers that the only man in Imani's life who has not tried
to exploit her in some fashion was Sugar-Groove who Imani herself had tried to seduce some weeks ago but who had gently
and lovingly declined her offer.

The symbolic connections between De Loretto/Imani and
Sugar-Groove are manifold. Like Sugar-Groove, Imani has been
haunted by visions of her lost mother. But Imani's situation is also
analogous to that of Sugar-Groove's mother, Sarah-Belle, as a
beautiful black woman exploited and ultimately destroyed by
men. Though Sugar-Groove has also been victimized by his father
and his step-brother, he has escaped from this fate and has
learned to understand the danger of trying to repossess the past.
He fears the Bloodworth curse of incest, which, for Forrest, represents among other things the terrible danger of ignorance about
the past combined with a passion to repossess it unchanged.
Indeed, one important dimension of *Divine Days* is its trenchant
satire of the quest for "roots" and related separatist and back-to-
Africa movements in African-American culture. Sugar-Groove has
learned to give up the attempt to repossess his past, and
instead, by passing on his story-heritage to Joubert has, in effect,
reinvented a son and a spiritual heir. Imani, however, has fallen
into the trap of believing that the only solution to her chaotic
state of mind is to escape into an idealized past of which she is,
in fact, almost totally ignorant—her lost mother actually exposed
her to physical and sexual abuse by remarrying; the lost siblings
she thinks she finds are disasters; and she only knows her African
heritage through the trumped-up fakery of Sambi! These fantasies culminate in her attendance at the disastrous encounter
group which drives her to her death.

Joubert's earlier interest in De Loretto/Imani primarily
reflected his own desire to possess her sexually. He resented her
obsession with her lost family because it was an obstacle to his
attempts at seduction. However, he comes at the end of the
novel to a new kind of insight into De Loretto/Imani's situation

and a deeper understanding of the tragedy of her life and death which prepares him for his culminating insights about Ford, Sugar-Groove and his own mission as a writer. He has been pushed to this new level of understanding by two earlier encounters. One has haunted him throughout the novel. During his service in Germany, Joubert had come to know a young boy named Hans Henson Hamilton, the son of a black American army sergeant and a German woman. One night before his departure he had come across Hans in a ditch being tormented by a group of white American soldiers and Germans who view his mixed race with hatred. When he sees that Hans has apparently been badly hurt, Joubert goes to a bar favored by American black soldiers seeking assistance, but, by the time he returns to the ditch Hans is gone and Joubert fears he has been killed.[7] Joubert's guilt at his inability to save young Hans recurs throughout *Divine Days* in a memory image of Hans in the ditch which Joubert keeps trying to repress, but which finally returns in full as the last major episode in the novel.

A second related encounter comes on Monday night toward the end of Joubert's week when he meets a young ghetto teenager, Cinderella Lilybridge, who has been impregnated by her own father. When Joubert meets Cinderella she is aimlessly looking for a woman who turns out to be her social worker and is actually De Loretto/Imani. Joubert is deeply touched by Cinderella's plight which reminds him of Hans Henson and he first tries to take the young girl home to her mother. When he realizes that Cinderella and her mother are homeless he attempts to persuade them to let him find a place for them to live. They agree, if he will attend a revival meeting with them. The service is another of Forrest's brilliant descriptions of African-American religious rituals,[8] and gives a momentary sense of ecstasy to Cinderella and her mother. However, Joubert realizes that he can probably do no more to help Cinderella than he could to save Hans Henson. As he remarks earlier, this is all part of the "chaos in the whirlwind of a Forest County Winter's night."

Joubert's own sense of guilt and futility helps him to understand the profound and fatal despair of De Loretto/Imani more deeply. But her tragic suicide also rouses him from his own confusion. In a scene which juxtaposes hilarious and farcical comedy with horror and tragedy in a mixture characteristic of many moments in *Divine Days*, the huckster Sambi! appears at De Loretto's apartment to reclaim his phony masks. Full of rage and grief, Joubert strikes out at him with a "Yoruba cane" which shatters into "a thousand fragments" revealing its construction of chicken wire and cow dung. Joubert, himself, is knocked out by Sambi!'s midget assistant and, when he comes to, finds that Sambi! and his midget, joined by seven youth gang members and their leader "the Purple Satisfier," have carried off Sambi!'s masks. In a rare moment of poetic justice amid the chaos of *Divine Days*, Joubert later hears on the radio that the police have arrested Sambi! and his gang associates and have discovered that the masks contain large quantities of cocaine.

Joubert now heads for his interview with Warren Wilkerson, where, as pointed out earlier, he is told of the final confrontation between Sugar-Groove and Ford. Now, against the background of his own wild week of return to Forest County Joubert is prepared to understand the significance of that cosmic encounter and its meaning to him as an aspiring writer. In the last pages of *Divine Days* Joubert relives in his imagination that moment on the mountain when Sugar-Groove's hours of mystical transcendence were interrupted by a lightning bolt which indicated the arrival of Ford. Joubert sees that, when he picked up his rifle to leave his mark on Ford's hinder-parts before being himself destroyed by the trickster, Sugar-Groove had arrived at his ultimate discovery:

That the harmony realized for a few days was wondrous; but perhaps it was deadly for human kind; so when Ford came upon him, it blasted Sugar-Groove back to the true chaos of the human enterprise. That he was born to live on the edge to know and not to know . . . to be and not to be . . . Sugar-Groove who had worked as a water-boy for gangs of men lining track . . . must have heard the gandy-dancers cry it out at the most secular moments possible, time and time again: "Jack the rabbit/Jack the bear,/ Lift it, lift it, just a cunt hair . . ." Lift what? Lift the lid of harmony by the weight of a feather; shift the load of human happiness by a fraction of an inch; sound off a 32nd note on the wrong beat, and you are back into the hell of the human predicament.

Joubert is also now able to see the connection between the confrontation of Ford and Sugar-Groove and the interplay between that contemporary avatar of Ford, the Black Muslim leader Elijah Muhammad, and the real spirit of the American Negro heritage which is exemplified by Sugar-Groove's ability to live on the edge and reinvent meaning out of chaos:

Blasting them with the necessary bolt of lightning to awaken them; that shock wave to the backbone and the soul. The Lamb of God had also deadened them into a group of thoughtless, mindless souls. Though in the beginning God knows they needed something like this to awaken them out of the horror and the havoc of the abominable coffin of death the whites had placed them into, on a long alabaster table. No doubt that religion is the opiate of the people; but it is an opiate that we cannot get along without. But it is the Negro in them that saves them. What saved them from the dead was that some remnant, some streak was still there of Negro, not African, and not European, but Negro—with that fabulous impulse to reinvent; to make a way out of noway. The Negro-American's will to transform, reinvent, and stylize until Hell freezes over . . . . Call no white man, Sir, for starters. Reinvention was what King and his spirit of Freedom Movement followers had attempted to do with Christianity; which we got from the white man, and re-made into something else that might even renew them.

V

Divine Days "transforms, reinvents and stylizes" many things, but certainly one of them is that *magnum opus* of modern literature, James Joyce's *Ulysses*. Just as Stephen Dedalus, in some half unconscious way, finds a spiritual father in Leopold Bloom, the orphan Joubert Jones discovers the significance of his inheritance from Sugar-Groove, in the process of which he becomes capable of writing *Divine Days*. He comes to understand that true creation, whether cultural or artistic, does not come through the imposition of order by trying to reject chaos, but through "making a way out of no way" or recreating life out of that chaos. Thus he comes to realize that his creative vision must incorporate the lost and doomed, like Hans Henson, Cinderella and the tragically divided De Loretto/Imani and the demonic trickster Ford, as well as the angelic hipster Sugar-Groove. This understanding enables him at last to rename (reinvent) Ford's mysterious star as DIVINITY'S DAIMON, the true symbol for DIVINE DAYS which "should be taken as a riddle, too, as metaphor for both the bliss-filled, and chaos-spewing shape of humankind's days upon this earth."

Finally, the transforming experiences of Joubert's week and a day enable him to set forth on his own perilous path as a "fabulous voyager" carrying with him the chaos he will transform into fictional vision and thus into life. Now he is at last able to fully understand (reinvent) Williemain's great folk legend of Sugar-Groove in heaven and its significance for him as a writer:

New bards will find new dazzling searchlights and even lighthouses within the spirit of the forever shape-shifting Sugar-Groove. For what was the saga about (when all is said and done) in the barbershop concerning Sugar-Groove upon the occasion of my return? How once Sugar-Groove got to heaven and was given a used set of wings . . . He was in fact issued an old patched-up set of shattered wings thrown in the Catholic Salvage section and over in the Free Will bin where other angelic vestments were tossed away, and cast asunder. . . . And not only that but how Sugar-Groove had to fly around heaven with one wing on the right, roped off and tied behind him . . . and how he reinvented himself out of all that so much that St. Peter himself was startled to amazement . . . *"I can't find the proper words to express the meanings of all your carryings on, your swerving cavorting . . . your."*

No St. Peter you can't . . . That's my job.

Notes

1. It also becomes evident in *Divine Days* that there are two Forest (Forrest) counties; Forest County is in the north, based loosely on Illinois' Cook County and the city of Chicago, and is a *reinvention* of a Southern Forrest County, in Mississippi, where the Bloodworth plantation is located.

2. Forrest informs me that "Aunt Eloise's column called *Eloise Etches,* is published three times a week in the *Forest County Dispatch.* "Eloise Echoes" and "Eloise's Elite" are sub-heads of particular sections of her column. The *Dispatch is a daily.* She is published Monday, Wednesday, and Friday. The paper is published Monday through Friday." Personal letter, Jan. 15, 1992.

3. This essay was completed before the published version of *Divine Days* became available thanks to Leon Forrest's courtesy in sending me a copy of the manuscript.

4. This story also reflects some of the Black Muslim mythology propounded by Elijah Muhammad.

5. In terms of the pervasive mythical analogies which underlie *Divine Days,* Wilkerson is a Proteus figure who when pinned down can reveal the fate of heroes and the way to go home.

6. *Imani* is a Swahili word which is listed as one of the principles of the Neo-African ceremony Kwanzaa. It is translated as "faith" and often glossed as belief in the importance of the African heritage of American blacks. De Loretto has also tried to rename her son Rhobert (named after a character in Toomer's *Cane* who symbolizes the materialism of

bourgeois culture) into Nia/Rhobert. *Nia* is another of the principles of Kwanzaa and is translated as "purpose."

7. In a typically Forrestian ironic and symbolic complication, Joubert enters the bar while the aging Lavinia Masterson is doing a shake-dance. Lavinia is a white Southern woman who has pursued her black lover William S. Body to France. Losing him, she has eventually settled in France where she marries another Negro-American solder during World War II. Now, "with her retired master-sergeant husband Lavinia ran a suc-cessful Barhaus in Gelnhausen, Germany which catered to black G.I.'s Only" (*The Bloodworth Orphans* xxxv). Joubert is not able to get help until Lavinia has finished her dance.

8. Just a brief sample: "Rev. Roper stands at the rostrum convicted and trembling, trying to burst his way back into the upheaving palaver of passionate singing and shouting voices; sweat lathered all over his fact, as a marathon runner, trying to break is way back into the front of the pack of long-haul track stars, in Jesus's name. Round and round this mountain. His eyes appear as one in a hypnotic trance. Orgiastic and hypnotic, the voices of Cinderella, and the lead songstress are fueled by the choir of twenty-one soaring voices" (1152). Joubert has had an important interview with this very same Reverend Roper earlier in his week.

Invisible Man by Sven Birkerts: Divine Days by Leon Forrest

Sven Birkerts

Leon Forrest is the invisible man of contemporary African-American letters. Born in Chicago in 1937, raised and educated there, Forrest has been publishing novels since the early 1970s, including *There Is a Tree More Ancient Than Eden* (1973), *The Bloodworth Orphans* (1977), and *Two Wings to Veil My Face* (1983). But public and critical reception have been minimal. Forrest's name does not come up much in discussions of writing; the indexes of scholarly studies march blithely forward without him.

I don't know that the publication of *Divine Days*, his megalithic novel, will change the situation much. I have not seen the book reviewed, or even mentioned anywhere. That it is a third again as long as *The Brothers Karamazov* is not likely to recommend it to readers short on time and stamina. This would be a shame, and an enormous loss. *Divine Days* is unlike anything else in our recent literature. At once a comic opera and a metaphysical tract, this great wordy beast stamps and blinks in the glittering light of the marketplace like something kidnapped from a more expansive age.

Unfolding over the course of seven days in February 1966, the novel carries us deep into the life of its narrator Joubert Jones, and at the same time layers around us the stories and myths—the great fabric of polyphonic talk—of an entire community. The place is a Chicago-like city in the author's own Forest County. Joubert, a would-be playwright whose work thus far has only met with rejection, has returned from a stint of military service in Germany. He plans to set himself up and resume his writing, but for a short run he has moved in with his feisty Aunt Eloise, who raised him after his parents died. Joubert also takes on the job of managing her bar, Eloise's Night Light Lounge, a place that he comes to see as a kind of stage for the tragedies and the comedies of neighborhood life. For all his determination to get on with his own work, Joubert finds himself utterly immersed in the human swirl around him. He tells himself that just by being present he is serving a dramatist's apprenticeship.

Joubert has been blessed with a special gift. He is susceptible to voices, and each one that he hears or remembers serves him as a pipeline to the speaker's soul. This is the source of his playwriting itch: he can hardly turn around without colliding with another inspiration. Once, he tells us, he thought of "trying to run a ladder up the hieroglyphics of Charlie Parker's tortured soul, then transforming this experience of his voice into a one-act play." His current fancy, which will occupy him increasingly as the book progresses, is to write a play "about the soul within the voice of Sugar-Groove." Traveler, talker, ladies' man, Sugar-Groove (also known as Sugar Grove, Sugar Shit and a dozen other "sugar"-based monikers) is a Forest County legend. Joubert knew him years ago and has been fascinated ever since. Reports that Sugar-Groove's body was recovered from a far-away mountain top will activate Joubert's memories; the man's enigmatic story will eventually give him answers about his own life.

Divine Days gets underway slowly, like a great long freight train clattering its couplers out of the yard. Joubert's world, past and present, is thickly settled. Both he and his aunt are vital agents in the life of the community. The cast of characters takes some time to assemble. And for a spelunking temperament like Joubert's there is a good deal more involved. Every person— waitress, lounge lizard or community stalwart—is not just a presence, but a history; and every history is for him a kind of root-system stretching back years, even decades.

But Joubert feels no compulsion to narrate quickly. Why, when narration is so interesting? Consider the excitements of the very first day, when Joubert finds himself embroiled in a knock-down shouting match with one Daisy Dawes, a sad, bewigged, dog-toting, spike-heeled old woman who has taken offense at an aspersion cast by Joubert at W.A.D. Ford. Ford, another legend, is the now-vanished huckster preacher, a "hermaphroditic" saver of souls who practiced his orgiastic messianism in his church, Divine Days, which is now the site of the lounge.

The Daisy Dawes confrontation begins as a "dirty dozens" trading of insults and jibes, with many of the onlookers chipping in. One of the regulars, Roy Ruffins, says of her dog Tosca: "that dog pisses perfumes, shits caviars and farts wine sauce . . . and if I'm lying, I'm flying." Joubert speeds and slows his report, taking time to fill us in on Daisy's past and on certain peculiarities of Ford's ministry. By the time we reach the climatic moment, with Daisy brandishing a .44 from her purse and then falling backward off her stool, we have taken the first of many tours of the human labyrinth that is Forest County. What's more, we have taken our first measure of the elusive Ford, the man who will emerge as Sugar-Groove's great antagonist and an emblem of the collective superstitions of the community.

In scene after scene, the pattern repeats. Nearly every one of Joubert's encounters is a point of departure for an anecdotal history. At first, naturally, there is some confusion. The reader keeps checking the back of the book to see whether a chart of identifications might not have appeared. But after a while the root systems begin to grow together. Characters start showing up in each others' stories, and we relax into the meandering momentum of Joubert's talk, bunching our brows perplexedly only when he offers some new piece of Ford apocrypha, such as his much bally-hooed Easter ascension at the end of a levitating umbrella, or an inventory of the cache he left behind in his storefront church, which included "the mighty egg-shaped shell and oval coffin box (he himself was known to take a ten or fifteen minute catnap there, only to rebound with the agility of an antelope); the stockpile of African masks about the wall; the seven sacred Hopi Masks; the one hundred bottles of snake oil . . . ." Forrest, word-glutted as Rabelais, is a master of the list, ticking off objects and names in endless catalogs, serving serial adjectives as appetizers to his nouns and contriving insult choruses that would scorch the wimple on the most liberal nun.

Characters, too, traipse before us in a vast processional. In what we must think of as the early pages—though many another novel would be in the end-game at this point—we meet and hear from, among others, Galloway Wheeler, a one-time teacher and Shakespeare scholar who peppers the proceedings, whatever they may be, with appropriate citations from the Bard; Williemain, the garrulous barber who presides over a select men's conversation society that Joubert has been invited to pledge; McGovern McNabb, a Falstaff-sized boozer who stops the action for thirty pages when he crashes unconscious to the barroom floor, to be revived only by a vigorously administered ice-pack on the privates; and a beautiful but haunted young painter who calls herself Imani, and who, in addition to covering canvases with the likenesses of her African-American heroes—Martin, Malcolm, and others—conducts desperate searches for the many members of her family who have gone missing. Joubert longs for Imani, believes he could love her, but cannot seem to find the path to her heart. Imani thinks that Joubert is denying his African origins and is turning his back on the struggles of his people; in one scene she gets so upset with him that she chases him from her apartment.

The reader trained to the expectations of the Anglo-American novel waits for the rising action, for some sustained engagement or conflict to develop between the principal characters. That reader may wish to shop elsewhere, for this is an altogether different sort of enterprise. So different, in fact, that we begin to understand why the critical establishment has not caught on to Forrest. If Ellison's *Invisible Man* can be seen as the liberation of the African-American novel, a claiming of new speculative and expressionistic options, then Forrest's work represents the transposition of these initiatives into the key of orality. What may from one vantage point look like a sprawl of chatter and association looks from another position like a heroic effort to plant the African-American novel in its original soil.

In his recent study, *To Wake the Nations: Race in the Making of American Literature*, Eric J. Sundquist has observed that, "Just as anthropologists are likely to misperceive the 'sounds' of another culture they attempt to record or analyze, so readers and literary critics . . . are likely to misperceive and misunderstand the signs generated by another cultural tradition when they force unfamiliar and hence potentially inappropriate paradigms."

Something of the sort, I suggest, has been happening with the work of Forrest. The largely white critical establishment seems to be missing the man's music. *Divine Days* is not a clomping foray into mimesis, it is a sluicing of the energies of black speech. It looms as a tour-de-force carnival of tongues. References to Rabelais, Shakespeare, and Joyce are not misplaced. Here is the soul of a community, and to a degree of a whole culture, exposed by way of speech—with Joubert Jones, hearer and interpreter of voices, as our guide. Now the presentation makes sense—its length, its anecdotal entanglements, its startling juxtaposition of kinds of talk, everything from insult to oratory to late-night philosophizing.

Forrest himself, in an essay entitled "In the Light of Likeness—Transformed," directs us to the central source of his vocal inspiration. "As a writer who comes out of a culture steeped in the eloquence of the Oral Tradition," he explains, "I've come to see the Negro preacher as the Bard of the race; and throughout my novels, that rich lodestone of eloquence has provided me with an important springboard." This is certainly the case in *Divine Days*, a novel that not only takes its name from the defunct church of the scurrilous W.A.D. Ford, but that features at intervals long passages of both religious and secular sermonizing. Forrest gives more than a few preacher characters a platform for their verbal strutting. And Joubert, attending, is rapt:

Deep within their voices I heard that old genesis grain—over, under, around and through; in and out of the window of the time—of the Negro singing voice: gone plucked, hardy, harp-haunted, accusational, grieving, roped off; time greased, woe-weary, wound-salted down; drum telegraphing, blues baked, hoe-cake fired; lightning mangled, fat-back foxy, bruised-blooded, merriment jangling; box-car coming, whistling and hushed over in Trouble.

So open is Joubert to what he hears that on one occasion, while at a service at the Anchor of Zion Missionary Baptist Church, he jumps to his feet, delirious, fully taken over by what he believes is the spirit of one Reverend Connie Dixon Rivers, all but stealing the show (and thunder) from the Reverend Lightfoot at the pulpit: "and suddenly I am, me, Joubert Jones, outdoing the visiting preacher's voice (with bloody testifying and confessing Rivers conversation in tongues of flames, like a man drowned up to his gills in fire water) just as Lightfoot took his sermon to another shrieking layer of climax and tried to razor me down with the signifying bad-eye look in order to offset my gradual takeover of his invitational sermon." The scene builds and builds, finally exploding into the richest comedy as Joubert faints, and then wakes to find himself in the solicitous hands of the seven Lockhart Laudermilk sisters, each fatter than the next, and each more covetous of securing Joubert for some extra-ecclesiastical comfort giving.

But while Forrest mines church speechifying for its humorous elements, he also uses the sacred idiom to tap into the reservoir of black spirituality. Indeed, it is finally of first and last things—of the soul entrapped in the confusions of the flesh—that he would speak. As he writes in that same essay, trying to come to terms with an epiphany he experienced once while listening to

Mahalia Jackson, "all great literature was and is and ever shall be, world without end, amen, about man's spiritual agony and ascendancy. A spiritual agony that I seemed steeped in, like a child baptized in the chilly waters of the Jordan." And from its middle on, *Divine Days* mobilizes its vast anecdotal energies on behalf of ultimates.

Taking a few hints from Dostoyevsky, one of the deities in Joubert's pantheon, Forrest sets up what finally proves to be an epic confrontation between good and evil—between the arduous and solitary search for genuine spiritual understanding and the temptations offered by false prophets. The two principal contenders in the drama, which unfolds in the thoughts and written meditations of Joubert, are Sugar-Groove and W.A.D. Ford.

Years ago, when Joubert was still an adolescent, Sugar-Groove had come to Williemain's barbershop to get his shoes shined. Joubert, then making his money with brushes and rags, was alone in the shop, and Sugar-Groove, for whatever reason, chose him to be the hearer of his extraordinary tale. For decades Joubert has kept a lid on what Sugar-Groove told him. But now, after his experience in the Anchor of Zion church and his many homecoming encounters, he is ready to puzzle out the story and its implications.

Sugar-Groove's narrative is convoluted—a Faulknerian agon from the deep South—and could not possibly be summarized here. Sugar-Groove, we learn, was the illegitimate son of a white landowner and his black servant; the mother died in childbirth. We read of legacies and ghosts, of a beloved half-sister murdered by a jealous brother. Sugar-Groove, afraid he will be blamed for the crime, flees North, carrying an illegitimate daughter from his own liaison. But before he leaves he is the victim of a cruel hoax perpetrated by none other than W.A.D. Ford, who in the guise of a medium tells him where he can meet the spirit of his mother—the first salvo in what will turn into a deathly rivalry. Once he arrives in Forest County, Sugar-Groove gives his daughter to a woman named Sweetie Reed to be raised. He sends money but refuses to show his face. Self-exiled from fatherly love, he becomes a rolling stone and ladies' man, hunting for a connection that continues to elude him.

The conclusion of Sugar-Groove's fabulous story is supplied by hearsay, as well as by a set of revealing documents. Joubert learns that after a long career, at once a search and a piracy, Sugar-Groove betook himself to a mountain top:

Sugar-Groove up there sought out the meaning of life. . . . Sought the radiance of not-only the face of God; but more—sought out the radiance from whence all creation poured from, and out of which the Maker Himself was but a manifestation. Sugar-Groove also sought to cast off that old skin of aggression and violence, too. Sought to strip himself down to the bone bare essentials so that he could come alive to something that went beyond the bestial to the beautiful to the sublime that is lodged away in the vow of pure poverty.

Sugar-Groove dies on the mountain top. At any rate, a body is found—a body from which the eyes have been plucked. Then we learn that Ford himself was known to be on the mountain, and the two, authentic seeker and spiritual con, had a final stand-off. As Joubert begins to sort this information, pondering it as one would ponder a runic inscription, he gets the news that Imani has killed herself. He is stunned. When he goes to her apartment, he finds her diary. There, in grievous syllables, is depicted another kind of struggle, not so much with spiritual ultimates as with a legacy of violence and personal loss. Imani, he sees, was striving, so long as she could, to transmute her pain, to put it somehow in the service of her people. But then, irony of ironies, the "brother" she had deemed to be one of the genuine keepers of the cause arrives to rescue his cocaine cache from some tribal masks he had given Imani. The face-off, we see, writ large and writ small, is between ideals and their perversion at the hands of the wicked, between the upwardly inclining soul and the terrible gravity of sordid circumstance.

By now it must be clear that no short appreciation can begin to encompass the fugal architectonics of Forrest's vast work. One after another the voices—aspirant, corrupt, fierce and sorrowful—vie for a place in the would-be dramatist's comprehending perspective. But while Shakespeare may have possessed an absolute negative capability, Joubert does not. He is not merely gathering material, he is looking for his own answers, laboring to forge his own identity. He understands at last that he must step aside from the chaotic plentitude of lounge life and face the silent page. He will let himself be guided by the example of Sugar-Groove, by his will to remake himself into a vessel for higher truths and by his openness at the end to the guiding powers of love. He will also heed, as much as he is able, the words of Dostoyevsky's Father Zossima: "Above all, avoid falsehood, every kind of falsehood, especially falseness to yourself.

Watch over your own deceitfulness and look into it every hour, every minute."

Divine Days is that rare thing in our self-conscious and ironic age—a full-out serious work of art. Cumbersome, complex and all-consuming, it asks the reader for a massive commitment. Forrest makes no concessions, apparently thinks nothing of tracking an encounter or a conversation over fifty pages. As if we had nothing better to do! But do we have something better to do, really? Here is a work that runs the octaves, carries us from street jive to the mysterious whisperings of the self in spiritual consultation. The world of the novel—the lore, the histories, the speech idioms—is African-American, but its reach, like that of the great literature its author so much admires, extends to all. Forrest may be, as yet, an invisible man, but invisible, as every believer knows, does not mean absent.

Beyond American Tribalism: Leon Forrest's Divine Days

Stanley Crouch

Like our economy, our cities, and our universities, our long fiction has been in trouble for years. The problem is as much spiritual as intellectual, for we need a far, far richer sense of the inner lives that give our nation its particular complexity. And because all Americans make their elevating to wacky variations on a set of essences, those essences need to be delivered with high and subtle style, a feeling for the labyrinths of our history, and a sense of the shifting dialogue across race and class, sex and geography, myth and fact. Most novelists duck the job, preferring to sink down into explications of ideology and statistics; or they hop the latest cattle car of academic convention from France; some even embrace the least revealing aspects of our popular culture, never determining what the relationship of the street is to the truly sophisticated expression of our protean national consciousness. If nothing else, they bush-whack the reality of our lives from behind barricades of ethnic and gender franchises.

But Leon Forrest has accepted the task of capturing our culture and has produced a novel that provides a signal moment in our literature, one that was largely missed when it arrived last year. With an equal level of ambition, he responds to the standards of fiction and the breadth of thought found in the work of Ralph Ellison, Albert Murray, Saul Bellow, William Faulkner, Herman Melville, James Joyce, Thomas Mann, and Marcel Proust. The resulting success of Divine Days is as startling for its narrative risks as for the sustained power of its author's literary will. Having spent twenty years working his way to this point through three earlier novels—There Is a Tree More Ancient Than Eden, The Bloodworth Orphans, and Two Wings to Veil My Face—Forrest has now moved to the forefront of American literature. All of the previous experiments and partial successes now read as a triptych of an overture to his masterwork.

Not one to satisfy himself with an imposing gift for mashing together the rural and urban sensibilities that make epic the Afro-

American language of our cities, Forrest has a big feeling for literature at large, and this 1,135-page novel reads the way a whale eats, swimming forward with its massive mouth open to ensure the continued substance of its bulk. Forrest gives us characters, tales, set pieces, sermons, rhythms, images, jokes, and a vision of our culture's mythic size we rarely encounter in this day of the little world, the little thought, and the devotion to a defeatist vision imported from Europe in the wake of the one-two punch of the world wars.

Even so, Forrest is no New Age Good Humour Man. He understands how we are duped by color, how unexamined or hysterical ideology often blinds us like intellectual mustard gas. But rather than crawl into that trench where engagement lies traumatized, Forrest successfully captures the struggle for the Afro-American soul that took place during the middle sixties. That soul has the feeling of multitudes and is a prism through which the spectrum of our nation at large appears: no matter how accurate the Afro-American texture, *Divine Days* provides us with a metaphor as resonant in its general meanings as it is commanding in the nuances of the particular.

Through the world Forrest summons with one brilliant thematic variation after another, we are able to see the struggles our democracy has in facing up to the prickly relationship between the individual and the masses. He artfully shows that the resentment we feel when faced with inevitable tragedy is what sets us up for the "happy endings" promised by purveyors of snake oil in every arena from the religious to the secular, the political to the psychoanalytic. The popularity of the intellectual, economic, spiritual, and physical surgery guaranteed to produce a "new you" is also fresh meat for the leaders of cults that stretch from the academy to the street corner. Our difficulty in combining intellect with style and style with intellect results in our accepting eloquent but empty-headed theories or being overly impressed by manner when we should also be looking for content. Our shallow, hand-me-down revisions of history and culture tear us from the transcendent grandeur of our human heritage, deny the endless miscegenations that complicate our national identity, and set us up for so many sucker blows that we end up culturally punch drunk. Finally, we can become so sanctimonious that we feel engagement is below us, or we can sneer at engagement because we have become convinced that every horror and disappointment is held in place by an invincible conspiracy.

These national themes come forward in the novel as the profane and empathetic flexibility of the blues spirit does battle
against the various puritanical visions that stem from either the
most restrictive versions of Christianity or the totalitarian cults that
combine ethnic nationalism with religion. In one corner is Sugar-
Groove. Sugar-Groove is a Mississippi-born half-caste and road
runner whose mutating legend is a gift to the Chicago black
people ever willing to spin a tale about him or listen when a fresh
one arrives. Though it is not immediately apparent, Sugar-Groove
dies seeking the meaning of life. He wants to get next to the light
that symbolizes both the bittersweet richness of his cultural background and the courage to face the burdens of existence with
tragic optimism. That affirmative courage sells out neither to innocence nor cynicism; it is the source of the wounded and optimistic love call heard in the pulsive swing of blues and jazz. That
wise and enlivening principle has made the people as charismatic as the music.

In the other corner is W.A.D. Ford. Ford is the demonic force
that rises from the recesses of black American culture. Through
Ford, *Divine Days* looks without a blinking eye into mad orders
and confidence men such as the Nation of Islam, Father Divine,
Daddy Grace, and Jim Jones. Ford possesses ominous charm
and knows that those black people who feel most intimidated by
the intricacies of a society demanding great sophistication often
harbor the desire to be part of an elite at any cost. Their rage,
insecurity, envy, and bitterness can be manipulated to the point
where they will end up accepting every repression of vitality in
the interest of order. Overwhelmed by so many choices equaled
by so many responsibilities, they will submit to one source for all
direction. "They were absolutely mindless before his powers," Forrest writes of two potential Ford followers, a borderline street
walker and a waiter, both marvelously drawn in their sass, preten-
sions, sorrow, and paranoia.

Though the spiritual contestants are quite clear, nothing
functions very simply in *Divine Days*. The novel takes place over a
week in the night world of Chicago's South Side, but much more
is going on than a few guppies warring in the miniature aquarium
of a pimp's platform shoe heel. Forrest weaves his complexities
with a multihued fishing tackle that will not break under the
demands of his epic ambition. His people have complicated
family lines, and their experiences, their educational back-
grounds, their interests, their terrors, and their hopes cross many

different lines of color and class, religion and career. Freed from the small talk of the contemporary provincial, the characters of *Divine Days* move across the country and around the world. Having done or wished for or failed at many things, they have much on their minds and memory trunks full of corkscrews and bent objects.

Joubert Jones is perhaps the hero, at least the narrator, a playwright just returned from two years of military service in Germany. Joubert intends to write a play about Sugar-Groove and has previously worked at bringing Ford's evil to the stage. This conceit allows the many literary allusions to work naturally, and Joubert's job as a bartender in his Aunt Eloise's watering hole supplies the novel with the rich breadth of characters either met during visits to the Night Light Lounge or remembered through the hooks of association.

The characters function as a narrative that is built upon *Invisible Man* in as original a way as that novel was built upon Richard Wright's *American Hunger*. (That is: the published *Black Boy* and the then-unpublished second half, which took the narrator to a disillusioning North, the book ending with his decision to become a writer and an allusion to the last lines of Tennyson's "Ulysses.") Forrest is taken by Southern experience and the seditious elements in the North that also infringe on individual identity. For Wright and Ellison, the conservative and brutal demon of racism was extended by the radical Northern demon that dismissed human specificity in favor of rote political theory. Setting his novel in 1966, Forrest brings us to the brink of the destruction of the Civil Rights Movement by the politics of black power. The writer revels in the vitality, humor, religious depth, sensuality, and lyricism of black American culture but sees its radical enemies as black nationalism and the romance of Africa, both of which are finally so disappointing that they destroy one of his characters, just as bitterness over the shallowness of The Brotherhood did in Ellison's Todd Clifton.

The work's exceptional strength arrives through the virtuoso fusion of idiomatic detail and allusions to the world of literature and religion. Though the playwright narrator will push his own sound into the mouths of people when he feels like it, Forrest knows so well the diction, the living patterns, the aspirations, the courtship styles, the dangers, and the brands of humor from the alley to the penthouse that he is quite free to deliver his black American world with three-dimensional authenticity, while creating an antiphony between that universe and—to give but a *few* examples—Shakespeare (especially *Othello*, *Hamlet*, *Macbeth*, and *King Lear*), Poe, Hawthorne, Joyce, Melville (*Moby-Dick*, "Benito Cereno," and *The Confidence Man*), Homer, Cain and Abel, Osiris and Set, Oedipus, Icarus, and Saint Paul. Having done a marvelous variation on it earlier, Forrest even tips his hat to Ellison's short story "Flying Home" for his finale. Those allusions allow Forrest to layer his renderings of the weights and wages of identity, murder, manipulation, greed, exploitation, ruthlessness, irresponsible uses of power, madness, and the heartbreak of the doomed romance. There are also copious references to black American writing, opera, boxing, popular songs, blues tunes, movies, cartoons, and the various kinds of technology that either support or destroy memory, threaten or sustain life.

As Joubert observes, interacts with, and contemplates the condition of the world he's in and the worlds he's known, Forrest critiques as often as he celebrates. In a masterful sequence, Forrest brings together criminals, church ritual, and the honoring of dubious martyrs. However much Joubert might be moved by the singing at the funeral of Aaron Snow, a scurrilous black drug addict shot to death by a black policeman, the narrator doesn't mistake the hot rhythm for substantial reflection: "They had all gone too far with this mushy-minded-mercurial palaver, in which the punk was elevated to a man on stilts, and turned into a kind of outlaw, as hero. I found myself disdaining the eulogizers, by and large, and pitying the blindness of the kids in the audience. . . . Oh, well, it is some burden to be known as a soulful people. Whoever heard tell of such chosen people, as also known for moderate lamentation? This was mindless celebration!" But it doesn't stop there. Soon "even the life of Emmet Till was echoed out here in the chapel in several statements concerning Aaron Snow." The concluding speaker announces the establishing of a scholarship "to do honor to Aaron Snow."

Joubert's pursuit of the facts about Sugar-Groove, the folk hero at war with the dictatorial W.A.D. Ford, makes *Divine Days* a Melvillian detective story of shifting styles. The following of clues opens up the novel to much irony and humor, erotic attraction and sexual repulsion, tragic disillusionment and hard, ruthless violence. The literary flat-footing pulls in elements of the gothic, the tall tale, the parable, the philosophical argument, the novel of ideas, the history lesson, the novel of manners, and the sort of close observation Balzac, Mann, and Hemingway would admire.

The technique of the novel is as musical as it is bold. Forrest prefers to lay his symbols out clearly so that the reader consciously watches him do his stuff the way an audience listens to jazz inventions on a standard song. He often sets up motifs—phrases, characters, colors, natural elements, conflicts, images, and so on—that form a chorus structure. With each successive chorus, the variations become more and more complex until they are either resolved or abruptly come to a conclusion, only to be picked up later. He also likes the extended dialogue, calling upon the precedents of Plato, Doestoevsky, Mann, Faulkner (especially "The Bear"), and the competitive invention of two jazz players foaming their creations at each other in four-bar units or entire blues choruses. Lengthy passages of evocative narrative in which the symbols are carefully submerged make obvious how well Forrest knows that the surreal nature of American experience often declares itself best when rendered accurately. The orchestral control from the first chapters to the last is apt to make our most serious novelists both grateful and envious.

As with every very long and great novel, there are passages that don't sustain force, fall into excess, or blubber into sentimentality. But, like a liberating hero who must rise over interior shortcomings, Leon Forrest never fails to regain his power and take on the details necessary for a difficult victory. *Divine Days* should capture the souls of all who truly love books and feel our national need for freedom from the rusty chains of an intellectual and aesthetic slavery that maintains itself by adding link after link of clichés.

Leon Forrest:
A Bibliography

Kathleen E. Bethel and Leigh Anna Mendenhall

BOOKS BY LEON FORREST

There Is a Tree More Ancient Than Eden. New York: Random House, 1973. (Reprint with an introduction by Ralph Ellison. Chicago: Another Chicago Press, 1988.)

The Bloodworth Orphans. New York: Random House, 1977. (Reprint with an introduction by John G. Cawelti. Chicago: Another Chicago Press, 1988.)

Two Wings to Veil My Face. New York: Random House, 1984. (Reprint with a forward by Toni Morrison. Chicago: Another Chicago Press, 1988.)

Divine Days. Chicago: Another Chicago Press, 1992. Reprinted in hardcover by W.W. Norton (1993) and in paperback by W.W. Norton (1995).

Relocations of the Spirit: Collected Essays. (Including essays on Billie Holiday and Elijah Muhammad.) Mount Kisco, NY: Asphodel Press, 1994. Reprinted in paperback as *The Furious Voice for Freedom.*

BOOK REVIEWS ABOUT *THERE IS A TREE MORE ANCIENT THAN EDEN*

Aubert, Alvin. *Library Journal* 98 (15 May 1973): 1599.

Baker, Houston. "Two Views." *Black World* 23 (1974): 66.

Bell, Pearl K. "Writers and Writing: The Red and the Black." *New Leader* 56 (July 1973): 15.

Book World 7 (17 June 1973): 15.

Booklist 59 (1 July 1973): 1007.

Broyard, A. *New York Times* 8 June 1973: 37.

Choice 10 (Oct. 1973): 1191.

Cohen, George. "Defining the Predicament of Modern Man." *Chicago Tribune* 8 July 1973: G4.

Colter, Cyrus. "Fiction with Feeling: The Historical Horror of the Black Experience. . . ." *Chicago Sun-Times* 27 May 1973: C14.

Davis, L.J. *New York Times Book Review* 21 Oct. 1973: 48-49.

Drown, Merle. *Southwest Independent Bulletin* 27 Sept. 1973.

Gilbert, Zack. "Two Views." *Black World* 23 (1974): 70.

Hairston, Loyle. "Exceptional Fiction by Two Black Writers." *Freedomways* 13.4 (1973): 337-40.

Kirkus Reviews 41 (15 Mar. 1973): 336.

Library Journal 98 (1 Feb. 1973): 446.

Minneapolis Tribune 20 May 1973.

Motley, Joel. *Harvard Advocate* 107.4 (1974): 59-60.

Philadelphia Bulletin July 1973.

Publishers' Weekly 203 (26 Mar. 1973): 68.

Washington Post 17 June 1973 (Briefly Noted).

BOOK REVIEWS ABOUT *THE BLOODWORTH ORPHANS*

Andries, Dorothy. *Evanston Review* 9 June 1977: 5+.

Booklist 73 (15 May 1977): 1399.

Broyard, A. *New York Times Book Review* 1 May 1977: 12.

Cohen, George. *Chicago Tribune Magazine* 8 May 1977: 7.

Cook, Bruce. *Washington Post* 24 June 1977: B6.

Frank, Sheldon. "Superb Fictioneer in Fits and Starts." *Chicago Daily News* 14 May 1977, sec. Panorama: 10.

Kirkus Reviews 45 (1 Mar. 1977): 239.

Major, Clarence. *Library Journal* 102 (1 May 1977): 1043.

Margolin, Victor. *Chicago* 26.5 (May 1977): 102+.

Phelps, Teresa Godwin. *Chicago Tribune Book World* 15 May 1977: G1.

Publishers' Weekly 211 (21 Mar. 1977): 79.

Thorne, Creath. "Orphans Too Ambitious . . . " *Chicago Sun-Times* 26 June 1977: S9.

Washington Star 26 June 1977.

BOOK REVIEWS ABOUT *TWO WINGS TO VEIL MY FACE*

Anderson, Michael. *Los Angeles Times* 25 Mar. 1984: B6.

Best Sellers 44 (May 1984): 45.

Booklist 80 (15 Feb. 1984): 845.

Carson, Herbert L. *The Grand Rapids Press* 1 Apr. 1984.

Cheatwood, K.T.H. *Richmond New Leader* 4 Apr. 1984.

Daily Iowan 6 Apr. 1984.

Davis, Thulani and Cheryl Everette. *Essence* 15 (Aug. 1984): 48.

Demott, Benjamin. "Sweetie Reed's Words of Wisdom." *New York Times Book Review* 26 Feb. 1984: 15-16.

Friend, James. *North Shore Magazine* June 1984: 16.

Heller, Amanda. *Boston Sunday Globe* 8 Apr. 1984: B10

Hutchinson, Paul E. *Library Journal* 109 (1 Mar. 1984): 508.

Kirkus Reviews 51 (15 Dec. 1983): 1265.

Los Angeles Sentinel 23 Jan. 1986: A15.

Pannell, Nancy. *Atlanta* 24 (June 1984): 32B.

Philadelphia Inquirer 8 Apr. 1984.

Publishers' Weekly 225 (6 Jan. 1984): 77.

Richmond Times Dispatch Apr. 1984.

Rodgers, Bernard. *Chicago Tribune Book World* 5 Feb. 1984: N33. (Interview conducted by Cerinda Survant.)

Seattle Times/Post Intelligencer 20 May 1984.

Seelye, John. *Chicago* 33 (Mar. 1984): 173.

Survant, Cerinda. "A Black Woman's Shattering Story." *The Plain Dealer* 8 Apr. 1984: D25.

Warren, Colleen Kelly. *St. Louis Post-Dispatch* 8 Apr. 1984: B4.

Young, Al. "Leon Forrest's Rich Ripe Great Momma Sweetie Reed." *Chicago Sun-Times* 25 Mar. 1984, Books Section: 26.

BOOK REVIEWS ABOUT *DIVINE DAYS*

Aldama, Frederick and Cybele Knowles. "*Divine Days.*" *African American Review* 29.1 (Spring 1995): 160-64.

Birkerts, Sven. "*Divine Days.*" *The New Republic* 208.22 (31 May 1993): 42-45.

Booklist 88 (July 1992): 1917.

Brady, Martin. "Out of Chicago, a Black 'Ulysses.'" *Chicago Sun-Times* 19 July 1992, Book Week: 12.

Byrne, Jack. "*Divine Days.*" *The Review of Contemporary Fiction* 14.1 (Spring 1994): 210-12.

Coates, Joseph. "A Vast Swirl of Voices." *Chicago Tribune* 2 Aug. 1992: N3.

Crouch, Stanley. "*Divine Days.*" *The New York Times Book Review* 25 July 1993: 14.

McPherson, James A. "The Promised Land." *Chicago* 42.1 (Jan. 1993): 55-56.

Publishers' Weekly 239.22 (11 May 1992): 52.

Robinson, Fredrick D. "Jazzed-up Storytelling Infuses *Divine Days.*" *Atlanta Journal and Constitution* 21 June 1992: N10.

Shuman, R.B. "*Divine Days*: A Novel." *Choice* 31.6 (Feb. 1994): 934.

Streitfeld, David. *Washington Post* 22 Nov. 1992, Book World: 15.

BOOK REVIEWS ABOUT *RELOCATIONS OF THE SPIRIT: ESSAYS*

Braun, Janice. "*Relocations of the Spirit.*" *Library Journal* 199.1 (Jan. 1994): 116-17.

Publishers' Weekly 240.50 (13 Dec. 1993): 54-55.

Watkins, Mel. "*Relocations of the Spirit: Essays.*" *The New York Times Book Review* 29 May 1994: 14.

BOOK REVIEW OF THE REPRINTS

Outlaw, Marpessa Dawn. *Village Voice* 34 (3 Oct. 1989): 54.

SHORT STORY BY LEON FORREST

"Oh Say Can You See." *StoryQuarterly* 15/16 (1982): 83-86.

POETRY BY LEON FORREST

"Ezekiel, Notes Towards a Suicide; Poem." *Negro Digest* 15 (June 1966): 48.

"Richard Hunt's Jacob's Ladder." *Black American Literature Forum* 18.1 (1984): 14-15.

WORKS PUBLISHED AS WORK-IN-PROGRESS

"That's Your Little Red Wagon." *Blackbird* (1966): Section from *There Is a Tree More Ancient Than Eden*.

"Jazz Odyssey." *Obsidian: Black Literature in Review* 1.1 (1975): 50-66. Section from *The Bloodworth Orphans*.

"Packwood's Sermon by Firelight." *Massachusetts Review* 18 (1977): 621-30. Section from *The Bloodworth Orphans*.

"Oh Jeremiah of the Dreamers." *Callaloo* 2.2 (1979): 73-80. Section from *There Is a Tree More Ancient Than Eden*.

"Big House/Praise Shack." *StoryQuarterly* 10 (Spring 1980): 177-90. Section from *Two Wings to Veil My Face*.

"Inside the Body of a Green Apple Tree." *Iowa Review* 14.1 (1984): 30-50.

"Sub-Rosa." *Tri-quarterly* 60 (1984): 254-83.

"Sugar Groove." *Callaloo* 10.4 (1987): 656-65. Section from *Divine Days*.

"An Avalanche of Creation." *Callaloo* 13.4 (1990): 703-26. Section from *Divine Days*.

WORKS EXCERPTED AND ANTHOLOGIZED

"There Is." *Giant Talk: An Anthology of Third World Writings*. Ed. Quincy Troupe. New York: Random House, 1975: 299-306. Excerpt from *There Is a Tree More Ancient Than Eden*.

"Noted with Pleasure." *New York Times* 24 Apr. 1988: G51. Excerpt from *There Is a Tree More Ancient Than Eden*. "from *Divine Days*." *Callaloo* 16.2 (1993): 368-91. Excerpt from *Divine Days*.

OTHER CREATIVE WORKS BY LEON FORREST

Theatre of the Soul, a three-act play, performed at Parkway Community House, Chicago, Nov. 1967.

Re-Creation, a one-act verse play, set to music by T.J. Anderson, presented at the studio of Richard Hunt, Chicago, June 1978.

The libretto for the opera *Soldier Boy, Soldier.* Composed by T.J. Anderson. Produced at the University of Indiana at Bloomington, Oct. - Nov. 1982.

OPERA REVIEWS

Porter, Andrew. Rev. of *Soldier Boy, Soldier. The New Yorker* 58 (13 Dec. 1982): 181-82.

Stroff, Stephen M. Rev. of *Soldier Boy, Soldier. Opera News* 47 (1 Jan. 1983): 38-39.

GENERAL ESSAYS BY LEON FORREST

"Faulkner/Reforestation: Faulkner and Yoknapatawpha." in *Faulkner and Popular Culture*, ed. Ann J. Abadie and Doreen Fowler. Jackson: University of Mississippi Press, 1990.

"In the Light of the Likeness—Transformed." In *Contemporary Authors. Autobiography series.* Vol. 7. Detroit: Gale Research, 1988. 21-35.

"Luminosity at the Lower Frequencies: An Essay on Ralph Ellison's *Invisible Man.*" *Carleton Miscellany* 18.3 (Fall 1980): 82-97.

"Milestones in Black History: A Basic Reading List." *Chicago Tribune Book World* 3 Feb. 1980: G3.

"Mortimer Adler's Invisible Writers." (Perspective) *Chicago Tribune* 3 Dec. 1990: 15.

"A Solo Long-Song: For Lady Day." *Callaloo* 16.2 (Spring 1993): 332-67.

"Souls in Motion (In Chicago's Black Churches . . .)." *Chicago* 34.7 (July 1985): 128+.

"Spiritual Flight of Female Fire." *Directions* (Newsletter of the Program on Communication and Development Studies, Northwestern University) 4 (1990): 5-8.

"Writers List the Books They Plan to Give as Christmas Gifts This Year." *Chicago Tribune* 9 Dec. 1984: N41.

BOOK REVIEWS BY LEON FORREST

"Forged Injustice." Rev. of *Leadership, Love and Aggression*, by Allison Davis. *Chicago* 32.11 (Nov. 1983): 146+.

Rev. of *The Art of Fiction*, by John Gardner. *Chicago Tribune* 1 Apr. 1984: N41.

Rev. of *The Autobiography of Black Chicago*, by Dempsey Travis. *Chicago* 31.4 (Apr. 1982): 112+.

Rev. of *Banco*, by Henri Charrierre. *Chicago Tribune* 20 Jan. 1974: G3.

Rev. of *The Book of Sand*, by Jorge Luis Borges and *The Gold of Tigers. Chicago Tribune* 9 Oct. 1977: G2.

Rev. of *Drylongso: A Self-portrait of Black America*, by John L. Gwaltney. *Chicago Tribune* 31 Aug. 1980: G2.

Rev. of *Going to the Territory*, by Ralph Ellison. *Chicago Tribune* 10 Aug. 1986: N44.

Rev. of *Just Above My Head*, by James Baldwin. *Chicago Tribune* 16 Sept. 1979: G1.

Rev. of *Six of One*, by Rita Mae Brown. *Chicago Tribune* 15 Oct. 1978: G4.

Rev. of *Son of the Morning*, by Joyce Carol Oates. *Chicago Tribune* 29 July 1978: G1.

Rev. of *The World Within the Word*, by William H. Gass. *Chicago Sun-Times* 2 Sept. 1978: S9.

Rev. of *Writers at Work: The Paris Review Interviews, Sixth Series*, ed. George Plimpton. *Chicago Tribune* 14 Oct. 1984: N39.

Rev. of *The Yawning Heights*, by Alexander Zinoviev. *Chicago Tribune* 17 June 1979: G1.

"Snapshots Portraiture from Parks." Rev. of *To Smile in Autumn: A Memoir*, by Gordon Parks. *Chicago Sun-Times* 16 Dec. 1979: C17.

"Three Different Views of the Fight for Equality." Rev of *Black Odyssey*, by Nathan Huggins; *My Soul Is Rested*, by Howell Raines; and *A Passion for Equality*, by Nick and Mary Kotz. *Chicago Sun-Times* 16 Oct. 1977: S20.

"Watching the Town Come to Life." Rev. of *The Avenue, Clayton City*, by C. Eric Lincoln. *New York Times* 8 May 1988: G7.

WORKS ABOUT LEON FORREST

Anania, Michael. "A Commitment to Grit: The Literary History of a Raw, Slangy Town." *Chicago* 32.11 (Nov. 1983): 200-07.

Anderson, T.J. "On *Soldier Boy, Soldier:* The Development of an Opera." *Black Music Research Newsletter* 7.2 (1985): 1-4.

Anderson, T.J. "On *Soldier Boy, Soldier:* The Development of an Opera." (Reprint) *Black Music Research Journal* 10.1 (1990): 160-66.

"Another Chicago Press Announces *Divine Days*, the Long Awaited Novel by Leon Forrest." *National Black Review* 5.2 (1992): 18-19.

Black Writers. Detroit: Gale Research, 1989: 202-03.

Blades, John. "Chicago Novelists Escape the Publishing Graveyard." *Chicago Tribune* 22 Nov. 1987: N3.

Bone, Robert. "Black Writing in the 1970s." *The Nation* 227.21 (16 Dec. 1978): 677-79.

Byerman, Keith. *Fingering the Jagged Grain: Tradition and Form in Recent Black Fiction*. Athens: University of Georgia Press, 1985. 238-55.

Cawelti, John G. "Earthly Thoughts on Divine Days." *Callaloo* 16.2 (Spring 1993): 431-47.

——. "Introduction (Leon Forrest: A Special Section)." *Callaloo* 16.2 (Spring 1993): 329-32.

Cohen, George. "Quintet: Five Writers of Indelibly Chicago Style." *Chicago Tribune* 8 June 1980: 154.

Contemporary Authors. v. 89-92. Detroit: Gale, 1980: 172.

Contemporary Authors. New Revision Series. v. 25. Detroit: Gale, 1989: 132-33.

Contemporary Literary Criticism. v. 4. Detroit: Gale, 1975: 163-65.

Fabre, Michel. "Leon Forrest." *Contemporary Novelists* 2nd ed. London: St. James Press, 1976: 299-300.

Franklin, John Hope. *From Slavery to Freedom: A History of Negro Americans.* 5th edition. New York: Knopf, 1980: 497.

Grimes, Johanna L. "Leon Forrest." *Afro-American Fiction Writers After 1955.* Ed. Thadious M. Davis and Trudier Harris. (*Dictionary of Literary Biography*, v. 33) Detroit: Gale Research Co., 1984: 77-83.

Grossman, Ron. "Tending the Past: Neighborhood Tavern a Backdrop to History in Its Ex-barkeep's New Novel." *Chicago Tribune* 10 Feb. 1993, sec. 5: 1+.

Harper, Michael S. "Corrected Review." (Poem) *Images of Kin: New and Selected Poems.* Urbana: University of Illinois Press, 1977: 64-65.

Land, I.S. "First Novelists." *Library Journal* 98 (1 Feb. 1973): 441.

Lee, A. Robert, ed. "Making New: Styles of Innovation in the Contemporary Black American Novel." *Black Fiction: New Studies in the Afro-American Novel Since 1945.* New York: Barnes & Nobles, 1980. 245-48.

"Leon Forrest Wins Carl Sandburg Award." *Atlanta Journal* 28 Dec. 1984: 3.

McQuade, Molly. "The Yeast of Chaos: An Interview with Leon Forrest." *Chicago Review* 41.2-3 (Spring-Summer 1995): 43-52.

Mootry, Maria K. "If He Changed My Name: An Interview." *Massachusetts Review* 18 (1977): 631-42.

——. "If He Changed My Name: An Interview." *Chant of Saints: A Gathering of Afro-American Literature, Art, and Scholarship.* Ed. Michael S. Harper and Robert B. Stepto. Urbana: University of Illinois Press, 1979: 146-57.

Muwakkil, Salim. "Rarities." *Reader* 30 Mar. 1984: 50-51.

Neville, Ken. "Novelist's Family and Students Inspire Plots." *Parents Quarterly* (Northwestern University) Summer 1984: 5.

Plumpp, Sterling. "Blues for Leon Forrest." (Poem) *The Black Nation* 5 (1986): 52.

"Profile of Novelist Leon Forrest." *Chicago Tribune* 5 Feb. 1984: N33.

"Quintet." *Chicago Sun-Times* 8 June 1980: I54.

Reich, Howard. "3 Black Artists Tell Forum of their Pains and Gains." (T.J. Anderson, Leon Forrest, and Richard Hunt) *Chicago Tribune* 28 Feb. 1991: 22.

Russell, Stephanie, and Kathryn Nash. "A Different Drummer." *North-western Perspective* 2.3 (1989): 8-11.

Schultz, Elizabeth A. "The Heir of Ralph Ellison: Patterns of Individualism in the Contemporary Afro-American Novel." *CLA Journal* 22.2 (1978): 101-22.

Scott, Nathan A., Jr. "Black Literature." *Harvard Guide to Contemporary American Writing.* Ed. Daniel Hoffman. Cambridge: Belknap Press of Harvard UP, 1979: 287-341.

Smith, Gary. "Leon Forrest." *Papyrus* 1 (Spring 1987): 19-37.

Taylor-Guthrie, Danille. "Sermons, Testifying, and Prayers: Looking Beneath the Wings in Leon Forrest's *Two Wings to Veil My Face.*" *Callaloo* 16.2 (Spring 1993): 419-30.

Thomas, H. Nigel. *From Folklore to Fiction: A Study of Folk Heroes and Rituals in the Black American Novel.* New York: Greenwood Press, 1989: 103-08, 158-73.

Varro, Barbara. ". . . But That Made Forrest an Author." *Chicago Sun-Times* 26 June 1977: S9.

Warren, Kenneth W. "The Mythic City: An Interview with Leon Forrest." *Callaloo* 16.2 (Spring 1993): 392-409.

——. "Thinking Beyond Catastrophe: Leon Forrest's *There Is a Tree More Ancient Than Eden.*" *Callaloo* 16.2 (Spring 1993): 409-19.

Werner, Craig. "Leon Forrest, the AACM and the legacy of the Chicago Renaissance." *The Black Scholar* 23.3-4 (Fall-Winter 1993): 10-28.

Williams, Andrea E. "Rediscovering the American Dream: The Fiction of Imamu Baraka, Leon Forrest, Wilson Harris, and Toni Morrison." (Unpublished paper; Yale University, Afro-American Studies Department; winner of the 1975-76 William Pickens Prize for a literary paper.)

AUDIOVISUALS

Illinois Reads with Illinois Authors, #10: Leon Forrest. (video recording) Wheeling: Library Cable Network, 1986. (VHS, ca. 30 min., sound, color, 1/2 inch)

HONORS

1978   Sandburg Medallion, Chicago Public Library

1984   Carl Sandburg Award

1984 Du Sable Museum Certificate of Merit and Achievement in Fiction.

1985 Friends of Literature Prize.

1985 Leon Forrest Day, declared by Chicago Mayor Harold Washington (April 14).

1986 Award for Fiction, Society of Midland Authors.

1993 Book of the Year Award for Fiction, *Chicago Sun-Times.*

Appendix 1

Leon Forrest:
A Chronology

1937 Leon Forrest is born to teen-age parents: Adeline Green Forrest (17) and Leon Forrest, Sr. (19), at Chicago's Cook County Hospital, January 8, 1937. Adeline Green's people migrated to Chicago from New Orleans, Louisiana. A mulatto from Bolivar County, Mississippi, Leon Forrest Sr. didn't know his father, Archie Forrest. Leon Sr., started working when he was six years old. With his mother, Emma, and his grandmother, Katie, Leon Sr. came to Chicago, in the late 1920's.

1942-1962. Leon, Sr., supports family (or himself) as a bartender on the Santa Fe Railroad. Family lives a stable, lower middle-class negro life, in a five-room apartment, on Chicago's South Side. The great-grandmother of Leon, Jr., Katie, lives with the Forrests until the boy is nine. Lenora Bell—a seamstress who never married—helps to raise Leon and also lives with the Forrests.

1942-1950. Leon Forrest attends a solid negro grade school, Wendell Phillips. Wins the American Legion Award, as the best male student in his class. Father takes eight mm. motion pictures of Leon's graduation. In addition to his photography, Forrest, Sr., writes lyrics for songs; a few are recorded with him singing the lyrics in his light tenor voice. Adeline develops interests in jazz/popular singers, particularly Billie Holiday. She sends off an occasional short story to magazines. None were ever published.

1951-1955. A chef on the Santa Fe allows the Forrests to use his address so that Leon can attend the highly regarded Hyde Park High School (which at the time ranks 3rd or 4th in the State and 15th amongst high schools nationally). Leon is a generally mediocre student, but shows real promise in Creative Writing under the guidance of Mrs. Edyth Thompson, a white teacher. He becomes President of the School's Creative Writing class. At this time, there is only one negro teacher at the school; the school is probably 60% white, 25% black, 10% Asian, 5% Hispanic.

1955-56. Leon attends Wilson Junior College, in Chicago.

1956. Adeline and Leon Forrest, Sr., divorce.

1957. Adeline marries an accountant, William Harrison Pitts. They open a liquor store on 79th and South Park (later King Drive). The 408 Liquors has a package goods section and a lounge. Leon works as a clerk in the package goods section and as a relief bartender while attending Roosevelt University, 1957-58. He also tries to study accounting, but shows no ability, nor appetite.

1958. Forrest is totally consumed by the music of Charlie Parker and the poetry of Dylan Thomas. Listens to recordings of Thomas reading his poetry, while reading the Welsh poet's work silently. Believes that these two artist may hold the key to bridge oral eloquence and intellectual eloquence that he is seeking in his writing. Believes that Parker's music may hold key to exploring the unconscious of African Americans, and that maybe he can translate all of this in writing. Comes under the influence of Eugene O'Neill's plays.

1960. Leon takes a playwrighting course with Norbert Hruby at the extension division of the University of Chicago.

1960-1962. Forrest drops out of college and is drafted into the army. He is stationed at Fort Leonard Wood, in Missouri, and Fort Hood, Texas, for the eight-week cycles of his Basic training in a infantry unit. He is sent to Gelnhausen, Germany for the remainder of his tour of duty. Switched from a line company to a Headquarters outfit, where he works as a Public Information Specialist—following troop training and reporting on it and writing feature stories for the 3rd Armoured Division Newspaper, *Spearhead*. Forrest pursues playwrighting in his off-duty hours; joins the theatre group at the Coleman Kaserne military base in Gelnhausen, as stage manager. On leaves he travels to London and Amsterdam.

1962-1964. Forrest returns to work at 408 Liquors, as manager and bartender. He takes classes at the University of Chicago, in the Extension Division. Takes a poetry workshop with the poet John

Logan. He takes a writing workshop with Perrin Holmes Lowrey. A long three-act play, entitled *Theatre of the Soul*, that Leon had started working on in the Army, is presented. In a class with Professor Lowrey on the Modern Novel, Forrest claims he is changed forevermore after reading Faulkner's *The Sound and the Fury* and re-reading Ellison's *Invisible Man*. He begins to move slowly away from his dream of being a playwright and starts to write fiction. Professor Lowery encourages Forrest about his dream of a writing career, particularly after reading a section from a manuscript that will eventually be a part of *There Is a Tree More Ancient than Eden*. Professor Lowrey lends Forrest a copy of Joyce's *Stephen Hero*, and suggests that he compare this novel with the masterwork, *A Portrait of the Artist As a Young Man*, one of the novels Professor Lowrey had assigned in the class. Through Lowrey, Forrest meets another U. of C. professor, John G. Cawelti.

August 28, 1963. Forrest goes on the March to Washington, with a group from St. Dorothy's Church.

August 21, 1964. Leon's mother, Adeline, dies suddenly, after an operation for cancer of the intestines. She is 45.

September 1964. Forrest moves into a small room in an old building on 61st and Dorchester, composed of musicians, painters, musicians, retired professors, and writers. He purchases a typewriter and starts working on the manuscript to his novel. Works as a part-time office boy and as a member of the Catholic Interracial Council's Speaker's Bureau.

June 1965. Professor Perrin Holmes Lowrey is killed in an automobile accident at Sweet Briar, Virginia.

1965-1968. Forrest writes for and edits local weekly newspapers on the Southside, *The Woodlawn Booster*, the *Englewood Bulletin*. Learns all facets of newspaper writing, including layout, headline writing. He works about 30 hours a week, allowing Leon to continue his pursuit of creative writing in the morning or evenings. He edits for a time the house organ for The Woodlawn Organization, a community self-help, self-determination group.

1966. Leon Forrest meets Allison Davis, the distinguished Social Anthropologist and Professor of Educational Psychology at the U.

of C., at International House. A seventeen-year friendship develops.

1966. Publication of "That's Your Little Red Wagon," a fictional fragment (which will end up as part of *There Is a Tree More Ancient than Eden*) in a short-lived magazine, *Blackbird*. Presents a copy to Prof. John G. Cawelti.

1969-1973. Leon joins the staff of *Muhammad Speaks* as an associate editor. Writes feature stories mainly on the arts. Promoted to Managing Editor, 1972-1973. Forrest is the last non-Muslim editor of this newspaper.
April 6, 1971. Leon Forrest, Sr., dies of chronic diabetes.

September 25, 1971. Leon Forrest marries the former Marianne Duncan.

1971. Forrest completes an early draft of his novel, which is called at this time, *Wakefulness*. Sends manuscript off to a recently promoted editor at Random House, Toni Morrison. Meets Morrison in October, and gets a contract from Random House in November. Manuscript goes through an extensive expansion, at Morrison's suggestion, in late 1971-72. Morrison comes up with the title that finally sticks: *There Is a Tree More Ancient than Eden*.

November 30, 1972. Leon Forrest meets Ralph Ellison. Interviews Ellison over a six-hour period, at Ellison's Riverside Drive apartment in New York, for a feature article published in *Muhammad Speaks* on December 15, 1972. Leon gives the author of *Invisible Man* a copy of the bound galleys of *There Is a Tree More Ancient than Eden*.

February 8, 1973. Ralph Ellison reads his endorsement of *There Is a Tree* to Toni Morrison over the telephone—and sends along the copy—which will become the foreword for the novel; Saul Bellow's statement also comes in to Morrison on the same day.

May 15, 1973. *There Is a Tree More Ancient than Eden* is published.

June 1973. Through the introduction of Jan Carew, chair of African-American Studies at Northwestern, Forrest meets with

Hanna Gray, Dean of the College of Arts and Sciences at Northwestern University. Dean Gray makes Forrest an offer of a position in the African-American Studies Department, as an Associate Professor, without tenure, with a five-year contract. Forrest joins the NU faculty in September 1973.

1977. *The Bloodworth Orphans* is published by Random House. Forrest is advanced to tenure by Provost Raymond Mack, June 10, 1978, after two committees had voted for tenure, but the Dean of the College of Arts and Sciences, Rudolph H. Weingartner had turned down Leon Forrest's bid for advancement. Leon's verse-play, *Recreation*, is set to music by the composer, T.J. Anderson, and performed in the studios of Chicago sculptor, Richard Hunt, June 11, 1978.

1977-1991. Leon Forrest takes occasional classes with Marvin Mirsky, a senior lecturer in the Humanities Division and head, at one time, of the Extension Program for Continuing Education, University of Chicago. Later Mirsky taught literature courses with gatherings of students on a private basis. Among the courses Forrest took with Mirsky were: The Bible (Old and New Testament); the novels of William Faulkner; the major works of Dostoyevsky; James Joyce's *Ulysess*; the major novels of Virginia Woolf; Proust's *Remembrance of Things Past*; selected plays of William Shakespeare.

1981. Forrest gives the inaugural Allison Davis Lecture, sponsored by the African-American Studies Dept. at Northwestern University, on Herman Melville's *Benito Cereno*. (Professor Davis attends the first two lectures in his honor; the second was given by Barbara Fields.)

1981-82. Serves as the first African-American President of the Society of Midland Authors. The opera, *Soldier Boy, Soldier* (music by T.J. Anderson) for which Leon wrote the libretto, is produced at the University of Indiana, at Bloomington, Oct.-Nov. 1982.

November 21, 1983. Allison Davis dies. Leon gives one of the eulogies at Bond Chapel, University of Chicago.

1984. *Two Wings to Veil My Face* (Random House) is published— the last of Forrest's novels edited by Toni Morrison; once again the famous writer suggests the title for Leon's book. Forrest wins the duSable museum Certificate of Merit and Achievement in Fiction; the Carl Sandburg Award; the Friends of Literature Prize; and the Society of Midland Authors Award for fiction.

Spring 1984. Forrest is promoted to the rank of full professor by Dean Weingartner.

April 14, 1985. By proclamation, Chicago's Mayor Harold Washington declares this day as Leon Forrest Day. The citation from the late Mayor stated in part: "This distinguished, major American writer is a native son of Chicago, whose outstanding achievements bring special recognition and praise to our great city."

August 1985-1994. Forrest serves as Chair of African-American Studies at Northwestern, where he also holds a professorship in the English Department.

1984. *Divine Days* is started. Leon completes the manuscript of 1829 pages in late August 1991.

1987. Lee Webster, publisher of Another Chicago Press, brings out all three of Forrest's novels in paperback, with new covers selected from catalogues of Richard Hunt's paintings. Professor John G. Cawelti writes the introduction to *The Bloodworth Orphans*; Toni Morrison writes the foreword for *Two Wings to Veil My Face*.

July 1992. Another Chicago Press brings out 1500 copies of *Divine Days*. Novel receives spectacular reviews. 125 copies were returned from bookstores to the publishing house. In the basement of Webster's Oak Park home, on Christmas night, smoke from an electrical fire damages all remaining copies of *Divine Days* (except for a few copies in possession of the author). Then the distributor for Another Chicago Press goes bankrupt. Three weeks after the fire, *Divine Days* is selected for the *Chicago Sun-Times* Book of the Year Award, for the best local fiction published in 1992.

May 1993. *Callaloo* Magazine, devotes a section of the Spring, 1993 issue to studies on Leon Forrest's works. John G. Cawelti edits this section, which includes critiques of Forrest's novels—one on *There Is a Tree More Ancient than Eden* by Kenneth Warren, as well as an interview conducted by Warren with Forrest; Danille Taylor-Guthrie's essay on *Two Wings to Veil My Face*. John G. Cawelti's long study of *Divine Days*, marks the first in-depth interpretation of the novel published thus far.

May 15, 1993. A five-hour benefit reading of *Divine Days* for Another Chicago Press is held from 12:30-5:30, at the Green Mill Jazz Club, 4802 North Broadway, in Chicago. Modeled on the yearly 24-hour reading of James Joyce's *Ulysses*, in Dublin. Writers Larry Heineman, Studs Terkel, Sterling Plumpp, Lerone Bennett, and Forrest were among those who appeared and read from selected sections of the novel.

May 27, 1993. Forrest undergoes surgery for colon cancer at Evanston Hospital. Although the operation is successful, Leon is directed by his physicians to take chemo-therapy for six months.

July 18, 1993. Leon delivers the convocation address for the College of Arts and Sciences.

July 1993. Through the intervention of Leon's literary agent, Faith Childs, W.W. Norton and Another Chicago Press collaborate and bring out *Divine Days* in hardback.

March 1994. Moyer Bell publishes Forrest's collection of essays, *Relocations of the Spirit*. Essays include compositions on Elijah Muhammad, Billie Holiday, Ralph Ellison, Toni Morrison, Herman Melville and William Faulkner.

April 16, 1994. Ralph Ellison dies. Leon delivers one of the eulogies at the private funeral.

June 1994. Forrest visits Berlin and Hamburg as a part of a ten-day exchange visit between Chicago writers and Berlin writers.

January 30, 1995. W.W. Norton brings out *Divine Days* in paperback.

A few of the reactions to Divine Days

". . . The Ulysses of Chicago's South Side. . . . Not since Joyce and Faulkner has a writer so brilliantly synthesized the whole range of qualities expressed in a place, a small group of characters, and a culture."

John G. Cawelti, Professor,
University of Kentucky, at Lexington

"An adventurous master work that provides our literature with a signal moment."

Stanley Crouch, *New York Times Book Review*

"Simply put, Leon Forrest's massive masterpiece is the *War and Peace* of the African-American novel."

Henry Louis Gates, Jr.

"Divine Days is like nothing else in our literature . . . a sluicing of the energies of black speech. It looms as a tour de force carnival of tongues. References to Rabelais, Shakespeare and Joyce are not misplaced. . . . It is a rare thing in our self-conscious and ironic age—a full-out serious work of art."

Sven Birkerts, *New Republic*

Appendix 2

Leon Forrest at the University of Kentucky: Two Interviews

a. On *There Is a Tree More Ancient than Eden*
December 1, 1994

This discussion took place between Leon Forrest and ten graduate students in a seminar on Faulkner and African-American literature directed by John Cawelti. The students had studied several works by Faulkner and a number of African-American writers including Richard Wright (*Native Son*), Ralph Ellison (*Invisible Man*), James Baldwin (*Go Tell It on the Mountain*), Toni Morrison (*Song of Solomon*) and Forrest's *There Is a Tree More Ancient than Eden.*

JOHN CAWELTI: This is a session with Leon Forrest where we'll go around the table with every person having a chance to ask a question.

STUDENT: (Asks about Forrest' relationship to the Harlem renaissance and whether he had met Louis Armstrong.)

FORREST: No, I didn't know Armstrong, but listened to him all the time. My great uncle went to school with him in New Orleans and knew him a bit. I certainly am in the tradition of the experimental African-American novelists. I guess the thing I would resist, of course, would be that the only writers who influenced me were African-American. My influences are all across the board like Ellison. I'm interested in breakthroughs in writing and the novel form, and even poetry wherever they happen. I am indebted to all of these writers. Then out of my reading and my experiences, I try to reshape something that has my own stamp to it and that is how style evolves.

STUDENT: I have a question dealing with the "Lives" section of *There Is a Tree More Ancient than Eden*. It seems to bear a strong resemblance to the "Appendix" to Faulkner's *The Sound and the Fury*.

FORREST: It certainly does. When I studied *The Sound and the Fury* for the first time at the University of Chicago, the "Appendix" was at the beginning of the book. Now they have it at the end. It was helpful having it at the beginning. I had actually written all of *There Is a Tree*, the 1973 version, and my editor, Toni Morrison said that in order to sell this to her fellow editors, the book needed some kind of introduction. She was fascinated by the material, but without some understanding of the characters which glue the text together it was too difficult to understand. Actually, the novel as it was originally written began with Chapter 2. I went back and wrote "Lives" and I did get the idea from Faulkner. No doubt about that. I wrote all of that in about two months, I was so hot to have a contract.

But I also like the idea of the competition. I knew that Faulkner wrote the "Appendix" about 15 years after the novel. It is wonderful material. Here was a chance to "box" the old man. No matter how much the young writer admires the older one, if he is worth anything he wants to beat him. That's probably a male perspective.

STUDENT: Was it a conscious decision to place it at the beginning?

FORREST: Oh, sure. I had to have something to help the reader get into the book. Faulkner offered a way and I was going to see if I could use that and then beat him at his game. That may be egotistical, but that's the way it was. The first section of the book that was actually published was in a little magazine called *Blackbird*. That was actually Chapter 3, which starts on page 46. It was originally called "That's your little red wagon." The phrase is kind of a put-down in African-American culture. It is a wild chapter in a book that is not known for modesty.

The reason that I went to Random House with the manuscript was this: One of the editors of the Muslim paper *Muhammad Speaks*, where I worked at the time, had a contact with Holt, Rinehart who had published Toni Morrison's novel *The Bluest Eye* in 1970. I sent the manuscript to them and the editor liked it a lot, but said "I can't make sense of it." He said "You might send it to

Toni Morrison, who is an editor at Random House and recently promoted. She might be interested." So, I called there and at that time, you could get right through to her. She was sitting at her desk. So I described the manuscript. She said "That sounds interesting. Send it to me." I did. She called me back the next week. I went up to New York to review a play by Melvin van Peebles for *Muhammad Speaks*. Morrison and I met and I gave her the section that was published in *Blackbird* Magazine. That was helpful to her in arguing with the other editors to get it published. You know how that works in a company. All of you are editors. If you have a manuscript you are interested in, you've got to convince the other people around the table. It is sort of a collective thing.

Morrison was a very good editor on several levels. She was an excellent line editor. She, too, is very much caught up in language. We had a tough fight to get my works through at Random House. She had to do some boxing there. I like to think that eventually I would have been published, but at the time I could not have done it without Morrison's help. She was indispensable. You must have a literary agent, today.

STUDENT: You can't just make a phone call?

FORREST: No, nothing as simple as that. As I mentioned, I wrote the "Lives" section after this. One of the things I was trying to do was to reconsider what I had already written. "Lives" ends with a section on Abraham Lincoln. I don't know which section is the heart of the book and I really don't even like to use that term, but the Lincoln section is pretty important in that it reflects the savagery of America. It's pulling up a leader and then destroying him. It's the way we use up things. African-American music has been used in this way, becoming tainted and destroyed by being commercialized, then corrupted.

STUDENT: Is this linked in with the "Transformations" section which you added later?

FORREST: The tension between destruction and resurrection, between death and rebirth, is central to *There Is a Tree* and this idea was instrumental in my decision to add the last two sections when the novel was republished. This section includes Sweetie Reed's letter, which is about the way the effigy of Johnson is destroyed, and the sermon on Martin Luther King, which is also about leadership and its destruction. The "Lives" section ends with Lincoln and now the novel itself ends with King, great leaders of the 19th and 20th century. The tension between the destruction and resurrection of leaders is also summed up at the end of the "Vision" section. Then there is an attempt to gather up what is left over in this remnant.

The "Lives" section is quite stark with many destroyed lives, Jamestown Fishbond, M.C. Browne, Lincoln, even the little section about Stale-Bread Winters who has such great potential and is driven to destroy himself. Many people, like Breedlove, develop great strength and survive. Louis Armstrong is an example. These people survive through the strength of several resources in black culture. These are the remnants of hope within the "Lives" section, as exemplified in Hattie Breedlove Wordlaw, Louis Armstrong, Frederick Douglass, Harriet Tubman, Jericho Witherspoon and Taylor "Warm Gravy" James, the jazz musician. They represent sources of strength in African-American life. Music, certain powerful historical figures of affirmation, and the tradition of religious faith.

CAWELTI: I think you said that *There Is a Tree* was originally titled "Wakefulness." How did you happen to decide on using a different title?

FORREST: That was Morrison's idea, and it was an excellent one, too. It was Morrison who gave me, ultimately, a title for the book. We had gone round and round on it. I sent her 40 titles one weekend. I wasn't sure of what it should be called.

CAWELTI: What were some of your early ideas for a title?

FORREST: They were outlandish. I can do a pretty good title as a newspaper man and was nifty at headlines for other peoples' stories, but the title of my book was different. I suggested "Deep Rivers of the Soul." At one point we were calling it "Of Eden and Thebes." Eventually Morrison came up with the idea of *There Is a Tree More Ancient than Eden*. I liked it very much. It seemed close to a Negro spiritual. For her, it may also have implied some African themes. Morrison also had the idea of using a different type face for the "Vision" section. It was helpful, I thought. You know she was easy to work with. The copy editor and even the person who sets the type are important in making a book.

STUDENT: I wanted to ask about the section where Jamestown and Breedlove argue . . . (Chap. 9)

FORREST: That's not Breedlove. That's Witherspoon.

STUDENT: Oh, I thought it was Breedlove.

FORREST: Oh, no. Breedlove would be much more religious. She probably wouldn't even have talked with Jamestown. But there are a lot of connections between Jamestown and Witherspoon. They were both men on the run. They were both individualists, quite arrogant and purposeful. Jamestown would be something of a kind of a figure, I suppose, for Nathaniel. He's something like Guitar in relation to Toni Morrison's Milkman.

The argument between Jamestown and Witherspoon also is somewhat like the implicit argument that is going on in *Invisible Man* between Booker T. Washington and W.E.B. DuBois. In the first chapter of that novel, the invisible man gets in trouble there at the battle royal by saying "social equality." It stops everything. He goes back to "social responsibility." This would certainly have had an influence and, in our time, the argument between Martin Luther King and Malcolm X would be there too. But I want to take it to another level. What I wanted to do with eloquence on paper was to go beyond Malcolm or Martin Luther King or any of them. I have the arrogance to think I can do that on paper. I can never match them as talkers. I would not even try. But with great respect for Dr. King I think I have to have the faith that I can do things that these eloquent men couldn't do. I have the benefit of history. I have the benefit of other literatures that I can bring in there, whereas in an orally-delivered argument, you would not have the time to do that. You wouldn't have the audience to do that.

CAWELTI: Would you say that there are echoes of Lincoln in Witherspoon's argument?

FORREST: The Lincoln section is very important to all of this. There you have an attempt to play with the agony of the man, even his looks. And to play with the myth of Lincoln and the mystery. They are connected.

STUDENT: Did it help you to have Morrison's endorsement for your book?

FORREST: I think Morrison was almost as unknown as I was at the time. It wouldn't have been much help to have her name on the book then. She was very helpful in getting me published. As to marketing it, I was benefitted by two things. One was that Ellison wrote the introduction. His introduction and Saul Bellow's endorsement came in the same day. Then I got a terrific review from Anatole Broyard in the daily *New York Times*. We used all of that. There was never any thought that it would sell very much. To some degree, it was a benefit that Random House saw this as yet another affirmative action thing, to help them get through this period. They didn't think that black writing would be around long, at the time. It is just like black studies departments. The idea was in many places. "Let's get them through this. They are not going to last." There was no idea of investing in my talent by Random House, though Morrison believed in it. Ellison's introduction was more important to me for his opinion rather than his influence on sales. I just hoped that it would sell enough and people would get interested a little bit, so I would begin to develop an audience. I never had any interest in being popular, a best-selling commercial writer.

One danger with things in this country is that anything that has any credibility to it and yeast to it is soon going to be commercialized and lose its effectiveness. Much of the genius in Afro-American life has already been taken off, commercialized, and marketed. It's always a struggle to recreate it and give some originality to it. That was what be-bop did with jazz. As a serious artist, I can't get too concerned with the commercialization of Malcolm X, but I do connect it with what we have done with Lincoln and other figures. There's death, there's assassination, and there's canonization and then there's destruction and commercialization. It will probably take writers and historians many years to really get some leverage on Malcolm. I thought one of the problems with the movie was that it down-played the over-arching power in his life of Elijah Muhammad. I knew Muhammad fairly well. He was nobody's fool. An encounter between the two probably was like a very charismatic politician running into a master precinct leader.

STUDENT: What new writers are you most interested in?

FORREST: I find myself increasingly going back to the writers that originally moved me. I very seldom find any new ones. One would be Rita Dove. I like her work a lot. I am always looking for those writers who will energize me because I am trying to fill each page with a certain turbulence and ecstacy and intelligence. I'm still particularly excited by the Russian writers, especially Dostoyevsky. Recently I've been transforming a verse play into a novel of voices with lots of monologues, and for that reason, I have been reading a lot of poetry. What I read depends a lot on what I am working on. If I am working on something where there is a lot of dialogue, then I will turn to plays. I am very fascinated by a lot of O'Neill and Archibald MacLeish, for instance.

STUDENT: Are you bothered that your books haven't become bestsellers?

FORREST: Not really. I can't be bothered about that. All I can worry about is trying to see if I can write a great American novel. Northwestern University has been kind enough to give me a job so I can buy a decent meal and take my wife out occasionally and buy a good bottle of bourbon. My tastes are quite simple. Cawelti here has said some nice things about my work and that means a lot. The point is that writing means everything to me, since I am a person who is drawn to seek and project in an ultimate way some sense of order in life. I'm very drawn to the life of this chaotic and crazy country, but the one place where I can get some leverage on this is in writing. In situation after situation, when I have been involved in churches, in bars, in love affairs, in all kinds of things, I was always sort of swept away. Writing is the one place where I can project this inner and outer chaos and transform it into something different. I didn't mean to sound as arrogant as I must have sounded earlier when I said I was trying to do better than Dr. King. I could never preach with these guys, but I can do something on paper, using their work as a springboard. I also admire the great jazz musicians, but I couldn't play any instrument. I took piano for about 5 or 6 years and can't play a tune. But I do seem to have a good ear for what is going on in music and taking that and making that into something else. No, you may not be able to do all these things, but if you are a writer, you can use these sources for transformation into something else. Finally a writer has to be a crazy blend of a person who is arrogant and at the same time quite humble.

I've been lucky to have a great heritage, that of African-American culture and I have benefitted from that. It was a tremendous heritage and this heritage of literature, both black and western stood in my favor. But I have to transform all of this into something else to mean anything. As I once told my father, it saved my life. I would be over there in skid row or probably waiting for a drink if I weren't a writer. Literature can give you an ennobling sense of yourself and lift you up and save you sometimes, even though when you actually meet writers you may think they are mean little beasts until you read their work!

STUDENT: Do you feel it is important to write about the past and the implications of history?

FORREST: Sure. It is important and it also is important to get past it. Because, you can get so overwhelmed by history, you can end up like one of Faulkner's characters, like Hightower, for example. There is a danger of becoming entrapped in the past and I think Morrison sees this. There's a problem, of course, with Black Americans and with what other Americans know about their past. A lot of it hadn't been recorded. A lot had been subordinated and left out of history books and literature and so on. On the other hand, you can get so trapped in going back, you don't do any new reinspection of the past. You sort of echo it. You get so involved in it that you can't free yourself. Blacks needed to do this, for sure and we all need to be aware that part of America's heritage is the slave past. My history is your history. Your history is my history. At the same time, you can be so entrapped by it that you don't go on. That's the great thing with the jazz musicians. People like Ellington, Armstrong, Billie Holliday, Charlie Parker faced all kinds of vicious insults and racism, yet look at the music they produced. Right in the face of it.

STUDENT: Which Dostoyevsky novels do you like?

FORREST: *The Brothers Karamazov* and, of course, *Crime and Punishment* and *Notes from Underground*. Dostoyevsky's sense of struggle going on within the embattled soul I found to be instrumental for my own dealing with the divisions in the African-American soul. Dostoyevsky also had the sense that a people can have a special mission. You've got that in the Civil Rights Movement and a lot of people felt, certainly King and others did, that something special had happened to us here that could be a great service to the country. Dostoyevsky was very much aware of how the Old Testament Jews were transformed into a new kind of people through their suffering; this was recombined in his imagination with the stories in the Gospel of the New Testament.

There is also his interest in family life of all kinds, certainly a compelling force in my writing. On another level, although I was quite influenced by Ellison, I wanted to stake out my own territory. He didn't do very much with family life, per se. For no matter how much the younger writer might admire the older one, he or she must find ways of getting around that lion or lioness of a literary consciousness and then you have to discover new ways in which the older writer didn't approach the experiences of life. . . . It's as if you were coming here to Lexington and all of you have heard about the strengths in each of the performances at local Baptist churches here. And you want to experience each one . . . and you discover that they have a great choir over at this one . . . at another church you find that there is great preaching to experience each Sunday . . . so you know what's going on at Ellison's church, you know what's going on in Baldwin's church, at Morrison's church, now I've got to show you, reveal to you what is unique at Forrest's church. Just as we could never confuse Billie Holiday with Sarah Vaughn, nor Ella Fitzgerald (that great trinity of female singers); so too, I would hope that you would discover the specialness of my work, in Forest County.

STUDENT: As Kenneth Warren points out in his article, *There Is a Tree* has become a different book because of the "Transformation" section. Could you tell us the process you went through to finally end up with the novel as we now read it, because that was added later?

FORREST: The "Transformation" section relates to the novel in many ways. There are several sermons in the novel, such as the sermonette of M.C. Browne, when he talks about his love of Jesus. I want to tell you a story about this. Browne is the boy who is beaten to death by his father because he is wearing a dress. Some time ago national public television approached Toni Morrison and requested that her work be used within the context of a gospel fest showcase, in Chicago. She suggested my work instead. They called me and I offered certain sections from all the works. The television producers decided on M.C. Browne's sermonette. A minister, who was scheduled to read the section, called me about 6 o'clock one morning. "Brother Forrest, I want to find out what is the meaning of this passage." I said, "Well, read it just as you would the Old Testament." He was sort of knocked back by that. What else could I have said? I might as well be arrogant. The weird thing about it all was the selection of this particular passage—given all the homophobia around. Black church people are as guilty of this as anybody else—despite the vital presence of gays at the heart and soul of some of the very best gospel singing.

But that is one of the sermonettes. There is also a sermon or sermonette which Hattie Breedlove Wordlaw delivers to Nathaniel. Someone asked earlier about the Vision section. That is presented as a kind of incantation—like a sermon. These all relate to the sermon that Pompey c.j. Browne (no relative of M.C.'s) gives in the "Transformation" section. Sweetie Reed's letter is very much in keeping with Lincoln and L.B.J. and the destruction of the leader. I can get a little bit more subtle on it, but that was the basic idea. I feel fully confident that the parts hang together—old with new. But I should leave that for the critics to say.

STUDENT: Here's the book under cover and on the shelves, but you have an opportunity to modify it.

FORREST: That's right. And again I stole something from Faulkner, this idea of putting something in later. I remember telling Toni Morrison about the additions (after she had been my editor for my first three novels). She said that she sometimes wished she had a chance to do something a little more with *The Bluest Eye*.

CAWELTI: Clearly one reason why you did that is that a new edition was coming out from Another Chicago Press. You might want to tell them about that.

FORREST: Well, Another Chicago Press is the kind of thing that gives you hope in this country, since this publisher is interested in bringing out quality books, instead of commercial smash-hits. That's the genius of this country in a way. The rise of independent publishers has become quite attractive. Now even the university presses in several places are publishing fiction. My publisher for the paperbacks and initially for *Divine Days*, Lee Webster, with Another Chicago Press, has been in the field for the last twelve years. He had learned of my work through his professor at UIC,

Michael Anania. Webster decided if he ever did get involved in publishing he would make certain that my books were brought back out in paperback. All of my novels were out of print when Webster approached me about bringing the novels out, which were originally acquired by Toni Morrison when she was senior editor at Random House. We had of course Ellison's introduction to *There Is a Tree*. Toni Morrison again came to my rescue and wrote the introduction for *Two Wings to Veil My Face*. Mr. Cawelti was so kind to give my readers an excellent map of *The Bloodworth Orphans*.

With Faulkner and all the stuff that was happening during the '20s with the jazz age and with literature, there has been a great tradition of experimentation and I wanted to keep that alive in my work. I am glad to see small presses like ANC coming along, because the commercial presses are so corrupt that all they want to do is cook books and photographic books and they are not open to experimentation. Even in my last novel, *Divine Days*, I was out there, looking for a publisher. Webster was the only one that would take it on, at the time. Of course, the manuscript was 1829 pages . . . and yet there was a time in this country when if some writer came along, an adventurous, first-rate editor would have taken this manuscript on. Once *Divine Days* was published and got marvelous reviews from all the quarterlies, there was a fire and perhaps 75 copies of the novel were smoke-damaged; they were all in my publishers' basement. *Divine Days* had practically sold out the initial run of 1500 copies. When that disaster occurred, we were able to get Norton interested in bringing the novel out (through my literary agent, Faith Childs). They brought the book out in hardback in July 1993, and they brought out the paperback in January 1995.

STUDENT: One of the questions this class has touched on this semester was the problem which black critics had with William Styron's *The Confessions of Nat Turner*. This relates to the whole problem of crossing the color line in fiction. Do you think there ought to be a sort of territorialization of fiction and that certain people are more qualified to write about certain subjects and be considered credible?

FORREST: I would expect that well-trained, well-educated black critics would bring something to the table and would unearth dimensions of both black and white novels that haven't been received before. That's what the rise of another people can do in the democracy and the laboratory of this country. Just as I would expect that women will tell us things, and indeed good sensitive feminist critics are doing this as well. However, I don't think it has to be a female critic or a black critic who can read sensitively. In other words the influence of sensitive women, if I am a good male critic, will enlighten me, so that I can look at texts by women and others in a new way. One hopes a kind of enlightened democracy can happen at this table, because of the diversity of the people here. Ultimately, as Morrison has shown, women can write about hunting scenes and any other kind of scenes. There's Joyce Carol Oates writing about boxing, for example. I believe in enlightened and sensitive, but tough-minded and open, criticism. I don't care, in the long run, for all these critical camps. They are camps. They have their limits. After awhile, you have all the women talking in a certain way; all the blacks talking, all the Hispanics talking a certain way. The danger is that you lose the sense of the daring possibility of the American experience and also the arrogance of my ambition. You know, Morrison has said herself that she's not always going to agree with everything that blacks and women say about her work. That's good. Diversity is all to our group health and our national truth.

STUDENT: But isn't that more the ideal than the truth? In most universities, they shy away from someone black writing about some white author, and they shy away from males writing about female writers. I find that a lot of times they shy away from white critics writing about black writers. I see a bit more leniency there than someone black coming in and writing about a lot of white writers. Particularly when there are no black characters in a book.

FORREST: I guess we have to go through all of this, as a country in process. But I think we try to maintain two things. You want to have a rich production by every new group. Gays, for example, have a lot to add to the richness of culture. I teach Baldwin a lot. But I do think we need good gay critics who can bring a certain perspective to many of his novels. Much as I often teach *Another Country* and have come to admire it in many ways, there is a sense you really do need a gay sensibility to deal with a lot of that novel. However, I think it's important that having said that,

I'm not going to stop teaching that novel and becoming more and more open to a gay sensibility in dealing with it. In the long run, it's how much you are willing to open your imagination up to the different sensibilities that are American. Yet, at the same time, we need to talk about what it means to be an American. That's the best part of Tennessee Williams. That is the best part of Ellison and Morrison, the best of Bellow, for instance. It is not only what it means to be Jewish, but how we find out what it means to be Jewish also has to lot to do with the way Jews have opened up the consciousness of this country. We are all part Jewish too. Certainly to be an American intellectual, you must be a Jew. That's all to the good. Now we are discovering that to be an American intellectual, you must be part black and maybe even discover you are part black. Later on we will see the influence of this, as we are seeing the way women are opening up our consciences. That is the great thing about the being an American right along with all the drive-by shootings and corruption in politics and all that.

STUDENT: When you were talking about the destruction and resurrection of America, is it a matter of democracy or capitalism or what?

FORREST: Well, much of the corruption could be traced to capitalism. Look at the slave heritage, the auctions . . . so much of the economy was based in slavery. At the same time, the other side of it is the American genius in making things. There's a wizardry really in creating things with such power and invention. We've got some very bad schools here, but we've got wonderful universities. Look at all the Americans who win a Nobel prize every year for scientific exploration. That is part of the oneness of experimentation. What we are doing in science and space and so on, and that is possible in time with our literature and possible with our art. I'm not a Marxist, but we have a problem with America. It is very hard for us because along with the freedom of the laboratory and the spirit, there is the excess we get into of commercialization and it has tainted our values. It is hard for us, maybe because we are very young as a nation, to learn a kind of balance, a mean.

CAWELTI: I think we are at the end of our time. Thank you, Leon Forrest.

b. On *The Bloodworth Orphans*
1988

This discussion took place between Leon Forrest and a group of graduate students in a course where Forrest's *The Bloodworth Orphans* was one of the texts studied.

CAWELTI: It's a great pleasure to introduce Leon Forrest. I've asked him to start out with a few remarks on how he came to write *The Bloodworth Orphans.*

FORREST: I thank Dr. Cawelti for inviting me. It may be helpful to know I had published a novel called *There Is a Tree More Ancient than Eden* the year before in 1973. I wanted to write a book that was filled with character and characterization. My first novel was very impressionistic. It tried to capture the consciousness of African-American people in this country , or some of it anyway, in an impressionistic novel influenced by *Portrait of the Artist* and other works. Almost as an answer to the critics of *There Is a Tree*, I wanted to create a novel filled with characters and a lot of character development. That was one impetus to *The Bloodworth Orphans.* The other was the idea of doing something on families. I was influenced not only by Faulkner, but by O'Neill and the rising sense of the crisis in the Afro-American family—indeed the American family. It was another genesis issue. Another was that in my family, there are any number of patterns of orphans: people who have taken in orphans, either by adopting them or raising them or otherwise helping them. This was particularly true of the Catholic side of my family (through the Catholic Family Bureau in Chicago) This gets enriched by the other side of my family tree, which is Protestant and Baptist on my father's side. In the Afro-American extended family any number of people that we knew were brought into the family preserves and raised, even though they were not related to us. They call the older people "aunt, uncle etc."—of course, that also has a southern genesis. Calling people aunt and uncle and cousin gets back to the connection of Negros and whites in the south. So there is always this kind of Southern black-like connection in groups.

There is an additional source. I was brought into the university community at that time, and moved from being a newspaper man to being Associate Professor of African-American Studies at Northwestern. I came into the university mainly with the idea of broadening my intellectual perspective. The writers I admired most, Ellison, Baldwin and Malamud had returned to the university and none were academics in the traditional sense. They had desperately sought in this American society so bereft of intellectual life to find some place of intellectual vibrancy.

At one time in this country, creative writers wrote for newspapers. Many of them are now working with universities. This really started after World War II. When the opportunity developed to come to Northwestern and teach, I thought this would be a possibility of growth. One of the interesting things about writers in this country, in this century, (perhaps separating us from Henry James) is the fact that many of our writers didn't finish college. I didn't finish college, either. I thought that one thing which separated us from the European and Russian novelists was that somehow our education was incomplete. I thought by going back to the university, I might complete that side of my education. What I didn't understand was that the writer lives a life of trying to complete his or her education. It is never completed. That is what I try to convey to my students at Northwestern in undergraduate school as well as in continuing education. At any rate, this experience got me to reading in a serious and a critical way works that I had read in a more general way. I was reading at the time several sources that go into this book. I was first assigned the task of trying to connect Afro-American literature and Native-American writing. I got very interested in reading and rereading certain Native-American writers. That got me back to the mythical aspects of traditional cultures. I became quite fascinated by the Orpheus myth, which appears in many many ways, in black culture, the movie "Black Orpheus" for instance. The myth is about this extraordinary musician in love with this extraordinary woman and she dies and goes to the land of the underground and the only way he can repatriate her is to sing her out a hymn. This spoke to me about Nat King Cole, Billy Eckstine and all these fantastic black singers. How many of your parents or grandparents fell in love while listening to some extraordinary black singer. I come from a people of singers and I have always been attracted to the great singers in literature. The great Irish writers are so helpful here. Joyce and O'Casey and O'Faolain, the great short story writer, that I read in high school. Of course the brilliance of Yeats. This led me to another great influence in my work and that is Dylan Thomas, who is connected as a Welshman to both the Irish heritage and the English. All of that became more vivid in my imagination now that I was at the university where I could read these people critically and intellectually and try to teach them. I was teaching things about oral tradition, not only out of my own heritage but also of the heritage that I also share as a westerner and also the Old Testament. This went into the formation of *The Bloodworth Orphans*.

Another element was the influence of Ellison and Faulkner. *The Invisible Man* and *The Sound and the Fury* are kind of similar works in my own development. In Ellison, it was important for me to see, for perhaps the first time, a black writer who took on the problems of how you translate the oral tradition into the eloquence of traditional literature. Ellison was the black novelist who was able to do this. Faulkner, who also comes out of a highly oral tradition, had the same problems and he was instructive in this. For instance, Faulkner has this extraordinary sermon that you have read in *The Sound and the Fury* of Rev. Shegog. I knew a lot about sermons through both of my heritages . . . my three heritages . . . my Afro-American-Protestant heritage, my Catholic heritage and of course the writers who had developed sermons in their works, such as Melville, and Moby Dick and then of course, Faulkner and Rev. Shegog's sermon. To me, it was just the starting of what I wanted to do. I wanted to do the broadest kind of thing in sermons. Ellison and Faulkner opened up for me the possibility of not only of how you can make a sermon novelistic and how that sermon can be the key to the novel.

Perhaps the third thing would be the connection with James Weldon Johnson, the black writer, who collected a group of sermons. That was oral tradition. I felt that I wanted to move past oral tradition to written tradition. Another key that Ellison offered me was the connection to Lord Raglan and his extraodinary book *The Hero* which was written by a man who was not a trained anthropologist, but who took on that idea of exploring other cultures. Oftentimes, clues to what you are doing can come from someone completely outside of your culture. Your culture, if you are deeply involved in it and if you are American, presents you with a sense of chaos. We are a nation of chaos. If you are an artist, you must make something of chaos, and turn it into art. It is absolutely essential; you will die as an artist or as a man or a woman if you can't do that. You will die, you will kill yourself, if you can't do that privately. All the great artists who killed themselves did so because ultimately they couldn't do it. Your drive is to make some order of this chaos, and oftentimes the clue to this comes from cultures outside of yours. That's one of the ironies of it. Lord Raglan presents a concept of the hero that has become very important to me, along with Ellison's notions about the hero. I was also reading (Heinrich) Zimmers' *King and the Corpse*, and much Eastern literature with the idea of gaining some sense of leverage over the chaos of Afro-American life. I haven't satisfied that and probably won't satisfy that.

In general, I wanted to use the sermon as a means of looking into the whole agony of being Afro-American. I wanted to suggest the spiritual, political, social, and intellectual dymamics of what it meant to be an American. Perhaps I've failed at that, but why is the country so caught up with the preacher? Where did he come from? Throughout my work I've been fascinated with the eloquence of the preacher and with the idea of working my way from oral eloquence to written eloquence, linking that to the problems of identity, of religion, of politics, and culture in society and making it a springboard within my own culture. Those were some of the issues I was involved with.

I wrote many scenes in the novel as monologues. I was very much interested in monologues. Here again Ellison, Faulkner and Dostoyevsky were very helpful. Also the tradition of monologue in our society, the preacher or the comedian—the standup comedian, who expresses his soul through monologue. This is probably the reason there are so many monologues in the world. The idea is that you can express a whole range of life, an epic, a world in a monologue. That was part of what intrigued me about monologues. I started *The Bloodworth Orphans* with the monologue of Carl-Rae Bowman. It happens early in the novel. He is a loose man and as I remember, (it has been a long time) one of the two sons of Rachel Flowers, the two sons she had by a white man in the south. The other one was Industrious. You hear Carl-Rae's last dying monologue there in a garbage can. There is this woman who is trying to save him then but he is a wanderer and a drifter and a lost man. Of course, that is the case with many of the lost souls in this novel and I was very inspired at that time, since it was the first thing I wrote in the novel.

After I left the Muslim paper *Muhammad Speaks*, I worked at home before I went out to Northwestern. I used to go home at night and listen to this song by the extraordinary blues singer Lyman Hoffman. There are some wonderful lines in it and some of them are "On this next train south, you can look for my clothes home but if you don't see my body, Mama, all you can do is mourn." That just haunted me all over. Every night I would go home and rewrite it. My method of writing is to take the most basic kind of line and improvize on it. After all, I am the child of the culture which created jazz. I would just take that line and improvize on it again and again and develop this monologue from it. "On that next train south, you can look for my clothes home. But if you don't see my body, Mama, all you can do is mourn." That got me into the idea of Carl-Rae and the relationship to his mother, and then out of that I began to develop many of the other themes of orphans. I had finished a stay with the Black Muslims and one of their themes was always the idea that Afro-Americans were a lost-found nation. I didn't agree with most of what the movement said but one thing they stood for was the idea that Afro-Americans were a lost-found people in this country. It seems to me that that was a very ironic statement since noone in this society is more American than blacks.

I worked on that theme of orphans with Carl-Rae and that brought in the orphans in my own family and the idea that blacks came to this country and were sold and shipped around and constantly given a sense of being orphans. Ultimately, after the civil war, the greatest quest among black Americans was to find their homes and find who they belonged to. The song which Regal Pettibone loves to sing should perhaps be the theme song of black America. "Sometimes I feel like a motherless child."

I would be glad to answer any questions.

STUDENT: Is this large number of orphans a result of breakdowns within the black family, or is it a broader thing of blacks being brought to this country and being abandoned by the white society?

FORREST: Blacks were forcibly brought into this country and separated early on from their families and their fathers. The search for wholeness and harmony in family emanates from that. But that is not only our condition as black Americans but it afflicts all Americans as this society is played out. In an immediate sense, we can say the black American family is in trouble, which it is for sure. But also the American family is in trouble, and the quest for the father is a very vital contporary concern. When I thought about contemporary life and contemporary black American life the idea of orphans seemed everywhere. I wanted to engage not only the Afro-American past, but contemporary issues. I was also hoping and dreaming, as any writer worth his (her) salt does, that my work would be something that would be helpful or useful to my country.

STUDENT: You mentioned an interest in O'Neill. I'm interested in the monologue. Do you see yourself primarily as a dramatist or as working that into the modern novel. Do you have any interest in doing something on the stage or will you continue to write novels?

FORREST: Initially, I wanted to be a poet. I wrote poetry for a long time, but I didn't have the discipline. That was part of the influence of Yeats, but particularly of Dylan Thomas and his use of monologues and how you could move from all eloquence in general (Dylan Thomas's father was a preacher) to a kind of literary style. I wanted to be a playwright for a long time. I wrote plays and I had one or two produced in reader-style theater. My problem was that I wouldn't work in the theater. I was a snob. Of course you have to work in theater to learn the problems of theatre. Our greatest playwrights have taught us this. Our greatest playwrights Shakespeare, Ibsen, Tennessee Williams, etc. I finally found out that what I was really in love with, after all, was the beauty of dramatic language. I wanted to try to keep alive all these interests, anyway, both in poetry and monologue and theater. I finally came to writing novels. A friend of mine, sort of a running buddy of mine, was in theatre, used to read my work, and he read an extraordinarily long play of mine once and he said "Leon, this is a novel, this isn't a play." It was the love of dramatic literature that I have tried to keep alive in my work. Probably more than I realized I was influenced by Strindberg, which I remembered loving so much. Strindberg was so helpful in these monologues. And Tennessee Williams with these extraordinary monologues of those great ladies. Well, I love ladies too. I also loved them in novels. O'Neill was helpful too, because O'Neill, like Faulkner was always dealing with relationships and emotions of family which lie beneath the surface, which are part of a kind of secret heritage that one does not want to admit. The playwrights were very important and I was also interested in the early '60s before I finally made my last transition in the British playwrights in that wonderful group of Osborne and the angry writers of the British theater and again you think about some extraordinary monologues there. So this was all a part of it.

STUDENT: Have you a collection of your plays? Are they published?

FORREST: No, they are not, but one long play was presented in reader-style theater and I did incorporate some of it in my first novel *There Is a Tree More Ancient than Eden*. The monologue that was by Madge Ann Fishbond. She also showed up in *The Bloodworth Orphans*. I was working as a journalist through all of this. I had this kind of background to work on when I turned to my fiction. Though the protests of the '60s were influential, I thought that the monologue would help me to get into the interior of characters. So often, no one got into the complexity of the black character. I don't think we have touched the surface of his complexity.

The other thing that I tried to do was to move past some of the people who had influenced me. O'Neill connected me with the Irish tradition and Irish literature, which I had already been interested in through reading Yeats and Sean O'Casey. Like African Americans the Irish had the experience of living as a suppressed people, and having to take over the language of the conqueror. This is the way black Americans have taken basketball from white people. They have taken the damn thing over. That's what I wanted to do with writing. Take it over. I learned something about that from the Irish.

STUDENT: I was very impressed by the sentence structure of your prose. I have noticed that it is more or less similar to Faulkner. Did you find yourself consciously using Faulkner's style as a model?

FORREST: I would be a liar and a fool to deny the influence of all I have read. Faulkner was certainly a strong influence, in general. Hardy was a great influence in high school (at Hyde Park); later on South American writers, especially Garcia-Marquez influenced me. But I think Faulkner also showed me a way of breaking open the sentence structure and opening it up so you could go for broke in it. That also helped with the monologues. Of course I was very interested in Faulkner's idea of a mythical kingdom, which also goes back to Hardy. Also, Faulkner's sensitivity to black life in a general way and his understanding of some aspects of the complexity of these relationships. I am certainly not the person to say how far I have gone past Faulkner in creating my own. Faulkner could certainly say, as Charlie Parker once said, that all musicians coming after him would have to pay their dues to him. I certainly have to pay my dues to Faulkner and I don't know if I have gone beyond him or not.

He certainly is an extraordinary influence and I am not the only writer influenced by Faulkner. Styron was, much more than I am; Toni Morrison, very much so; Ellison, Albert Murray. I think the best of Faulkner is involved with black life. With the exception of *As I Lay Dying*, it's only when he deals with this negro presence, that he is onto the tragedy of the south, and indeed this country. Faulkner also is very helpful in terms of clues. You can mention what he did with Rev. Shegog's sermon, for example. I have to go beyond that. There's certainly this competition as Faulkner himself said, "The young writer if he is worth his salt, he wants to beat the old guy." But it's hard to be a better hitter than Ted Williams.

STUDENT: Could you tell us what you see as the central theme of *The Bloodworth Orphans*?

FORREST: I would say that the novel is about African-Americans trying to find a home and the difficulty of that, the difficulty of ever finding some home. In the search for that and the chaos of it. Maybe Africa and the South came together to make this new people—Afro-Americans—in this country. My own thought is that this is ultimately being an American. For Americans, there are none of these ultimate touchstones that you can say are home. You carry home with you. This is what Thomas Wolfe perhaps didn't understand. You carry home with you and you keep going into new territory and facing new problems and chaos and you don't know how much of the old world will keep you alive.

STUDENT: Gospel music seems to play an important part in your work. Could you discuss that?

FORREST: There is a powerful relationship between sexuality and spirituality which seems to me to be the glory and the power of negro gospel music. This marriage of sexuality and spirituality is at the heart of gospel music which is a union between the blues and the spiritual. At one time the notion was in black life that you could never mingle the two. Blues singers would say "Well, you just keep these separate." For a long time, in the middle-class Baptist churches in the north, people like Mahalia Jackson were not allowed. Ultimately, gospel music became important because there was a need to somehow bring together the secular and the spiritual, to find a kind of art form to match up with the growing complexity of black American life in the North.

STUDENT: Your novel is so much concerned with chaos and disruption in the family. Do you see this as a special problem of African-American life, or is this family violence more universal as a theme?

FORREST: I hope you will forgive me, for kind of a short handed answer to this excellent question. I was thinking about this after a book party for my last novel in April 1984. We had had a wonderful day and left this bookstore. Someone stopped us at the door, and said "you know, we just got word that Marvin Gaye was killed by his father." What a terrible family tragedy this was, almost like something Greek. We have a mother, father and son in this house, which was built by the son. But the son is despised by the father, while the mother plays the two off against each other. Women and narcotics are also involved. But this is not just African-American, it's contemporary America. It made me think, once again, that, in the most marvelous ways and in the most horrible ways black Americans are at the center of this society. I don't say this in any bragging. This may be why black American women writers are becoming more and more popular. Perhaps there's a sense that the experience they write about is deeply symbolic of our national experience. Just as when I was growing up Eugene O'Neill seemed so important. He was doing something similar for Irish families. So this whole theme of family chaos and disruption seemed to me suggestive of a broad range of American life.

CAWELTI: In your third novel, *Two Wings to Veil My Face*, you deal with the experience of slavery, like Toni Morrison in her latest novel, *Beloved*, which has made such a tremendous impact on the American public, both white and black. Do you see this as a significant move in Afro-American literature, trying to imaginatively recapture that terrible era which has, until now, been largely absent from African-American fiction. Unless I'm greatly mistaken, there was a period of slave narratives, Frederick Douglass, but that since then that time has been significantly avoided.

FORREST: That's true and I think there will be more of that. I think for me and maybe some of the others, it is a way for us, as Americans to see how entangled we are as a people with our heritage. In the novel *Two Wings to Veil My Face* the main character is a woman, who is 91. The novel is set in 1958. The woman was born two years after the end of the Civil War and four years after the Emancipation Proclamation. My own great-grandmother was born in 1877. I am 51 now. I knew many people, when I was coming along whose grandparents were slaves. It would be true of many people today. So, we are not that far removed from slavery. For the novelist with his larger sense of time, events that were a hundred years ago are not that long removed. Of course, we are still just coming out of the last shadows of the Civil War. Many recent events suggest this. Jesse Jackson's campaign is a phenomenon which poses the question of whether we can elect to the presidency a man whose great-grandfather had been a slave. Generally, there's been very little from our great American writers on slavery. Obviously we have a rich harvest of histories but these are mainly by white historians. There were few black historians historians writing on slavery. But now, we are getting a sense of the complexity of the relationship between slaves and masters so I am interested in trying to evoke that and use that as a way of our understanding our own time. A hundred and twenty years is certainly not a long time in the life of a people, a race or a country. Toni Morrison's last novel is very interested in that. I have been, continually. For me, the theme is more important as it is linked to families. There are many slave families, in this novel, and some of the characters in this novel who are are also presented in my earlier works will probably continue to develop in my novels to come.

I think I am different from Haley in that I am interested in the human complexity of slavery and in what I can do with this as an artist. I like to let the imagination go wherever it might.

STUDENT: What kind of similarities do you see in the black experience as captured by white writers and as captured by black ones, say Faulkner versus Ellison?

FORREST: Well, I don't know if I am a student of these things. In a general way, there is a general failure for me. Maybe I wouldn't be a writer if I didn't think earlier writers had failed, and I wanted to do something different. Most black writing and white writing about black characters is limited. And particularly when it involves black characters pitted against or in confrontation with whites. Of course, there have been certain extraordinary exceptions but some of the exceptional writers did this well on some occasions and didn't on others. I think Faulkner's successful in some things and he falls into very stereotypic characters in others. Richard Wright is oftentimes a failure. On occasion his characters are interesting and somewhat complex, but often they are less complex as characters and more important symbolically. Ellison's characters, in his one great novel, are always very intriguing. Certainly, William Styron's attempt to deal with Nat Turner was extrordinary. So, I want to look at the work. I don't care if its white or black. I don't agree that "if you're white, you can't write." I want to see what they can do. I also don't believe that because I am a man, I can't write about women. I had better quit writing, if I can't write about women. Why can't women write about men? It's talent that's important. Many southern whites could write rings around black northerners. It is true that some white writers have had a unique advantage. Faulkner had an extraordinary advantage that no black American has had that I can think of. He was able to walk around and touch every level of society. Poor white, black, white aristocracy, etc. though he didn't ever touch the black middle and upper middle class and that was his limitation. That's why you never see that in his writing. You would almost have to go back to Russian literature to find someone who could have the feel of every strata of the society. It is hard to imagine anyone having this today, because we are so separated and segregated in this society. Yet, Faulkner with his extraordinary talent did touch so many areas of Southern society and that allowed him to know all kinds of things about a wonderful range of black voices and black heritage. He had a sense of their rage for freedom. Where Faulkner stops is where a black writer should begin. Perhaps Joe Christmas is a good example of that. Often the black characters in Faulkner are symbolic more than they are fully developed characters, but his achievement is extraordinary. Many times the characters of Richard Wright are very limited, but, on occasion, he is really on to the great quest for freedom. Being good as a writer is a matter of how much you love the genre that you are working in and how much talent and drive and appetite for human character you have and your imagination and your willingness to take on things that you are attracted to and don't know all that much about. That's typical of novels. You want to write about something you know a little about but are attracted to, partly because it's so different from you.

STUDENT: Does this mean that the writer must move beyond his personal experience?

FORREST: That's right. You burn out early on about autobiographical stuff. Your talent has to do with how much you can imagine in a felt way, in a yeasty way, in an emotional way. How much you can make your readers dream of reality, how much you can take over your readers imagination. When you think about it, there's not an awful lot in what Rev. Shegog says in that sermon, but it's a powerful presence. That's Faulkner's talent.

STUDENT: What do you think has influenced you most about your own background?

FORREST: I was raised Catholic on my mother's side and attended mass regularly. I didn't go to Catholic school, but I went to Catholic catechism classes one day a week on Wednesday. That's how I got my Catholic training in a specific way, so I could take first communion and get my confirmation. That's quite different from other cousins in my family. I used to spend regular weekends with the Protestant side of my family, my fathers' people, and go to church occasionally. Again, it has to do with the complexity of Afro-American culture. You might be divided between these worlds. From the Catholic side, I was always attracted to the ritual of it and to the grandness of the tradition, the concept of original sin and the secret self of confession. Maybe that's where my interior monologues come from. On the Protestant side, my father sang in the Pilgrim Baptist Church in the choir there and was leader of the junior choir. I became very interested, although I was not conscious of the interest as a child, in the thrust of negro spirituals and gospel music and the great sermons. As a matter of fact, the man of eloquence, someone like Jesse Jackson, and before him King, has a long heritage. One of the preachers in Chicago who was so eloquent and known nationally, though he wasn't connected with any kind of political movement was Rev. Austin (J.C. Austin) at the Pilgrim Baptist Church. President Roosevelt said he had the greatest speaking voice of any public man in America. His son is now the pastor of that church. Adam Clayton Powell was known for his power of eloquence. It was the Baptists on the Protestant side, that made me aware of eloquence as a form, not only a protest, but as it evoked the anquish and the celebration of black life on a larger stage. It wasn't writers, because after all, when I was coming along, there weren't that many well-known African-American writers—*Invisible Man* wasn't published until the 50's and so on. It was the eloquence of these great public speakers, mainly preachers, and also the eloquence and style of black athletes that shaped me. It made me want to try to something in a grand manner, in the grand style. It's apparent this caught some light in my imagination, when I started to write. Also, I was interested, from my Catholic side, in the New Testament. I used to read the epistles and the gospels to an invalid aunt of mine who couldn't go to mass on Sundays. My great grandmother, on my father's side, lived with us until I was about nine or ten and I used to read to her the Old Testament. I've gained much from these two heritages. For a long time I could never think about how I was going to write, because this all seemed to me to be rather chaotic. Anyway this was part of me. The Catholic side gets me back to New Orleans, my mother's people; my father's people, and the Protestant side, were from Mississippi. There is a long tradition, in Chicago, of blacks coming from Mississippi and Louisiana. What I tried to do was create an artistic version of that great migration.

STUDENT: I have noticed that the current black women writers like Alice Walker have all acknowledged Zora Neal Hurston. You haven't mentioned her. Did she have any effect on you?

FORREST: No, because I didn't read her until I was in college. Of course, I've taught her regularly. I think your point is very important. There is a link between women writers like Hurston and Walker. You could go on with others like Toni Morrison. Hurston is sort of the grand mama for women writers, the way many white female writers would trace their lineage to Virginia Woolf. No, my linkage would be to Ellison and Faulkner. Of course, when I was in college, I began to know Hurston. Obviously, if you were talking to a black female writer, her perceptions would be different.

CAWELTI: Well, we've got time for one more question. I would like you to talk about names. Names, seem to me one of the central themes in your work. Not only are you marvelously inventive in thinking up different names, but the recurrent phrase "he changed my name" seems to crop up very often in your novels.

FORREST: That is from a spiritual. "I asked Oh Jesus, if that was all right if He changed my name. And Jesus said, I would have to live humble if he changed my name." Changing your name is a kind of initiation. In that case, into the spiritual; one changes one's name in terms of a new spiritual identity, based on the idea of the way names were changed through slavery and, as slaves were moved from one plantation to another, its conceivable they got a new name each time. Then there is the other traditon of nicknames coming along and those names in Afro-American culture, having a greater significance than the names one received from one's parents. I was very alive to that as a kid coming along. This was one of the ways one might reinvent oneself. Reinvention is very important to me as a writer. That is one way in which I think my work is connected to Morrison's and Ellison's, this idea of the reinvention of life, of making one's character in life constantly new, taking what's left over and remaking it into something else and adding a stamp of eloquence and style to that. That style and eloquence is everything. That is so much a part of the culture that black Americans offer which is stunning and new and different. That is the cudgel under which every jazz musician operates. He had to create anew every night on the set. So this was a part of my growing up, the idea of being alive to change and transformation. The problem is to take this tendency within the culture and to make it new again. So I do not want to take some wonderful, interesting name that I've heard. I have to do something else to it. Maybe link it to other things I'm doing in the novel and to reinvent it again. That is another part of the difference between oral traditon and written tradition. I just don't want to take a name I heard and reecho it in my novel or like Langston Hughes, who takes what he hears and just puts it down that way. I want to take that and remake it again. What helps me to remake it again is my debt and my relationship to traditional literature. I am thinking about what Hardy did with names. So extraordinary with so many wonderful names around me. He's helpful, too in this idea in making a world of the imagination based on a recreation of reality.

This is also something characteristic of other traditions and other writers, like the Irish, who have faced the same problems. Joyce heard these extraordinary sermons, but he wrote sermons that go beyond what he had heard among the Jesuits. I can't preach with King. I can outwrite him. He wasn't a writer. I can take what he gave me, as a writer and go beyond that. At least I think that is what would make him proud of me, anyway.

Contributors

Jeffrey Renard Allen has published poems and stories in *Caliban, Obsidian II, Black American Literature Forum,* and other journals and is working on a novel *Rails Under My Back.* He is Assistant Professor in American Literature at Queens College.

Kathleen E. Bethel is the African-American Studies Librarian at the Northwestern University Library.

Sven Birkerts is a critic, essayist and reviewer who often contributes to such periodicals as *The New Republic* and *The Atlantic Monthly.* He teaches at Emerson College.

Keith Byerman is Professor of English at Indiana State University and Associate Editor of *Black American Literature Forum.* He has written *Fingering the Jagged Grain: Tradition and Form in Recent Black Fiction* and, with Erma Banks, *Alice Walker: An Annotated Bibliography.* His recent book on W.E.B. Du Bois is a major contribution to the analysis of that crucial figure. Byerman has published articles on black fiction and autobiography in *American Literary History, American Literary Realism, Studies in Short Fiction,* and *Callaloo.*

John G. Cawelti is author of *Adventure, Mystery and Romance, The Six-Gun Mystique, The Spy Story* and other books as well as the Introduction to Another Chicago Press's edition of *The Bloodworth Orphans.* He edited a special section on Leon Forrest in *Callaloo.* He is Professor of English at the University of Kentucky.

Stanley Crouch is a distinguished literary and jazz critic and a contributing editor to *The New Republic.* He is author of *Notes of a Hanging Judge,* and *The All-American Skin Game.*

Veena Deo teaches courses in African-American Literature, World Literature and Women's Studies at Hamline University in St. Paul. She served as a member of the Board of Associate Editors for

Signs: Journal of Woman and Culture in Society (1993-1995) and the editorial board of *Critique: Journal of Critical Studies of Iran and the Middle East* (1993-1994). She has presented papers and published essays and review articles on African American writers, Dalit Marathi writers and Asian American artists defining community through the arts.

A. Robert Lee teaches at the University of Kent at Canterbury, England, where he is currently Chair of American Studies. He has been a frequent Visiting Professor in the United States, having taught at Princeton, The University of Virginia, Bryn Mawr, Northwestern, Colorado. and the University of California-Berkley. His publications include the Everyman Moby Dick, *Black American Fiction Since Richard Wright* and twelve volumes in the Vision Press Critical Series, among them *Black Fiction: New Studies in the Afro-American Novel since 1945, Herman Melville: Reassessments, Scott Fitzgerald: The Promises of Life*, and *William Faulkner: The Yoknapatawpha Fiction*. He has written widely on African-American, Lation, Native-American and Asian-American literature. He also broadcasts with the BBC.

Bruce A. Rosenberg has written a study of the American Folk Preacher as well as books on *Custer and the Epic of Defeat, Folkore and Literature*, Ian Fleming, and Western folklore as well as many articles on medieval studies, folklore and American studies. He is a Professor at Brown University.

Danille Taylor-Guthrie received her Ph.D. from Brown University and has taught at the Art Institute of Chicago, Northwestern University and Indiana University-Northwest. She has also written essays on Toni Morrison, Leslie Silko and Gerald Vizenour.

Kenneth W. Warren recently moved from Northwestern to the University of Chicago. His book *Black and White Strangers: Race and American Literary Realism* was recently published by the University of Chicago Press.

Craig Werner teaches courses in literature, music, and multicultural philosophy in the Department of African American Studies at the University of Wisconsin-Madison. He has written many books and essays on modern literature and African-American literature and recenty published *Playing the Changes*, a major study of African-American literature in its twentieth century contexts. He is a member of the multicultural theater/music groups Abreaction, whose LP, *Game Theory* was released by Riah Records.

Index

317